The Gardening Book

Contributors
**Ann Bonar
Richard Gorer MA
Denis Hardwicke
Cyril Harris BSc ARCS
Peter Hunt FLS
John Mitchell
Brian Walkden
Richard Weeks**

The
Gardening Book

**Edited by
Peter Hunt**

OCTOPUS

CONTENTS

First published 1978 by
Octopus Books Limited,
59 Grosvenor Street, London W1

© 1975 Hennerwood Publications Limited

ISBN 0 7064 1044 0

Produced by Mandarin Publishers Limited
22a Westlands Road, Quarry Bay, Hong Kong
Printed in Singapore

MAKING THE MOST OF YOUR GARDEN SPACE

Faced with an expanse of earth and plants, possibly for the first time, the temptation to start moulding it as you would like it at once, without any preliminary thinking, is almost overwhelming. Whether it is an apparently endless bare patch left after the builders have done their worst, or an old but neglected garden in which the laws of the jungle now seem to be prevailing, you, as the new owner, are likely to hurry out with your favourite plants, scrabble them hastily into the ground, hack down all the under-growth in sight, and dig as much ground as you can manage before your back gives out.

Unfortunately the result is often a more than unusually fine crop of weeds which rapidly overwhelm your cherished plants – if any do survive, they are in any case invisible from the house, or totally unsuited to the soil.

This is not the way to go about using that piece of ground which is so precious in this crowded island. Today, more than ever before, it pays to sit down and think about the way you are going to use your garden space before you actually start working on it. There are so many possibilities, whatever the size of the garden – even the tiniest can contain specialist collections of, for instance, rock garden plants, miniature bulbs or herbs.

Then, when you do start to put your ideas into practice, there is a good chance that they will be successful, and there is nothing like success for breeding enthusiasm and generating more ideas – in no time you will be opening your garden to the public!

Whether the garden is an old or a new one, the first point to consider is: what are your priorities? What are the features you must have? The ones you and your family would like can be considered later, but for the moment it is the essentials which take first place. For instance, is a play area needed, for children and pets? Do you need to grow your own food? Home-grown vegetables, fruit and herbs have so much in their favour you cannot really afford to be without them

nowadays. Should there be somewhere to hang the washing? Of course, one priority is that the garden satisfies the decorative side, so there will need to be an area for flowers and foliage, colours and fragrance. Then again, perhaps someone in the family has a special garden hobby, such as dahlias or old shrub roses. You yourself may like the idea of climbing plants. A greenhouse is a very special feature, with its possibilities for growing more exotic plants than out-doors, and for providing flowers and plants for the house.

So the list could go on, but, provided you can get your basic requirements on paper first, you should eventually end up with a satisfying garden. The next step is to draw a plan – it need not be draughtsmanship accurate – which shows the shape of the garden, including the house, using squared paper. Give yourself a scale, for instance so many feet per square or squares, having measured the boundaries of the garden first. On this you can mark in the features you need, but it is likely that you will redraw this plan several times as there are a great variety of considerations to be taken into account. Even then, when you set out to dig and plant, weed and build, you may well find that the design alters as you go along. A good garden is a blend of skilful advance planning and on the spot alterations over the years to allow the garden to 'grow' its own character. Although a plan is necessary, it should never be rigidly adhered to, otherwise the garden will be 'stiff' and out of harmony with its surroundings. Remember that a garden consists of living things that are constantly altering their size and shape; nothing is static, nothing grows in ruler-straight lines, and compromise and adjustment are needed all the time.

When you are considering your plan, the climate of the garden and the type of soil it contains are extremely important, as it is these that will determine the kind of plants you grow. The climate and aspect will be just that little bit different to your neighbour's: enough to mean that you may be able to grow an exotic plant like a magnolia, which he cannot because his garden is exposed to a prevailing north-easterly wind. Similarly, rock roses which come from the sunny hillsides of the Mediterreanean countries will languish miserably in a shaded, damp place, while ferns or plantain lilies would flourish.

So one of the first things is to find the sunny and shady parts of the garden, the sheltered and windy bits, and where there are some nice warm sunny nooks; the draughty places, the parts where the frost does not leave the ground until midday, the bits that are always moist, and the bits that are mostly bone-dry. The times of day when various parts get the sun, and the times of year, too, are important.

Don't forget that deciduous trees in winter let in a good deal more light than they do in summer, and that the angle of the sun changes through the year. Don't forget, too, when deciding where to put plants, that trees and shrubs in particular will make a difference to light and shade over the years. It is better to wait a season before starting an all-out planting programme; in any case, planting the whole garden at once is both time-consuming and expensive, and it will pay to make haste slowly.

I mentioned earlier that the choice of plants for the garden will be partly determined by the soil type. Plants can be divided into two kinds: those that will grow in what is known as acid soil, and those that will grow in chalky, or alkaline, soils. Usually the acid soil plants will not grow well, if at all, in the chalky soils, though plants happy in chalk will also grow in acid soils. You can find out which yours is by using a simple soil-testing kit supplied by

your local garden shop. There will be instructions with the kit on how to carry out the soil test.

Once you have found out how your soil reacts, you can then assess the structural type, that is, whether it is basically sand, peat, clay, chalk or stony; very occasionally it is a combination of these elements in such proportions as to produce the garden loam which plants like best.

A simple but effective way of deciding what soil type you have is to take teaspoonfuls of soil from various parts of the garden, at depths varying from the surface down to about 18 in., mix all the samples together, and then put a teaspoonful in a test tube or similar narrow glass container, fill with water and shake hard. Leave the contents to settle, and when the water is finally clear again, the soil will have settled into layers. It will do this more obviously if you can add a little barium sulphate (obtainable from a chemist) to the solution before shaking.

Any humus (rotted organic matter) will rise to the top, and the remaining layers will consist of successively larger particles, starting with clay, the smallest, down to sand and grit at the bottom. If one of these layers is much larger than the others, that will determine the basic type of soil, and you will then have a better idea how to treat it.

Another way of deciding on your soil

ABOVE: *An abundance of flowers can be grown in a small space. Here border flowers, small shrubs and climbing roses give variety of size, texture and colour.*
OPPOSITE: *A small town garden which has been paved to give the minimum amount of work in attending to it. Climbing plants are used to soften the otherwise bare lines of the house and walls.*

type is by hand, feeling the soil and squeezing it into a ball. A sandy soil will feel gritty when rubbed between fingers and thumb, clay will be sticky to the touch, and peat will be spongy and springy. Silt is difficult to determine, as the particles are small, like clay, but it is 'silky' rather than sticky. Chalky soils are usually pale in colour; a red soil, like the Devon soils, is usually very fertile, so are the black Fen soils. Town garden soil is generally lacking in humus and nutrient, and is rather acid and very quick-draining – it is one of the poorest soil types.

You can improve the structure of your soil mainly by adding rotted organic matter and also, in the case of the heavy and badly drained soils, by mixing in lime or gypsum. Organic matter is anything which was once living, vegetative or animal, and in the garden rotted vegetation is most generally used, for instance leaf mould (rotted leaves), rotted straw, spent mushroom compost, spent hops (left over from making beer), fibrous peat or garden compost. Animal manure such as rabbit and pigeon droppings and poultry manure can also be used, but mainly for their food content rather than their organic matter. Well-rotted farm and stable manures are good.

Garden compost is the easiest to obtain in the long run, because it can be made on the spot, but for initial improvement it may be necessary to buy manure. However, you can at least start a compost heap with the vegetation cut down when clearing the site.

The compost heap is best built about 4 × 5 × 2 ft. high, using a base of woody twigs and branches. It can be contained with wire netting with a post at each corner; another in the middle, removed when the heap is completed, will ensure that air can reach the centre. An approximately 6-in. layer of vegetation should be alternated with a sprinkled layer of lime and one of a nitrogen-containing fertilizers, such as sulphate of ammonia.

By building the heap like this, it is supplied with air (oxygen), moisture, warmth and nitrogen, all of which are needed by the organisms responsible for the process of rotting. Any vegetation can be used: leaves, soft stems, flower heads, soft prunings, annual weeds (without seedheads), grass mowings, tea leaves, and so on, but not woody material as it takes years to rot down. The heap will be ready for use when it is dark brown and crumbly.

Organic matter should be applied to the soil in large quantities – an inch-thick layer is not too much, though in a heap it may seem an awful lot. If the soil is heavy and sticky, hydrated lime at up to 1 lb. a square yard can be used to break it down; if a soil test has shown the soil to be alkaline, then

gypsum would be better, as it is neutral in reaction but with the same structural effect. It is applied at the same rate as lime. Grit or coarse sand are a further help to heavy soil improvement, but rather expensive to use, as at least 7 lbs. per sq. yd. are required.

Sandy, stony or quick-draining chalky soils can also be improved with organic matter, which acts as a sponge to retain the water and plant foods. Again, as much as possible is needed. Another way of helping to improve this type of soil is to grow a quick-maturing green manure crop, such as mustard, rape, annual lupin or rye grass. Sow the seed broadcast from spring to August, allow the crop to grow until it is just about to flower, and then dig it in. Remember to add a nitrogen fertilizer while you are digging in, to help with decay and prevent a temporary nitrogen shortage.

Another very important point when considering the state of your soil is the plant food content. Plants are just like humans, they need food as well as drink, and for them food partly takes the form of mineral particles in solution, which they absorb from the soil. The most important elements are nitrogen, phosphorus and potassium, needed in relatively large quantities, and a variety of others (called 'trace elements'), such as magnesium, boron, iron and copper, which are just as necessary but in minute amounts. Town gardens in particular are radically short of such plant foods but, with any garden, it pays to use some fertilizer.

You will find that whether it is a compound fertilizer, containing several different minerals, or a 'straight' fertilizer, the percentage of minerals is given on the container, along with instructions for the rate of application. Such fertilizers can be dug in before planting or sowing, or used as topdressings on the soil surface while plants are growing.

I have gone into the subject of the garden soil in some detail, because without a good soil your hard work will be sabotaged from the start, and you will never have a really good garden, with flourishing plants and abundant growth.

Whatever the soil type and climate of the land you are dealing with, you will be presented with one of two problems: either a new garden which is as the builders left it after the house was finished, or an already established garden.

In some ways, laying out a completely new garden is easier than one which has been going for some years; you can indulge yourself, and put in whatever features you like, wherever you like. But the devastation left by builders can be heartbreaking; the topsoil is often covered with useless foundation subsoil, and heavy equipment will have been over the ground repeatedly so that it is either rock hard or a morass of mud. It will be full of brick, the remains of sand and concrete heaps, pieces of wood, pipes, glass, wire and so on. The only thing to do is to tackle the clearing section by section, taking a pick-axe to some parts if need be.

ABOVE: *Formal paving slabs are best used in a muted shade, leaving the shrubs to provide variety of colour and form.*

TOP: *The plants in this town garden have been carefully chosen to give a soft old-fashioned colour combination.*

TOP LEFT: *The vertical forms of iris and lavender contrast here with the lower, bushy growth of thyme and ballota.*

and borrowing or hiring a rotary cultivator for preliminary cultivation after the rubbish has been removed. For any kind of future success at all, the subsoil layer should be removed. This part of the work, clearing the ground, will easily be the worst in the creation of the garden, so take heart, and do the job slowly and steadily.

An old overgrown garden will have rather too much vegetation instead of too little; your problem here will be to get rid of the jungle-like growth of grass that was a lawn, and disentagle the cultivated plants in the beds from the native ones.

A rotary grass cutter is a good machine for long growth on a lawn, and will not jib too much at the anthills, nests and tussocks of grass amongst it; small areas can be cut by hand, using a grass or bagging hook. The cut vegetation can be used for starting a compost heap. When you have cleared the lawn to this stage, raking and then brushing will get rid of the mat of dead leaves and twigs, insects and other debris on the surface. Dig out any clumps of coarse grass, and then cut the grass with an ordinary mower, but with the blades set high, lowering them as the grass improves.

A food and weedkilling dressing can be put on in late spring and a topdressing of loam, peat and sand and a winter fertilizer in autumn. Regular mowing will have helped to drive out much of the coarse grass; the remainder can be cut out with a knife, and bare patches sown with fine seed mixture.

When it comes to tackling the state of the beds, as with the new garden, clear one section at a time. There may be bulbs dormant in the ground in summer, or perennials which have died down for winter, so dig with care. Don't worry about the weeds growing up all round you and all the other jobs crying out to be done. Stick to clearing one piece completely and planting it, and then go on to the next. A desperate attempt to clear the whole garden at once will only result in more trouble; inadequately cleared ground will be weed-ridden again in no time. Remember that chemical weedkillers are a very useful tool for preliminary clearing even if you prefer not, for environmental reasons, to use them regularly later on.

Top and soft fruit in old gardens can be in a very sorry state; it is often advisable to grub out the bush and cane fruits and start again with new stock. Top fruit will need pruning spread over two or three winters to take out old unproductive, diseased and crowded shoots and branches, and to let sun and air in to the centre of the trees. Some of the old varieties are exceptionally well-flavoured and may be quite rare, so they are worth preserving, but here again you may eventually decide to take out all the top fruit and put in new dwarfing trees of modern varieties.

To come back to our plan, besides marking features such as the area for borders, the lawn, the greenhouse or kitchen garden, it

is a good idea to position the paths. The most obvious route from A to B is not necessarily the best; it may be that A and B are points that are not particularly important, or that one wants to go to C from A rather than from B. So draw in the paths, but don't lay them permanently until you have used the garden for a while. The essential paths will come of their own accord, and you may even find that some features need to be re-sited as a result.

The relationship of one feature to another, and to the house, is worth thinking about. The transition from the angular lines and rigid inert material of the house to the fluidity and movement of the living plants can be made less abrupt by using climbing plants on the house walls, by extending paving out from the house and interplanting spaces in it with carpeting plants, and by building low raised beds or low double walls alongside the paving which can be planted with trailing plants. Similarly, parts of the garden should merge into one another, the eye being led on by a carefully placed tall narrow tree, an informal hedge or a path.

The garden which does not reveal all its charms at once is the most visually satisfying – what is behind that hedge, what is round the curve of that path? What does that shrub hide? Maybe only the compost heap, but it has to go somewhere, and a charming screen for it in the shape of a blue-flowered ceanothus is much better than some old pieces of wood or corrugated iron.

The view from the house windows is important, especially in winter. Here flowers come into their own, whether they are herbaceous plants, bulbs, flowering shrubs or roses. When you are choosing them, their season of flowering, as well as their colours, are important. Plants which

flower in winter are best put near the house so that they can be easily seen; no one is going to go right down to the end of the garden in wet or snowy weather to admire a winter-flowering cherry, or to pick Christmas roses.

Colour is without doubt the most obvious part of an ornamental plant's attraction, and the most important to the majority of gardeners. A dazzling, riotous display of colour from spring to autumn is generally the ideal for beginner gardeners. But as time goes on and experience accumulates, this aim gradually changes as you realize that more subtle but more satisfying blendings can be obtained, in which colour is mixed with white, or cool greys and silvers, or with plants grown for their leaves in a variety of greens.

A blaze of all the colours of the rainbow is difficult to absorb all at once; it has the same effect as being hit with a sledge-hammer. Much better to group the plants in types of colour, and merge each into the one adjacent to it. Pink, purple, rose, grey, lavender, blue and lilac makes one group; yellow, cream, orange, bronze, brown, light red another. The reds will graduate into shades of rose, lavender and so to blue; or on the opposite side into scarlet, vermilion, flame and finally yellow. Grey-leaved and white-flowered plants will calm down the brighter colours, and mix beautifully with muted shades.

If you want a bed of one colour, be careful. It can look most striking, for instance with flowers in all shades of red, if you include plants whose leaves have reddish tinges ('Rosemary Rose', dahlia 'Bishop of Llandaff', *Salvia coccineus*) and use a mixture of herbaceous plants, shrubs, bulbs and grasses, but an unmitigated planting of dahlias or poppies would be

gaudy and boring.

There is no better way of breaking up blocks of colour than by planting leafy plants. There are many species whose leaves are handsome in shape, agreeable in colour and pleasing in texture; they deserve planting in their own right. The softly haired leaves of the mullein (*Verbascum bombyciferum*) are like grey velvet; the large, rounded leathery leaves of bergenia are evergreen, and dicentra (bleeding heart) has delicately cut, frond-like leaves. The green and yellow spears of variegated iris, the shield shape of nasturtium, and the prickles of acanthus are just other examples of foliage plants which could be used to play up (or down) the flowering plants.

Colour in the garden in winter may seem impossible, until you realize that there are plants for whom winter is the natural time of flowering. Certainly you will not get a great deal of bloom – that would be too much to expect – but you will find, if you look through the catalogues of the leading nurserymen, a surprising variety of plants which will take up where the summer plants left off, and flower in succession through the otherwise dormant months of the year. Such shrubs as winter sweet, witch hazel, laurustinus, some of the rhododendrons, corylopsis, mahonia 'Charity' and mezereon, and herbaceous perennials, hellebores, snowdrops, *Iris reticulata* and *I. unguicularis* (the Algerian iris), bergenias and some of the violets, are all winter-flowering.

To add to winter colour, there are the evergreen plants whose leaves are plain green or green variegated with yellow or white, such as holly, and the conifers in blue, grey, green or yellow. All these mean that the garden can continue to be clothed and ornamental in winter; in fact, a really well-designed and thought-out garden will look

just as good, though in a different way, in winter as it does in summer.

When you are drawing out your plan on paper, this is the time to consider the overall design, and to make certain that the garden will be both decorative and useful in a practical way. The placing of the vegetables, herbs and fruit in relation to borders, shrubs, lawn and so on, should ensure that they flow from one into the other, as though they just happened to have occurred naturally in the arrangement which you have in fact planned.

A variation in levels and a variation of plant heights all help to add interest; for instance, a herbaceous border can all too easily have a single horizontal level. Break it up with the smaller, vertically growing conifers, juniper 'Skyrocket', the fastigiate Irish yew or evening primroses (oenothera). Use shrubs as a change from herbaceous plants; go in for bulbs – these can vary from the tiny front-of-border snowdrops and crocuses to the 3-ft. crown imperials and summer hyacinths (galtonia).

The herbaceous border, when first conceived, contained plants graded in height so that the lowest were in front and the tallest at the back; it was meant to be looked at from only one side. When successful it was superb, but it was difficult to achieve and often difficult to cultivate. The modern idea has commuted this a little to the 'island border'. This is a bed of irregular curving shape, cut in turf or surrounded by paving, containing perennials arranged so that the tallest are more or less in the middle, and the carpeters at the edges. The shapes of these beds can be very pleasing and, being islands, they are more easily cared for, particularly if no-staking perennials are grown.

This last point is not to be overlooked in planting. The more time you have to

spare, the more you can improve the garden, and enjoy it, too; a garden which is always needing attention becomes a tiresome job which has to be done, instead of being a place for pleasure and interest, as it should be. Shrubs are plants which do not need a lot of care, on the whole, but which can provide much in the way of flowers, fruits and foliage. Ground-cover plants will fill in spaces between perennials and shrubs so that the weeds cannot spread; ivy, periwinkle, heathers, London Pride, St John's Wort (hypericum), creeping thyme and saxifrages, once established, need virtually no attention.

If you do not want to be tied to the weekly chore of mowing the lawn, paving will take its place in small areas, or, if you are not too particular about the fineness of the grasses in it, you can treat it with a grass-growth inhibitor every six weeks or so. Using bedding plants and growing plants from seed are time-consuming ways of gardening, though they do provide colour quickly, and give variation in design and colour schemes from year to year. Bulbs are a mixed lot: some, like daffodils, can be left to their own devices for years; others, like tulips, need lifting every year.

Many gardeners are now thinking of growing vegetables and fruit for the first time. There isn't any doubt that vegetables, particularly the leafy kinds and the salad crops, straight from the garden to the table have much more flavour and are much more nutritious than even the best of the shop-bought kind.

This is an area of gardening where planning is particularly important, as it is possible, with careful thinking, to have a succession of vegetables all year round, from lettuces and new potatoes in June round to spring greens and overwintered lettuce in

ABOVE: *A great variety of fruit and vegetables can be grown in even the smallest space. Sweet corn is a rather exotic vegetable which can be successfully grown in this country.*

TOP: *Achieving a balance between vertical and horizontal growth is important in successful garden design. Care over this can do much to make a small garden seem larger.*

OPPOSITE PAGE AND TOP LEFT: *A three-dimensional sketch – even if only rough – adds to the value of a careful plan. It is a reminder of the height of fences and gives perspective to the gardener's ideas. Stepping stones avoid people treading on young plants and give easier access to the rear of deep beds.*

May. You do need to sit down and think about it in advance, however, especially deciding where the vegetable garden is to go.

If a space for it can be managed near the house, so much the better for the cook's sake, and it should be large enough to be divided into three sections for rotation. Switching groups of vegetables so that each is grown on a different section each year ensures that pests and diseases do not build up in the soil, and that all the food is equally used over a period of time, otherwise one crop might absorb all the potassium, for instance, resulting in a deficiency.

If you are short of space in the garden as a whole, remember that there is no reason why the vegetables should not sometimes be mixed in with herbaceous plants. Carrot leaves are very decorative; the reddish leaves of beetroot, the fronds of asparagus and the leaves of Jerusalem artichokes are snapped up by flower arrangers. Runner beans grown on tripods as well as in straight rows make good dividers.

It also pays to choose the smaller-growing varieties; peas vary between $1\frac{1}{2}$ and 5 ft., for instance, and Tom Thumb lettuce can be grown much more closely than Webbs Wonderful. With a bit of ingenuity, and thinking round the problem of a small space, it is surprising how much can be fitted in. The old idea of a kitchen garden with all the vegetables and herbs in one place was fine when there was land to spare, but a new outlook is needed nowadays.

Herbs are easily grown, and picked fresh or stored in the deep freeze make such a difference to food with their aromatic and individual flavours. They can be grown in a group together, but they also lend themselves very well to edgings for borders, or to being grown in containers and troughs near the kitchen so that they are handy for picking in a hurry.

As far as fruit is concerned, here again there is no need to keep it all together in one place. If you can do this, it will be easier to protect it from birds by putting netting over all of it at once, but it can also be spread about the garden, doing double

ABOVE: *Climbing roses can effectively mask and make an attractive feature of a pillar.*
ABOVE RIGHT: *This corner of a paved garden again utilizes various leaf shapes and plant forms as well as colour to give variety. The open design walling is an unusual feature.*
LEFT: *A small vegetable plot can be made into a decorative feature.*

duty. Black and red currants can be grown as an internal hedge to separate the vegetables from the lawn or borders; blackberries, loganberries and raspberries can be grown along wire fences so that they act as dividers. So, too, can apples and pears grown as oblique cordons; spacing should be about 2½ ft. apart, and each tree will produce about 3–5 lbs. in a season.

Apples and pears are grafted plants, for which a variety of different stocks are used, influencing the growth of the trees. The dwarfing stock is best for limited space, and your nurseryman will give advice on this. Strawberries can be grown as edgings – in a good year they can produce two crops, the second a smaller one in autumn. Alpine strawberries, whose berries are small but deliciously and strongly flavoured, will crop continuously all summer. Walls are ideal for fan-trained peaches and plums.

It is all a matter of thinking in advance, and often of abandoning the old ideas or adapting them to today's needs. As I have said before, rigidity in gardening is out – it needs an adaptable approach, flexibility and willingness to think ahead, and then the ability to alter in the light of experience and conditions.

Whether you have a lot of space or not, a thousand square feet, a quarter of an acre or two acres, you will want to make the best use of it that can be managed. Filling

up the horizontal space is obvious, but what about the vertical space? The walls, whether boundary, house or internal separating walls, the fences and the spaces where dividers are wanted all come into this category. There is a tremendous variety of plants to choose from to clothe this space: roses, clematis, honeysuckle, winter and summer jasmine, the trumpet vine, large- and small-leaved ivies, wisteria, Virginia creeper and ornamental grape vines.

Then there are the temporary climbers, like hops (there is a golden-leaved kind), nasturtium, morning glory, sweet peas, and *Cobaea scandens* (cup-and-saucer plant). There are the wall plants, which are not strictly climbers but do better grown against a wall for support, such as the fishbone cotoneaster, firethorn, the New Zealand bottlebrush for warm walls, abutilon, and many others.

Informal hedges make a change to the formal kind and save on work, as they should not be clipped much, if at all. Here some of the roses are excellent: *Rosa rugosa*, the musk roses, the bright yellow rose 'Canary Bird'; also forsythia, hydrangea, fuchsia (in the West country), broom (cytisus) and rhododendron. The hedge can perhaps be two species alternated, to spread the period of flowering, or to ensure some evergreen for winter effect. Don't forget that climbing plants can be used to trail as well as to climb, and can sometimes be conveniently used on steep banks or down containing walls.

If you want to make a feature of walls and dividers to show off the construction material as well as the plants, there are many excellent kinds to choose from. The traditional brick wall takes a lot of beating, whether the bricks are laid in the garden wall bond, English or Flemish bond or other patterns. You can have a solid brick wall, or insert concrete screen blocks at intervals, or build a wall entirely of these concrete blocks which come in many patterns. Concrete blocks are especially good for patio walls and courtyards, as they help to increase the feeling of space.

Dry stone walls are attractive in their own right, but they can be made even more so if you insert plants at intervals as the wall is built – rock plants do very well grown like this. As low walls, 2 ft. or so high, round a terrace, they provide a link between house and garden.

If you prefer the less solid look you get with fencing, here again the choice is wide, from rail or ranch style, trellis, interwoven lathes, chain link, wire and wooden posts, or square wire mesh. Rather more solid fences consist of palisade (poles) fencing or overlap (planks); they are more expensive but longer-lasting, and provide more support.

Your planning of the garden framework will also include provision for paths, their placing, building and maintenance. I said earlier that you may find with use that their position has to be changed because the natural routes have proved to be different. The choice of materials will also need to be considered. You can simply have a beaten-out track, which comes naturally as the result of constant traffic, but it will be very muddy whenever the weather is wet and a properly constructed path will be more practical and better to look at. Its width should be such that it will take your wheeled machinery – wheelbarrow, mower or garden cultivator – comfortably, without the wheels coming off the edges.

The most hard-wearing and simplest path to make, though utilitarian in appearance, is the concrete path, constructed of a layer of rubble (hardcore) – broken brick, and stones – about 4 in. deep, packed solidly together, rammed well down, and covered with concrete, which is then beaten flat. The foundation should be dug out to a depth of at least 6 in., and shuttering boards will be needed on each side to retain the shape of the concrete while it sets.

Other materials for paths and drives include bricks, stone slabs, crazy paving, concrete tiles (there are non-slip kinds), in neutral shades or coloured, logs, cobbles

and concrete slabs; asphalt can also be used. Crazy paving can be concrete, marked with lines while wet, to simulate the real thing, or you can also use broken York stone or plain concrete.

With any of these materials, the foundation for the path is extremely important if it is to stay in place and not 'creep' in the course of use, or break up. In general, paths are dug out to a depth of 6–9 in., the bottom soil is firmed and levelled (use a spirit level), and hardcore 3–6 in. deep, or a layer of coarse sand about 2 in. deep is added, depending on what material is being used for the path.

Hardcore is necessary for crazy paving, stone cobbles, brick and asphalt; a 2-in. layer of sand on top of this is also needed for crazy paving, bricks, and bricks mixed with tiles placed end on. Sand alone can be used in the dug-out path for logs and stone and concrete slabs, though they are more satisfactory with a hardcore base. Concrete slabs are kept in place with mortar on the sand at each corner of each slab; cobble setts are also laid in mortar on sand. Asphalt paths should have fine chippings scattered over the hardcore as a base on which to lay the asphalt. The kind supplied for garden use can be laid cold.

Whichever material you choose, you should finish off the laid path by scattering

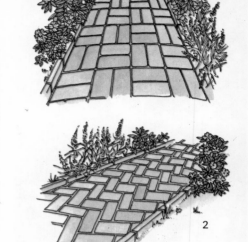

ABOVE: *Bricks laid in different patterns (1 basket-weave; 2 herring-bone) make unusual and effective pathways.*
BELOW: *Different shapes of plants make for variety, especially in a small garden.*
OPPOSITE: *Dry stone walls need careful construction and firm foundations, but they are very decorative.*

coarse sand over the surface and brushing it well into the cracks to fill them up. The level of the path should be checked frequently in the course of construction, to avoid irregularities in which water can collect. As an added refinement, the path could slope very slightly to each side for drainage.

With the ornamental side of the garden goes the area which in most gardens is covered with grass. In very small gardens this can be replaced by paving, in which spaces are left for planting, but a large expanse of paving is boring and really only for those who dislike anything to do with plants, and who would not therefore be reading this book.

Grass can be divided into one of two categories: that which provides a pleasant expanse of green, albeit consisting of a mixture of grass and a variety of leafy, mat-forming weeds, and that which is purely fine velvety turf. The latter requires constand detailed attention the year round; such a lawn can be more time-consuming than the rest of the garden put together. It is something to aim at when you have the garden more or less under control and can give it the time and care that it needs, but for the time being you can produce a reasonable turf which will serve as the garden's 'carpet' and set off the main features, with

a minimum of management.

The lawn can be grown from seed or turf; seed is sown in spring or autumn, turf laid at any time between October and March. It costs at least seven times as much as seed but does have the advantage that there is your lawn at once, as soon as the laying is finished.

A lawn grown from seed will take a fortnight to germinate, longer if the weather is dry, and a season before it can be said to be thick enough to be called a lawn. Moreover, it should be walked on as little as possible during this time, particularly in the first couple of months after germination. In the long run, though, it will probably prove to be the better lawn of the two.

If you decide to use seed, remember that it is possible to obtain different seed mixtures for different needs and sites. Seedsmen make up their own mixtures, or will supply one to your own requirements; proprietary brands are sold especially for fine lawns, hard wear, shade and so on, and it pays to obtain a selection of seed catalogues and study the different mixtures and their prices.

The rate of sowing is about $1\frac{1}{2}$ oz. per sq. yd., but it varies slightly with the different mixtures. If in doubt, $1\frac{1}{2}$ oz. is a good average.

Before you start to sow, the site for the lawn should have been thoughly prepared:

weeds and large stones completely removed, organic matter, lime or gypsum and sand added as required, and a pre-sowing general fertilizer mixed into the top few inches a couple of days before sowing. Check the site to make sure that it is quite level, and firm the soil by treading and raking alternately until it is well broken down to a crumb-like state, so that the seed can germinate and establish as rapidly as possible. Warm showery weather is ideal for the germinating period.

Choose a day when there is no wind, and sow the seed evenly by hand or, if the area is large, with a seed distributor. Rake the soil lightly over it so that it is barely covered, and put up bird scarers, or use black cotton stranded across it. You can buy seed which has been specially treated to prevent attack by birds.

A lawn grown from turf will 'knit' most successfully if the turves are laid in wet rather than dry weather, and provided they are laid really tightly packed. Turf is supplied in various grades, and in general each turf is 3 ft. × 1 ft. in size, and about $1\frac{1}{2}$ in. thick. When delivered they will be rolled up and if you are not going to use them at once, they will keep in better condition if they are unrolled and laid flat until required.

Prepare the ground as for sowing seed, except that it need not be so finely broken down; an added refinement is to put a layer of sharp sand on the surface to help knitting, but it is not essential. The turves are then laid up and down the site, starting at one side. A complete line is laid, if necessary with half a turf at one or other end. This ensures that the next line laid against the first will be 'bonded', in other words, a join between the ends of two turves comes in the middle of the side of the previous turf.

Each turf should be laid slightly humped; when a line is complete, gently thump each turf down to lie flat, which will give a tight fit between each turf. As each row is laid, it should be knocked up against the previous row, and in this way the thorough knitting together of the grass is ensured.

While you are laying the turves, you can avoid compacting the prepared soil by standing on a plank placed on the row which has just been laid, and working from this. Use a spirit level at frequent intervals, and add or remove soil below turves if necessary. When the whole lawn has been laid, put a light dressing of compost or coarse sand over it, and brush well into the cracks between the turves. If you lay the lawn in this manner, there will be no need to roll it, and in fact would be harmful.

Whether the lawn is grown from seed or turf, the first cutting should be given when the grass is about 2 in. high, just taking off

the top with really sharp blades. The height of cut is gradually lowered thereafter, as the grass becomes established and stronger.

When you are considering the planning of your garden, you should take into account its final overall style. The tendency nowadays is towards the informal, in which different features are married one to another. In the Victorian age, formality was the rage, with grass precisely clipped, beds exactly placed in geometric arrangements, flowers placed in dead straight lines, and hedges straight up and down. The same theme applied in Elizabethan gardens, though it was interpreted differently, with gravel paths and knot gardens.

Whatever style you adopt, which you think is best fitted to your surroundings, and which accords with your own taste, there are all kinds of features which can be included, besides the ones I have already suggested. Rock gardens, for example, have always had a fascination for most people and now that they have graduated to their present high standard of construction and design, together with the tremendously wide selection of plants that are now available, they can be a considerable attraction in any garden.

Rock plants need a situation which gets sun for some if not all of the day in spring and, above all, they must have moist, well-drained soil, kept cool by the addition of stone and rocks, as in their natural surroundings: an open site away from trees is ideal. The rock garden itself need not be on a particularly high mound, unless this occurs naturally. It can be blended in with the rest of the garden with mown grass on the foot-hills, so to speak, or by finishing off with low stone walls, planted with rock plants and trailers such as aubrieta, alyssum, the small periwinkle and so on.

All too often the rock garden is built on the soil thrown up by the builders when excavating the foundations of the house, and nothing could be worse. This is subsoil, lifeless and poorly drained and practically without plant food; it should never be used. Instead, good garden soil should be built up to the height required, and rock placed as high as possible, as it would occur naturally. Stone with obvious strata lines should be positioned with the strata running in their natural direction, either horizontal or vertical. They should be set back into the slope at an angle, so that water runs back into the soil. Stones placed close together can simulate rock crevices, in between which you can grow small plants; whatever else you do, try to avoid the effect of a suet pudding dotted with raisins.

A garden which has a great variation in levels will take kindly to the inclusion of a rock garden; a garden on a rather flat site, or one which slopes gently down to one end or side, will accept a pool. Water in the garden, whether still or moving, gives it an extra, almost otherworldly quality. It is always fascinating, and provides another dimension of interest with the fish, frogs, newts and other small water animals which will inevitably make it their home.

When you are choosing a site for the pool, you should, as with the rock garden, ensure that it is well away from trees, to avoid trouble with falling leaves in autumn. The bottom of a slope is always a good place for it, especially if it is to be a natural pond, lined with clay. This also overcomes the problems of trying to grow ordinary plants in badly drained conditions, as the pool can be surrounded with moisture-loving and swamp-type, for example primulas, the American yellow arum, ferns, Japanese irises, astilbes and so on.

Other specialities besides pools and rock gardens that you might consider are those which are of particular interest to you, or a member of your family. For instance, dahlias arouse great enthusiasm with their dazzling colours – they make excellent plants for the show bench – and chrysanthemums are another group whose subtle colours, incurving blooms and long season of flowering have also won a large body of worshippers. The elusive charm of the old shrub roses is bringing them back into favour; their heavy perfume and crinkled and quartered blooms can provide, for some people, much greater pleasure than the hybrid tea and floribunda roses.

You could set aside a border for flowers and foliage purely for cutting for the house; the flower arranger will be very thankful for this, and the appearance of the borders will not be spoilt by raids on the plants for their flowers and leaves. A part of the garden in which flowers are grown for their fragrance is always delightful; sunny and sheltered, it will be a haven for bees, and could include herbs like lavender, rosemary and thyme.

One final feature which can give more pleasure than the whole of the rest of the garden put together is a greenhouse. The extra warmth and shelter from wind that it provides, even if it is unheated in winter, mean that the range of plants is widened very appreciably. It also means that they can certainly be grown to perfection, not always possible outdoors where there are the risks of drought, frost, hail, heavy rain, cats and dogs, gales and children destroying a cherished display or crop.

A garden room attached to the house is a variation on the greenhouse, and the lean-to against a wall cuts down the costs of erection tremendously. A lean-to will also be less expensive to maintain.

FLOWERS TO GROW FROM SEED

When you look at a border crowded with flowers of many different colours and varieties have you sometimes thought about where they all came from? The art of gardening goes far back into history until its origins are lost. We can only suppose that back in early times settled populations collected useful plants which they found growing wild: herbs and others that were good to eat, believed to be valuable medicinally, or which would produce dyes for cloth. These were perhaps replanted and cultivated close to the dwelling to save trouble, and as time went on further additions must have been made of flowers that were simply attractive to look at or had a sweet smell. There is no reason to believe that early man was too primitive to take pleasure in such things, for we know that he not merely painted pictures with great skill but also that he used personal ornaments of many different kinds.

These early peoples could not have failed to notice that some of the plants which they had imported into their gardens continued to grow in the same place year after year, while others died down, but shed their seed so that next year they were all over the place. As a result of this, certain kinds were soon crowded out by the more vigorous and prolific species, so that the gardener had to intervene by weeding and replanting or by saving and sowing the seed in the same way as he did with his crops of corn.

So he soon learnt to distinguish between the *perennials* that went on and on, and the *annuals* which could be sown from seed to flower in the same year, and *biennials* which produced their flowers in the year following the year of sowing.

As the art of gardening developed valuable or attractive plants caught the eye of travellers, who brought home the seed from climates more genial than those in which they lived. There must have been many disappointments when these failed to germinate or were cut down in infancy by frost,

but it was found that if they could be given protection until the danger of frost was past they could be coaxed into flourishing in places where they did not naturally grow. Alternatively, if they were fast growers, their sowing could be delayed until the seedlings would be safe, to produce a late display. These are the plants that we now call *half-hardy annuals*, and the modern gardener gives them the protection from frost that they need by sowing them under glass and planting them out after the danger of frost is past, or uses the method of sowing late in the open just mentioned. When autumn comes and the frosts return, that is the end of the half-hardy annuals.

But the dividing lines between these classes of plants are not quite absolute.

According to the climate or district in which your garden is situated, short-lived perennials such as wallflowers can be grown as biennials, and perennials such as antirrhinums can be grown as annuals.

From the earliest times some form of plant-breeding must have been practised for both farm crops and garden plants, by always selecting the best plants to provide next year's seed. In this way the strains were gradually improved, but if this process of selection were not kept up plants would soon degenerate into their wild state again – the state in which they could best survive naturally.

In the cottage garden of the old days a considerable amount of saving of seed from this year's flowers to be re-sown next year

ABOVE: Convolvulus 'Royal Ensign' has trumpet-shaped flowers of bright deep blue with brilliantly contrasting white and yellow centres.

LEFT: A giant dahlia-flowering variety of zinnia, in a wide range of autumn colours.

was practised. Or sometimes the flowers were simply allowed to seed themselves so that they grew in roughly the same place year after year and were then weeded out when they started to get out of hand. But to keep more varieties and get better blooms it was necessary to go back to the plant-breeder for seed produced by crossing under controlled conditions.

This brings us to one other class that should be mentioned. The hybrids that produce some of the gardener's finest effects are by nature unstable, and their seed unlikely to produce such good results next year unless it is produced by the scientific plant breeder.

Such seed is known to the scientist as seed of the 'first filial generation', an expression that is mercifully abbreviated in seed catalogues to F_1 Hybrids.

CULTIVATION OF HARDY ANNUALS

As you have already seen, hardy annuals are so called because you can simply sow the seed in the open where you want the plants to grow. While there are a few species, such as nasturtiums, which seem to flourish quite well on poor soil, you should make it

the general rule to give hardy annuals better conditions if you want to get good blooms. So select sunny, open and well-drained situations and prepare the ground before sowing.

You must first create the conditions in which the mature plants can thrive, and second, work up the soil surface to give the seed the best chance of germination.

After the soil has been dug properly and has been broken up by the weather, fork the ground over a few days before sowing, and incorporate about 2 oz. per sq. yd. of bonemeal in the top 3 in. if you have any doubts about the fertility of the soil. It will be a little while before the soil gets the benefit of this but by the time the plants have put down their roots, the extra nourishment will have become available. Do not dig in fresh manure as it encourages leaf growth instead of flowers.

If you have previous gardening experience you will know by instinct when the soil is in condition to produce a good tilth for the seed bed, and will know that you have to wait for the right day, particularly if the soil is at all heavy. Rake the surface level and remove stones and lumps with your fingers. When conditions are right, light raking will bring the soil to a fine fluffy and crumbly condition which the seeds like. It will not do this if it is wet.

Do not scatter seed thickly from the packet. If the seed is of good quality you can expect a high rate of germination, and it will go much further if you sprinkle it thinly, a small pinch at a time, and even then some of the plants will have to be thinned out. This is not simply wasteful, for if the seedlings are tightly packed thinning will disturb those that are left and may check them. With pelleted seeds the task is made easier, as they are larger and may be sown more sparsely so that there is less need for subsequent thinning.

Cover the seed lightly with fine soil to about twice the thickness of the seeds and, using a fine rose on the watering can, sprinkle enough water to moisten the surface soil. Needless to say, this will evaporate quickly in a hot, dry spell, so it is a good thing to give the newly-sown seed a little shade at such times. Evergreen or other twigs will provide shade and also some protection against birds and excavations by cats.

Cloches can be a great help by keeping the seed-bed warm and protecting it from heavy rain and once again birds, if the ends are closed with glass sheets. But beware of brilliant sunshine, when the temperature can quickly become too fierce for the tender young shoots whose roots do not yet reach down far enough to get to the moister soil below.

CULTIVATION OF HALF-HARDY ANNUALS

As half-hardy annuals are plants which have been introduced from climates in which frost seldom occurs (and where many of them are perennial) their cultivation consists in artificially giving them conditions which are like those of their country of origin.

You can provide these conditions by sowing the seed in the artificial heat of the greenhouse or in a frame, unless they are to be sown late outside. The late sowing method can be adopted for asters, cosmos, African and French marigolds, mignonette, and zinnias, all of which should be sown in late May or early June. The last two in particular are best handled in this way because they do not transplant well and germinate best in well-firmed soil.

For the others, since you are not growing the seed in beds, and want to plant the young seedlings out later, you should use pots or boxes in which you can provide the most favourable soil conditions possible, in the form of specially prepared seed-compost obtained from garden suppliers. Fill the pot or box with compost and press it down firmly but not too vigorously with the bottom of another pot or a flat piece of wood. You will then find that the surface is about $\frac{1}{2}$ in. from the top. Sprinkle the seed very thinly onto this prepared surface, cover it over just as you would annual seed sown in the open, and over the top place a sheet of glass and a sheet of brown paper to give the seeds the darkness that they like for germinating. The prepared compost should contain sufficient moisture not to require the watering that you would have given annuals, but as there will be a lot of condensation beneath the glass, from which large drops of moisture will drip, remove and wipe the glass daily, and replace it the other way up. Both glass and paper should be removed once the seeds have germinated, and the box or pots placed where the light can reach them and watered.

Seedlings are ready for replanting usually by the time they are showing two pairs of leaves. At this point you will appreciate the advantage of having sown them thinly. They should then be levered up with a wooden label or spatula, and carefully lifted out without handling the roots. Pick them up gently by the tops. They are not yet ready to put outside until May, but should now be replanted in other boxes or pots, about 2 in. apart. On this occasion they should be gently watered again and kept under cover until early May when, in mild weather, they can be brought out in the boxes to stand in the open for hardening off before their final replanting. If they are under frames there is no need to move them

at all; it is enough simply to lift the lids off the frame. It is important to keep the bottoms of the boxes or pots in contact with a firm base of soil to prevent their drying out from underneath. When they have had their period of hardening they are ready for the final planting out. Give them a good watering an hour or so beforehand so that the soil which is attached to their roots during this process will be moist. Then water them again when they have been planted out.

CULTIVATION OF BIENNIALS

Plants classed as biennials are those which will not flower until the year after the seed is sown. This does not necessarily mean that they are delicate, but because they are not to flower within the year of sowing you may as well give them the best possible conditions by leaving sowing in the open ground until late June or July. At that time they should germinate and go ahead well if the seed bed is kept moist during these sunnier months.

With hardy plants there is nothing to be gained by giving them artificial heat. It is, indeed, best avoided. However, the method of sowing in a cold frame or unheated greenhouse earlier, in March or April, in boxes or pots is commonly adopted for plants that are not required in large numbers. The cold frame in particular should be kept well ventilated to prevent overheating, and the boxes or frames shaded during germination to conserve moisture as with annuals.

Certain biennials, notably foxgloves, forget-me-nots; mulleins, and hollyhocks are so readily self-seeding that they can be left to perpetuate themselves without any of the procedures which have just been described.

USES OF ANNUALS AND BIENNIALS

If you are starting with a brand-new garden you may find that you will have to lean particularly heavily on annuals in order to get some kind of a display as soon as possible while your hardy herbaceous perennials are growing up. If you can sow your seed in March or April, you should have a display from May or June onwards.

Because annuals are renewed each year you can recompose the colour-groupings of your beds and borders each year within the overall framework of the hardy herbaceous perennials, shrubs, and trees that remain at their stations from one year to the next. To use an analogy, you can give your garden a new summer frock each year. If you are a photographer, recording colour pictures taken each summer can be very interesting

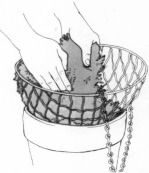

in retrospect, and a great help in planning future displays.

Once you have got the garden running, your main show of flowers will last from May to November. A lot depends on how much time you have, as large beds of annuals grown in profusion will demand a fair deal of attention with watering, sticking and staking, and weeding. If you have a rather exposed garden you may do well to avoid the taller kinds and concentrate on the low-growing annuals which are easier to care for. It may go hard to dispense with lofty clumps of larkspurs, but you will be spared the pain of seeing them in ruins after a gale.

Annuals come in all sizes, and it is an obvious fundamental rule when you are planning a border to grow the tallest at the back and the shortest at the front. Right at the very front come the dwarfs, of which there is a large variety, to form edgings that can be allowed to stray here and there over the paths, or even be grown in crevices in the paving. This is not merely decorative but will help to keep weeds from growing there instead. Where there is room, many gardeners leave small spaces among the stones or bricks for this purpose. Among the small annuals may be mentioned *Limnanthes douglasii*, which is self-seeding though not inclined to run riot and has quite large white

ABOVE: *Making a hanging basket for flowers. Line the basket with moss which has been soaked in water, wringing out the excess moisture. Fill with compost and plant flowers ready-grown in pots.*
BELOW: *The finished basket.*
BOTTOM: *Blue pimpernel,* Anagallis linifolia, *has brilliant scarlet or blue flowers.*
OPPOSITE: *The beautiful pink flowers of* Mesembryanthemum criniflorum, *properly called* Dorotheanthus bellidiflorus, *come in many other brilliant colours.*

flowers with yellow centres, mesembryanthemum, also with daisy-like flowers, anagallis (pimpernel), creeping zinnia (*Sanvitalia procumbens*) with blooms like miniature sunflowers.

Town gardeners with patios, or country gardeners with courtyards, can get fine effects with half-hardy annuals. These can be grown from seed as already described, or bought as seedlings for planting out in May in tubs, pots, window-boxes, or jardinières. Lovely shows can be obtained with antirrhinums, petunias, fragrant stocks, annual chrysanthemums, cherry pie (heliotrope), lobelias, *Phlox drummondii*, and African and French marigolds. For hanging baskets heliotropes, trailing lobelias, free-flowering nasturtiums, and petunias may be used.

Cut flowers

In the A–Z section annuals and biennials that are particularly useful for cutting are noted. In order to ensure an adequate supply you might consider devoting part of the vegetable garden for a few of the kinds that are specially useful for this purpose. If there is a sudden call for flowers indoors it is then not so necessary to raid the beds, and your local church will always be grateful for your flowers, even if it does not get the benefit of your attendance.

Biennials

Biennials need only be considered separately as flowers for the border because they will remain in their positions when the autumn comes. By then the annuals will all be finished, the beds possibly covered with autumn leaves, and the job of clearing up for the winter can be undertaken. If you grow biennials you should mark them or keep an eye on where they are so that you do not rake them up with the dead leaves in your enthusiasm for having everything looking neat and tidy.

One of the most familiar biennials is the wallflower, which is not only available in the most beautiful shades of rich golds and deep reds but also has a curiously haunting fragrance which is particularly noticeable on warm days in May. They are not always easy to establish in walls, where they seem happiest, but once a few decide to take up residence in ruined masonry or old brick-work, where there are plenty of crevices, they will often continue to spread by self-seeding without much further attention. For the flower-beds there are the 9-in. 'Tom Thumb' varieties, which can be brought well to the front and do not straggle so much as the standards.

All such biennials may be planted in position either in early autumn or, if winter proves unusually severe, in March. They will still grow well, though their roots will be less well established than if planted before winter.

Other favourites among biennials are the equally sweetly-scented Sweet Williams – old-fashioned-looking flowers which are obtainable in a wide variety of the most delightful colour combinations. Canterbury Bells can provide masses of their different shades of blue, pink, and purple, which gives a delicious contrast with the more sophisticated hues of many other border flowers, but in some gardens they romp all over the place like a pack of school children. However, you can pull them up wherever their impertinence is beyond bearing.

Cynoglossum has flowers like forget-me-nots; there are innumerable varieties of polyanthus, violas, pansies, and Iceland poppies (*Papaver nudicaule*). There is also that piece of garden Victoriana, honesty, whose peeled flat seed-pods look like mother-of-pearl. It makes a useful if bulky house-decoration for winter, but it is another grossly invasive plant in the garden, in that it seeds itself readily, though unwanted seedlings are easily pulled up.

ANNUALS AND BIENNIALS FOR THE COOL GREENHOUSE

It has been already mentioned that many plants that are annuals in the more northerly

climates are able to survive winter and grow as perennials in warmer parts. This will often be true when they are given an artificial warm climate in a cool greenhouse at a minimum of about 45°F (7°C). Here, also, of course, you can cultivate various flowers that you would not otherwise have at all. John Innes Seed Compost, or a peat-based soilless compost are suitable for sowing seeds of such plants.

Among these plants, for instance, is *Cobaea scandens*, the Mexican cup-and-saucer vine, whose purple flowers will continue for a long period. But do not entertain it if your greenhouse is a small one. It is very fast growing and quite capable of taking the greenhouse over. On a sunny wall in a large conservatory it will climb to 20 ft. in one season.

Morning glories (*Ipomoea* or *Pharbitis*), grow to only half this height, with their blue bell-tent flowers. *Eccremocarpus scaber*, the Chilean glory vine, is another climber with a long blooming season of bright orange tubular flowers; it can also be grown outside if a sunny, fairly sheltered spot can be found for it. All this group may also be grown in pots.

For germinating the best temperature is around 65°F (18°C), with a moist atmosphere. This temperature should be maintained during germination, after sowing under glass in March, and thereafter it can gradually be reduced. Provided an even temperature of 45°F (7°C) can be provided there will be no need to have a fully heated greenhouse. The higher temperature required for germination can easily be provided by a soil-warming cable under a bottomless wooden box with a sheet of glass over it, which forms a propagating frame.

The use of glass and brown paper to provide darkness and moisture for the germina-

tion period has already been mentioned. After germination the glass should be removed, but this must be compensated for by slightly increased watering. Some shade may, however, still have to be provided for the very young seedlings if the sun becomes at all fierce.

Around Christmas people pay high prices for cyclamen plants in pots. Cyclamens are mentioned here, because although strictly speaking they are perennial tuberous-rooted plants, you can raise them yourself from seed in the cool greenhouse. They take 15 months to come to flower so you can sow them in August for the Christmas after next. This sowing time is, of course, at the height of summer, and the seeds require a temperature of only 60°F (15°C) for germinating. So you may need to shade the greenhouse, keeping the atmosphere moist by wetting the floor, and when the seedlings have made two leaves, prick them out into trays or small pots and grow them on in gentle warmth. When the little corms have formed transfer them into their final pots, taking care to press the corms firmly into the soil but not to bury them. Many shades can be obtained in salmon, crimson, mauve, and white, or the Japanese 'Kimono' strain in mixed colours. *Cyclamen persicum*, the grandfather of the modern hybrids, remains one of the most delightful with its fragrant flowers in spring. Cyclamens should be re-potted every year in later summer or early autumn.

Other plants that can be easily raised from seed to provide colour in the cool greenhouse during winter and early spring include *Primula malacoides* and *Primula denticulata*, which is a hardy perennial. Both have strong stems, the former with flowers of pink, lilac, and mauve; the latter in purple, mauve, and white. Fragrant polyanthus and primroses of various colours will flower for many months in the cool house.

From February onwards cinerarias sown in June will flower, at the same time as *Limnanthes douglasii* and nemophila, which should be grown in partial shade. Schizanthus, the butterfly-flower, will also flower in February and onwards in innumerable shades of lemon, apricot, pink, mauve, and purple, with attractive markings. Calceolarias sown in the previous May will start to flower in March.

Salpiglossis has richly-coloured trumpet-shaped flowers with veined markings in rose, crimson, purple, and cream, and has dwarf forms about 1 ft. high and large-flowered hybrids up to 3 ft. This flowers in May from sowings in the previous August or September.

Various varieties of *Coleus blumei* are grown for their leaves. They enjoy a jungle-like environment of warmth and moisture and should be sown in warm conditions in February. They are usually treated as annuals. The blue flower-spikes should be pinched out to encourage them to produce more of their nettle-like leaves in shades of red-bronze, yellow, green, and maroon.

Celosia plumosa produces bright-red feathery plumes in summer. It should be sown under glass in March in rich soil and given plenty of light.

Californian poppy (*Eschscholzia*) is an annual which dislikes being transplanted, so it should be sown thinly in the pots in which it is to flower. After the seeds have germinated the seedlings are thinned out to 5 or 6 plants in a pot to produce orange, copper, yellow, carmine, and ivory flowers. Other plants treated in similar fashion are linaria, viscaria, and mignonette (reseda), which has sweetly fragrant flowers.

In the cool greenhouse you can also grow antirrhinum, brachycome, *Campanula isophylla* (which is suitable for hanging baskets), *Campanula pyramidalis* with pale blue flowers on erect stems 5–6 ft. high, and clarkia which is sown in autumn to flower in the following spring. Annual and biennial stocks (*Matthiola*) are sown at different times of the year for their colour and fragrance.

Hybrid petunias make excellent pot plants which can also be grown in tubs or hanging baskets. They are very long lasting and available in many colours and types.

A–Z OF FLOWERS

Adonis (Buttercup family) (pheasant's eye). *A. aestivalis* has small crimson flowers and attractive, deep-green, finely cut leaves. Sow in a sunny position in spring for June and July flowering.

Ageratum (Daisy family) (floss flower). The fluffy flowers, mainly in shades of blue (but there are white varieties) continue from July until the autumn frosts, without fading. 'Blue Mink', powder blue; 'Blue Mist', mid-blue and early flowering; 'Fairy Pink', pale pink. All are about 6 in. high. *A. mexicanum* has lavender-blue flowers. Sow in February or March under glass for planting out towards the end of May in a sunny bed, window box, etc. Dwarf kinds are grown in pots to flower in a cool greenhouse.

Agrostemma (Pink family) (corn cockle). Single magenta flowers are borne throughout summer on stems 18–24 in. tall. 'Milas' is a decorative variety whose large rosylilac flowers show dark streaks along each petal; a useful variety for cutting on account of its long, stiff stems. Sow in the open in autumn or spring.

Althaea (Mallow family) (hollyhock). The biennial hollyhocks are easily raised from seed in the open during May or June. Transplant the seedlings once before moving to

their flowering positions in autumn or early spring. They will flower the following July and August. Single or double varieties are available in the familiar shades of crimson, pink, yellow, and white. Sow the annual form under glass in February or March and out in May. All the hollyhocks grow to 5 ft. or more.

Alyssum (Cabbage family) (sweet alyssum or alison). *A. maritimum* gets its popular name from the fragrance of its small flower heads, which are abundant in summer and early autumn. Varieties include 'Lilac Queen'; 'Little Dorrit', white; 'Rosie O'Day', deep rose-pink; 'Royal Carpet', violet-purple; 'Violet Queen'. Raise either from seed sown in the flowering position in spring or sow under glass in late winter and plant out about mid-May. It thrives in pavings and window-boxes, and is excellent for edgings.

Amaranthus (Amaranth family) (Lovelies-bleeding). The crimson tassels from which this half-hardy annual, *A. caudatus*, takes its name appear throughout July to September. The variety 'Viridis' has greenish-yellow tassels. Sow the seed in the open ground in April. The position should be sunny, and the soil well drained, but it requires plenty of moisture for growing. Plants grow about 36-in. high.

ABOVE: Agrostemma *'Milas', the most decorative variety of corn cockle.*
BELOW: Amaranthus caudatus, *popularly known as Love-lies-bleeding.*
OPPOSITE: *Gazanias, often called the treasure flower.*

Anagallis (Primrose family) (pimpernel). *A. linifolia* is available in the traditional scarlet, or blue, for open sowing in the rock garden or border. The site should be well drained and warm to produce 6–12 in. high plants with brilliant flowers throughout most of the summer.

Antirrhinum (Figwort family) (snapdragon). This familiar flower offers a range of colours in various combinations of reds and yellows, and also white. It can be obtained in standard sizes up to 36 in. down to 9-in. dwarfs. Antirrhinums can be sown in the open in April, but for much better results sow in boxes or pots in a warm greenhouse in February or March, and plant out in a sunny situation in May. They are best treated as annuals except in very mild districts. Rust has been a serious problem, but there is now an excellent selection of resistant hybrids.

Arctotis (Daisy family) (African daisy). Available in many colours, and with characteristically attractive grey leaves, these grow up to 24 in. high. In Britain arctotis is not perennial, but should be sown under glass in March at about 65°F (18°C), and hardened off before planting out in mid–May. The site should be well drained and sunny. Pinch the young plants back when they are 6-in. high to encourage bushing. *A. grandis* has a mauve centre and a golden band.

Bellis (Daisy family) (double daisy). *Bellis perennis* 'Monstrosa Flore Pleno' grows to 6 in. with crimson, rose, or white buttons which make an attractive contribution to the spring border. Sow the seeds in open ground in early summer and transplant in the autumn.

Brachycome (Daisy family) (Swan River daisy). This has starry blue or white flowers with a dark disk. It grows to 12-in. high and flowers throughout summer until autumn frosts. *B. iberidifolia* can be treated as a hardy annual, but it is best sown under glass in March for May planting in a dry and sunny position, where it will grow well. Or it may be grown as a pot plant in a cool greenhouse.

Calendula (Daisy family) (pot marigold or friendship flower in the USA, whence many varieties come). The plant is so called because of its use for flavouring soups, not because it is grown in pots. It is hardy and easy to grow almost anywhere, but it rejoices in sunshine and will flower on throughout summer and autumn, growing to a height of 24 in. Sow it in spring or autumn where it is to flower. Transplanting is easy, if required. It is self-seeding but apt to deteriorate unless fresh seed is purchased annually. 'First Lady', bright yellow; 'Gold Galore', golden; 'Indian Maid', orange with maroon centres; 'Lemon Beauty'; 'Radio', orange balled flowers, are among the many cultivars.

Callistephus (Daisy family) (China aster). These offer an immense colour range of double and single flowers on plants up to 2½ ft. high, which are quite invaluable for the border and for cutting. Sow them in March or April in a cool greenhouse, or outdoors in early May in a sheltered open site. Transplanting is easy when the seedlings are small. They are at their best when massed, and this is just as true when growing the shorter varieties in window boxes. For cutting 'Ostrich Plume' and 'Princess', growing to 24 in. are recommended.

Celosia (Amaranth family) (cockscomb). Of tropical origin celosia should be given well-drained light soils and plenty of sun. 'Thompsonii magnifica' is a fine 24-in. specimen of the feathered form of *C. argentea cristata* with plumes in shades from red into yellow, which appear from July to September. The seed is sown in a warm greenhouse in March, and the seedlings potted individually for planting out in mid-June in southern England. Some may be retained in the greenhouse as pot-plants.

Centaurea (Daisy family) (cornflower, sweet sultan, bluebottle). *C. cyanus* will grow to 3 ft. with flowers of a clear clean blue, and also paler shades: lilac, pink, and white. Dwarf varieties do not exceed 1 ft. Give them sunshine, and sow from March to May, or in September where there is some drainage. Sweet Sultan is *C. moschata* with large lilac-coloured fluffy heads which are scented. There are also giant varieties in mauve, purple, rose, yellow, and white, and these are sown in the same way. It is a useful cutting plant which survives well in the house if cut young. All kinds grow well in chalky soil.

Cheiranthus (Cabbage family) (wallflower). Most wallflowers grow to about 15-in. high, giving out their fragrance on warm summer days. Their typical colours are yellow and blood red, but there are many other varieties in purple, pink, and ivory white. The common wallflower is *C. cheiri*, best treated as a biennial, sown in an open seed bed in May and replanted in October, where the plants are to flower. *C. × allionii* is the Siberian wallflower with bright orange flowers from March to May. 'Golden Bedder' is mellower in colour. Sow these in June, and transplant as above. 'Persian Carpet' is a strain of mixed colours, while 'Tom Thumb' is a 9-in. version in various colours, suitable for small beds, window boxes or for filling in borders.

Chrysanthemum (Daisy family) (painted lady, crown daisy, corn marigold). Annual chrysanthemums have either single or double daisy-like flowers with white or cream petals, often with coloured rings.

ABOVE: Cleome *'Pink Queen'*, the spider flower.

TOP: Centaurea *'Polka Dot'* is one of the dwarf cornflowers.

OPPOSITE: *A fine display of wallflowers,* Cheiranthus.

Give them a sunny position where it is not too wet, and sow the seed in April where the plants are to flower, or in September for the next year's early display. Unfortunately the thinnings are of little use for transplanting. *C. carinatum* (painted lady) grows to 2 ft., *C. coronarium* (crown daisy) to 3 ft., and *C. segetum* (corn marigold) to 1½ ft. These are among the best hardy annuals for summer, and almost indispensable for cutting.

Clarkia (Evening Primrose family). *C. elegans* hybrids with double flowers are generally preferred. These have spikes of salmon-pink, carmine, rosy-purple, or white flowers to 2-ft. high. Sow seeds in the open in March or April, or in September for flowering the following May or June. The site should be sheltered, and the young plants supported with twigs, as they are vulnerable to wind. Never give clarkia a heavy soil or soggy position. Sow under glass in autumn for a cold greenhouse display in spring.

Cleome (Caper family) (spider plant). *C. spinosa* has erect, thorny stems reaching up to 4 ft. high, surmounted by large open flower-trusses of pinky-mauve, apple-blossom pink ('Pink Queen') or white. It gives its best effect in the border when grown in clumps. Sow in March in a warm greenhouse for planting out in May and for flowering from June to September. It likes well-drained soil but requires plenty of moisture to support its rapid growth.

Cobaea (Polemonium family) (cup-and-saucer plant). *C. scandens* should be grown on a warm wall, where its stems will reach to 20 ft. The flowers, which open green, turn violet-purple (there is a white variety) and resemble Canterbury bells. Out of doors it is an annual, but is perennial in a cool greenhouse. In March soak the large seeds for a few hours before sowing them on edge in pots in the greenhouse. Pot on and plant out in early June.

Convolvulus (Bindweed family). *C. tricolor* (syn. *C. minor*) is a bushy plant up to 15-in. tall. The funnel-shaped flowers are generally deep blue, yellow, and white, and continue throughout summer. It should be given full sunshine but will grow well in poor soil. Sow in position in March, April, or September. Varieties are 'Cambridge Blue', 'Crimson Monarch', and 'Royal Ensign', a royal-blue trailer.

Coreopsis (Daisy family) (tickseed). This may be found in catalogues as calliopsis. The flowers are large, with broad, pleasingly marked petals of yellow, brown, and crimson. Sow the seed in the open in April or under glass in March. Give it sunshine. It will thrive in quite poor soil, reaching a height of 2½ ft.

Cosmos (Daisy family) (cosmea). The large, daisy-like flowers are single or double in hues of orange, yellow, deep rose, vermilion, red, and white, accompanied by attractive, fern-like foliage. Growing between 2 and 3 ft. high, it is very useful for cutting from July to October. Sow under glass in February and March at 60°F (16°C), prick out the seedlings and plant them out in May. Give the plants full sun and well-drained soil.

Dahlia (Daisy family). Dahlias grown for bedding are sown thinly in boxes in late March, and will germinate in a warm greenhouse in 10 days. Prick out the seedlings or pot individually for planting out in the middle of May. They should be given a sunny situation, good soil, and plenty of moisture while growing. Plants are often discarded after flowering, although after the first autumn frost tubers may be lifted, washed, dried, and stored for the winter away from frost. These tubers, planted out in the following spring, will flower from July. Cuttings may be taken from tubers put into a warm greenhouse in April.

Delphinium (Buttercup family) (larkspur). Larkspurs are obtainable in blue, pink, lavender, mauve, rosy-scarlet, and white, either as 3-ft. standard kinds or in dwarf varieties half that height. They do not transplant well, so in March or April the seed should be sown where the plants are to flower in July. For an earlier show sow them in the open in autumn. Cuttings may be taken from the tall varieties with branching, stock-flowered spikes.

Dianthus (Pink family) (pink). There are many varieties, such as the Chabaud carnations (*D. caryophyllus*), Japanese pink (*D. chinensis* 'Heddewigii'). In February and March sow thinly in pots, covering lightly with sifted soil, to germinate in a week to 10 days in a warm greenhouse. Prick out as soon as possible and plant out in May after hardening off. Give them sunshine and well-drained soil. Heights vary from 9 to 18 in. The Sweet William, *D. barbatus*, is sown in April and planted in July, to flower the following spring and summer. There is a wide choice of beautiful colourings.

Digitalis (Figwort family) (foxglove). Though naturally a woodland plant which grows well (4–5 ft.) in shade, *D. purpurea* does just as well in sunshine. 'Excelsior Hybrids' have flowers arranged horizontally around the stem revealing the attractive markings of the florets. The 'Shirley' strains are especially fine. Colour ranges from pink, to purple, cream, and white. Sow seed in May to July to flower the following year.

Dimorphotheca (Daisy family) (star of the veldt). *D. aurantiaca* produces 1-ft. plants with large daisy-like flowers in salmon, pink, apricot, buff, and orange, with greenish-black centres, which remain closed in dull weather. The 'Glistening White' variety has a spreading habit. In southern England sow in May to flower in 6 weeks' time if the weather suits. Elsewhere sow under glass in March and plant out in May.

Eccremocarpus (Bignonia family) (Chilean glory flower). A climber attaining a length of 10 ft., *E. scaber* produces clusters of orange-scarlet, yellow-tipped tubular flowers throughout summer and autumn. Sow under glass in March and plant against a sunny wall after the frosts. It is a rapid grower.

Eschscholzia (Poppy family) (Californian poppy). *E. californica* has single, semi-double and double poppies in hues of yellow, orange, copper, and ivory to 1½ ft. high. Easily raised from seed it can be left to seed for itself.

Gaillardia (Daisy family) (blanket flower). *G. pulchella* is the annual (1½ ft.) form with crimson-purple flowers tipped with yellow. 'Indian Chief' is copper-scarlet. Sow under glass in March in gentle heat or in the open in April to flower from July to October. Give it sunshine and good drainage. It is useful for cutting.

Gazania (Daisy family) (treasure flower). Sow seed under glass in March in a moderate temperature, and plant out in sunny

ABOVE: Eschscholzia californica, *the Californian poppy, is easily raised from seed.*
TOP: Helichrysum bracteatum monstrosum *is an excellent dried flower.*
RIGHT: Iberis umbellata, *the common form of candytuft.*
FAR RIGHT: *'Monarch' is one of the dwarf varieties of* Godetia.

positions in mid-May. The modern hybrids are yellow, orange, brown, pink, and ruby daisies 6–9 in. high, with contrasting centres. Sow them in spring in light, well-drained, sunny positions.

Godetia (Evening Primrose family). Godetias have large, cup-shaped double or single flowers in pink, mauve, salmon, and white. The dwarfs grow to 1 ft., and the taller kinds, which are excellent for cutting, to 2½ ft. Sow them in March or April or in autumn in a sunny situation and light soil. The seedlings do not transplant well.

Gypsophila (Pink family) (baby's breath). *G. elegans* produces dainty, white flowers on slender 1½-ft. stems. Those of 'Rosea' are pink. This is a fast grower which, if sown in the open in April and at intervals of 3 weeks, will flower from June onwards. It prefers chalk, but will thrive in most good soils, and is a very useful 'fill' in flower arrangements.

Helianthus (Daisy family) (sunflower). Too well known to need description, sunflowers will grow in most soils, but like sunshine, and will reach for it to a height of 7 ft. For shorter varieties, 'Autumn Beauty' (3 ft.) is sulphur-yellow with a copper zone; 'Sunburst' (4 ft.) is multicoloured. Sow in the open in April or in boxes under glass and plant out in mid-May.

Helichrysum (Daisy family) (everlasting flower). These are used when cut and dried for winter house decoration. The Australian varieties are the best known. There is a double form 'Monstrosum' of *H. bracteatum* in crimson, rose, silvery pink, bronze, and white, and also dwarf, compact border varieties. Give them sun and a light soil.

Iberis (Cabbage family) (candytuft). *I. coronaria* is the giant-flowered candytuft, and *I. umbellata* is the common form. These are best massed in the border, but the seed need not be thickly sown. Dwarf varieties are in shades of lilac, rose, and white. Sow in the open in September for early summer-flowering, or in March and April. Give them moist, rich soil.

Ipomoea (Bindweed family) (morning glory). This is truly *I. tricolor*, though often listed as *I. rubrocaerulea*. The large, sky-blue trumpet flowers are 4-in. across, and show from July to September. Germination is not very reliable, but it helps to chip the hard seed covers carefully with a sharp knife before sowing them singly in small pots in a warm greenhouse in March. Plant them in a warm, sheltered spot in well drained soil in May. They attain a height of 8 ft. or more. Although they belong to the bindweed family, they are not weeds as they die off in autumn.

Kochia (Goosefoot family) (summer cypress, firebush). A 3-ft. foliage plant, this is called 'firebush' because of the fiery colour of the finely-cut leaves in autumn. The seeds of *K. scoparia tricophylla* are either sown singly in small pots, or in threes in 3½-in. pots and thinned to single plants. Plant out in late May, and be cautious over watering the young seedlings.

Lathyrus (Pea family) (sweet pea). There is a huge variety of modern hybrids of the sweet pea, in all sizes from dwarfs such as 'Bijou' (1 ft.) through mediums such as 'Knee-hi' (3–4 ft.) up to 8 ft. 'Galaxy' is early flowering. Sow the peas in pots or boxes in autumn and overwinter them in a cold frame that is as mouse-proof as possible. Plant in the open in mid-March or early April to begin flowering in June, 1 ft. apart with 1 ft. between rows. Pea sticks, netting, or tripods are all used to give them climbing room. Give them deeply-dug, fertile soil in a sunny situation.

Lavatera (Mallow family) (mallow). *L. trimestris* may attain 4 ft. and bush out to 3-ft. wide, with hollyhock-like flowers throughout summer. 'Loveliness' is a variety with bright carmine flowers, and a white variety is also obtainable. Sow thinly in a sunny flowering position in March or April, giving it enough room.

Limnanthes (Limnanthes family) butter and eggs). This is about 6-in. tall, with a spreading habit, shiny green leaves and fragrant, bright yellow flowers. Sow *L. douglasii* in an open, sunny position, in September for spring flowering, or March to mid-May for summer flowering.

Linaria (Figwort family) (toadflax). This grows to 9 in. with many small snapdragon-like flowers. *L. maroccana* should be thinly sown in March or April to flower from June to September. The 'Fairy Bouquet' strain provides flowers in pink, yellow, lavender, and salmon.

Linum (Flax family) (flax). The common flax with baby-blue flowers is *L. usitatissimum*. *L. grandiflorum* 'Rubrum' is scarlet. Both grow to 15 in. Choose sunny positions and sow for clumps in spring for summer flowering.

Lobelia (Bellflower family). *L. erinus* grows 4–6 in. high, and has also trailing varieties suitable for hanging baskets or window-boxes, where they need regular watering. Apart from blue varieties there are 'Rosamund', deep carmine-red, and a white variety. Sow the tiny seed thinly in pots of sandy compost in February or early March in a warm greenhouse. Prick out a month later to produce bushy plants for end-of-May planting.

Matthiola (Cabbage family) (night-scented stock). *M. bicornis* is grown for its summer-night fragrance when the lilac-mauve flowers open at evening. Candytuft interspersed will supply colour during the day. Sow it in March or April.

M. incana (ten-week stocks) grow to 1–2 ft. high and are available in a wide colour range. Sow these under glass in March and prick out as soon as possible. When bushy plant out 1 ft. apart.

M. incana (East Lothian or intermediate stocks). These are vigorous, branching stocks, a little higher, which flower in late summer and autumn. Management is as for ten-week stocks, but seed may be sown in February. They are available in crimson, scarlet, rose, lavender, and white. In sheltered gardens they may be biennial.

Mentzelia (Loasa family) (blazing star). *M. lindleyi* is still appearing in some catalogues as *Bartonia aurea*. It has large, single, golden flowers with masses of golden stamens, produced on plants growing 2 ft. high, from June onwards. It will grow easily when sown in March or April in a sunny position.

Mesembryanthemum (Mesembryanthemum family) (the Livingstone daisy). Properly this star-like flower of many brilliant colours is *Dorotheanthus bellidiflorus*. It grows 6 in. high and will spread and trail over a dry wall or in crazy paving. It wants much sun and rather dry soil. Sow under glass in

March or April and plant out in May.

Moluccella (Labiate family) (bells of Ireland) is grown mainly for its large, pale-green, netted calyces, the little white flowers themselves being insignificant. The flower-heads may be dried for use in winter. Sow *M. laevis* under glass in March or April at 65°F (18°C), but germination is unpredictable. It may germinate in the open with light and warm soil in early May, attaining a height of 2 ft.

Myosotis (Borage family) (forget-me-not). Forget-me-nots will grow in sun or partial shade, from 6–12 in. high. Named varieties offer shades of blue, carmine-pink, and white. Sow them in the open ground in June and transplant in autumn to their sites. They are freely self-seeding.

Nemesia (Figwort family). Nemesia flowers freely in numerous colours. Sow *N. strumosa* in mid-March in a cool greenhouse. Grow them steadily, prick the seedlings out into boxes, harden them off and plant in late May or early June. Never allow the soil to dry out. For winter flowering under glass as pot plants, sow in August. Height: 8–12 in.

Nemophila (Hydrophylla family) (baby blue-eyes). A 6–8 in. spreading plant with feathery foliage and white-eyed sky-blue flowers, this is suitable for the border or rock-garden. It likes a moist situation in sun or partial shade. Sow seeds in the open in March or April, or in autumn if there is a sheltered garden. There is a white-flowered form.

Nicotiana (Potato family) (tobacco plant). *N. alata* is grown in particular for its evening fragrance, but in partial shade the flowers may remain open by day. The strain 'Sensation' does remain open in daylight and has flowers of mixed colours. Those of 'Lime Green' are greenish-yellow. It likes rich, moist, deeply dug soil, and flowers from July to September. Sow under glass in moderate temperature in March and plant out when frosts are over.

Nigella (Buttercup family) (love-in-a-mist). *N. damascena* 'Miss Jekyll' has sky-blue flowers and feathery foliage. 'Persian Jewels' has pink, rosy red, mauve, or white flowers. Plants prefer well-drained soil in a sunny situation and seeds should be sown where the plants are to flower. Sow in March or April for a long flowering season from May onwards.

Omphalodes (Borage family) (Venus's navelwort). *O. linifolia* grows to 1 ft. tall and bears great numbers of white flowers and grey-green leaves. It somewhat resembles forget-me-not. Sow seeds in spring or early autumn in light, well-drained soil at the front of a border or in the rock garden. Omphalodes flowers in mid-summer from June through to August.

Papaver (Poppy family) (poppy). Sow poppies in March, April, and May. The Shirley poppy (derived from *P. rhoeas*), may be sown in September and will flower from May. *P. somniferum* is the opium poppy and may be double paeony flowered or double carnation flowered, in a number of colours. 'Pink Beauty' is a variety with double flowers and grey foliage. Heights vary from 1½–2½ ft.

Petunia (Potato family). These sun-loving plants are available as modern hybrids in many colours, multicolours, and of varying habit, with single or double flowers. There are forms suitable for bedding, hanging baskets or window boxes. F$_1$ hybrids are particularly vigorous, with large, trumpet-shaped flowers. Sow seeds under glass in March, grow steadily and prick out when possible to grow on in the greenhouse. Harden off in a cold frame before planting outdoors in May or early June in light soil and a sunny situation.

Phacelia (Hydrophylla family) (Californian bluebell). The large, brilliant blue bellflowers with greyish-green, red-tinted leaves are produced on plants 9 in. to 2 ft. high. *P. campanularia* is a neat plant and should be sown in spring for June flowering in light, well-drained soil in a sunny position. *P. tanacetifolia* is a tall, hairy-leaved species, with spikes of lavender-blue flowers, cultivated by bee-keepers.

Phlox (Phlox family). The popular bedding plant is *P. drummondii*, which may have pink, salmon, crimson, violet, or purple flowers often with a white eye. Smaller varieties may be only 6-in. high, or the 'Grandiflora' hybrids may grow to 1 ft. Sow in gentle heat in March and plant out from mid-May onwards in a sunny situation. They flower from July to early October. Water the young plants well.

Reseda (Reseda family) (mignonette). This is grown especially for its delightful fragrance, but it is also of charming appearance. The variety 'Goliath' has large, very fragrant, reddish spikes. It likes lime. Sow in well-drained soil in April and May, firming the soil down and very lightly covering the seed with fine soil.

Ricinus (Spurge family) (castor oil plant, castor bean). Grown for its decorative foliage, the leaves of *R. communis* has a span of 12–18 ins. and the whole plant may attain 6 ft. in height. The oil comes from the bean-like seeds. Sow singly in small pots in March in a greenhouse at 60°F (15°C). Pot the seedlings on and plant them in June. They like a rich, moist soil, and may need staking in exposed positions.

Rudbeckia (Daisy family) (coneflower). These are gay annuals, 2 ft. high, raised from seed sown under glass in March and planted out in May in a sunny situation. *R. bicolor* 'Golden Flame' is golden-yellow with a dark centre, and 'Kelvedon Star' is deep yellow with a brown central disk and mahogany zone.

Salpiglossis (Potato family) (painted tongue). This grows 2–3 ft. tall and has veined, trumpet-shaped flowers in a range of brilliant colours. Sow seeds in February and March in a warm greenhouse. Prick out the seedlings singly into small pots and grow on steadily for planting out in June. They require rich soil, warmth and shelter, and make good pot plants in a cool greenhouse.

Salvia (Labiate family) (Sage). *S. splendens* is a vivid scarlet perennial, 1–1½ ft. high, treated as a half-hardy annual. Sow it under glass in February or March at 68°F (20°C). Pot the seedlings singly, grow on steadily, and harden off before planting out in late May or early June. Give them a sunny position. *S. horminum*, 1½ ft., purple, is sown in spring where it is to flower. The variety 'Blue Beard' has blue bracts.

Scabiosa (Teasel family) (sweet scabious). *S. atropurpurea*, pincushion flower, 1½–3 ft. tall, normally flowers well from July onwards, but can be had earlier by sowing under glass in March and planting out in May in a sunny border. Support the taller varieties with twigs against summer gales. Mixed colours are available. They are good for cutting.

Schizanthus (Potato family) (butterfly flower). If they are to be grown in the open, schizanthus hybrids should be sown under glass in March and planted out at the end of May in a sunny, sheltered position. Strains 1½–3 ft. high are available, with beautiful petal markings in salmon, apricot, pink, yellow, mauve, and purple.

Tagetes (Daisy family) (African and French marigold). The African marigold, *T. erecta*, branches up to 3 ft., and there are many modern F$_1$ hybrids in softer shades of

ABOVE: Tagetes erecta, *the African marigold, is a very popular garden flower. This species is called 'Picador'.*

TOP: Salpiglossis *comes in a rich variety of colours.*

OPPOSITE: Nicotiana alata, *the tobacco plant, is grown mainly for its fragrance.*

yellow, orange, and lemon. Raise from thinly sown seed in a cool greenhouse and plant out at end of May in a sunny situation. American dwarf hybrids, 1 ft. tall, are available. The French marigold, *T. patula*, is compact, about 9 in. high, with single and double varieties in pale yellow, orange, gold, and mahogany, some with dark foliage.

Tithonia (Daisy family) (Mexican sunflower). *T. rotundifolia*, 4 ft., is a vigorous plant with large, orange-red broad-petalled flowers. Sow in March under glass, pot, and plant out in light soil and full sun towards the end of May for August and September flowering.

Tropaeolum (Nasturtium family) (nasturtium). *T. majus* is a 9-in. trailer and climber which performs better on poor soil than rich. Do not risk sowing before the last late frost, late April being early enough in southern England. Single, semi-double, and double varieties are available in scarlet, golden yellow, cherry-rose, and mahogany red. *T. peregrinum* is the Peruvian 10-ft. climbing species with fringed golden-yellow flowers. This species likes rich soil, and is sown in sun or shade in late April or May for flowering from July onwards.

Ursinia (Daisy family). It has large masses of daisy-like flowers and attractive foliage, growing from 9–15 in. high. Sow it under glass in March and plant out in mid-May in full sun and light, well drained soil. The taller *U. anethoides* has large orange flowers with a chestnut zone in July and August. The dwarf *U. pulchra* is also orange with a dark centre and will suit the rock garden or border front. 'Aurora' is orange and crimson-red. Another recommended variety is 'Golden Bedder'.

Venidium (Daisy family) (Namaqualand daisy). *V. fastuosum* has large, orange flowers with purple-black zones and shiny black centres. It flowers from July to September. Sow it under glass in March and plant out in mid-May in good loamy soil. Give it plenty of sunshine. There are straw, orange, and cream hybrids with darker blotches at the bases of the petals. It grows to $2\frac{1}{2}$ ft.

Verbena (Verbena family). Raise the 6–15-in. hybrids from seed in a warm greenhouse in February or March. Germination may be delayed for several weeks. Prick out and harden off before planting in May in sunshine, where it should flower freely from June to September. Available in scarlet, rose, salmon, deep blue, and lavender, some with a white eye, and white. The compact varieties are most suitable for window boxes or borders.

Viola (Violet family) (pansy, viola). Both grow from 6–9 in., the pansies with the larger flowers. Violas are best treated as hardy biennials. There are many special strains, and winter varieties. Sow them in seed boxes in a cold frame in June or July. Keep cool and moist, and prick out into rows. Plant out in September or October. Give them rich soil, in sun or partial shade, and never allow to dry out. Alternatively, sow in March or April where they are to flower.

Viscaria (Pink family). This is a freely-flowering plant with pink, scarlet, crimson, blue, and white, or mixed coloured flowers, at its best massed at the front of the border. Sow in March or April in the bed. Varieties of *V. elegans oculata*, 6–15 in. high, may also be kept as pot plants in a cool greenhouse.

Zinnia (Daisy family). There are giant-flowered and giant dahlia-flowering varieties up to $2\frac{1}{2}$-ft. high, and the 9–12 in. dwarfs 'Lilliput' and 'Pompon' down to the American 'Thumbelina' only 6-in. tall. They may be scarlet, pink, orange, lavender, yellow, or white. Sow them in April in a warm greenhouse. Earlier sowing may result in damping off in a cold spell. Prick out into boxes or singly into small pots. Harden off in a cold frame before planting out in a sunny situation and rich, well-drained soil in early June.

31

HOW TO INCREASE YOUR PLANTS

Apart from the interest it engenders, it is valuable for a gardener to be able to propagate his own plants, particularly in view of their high cost nowadays. The methods of propagation fall into two categories, (i) raising from seeds, which is termed *seminal* reproduction, and (ii) vegetative. Although there are some rather more complicated practices, which are used by professionals, they are mostly within the power of an amateur gardener to carry out.

Raising plants from seeds

Although many plants can be reproduced by this method, it must be remembered that so many are inbred so extensively that it is nearly impossible to get true reproduction. Except where true species are concerned, it cannot be used for roses and their cultivars and special forms of trees and shrubs. It is, however, applicable to species, generally perennials, annuals, alpines, vegetables, and some fruits.

Seeds are usually sown in a seedbox, pan, or pot. It is essential to have good drain holes in the bottom of any container used. To assist drainage, place at the bottom of the pot a layer, about $\frac{3}{4}$ in. thick, of broken pot (crocks) or small stones. The container is then filled to within a $\frac{1}{2}$ in. of its top with John Innes Seed Compost, or a suitable soilless seed compost.

The secret of success in raising from seed is not planting too deeply. Generally seeds should not be covered by more than their own diameter of soil. Very fine seeds should be mixed with a little dry sand to facilitate distribution. The other 'don't is not to sow too thickly. When sown the containers should be stood in a cold frame or a greenhouse, according to their requirements. They should be covered with paper and a sheet of glass until the seeds have germinated and then brought into the light. So that they do not get overcrowded, it is important to thin out the seedlings as soon as they are large enough to handle. All the seedlings should be hardened off before they are planted out.

To be sure that moisture penetrates readily after sowing, some seeds with tough coats, such as sweet peas, should be soaked in water for 48 hours before sowing, or, if the seeds are large enough, the skin can be nicked with a sharp knife. Due to the need to remove the flesh, to break down the hard shell or possibly to eliminate any chemical inhibitor that retards germination, the tough seeds of some trees, shrubs, and alpines need to be chilled. When dealing with comparatively few, they should be sown normally in pots and placed outdoors in a plunge bed for the winter. When the number is large, the seeds should be planted in layers in seed compost in a seedbox and stood outdoors for the winter. This is known as *stratification*. On germination the seedlings are potted up.

Vegetative propagation

This process takes two forms, firstly, inducing roots to develop on the portions of the plants to be propagated and secondly, uniting the part of one with another that is already growing on its own roots. In the latter process the plant being propagated is called the *scion* and the rooted one, the *rootstock*.

Rooting cuttings This is one of the easier methods. It is applicable to trees, shrubs, herbaceous perennials, alpines, and others. In this form of propagation portions of a plant are induced to develop roots of their own. The most common types of cuttings are stem, which are either soft, semi–hard or hardwood, and heel cuttings. Hardwood stem cuttings are usually 6 to 12–in. long and taken in autumn. They are trimmed level just below a joint or a bud. Soft and half-ripe cuttings are taken in the same way, usually in late summer, and should be about 4 in. long. Heel cuttings, (hard or semi–hard) which in some instances root more readily, are taken by gently tearing off a shoot from a main stem, carrying with it a small piece of bark and wood, which should be trimmed to remove any raggedness and the tail of bark.

In all these types of cuttings the leaves likely to be below the ground are removed. The success of rooting cuttings lies in giving them the correct soil and environment and in being sure that they are planted firmly to a depth of $\frac{1}{2}$ to $\frac{2}{3}$ of their length so that they do not move. Some cuttings that are difficult to root need to have their lower end wetted and dipped in hormone rooting compound. Generally cuttings are planted in about an inch of sand in a V-shaped trench of the appropriate depth, about 6-in. apart, either in the open, for most hardwood cuttings, or in a cold frame for semi-hard. Replace and firm the soil around them so that they are vertical. Some cuttings, including softwood ones, often need the protection of a greenhouse or frame. Softwood cuttings root more readily if they are provided with bottom heat. Cuttings planted individually in pots, covered with a polythene bag and watered from the bottom, strike satisfactorily and quickly; usually roots will have developed by the following spring.

Plants with very fleshy leaves, such as begonias, saintpaulias and sedums can be rooted from leaves, by inserting them vertically in the compost.

Some woody evergreens, such as camellias, are propagated by means of *bud cuttings*.
Bud cuttings These are taken in the summer by scooping out from a stem a bud with a leaf and a sliver of wood, using a sharp knife. They should be inserted in soil in a container, so that only the leaf shows above the surface, and placed in a propagating case at 59°–64°F (15°–18°C).
Layering This is a method of propagation that is used for plants which have pendulous stems and can easily be bent down to ground level without breaking, such as rhododendrons, heathers, and carnations.

ABOVE: *Taking chrysanthemum cuttings.*
TOP: Sedum spectabile, *the butterfly or rice plant, one of the fleshy-leaved plants which can be propagated by planting leaf-cuttings in compost.*

Layering is achieved by pulling down a young, non-flowering, flexible shoot to the ground. The flow of the sap at the point where it contacts the soil is stopped by making an incision just behind a bud. Keep this incision open by inserting a small stone in it, or by bending the stem sharply away from it. Holding the tip of the shoot vertically, bury the U-bend, so formed, in the soil and fix it in position by means of large hairpin-shaped wires or a heavy stone. The tip of the shoot should be tied to a stake. Most plants are rooted in 12 months and can be cut away on the parent plant-side, close to the root. Rhododendrons and magnolias may take up to two years to root.

Air-layering is another method of rooting which is sometimes used, particularly with house plants. It consists of ringing the bark on a shoot in a selected position and wetting and dusting the cut with hormone rooting compound. A mixture of just moist sphagnum moss, peat, sand, and loam is packed around it and enclosed in a plastic sleeve, securely sealed at each end with adhesive tape. When the roots are seen through the plastic sheet to be well-developed, the new plant is obtained by cutting the stem near it on the side of the old plant, and potting up the newly-rooted air-layer.

Division is the easiest way of propagating plants and is largely applicable to herbaceous plants and alpines. It is usually done by dividing the plants into several smaller pieces, each carrying roots. Where tough herbaceous perennials are concerned, this is best done by inserting two forks back to back, tines vertical, in the centre of the clump and pulling the handles together. With more delicate plants, division should

be made by cutting through with a knife, or even by pulling them apart by hand.

Division of rhizomes, tubers, bulbs, and corms The rhizomes of irises are divided by splitting off and retaining only the young, vigorous fans with a rhizome and strong root. Dahlia tubers are divided in the spring by cutting down the centre of the stem through the tuber between two 'eyes' (buds). Further division is possible, but each portion must contain a piece of stem and a bud. Bulbous and cormous plants undergo a process of natural division by forming offsets in the shape of bulbils and cormlets. On lifting, these can be separated and planted out in a nursery bed. They will flower in about two years. Some species of lilies and hybrids of lilies produce small bulbils in their leaf axils. These can be gathered in late summer and set $\frac{1}{2}$ in. deep and 2 in. apart in seed compost. They will be flowering after two or three years.

Suckers Certain shrubs and trees produce suckers freely, offering a simple means of propagation. They can be severed from the main plant by cutting with a sharp spade. This applies only to plants growing on their own roots and not to grafted or budded ones.

Budding and grafting These two forms of propagation are particularly valuable means of reproducing cultivars and special forms that do not come true from seeds.

Budding This is a method of propagating fruit trees, some ornamental trees and shrubs, including roses, by inserting a single bud of a named variety or scion into a root-stock, so that their tissues knit up and form a new rooted plant. (See under Roses for full details.)

Grafting is practised by nurserymen to propagate a particular species or variety and, in fruit trees, to produce a plant of known vigour and performance by using special rootstocks. The most common form of grafting used commercially is what is termed *whip and tongue* grafting. This consists of slicing off the top of the rootstock and the bottom of the scion obliquely so that they fit snugly together. A small incision in the cut surfaces at a sharp angle forms two small tongues that fit into each other when the stock and scion are pushed together. The two components are bound together with raffia and sealed with grafting wax. *Crown or rind* grafting is another common method, which consists of inserting the scion between the wood and the bark after a slit has been made. In *cleft* grafting, two scions are inserted in a fair-sized limb, which has been split open with an axe and kept open during the operation with the pointed edge of a wedging tool. The stock is bound with raffia, the split filled with clay and sealed with wax.

BULBS FOR YEAR-ROUND COLOUR

The group of plants called bulbs, corms and tubers is a particularly attractive and easily grown section of garden plants, and will provide colour and beauty all the year round without the need for intensive or difficult cultivation.

The group is defined by the type of growth it produces below ground; this is not necessarily a true root, but may be a leaf or stem modified to store food. The plants have developed these storage organs to carry them over a period when conditions for growth are not suitable, though they must in fact continue to function to some extent. To all intents and purposes, they are dormant, and this dormancy occurs in most cases during periods of drought.

A store of concentrated food is contained inside them, and sometimes also embryonic flowers and leaves, so that when growing conditions are once more suitable, they can develop these very quickly indeed. Bulbs, corms, and tubers are in fact prepacked plants: simply add water and warmth, and growth follows rapidly. Because they are at a standstill when dormant, they can be dug up, moved and marketed without causing them any harm.

Bulbs are distinguished by having swollen leaves, reduced to scales, tightly or loosely packed, and coming from a very compressed stem which forms the base or 'plate' of the bulb on its underside. The true roots come from the underside of this plate. Tightly packed scale leaves forming a solid, hard bulb are found in tulips, daffodils, and hyacinths; the kind whose scales are loosely packed around the bud are typified by lilies. The old bulb will continue to grow and flower, for several seasons in some cases, but at the same time producing new bulbs at its side from the basal plate.

Corms are different in that the food reserve is contained in the stem, and it is this which is swollen and sometimes flattened, with a thin brown skin or 'tunic' enclosing it. Usually a new corm is formed on top of the old one, sometimes beside it, and the old one withers, though it may take more than a year to do so. The plants which produce corms are members of the iris family which includes such plants as crocus and colchicum.

Tubers are storage organs which may be the swollen part of an underground stem, or they may be root tubers. Stem tubers will readily produce roots, but root tubers will practically never grow another bud, if they lose the one they have. Tubers also differ from bulbs and corms in that they do not produce smaller editions of themselves, and so cannot be used for increase in this way.

When to buy Most bulbs, corms and tubers are planted during the autumn from the middle of August to the end of November, for flowering the following spring or early summer. It is possible to plant some of them even later, but they do tend to flower late, for instance March–flowering tulips planted in December will not flower until mid–April. Some bulbs flower in autumn, either with only traces of leaves, or with none at all. They rest for only a little while, in July and August, and will be found for sale in garden shops at that time.

Lilies have an unusually long growing season; they will start to produce leaves and shoots in late autumn and continue to develop right through to July or August the following year. They are generally planted in early autumn, but are sometimes late arriving in this country. If that happens, they are best potted as soon as bought if they cannot be planted outdoors at once because of climatic conditions, and then planted out in spring. They should never be stored.

'Prepared' bulbs are those which have been treated with extremes of temperature to hasten or delay flowering and to ensure that this occurs at a particular time, usually Christmas. These will be for sale in August and early September, and need to be potted at once for indoor flowering in December; hyacinths are the bulbs most commonly treated like this.

Some of the corms are not completely hardy through the winter, though they are dormant. Frost in the ground can kill them, so they should be stored away from frost, and will be on sale between late January and the end of April – for planting when the soil is free from frost. Alternatively, they can be brought on a trifle earlier, if preferred, by potting them up and keeping in a frost-proof greenhouse. Providing they have been hardened off, they can then be planted out when all danger of air frost is past.

Bulbs for the greenhouse include those which need more warmth during the winter than they would get out of doors in Britain; they are native of such places as South Africa. They may also be of the sort which make growth during the winter. The latter can be obtained in autumn, and are best potted then, or planted outside, if the garden is sheltered and in a mild district. Those which need warmth during winter are planted at greatly varying times, partly depending on how much heat can be given.

The greenhouse can also be used for 'forcing' bulbs which are perfectly hardy, but which are also suitable, depending on variety, for bringing on in extra warmth so that they flower much earlier than their normal season. The extra heat given should not be too much, otherwise they will only produce leaf, and abort. Narcissus and tulip varieties which can be forced like this will be so marked in specialist bulb catalogues.

CHOICE OF BULBS, CORMS AND TUBERS

When buying any of this group of plants, the temperature of the shop in which they have been kept is important, since cold and even frost will injure the tender bulbs. Too much heat will dry them up, or start them into early shoot growth without the support of roots. Damage to tissue in this way allows bacterial and fungal disease to enter;

it can even invade where there is merely bruising. Bulbs which have been 'prepared' will lose the effect with great temperature variations. Tubers which can shrivel, such as dahlias, should have been packed in polythene and costly bulbs, like lilies, should only be sold packed in peat, sawdust or wood shavings.

Size of bulbs is important; the larger ones are not necessarily the best for flowering. For instance, anemone tubers should not be more than about 1 in. in diameter, to give the best flowers; the large corms of 3 in. and more are old and nearly worn out, and produce poor flowers. Narcissus (daffodil) bulbs are sold with one, two or three stems or 'noses'; each will produce a flower but it is a question of whether one bulb with three noses will give a better display than three single-nosed bulbs.

Hyacinths of medium size will give one very good flower spike, as opposed to a large bulb with one moderate spike and one tiny one; small to medium cyclamen corms have a longer life ahead than the enormous plate-like kinds of great age.

One point to remember when planting narcissus is that a job lot of small bulbs, which may have been sold cheap, may not flower the same year or even the year after.

Have a look at the bulbs before buying to see whether they are clean, as soil can carry disease and it may mask injury and bruising. Handle them if possible – lightweight bulbs which are soft to the touch indicate possible infestation by narcissus fly maggots, which feed on the inside of the bulb – and do not buy any from a batch containing such specimens.

Look underneath the outer scales of lilies for fungal growth or wetness; avoid them unless you have a fungicide to treat them with. Avoid iris corms which have sooty black patches on them, and tulips with scabby patches. Bulbs which have scales actually falling off will undoubtedly be infected in the basal plate and should be burnt, if bought by mistake.

Virus diseases cannot unfortunately be spotted on the bulb; they are only seen on the top growth as yellowing of the leaves or mottling of the flower colour. There is no cure for these diseases. Sometimes green-fly eggs may be laid on the scales, or under them, and are not noticed until greenfly are present. They are particularly attracted to lachenalias. If you do spot greenfly trouble, deal with it at once with derris or malathion aerosol or spray, as greenfly feeding is the means by which viruses are spread.

Make sure that bulbs are properly labelled and named when you buy them, and that you get the grade you have asked for and paid for. See that bulbs are handled properly when being bagged, and that the buds are not knocked off, especially when a metal scoop is being used. Keep them in the cool when you get home, but free from frost and undue warmth.

GENERAL CULTIVATION

Bulbs carry a season's supply of food stored inside them, but once this has been used up on leafing and flowering, they will either die, or produce weak growth only, unless they are supplied with more food from an outside source. In nature this may come from animals or birds, from moisture running down off hills and mountains, and from decayed vegetative material in the nearby soil.

In the garden there is much competition for the mineral nutrients of the soil from other plants, and so it is a good idea to put plenty of food into the bulb site before planting, and to give it regularly each year thereafter. Tulips, crocus, and the smaller iris and the highly-bred hyacinths benefit particularly from this.

All bulbs do best in a well-drained soil, and if you do not have a sandy or stony one naturally, it should be lightened by the addition of peat and sharp sand before planting. Coarse hoof and horn meal and bonemeal, mixed into the soil a few days before planting, will help establishment and root growth, and it pays to treat the whole bed, instead of only planting holes, otherwise you may find that these act as drainage sumps and the bulbs then rot.

When planting, put the bulbs on the surface of the soil where you want to plant them, and then dig and plant hole by hole, with a trowel or bulb planter, covering as you go.

For naturalizing in grass, simply throw the bulbs on to the grass, and then plant them where they have fallen; this is most easily done in turf with a bulb planter. Small bulbs are best set by skimming the turf up, putting the bulbs underneath and then replacing the turf. It should not be beaten down, but watered instead, to help settle it.

Depth of planting Bulbs which are to be grown outdoors should be planted so that there is twice their depth of soil above them; it should on no account be less than their depth. For instance, a bulb which is 2 in. from the base to the tip of the nose should be planted between 4 and 6 in. deep. If not planted deeply enough, some will produce contractile roots, which literally pull the bulb down; others grow 'droppers' (short stems) which do the same job. Sometimes a half-hardy bulb can be protected from frost by depth of planting, or by putting a deep mulch over the top, but this

is not always effective, as some bulbs will work their way upwards.

When bulbs are grown in containers, such as bowls, troughs, pots or tubs, it is usual to plant the bulbs less deeply, with perhaps only ½ or 1 in. of compost above them; large bulbs should actually have the tips above the surface, so that about ½ an inch or more is exposed. It is important to use a container which really is large enough to take the bulb or bulbs. So often a large hyacinth is crammed into a pot at least an inch in diameter too small for it, so that the roots go round and round, and eventually come up through the surface. The compost should be packed in hard round the bulb, but it should not be compressed immediately below it; a hard bed for the bulb to sit on can also result in the roots growing upwards instead of downwards.

As with any other container-grown plant, a space should be left at the top for watering, and for adding topdressing later, to feed the bulb when it has flowered.

When planting a collection of bulbs in one container, a very good show can be obtained if they are planted in two layers, staggered. The lower layer may be at about 6 in., and the compost is filled in round them so that the tops are just showing; then the next layer is put between them and compost filled in again to cover them completely. This method does need a good deep container and good compost.

Bulbs grown indoors can be put into bulb fibre or a John Innes Potting Compost. Bulb fibre contains 6 parts fibrous peat, 2 parts oyster shell and 1 part crushed charcoal, and is generally used in containers that have no drainage holes. It can be bought made up, if required and has practically no nutrient content; the charcoal helps with the drainage.

Bulbs should always be planted in moist fibre, soaking it overnight if need be, and then squeezing out the extra moisture by hand before planting. If the plants are over-watered while growing, the containers can be tilted and the surplus water drained off, with one hand spread over the surface of

the fibre. Bulbs in fibre do not need to be fed with liquid feed while growing, unless required for use the following year when they are unlikely to make much display, as fibre is really only suitable for one season's flowering.

The use of a potting compost containing loam, peat and coarse sand, together with fertilizer and chalk, will ensure that the bulb is able to build up a food reserve again, and develop embryo flowers or new buds for the following season. The John Innes Potting Compost is very good, provided extra grit is added to it. There are three grades of this compost: No 1, which has one unit of fertilizer, No 2, which has twice as much, and No 3, which is the richest of all, with 3 units. The proprietary soilless composts, containing peat, sand, and some fertilizer, depending on the brand, are also good, probably best used for the smaller bulbs, and for indoor kinds.

Bulbs which are to flower in the house must be potted and placed in the dark and the cool for at least eight weeks, and sometimes ten or eleven, to encourage them to make plenty of root growth. This will sustain the new shoots, which will be forced into growing a little more quickly than usual by the extra warmth of the home.

These bulbs can go in an outside shed, where they should be looked at occasionally in case they need to be watered, or put in the garden in a plunge bed, that is, sunk into the soil to their rims or placed on the flat, with peat, sand, and ashes packed round and over them to a depth of about 2 in. A frame is a convenient site for a plunge bed; the packing medium ensures an even temperature and constant moisture.

When brought into the warmth and light, the bulbs are best introduced gradually, first to semi-shade and only slightly higher temperature; then to increased light and rather more warmth. Too much light and heat all at once will produce a lot of elongated leaves, and possibly no flower at all.

Feeding Because a bulb contains its own supply of food, it will not need extra

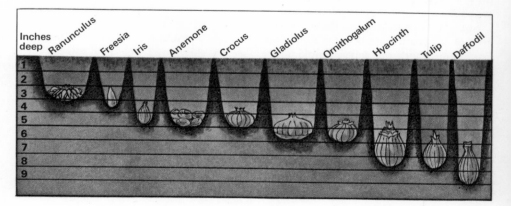

36

feeding. For about six weeks after potting, the food contained in the growing medium, where this is a soil-based compost, should be enough; then it can be fed regularly with a liquid feed, preferably one which has plenty of potash in it. This will help with ripening, and so with the production of next year's flowers. The compost to which the fertilizer is added should always be moist, so water it first if it is dry. Some bulbs will be growing during the winter, and should be fed at that time.

Watering Bulbs should never go without water, particularly when they are in the preliminary stages of making root, otherwise individual florets may wither, or an entire flower spike may come to nothing. However, unless they are growing very strongly, they will need only moderate amounts of water, and care should be taken to see that it does not fall on to the leaves – fungal rots can very easily be produced if this happens.

Ripening A good many bulbs ripen naturally under conditions of drought and baking heat, which start sometime before the leaves die down and continue after they have gone. They also need potash for the process. Nerines are an example, as they undergo drought conditions during their resting period. Outdoor plants which need sun to complete their ripening should be kept free from weeds and other plants.

Resting Bulbs enter into their resting period as the leaves begin to turn yellow; if they are to be lifted, they should be left until the leaves have died down and disappeared completely, as they are usually the means by which the bulb builds up its stored food and initiates its buds and flowers for the following season. However, if they have to be lifted while still in green leaf, as in some bedding schemes, they should be immediately replanted or heeled in in a sheltered place, in a shallow trench, with the soil filled in over the bulbs and the leaves above ground. This is a measure of expediency, and if the bulbs can be left in their original place, the following year will show better results. Where it is possible to leave them, marking the site is a good idea. Once the leaves have withered, it is very easy to forget where they are, and in the autumn you might plant a perennial straight on top of them.

If bulbs have been growing in grass, do not cut or mow until the bulb leaves turn yellow; never pick the foliage with the flowers.

Starting into growth Sometimes bulbs and corms will start into growth of their own accord, in the containers in which they have been resting. Cyclamen, for example, will often show signs of life in late July or early August. They can then be transferred,

PREVIOUS PAGE: *The magnificent yellow trumpet hybrid lily, 'Honeydew'.*
ABOVE: *A selection of St Brigid anemones, in traditional colours.*
LEFT: *Chart showing the correct depth to plant your bulbs.*
RIGHT: *Planting indoor bulbs.*
1. *Half-fill a pot with moist bulb fibre.*
2. *Put the bulbs on top.*
3. *Fill the pot with more fibre, pressed gently around the bulbs, leaving the tips exposed.*
4. *Cover with polythene.*

as they are, to a larger pot, filling in round the sides and on top with new compost, or they can have the old compost removed, and be repotted completely fresh. They can also be left in their original pots, the top inch or so of compost removed, and top-dressed with fresh compost. Watering will be required, but to start with only small amounts will be needed.

BULBS IN THE GREENHOUSE

As with plants grown in the home, green-house bulbs are put into a John Innes Potting Compost (JIP), with broken crocks at the bottom for drainage, or a soilless compost can be used. Small bulbs are covered with their own depth of soil; large ones are only half covered. Alpine bulbs are put into pans, with really first class drainage, unless they require a specially good depth for their roots. Bulbs whose flowers are wanted for cutting are put into boxes, since their appearance is not so important.

Greenhouse bulbs or corms can be left in their containers during their resting period until the season for replanting comes round. In this way they are kept free in winter from extreme cold, and are prevented from withering. Some can be allowed to become completely dry and subjected to great heat, if resting in summer. Tulips, for instance, which are mostly natives of the Mediterranean and the Middle East, can be treated in this way.

Bulbs which have been forced in the greenhouse for home display or for cutting cannot be forced again the following year. After the flowers have been cut, the plants should be allowed to die down and rest, and then planted outdoors if hardy, or into containers with fresh compost. They will flower again, though it may take two seasons before they are in good condition.

SUITABLE SITES

There are all kinds of places in the garden or greenhouse where bulbs can be grown and, conversely, there is a suitable bulb, corm or tuber for any position, though in general they prefer a sunny position.

The following list gives some of the possible sites:

Naturalized in grass: if long, daffodils, and if short, the miniature daffodils, fritillarias and muscari.

In mixed borders: crown imperial, camassia, some lilies, galtonia, summer snowflake.

As bedding growing through other bedding: tulips through forget-me-nots, cannas through annuals.

As bedding in rows: tulips, hyacinths, narcissi.

In beds for cutting: gladioli, iris, St Brigid and de Caen anemones, narcissi.

As edging to beds: alliums, muscari, crocuses, chionodoxa, scilla.

In warm sheltered borders facing south: nerine, amaryllis, crinum, sparaxia.

In warm but moist borders: ranunculus, chincherinchee, tigridia.

On rock gardens: miniature narcissi, greigii tulips, crocus, alliums, small iris, fritillarias.

In woodland: bluebells, erythronium, snowdrops, ornithogalum, *Anemone blanda*.

Under shrubs: lilies, colchicum, cyclamen, eranthis, snowdrops.

Containers on a patio or terrace: hyacinths, cannas, lilies, tulips, galtonia, daffodils, nerines.

Window boxes: double and greigii tulips, crocus, hyacinth, daffodils, *Iris reticulata*, alliums, achimenes.

In the home: hyacinths, daffodils, early tulips, vallota, hippeastrum, small spring bulbs.

In a cool greenhouse: lachenalia and other spring flowering kinds, nerines, lilies, freesia, chincherinchee.

In a warm greenhouse: cyclamen, vallota, achimenes, gloxinia, gloriosa.

PROPAGATION METHODS

Bulbs and corms of all kinds are very easy to propagate, as every year many of them naturally produce offsets or small bulbs from the parent plant. For instance, a double-nosed daffodil will finish the season with at least two extra bulbs. The single corm of a gladiolus will develop a lot of cormlets or cormels around it, and any of these will grow, in one or two seasons, into a flowering-size corm, provided they are in a frost-free site. They can, if liked, be detached, and grown on in a frame to flowering size, to produce blooms exactly like the parent. Sometimes bulbs produce several small new ones instead of one large flowering-size one; tulips are prone to do this unless really well fed. Many lilies can be increased from bulb scales; they are removed from the parent, placed lower edge downwards in a mixture of sand and peat, and kept warm and close. In due course, tiny bulbs form on the lower edge of the scales.

Some lilies can also be increased from bulbils. These are small round, dark-coloured balls formed in the axil between the leaf and the stem during June and July. When they are ready to drop of their own accord, a tiny root will start appearing from the lower side, and they can be detached, planted at once and grown on.

Most bulbs and corms can be increased from seed but the plants obtained from hybrids may not be the same as the parents. They will take, in general, several years to

ABOVE: Allium ostrowskianum, *the pink-flowering ornamental onion, is a popular dried flower.*

TOP: Amaryllis belladonna, *fragrant as well as beautiful.*

OPPOSITE ABOVE: Anemone apennina *is one of the star-like daisy-flowered anemones, very different from the poppy anemones.*

heads at the top of stems 3 in. to 4 ft. tall, depending on species. They are hardy, and do best in a sunny place, on a rock garden, or scree, as edging and in mixed borders. Surprisingly, some are good cut flowers. Those that have a strong onion smell when brushed against are preferably planted back from a path or edge. *A. caeruleum*, 1–2 ft., flowers blue in June–July; *A. elatum*, 2½–3 ft., flowers rosy-purple, end May; *A. flavum*, ¼–1 ft., flowers yellow, bell-like, July; *A. moly*, ½–1 ft., yellow, star-like, June; *A. roseum*, ¾–1 ft., pink, June–July; *A. sphaerocephalum*, 1–2 ft. flowers purple, June–July. There are many more good species, and the above is a selection only. Plant in well-drained soil and a sunny place in autumn, and increase from offsets or from seeds sown in spring in a rich and gritty soil.

Amaryllis (Amaryllis family) (belladonna lily, Jersey lily). A slightly tender bulbous plant with very beautiful rose-pink flowers, *A. belladonna*, 2–2½ ft., flowers rose-pink, lily-like, fragrant, September, before the leaves; 'Hathor' is a good white form, with a yellow throat. Plant the very large bulbs just below the soil surface in September, at the foot of a warm south-facing wall. They are unlikely to flower the first year after planting. Well-drained but rich soil is preferred, and they can be left for many years before lifting and dividing is required. Mulch them well just before frost is likely. Feed and topdress every year. Propagate by division of the bulbs, or by seed which takes seven years or more to flower.

Anemone (Buttercup family) (wind flower). Two kinds make good plants grown from tubers. The poppy anemones have large, brightly coloured flowers at various times of the year, according to planting date, and the star-like flowers of the other form come in March. *A. coronaria*, 9–12 in., flowers red, violet, purple, white, and blue, spring, leaves fern-like; the de Caen varieties are single, and the St Brigid semi-double. Plant tubers 6 in. apart in April, June or September in a light but rich soil and a little shade. Protect autumn-planted tubers with cloches for winter flowering. Lift when crowded and increase by division, or seed. *A. blanda*, 6 in., flowers blue, January–March, with white, pink, and carmine forms. Soak the tubers before planting in autumn in a sunny place.

Camassia (Lily family) (quamash). Hardy bulbous plants from North America, the quamashes can be grown in a border, and also naturalized. *C. leichtlinii*, 3 ft., flowers cream, June–July; *C. quamash*, 2–3 ft., flowers purple-blue to white, in a spike, June–July. A reasonable soil and open place are best; plant in October or February, at least 4 in. deep. Topdress with leafmould

reach flowering size. Tulips and daffodils can take from five to seven years; the South African corms and many lilies will, however, flower in the third year; occasionally one comes across bulbs which will flower from seed in only one year.

Tubers do not have the convenient habit of dividing themselves into several baby tubers; one plant will certainly produce several tubers in a season, but unless there is more than one growth bud or 'eye' on each tuber, it will only produce one new plant. Where there are two or more eyes, the tuber can be cut up so that there is one eye to each piece, growing each of these on. Cyclamen are increased from seed, other bulbs such as gloxinias, by cuttings. If tubers have to be bought, the smaller ones will have a longer life.

SOME COLOURFUL FAVOURITES

Achimenes (Gesneria family) (hot water plant). The achimenes, from Mexico and Brazil, are plants for the greenhouse with small trumpet-shaped flowers all summer. They look particularly attractive in hanging baskets; most have trailing stems, though

some will grow upright. *A. longiflora*, 1 ft., flowers violet, August; *A. coccinea*, 1 ft., flowers red, August. There are a great number of named hybrids with larger and smaller flowers in all shades of purple, red, white, yellow, and pink, flowering profusely between late July and September. The small, scaly rhizomes are started into growth in peat and sand from February to April, in at least 55°F (13°C), 1 in. apart and 2 in. deep. They are very slow to start and take four weeks or longer to produce the first leaves. When well away, they are transferred to their permanent containers, spaced 3 in. apart in them, and kept slightly shaded and in a humid atmosphere, never allowing them to dry out. JIP 1 is a good compost; pinch out the growing tips to encourage bushiness, and stake, if not grown in a hanging basket. After flowering dry off gradually, and store in their containers at 50°F (10°C) in a dry place. Increase by division of rhizomes, by seed sown in spring in 70°F (21°C), and by tip cutting in warmth.

Allium (Lily family) (ornamental onion). This is a bulbous group of plants with grass-like leaves, whose flowers come in round

every year and lift and divide every four years. Increase by offsets, or seeds sown outdoors in March.

Canna (Canna family) (Indian shot). The cannas are tender plants with swollen rootstocks, making good summer bedding plants or warm greenhouse specimens. *C. indica*, 4 ft., large flowers yellow and red, in a spike, summer, leaves large, green or bronze; hybrids in yellow, red, orange, and pink, and also dwarf forms. Growth starts in March, with moderate watering and potting in JIP 3, and they can be planted outdoors in late May, bringing in before the frost comes in the autumn. They can be allowed to dry completely during resting, from October–March, or packed into moist peat, or left in their pots. Increase by division in spring or in February by seed soaked in water for 24 hours, notched, and then put in a temperature of 85°F (30°C).

Chionodoxa (Lily family) (glory of the snow). A small hardy bulb flowering in spring, which is suitable for edging, rock gardens and in containers. *C. luciliae*, 6 in., flowers blue, white-centred and star-like, March–April. Plant in autumn in sun or a little shade and divide only when the bulbs become crowded. Also grow in pans in JIP 1 for the greenhouse. Increase by offsets or seed sown in August in a cold frame.

Colchicum (Lily family) (autumn crocus). The autumn crocus are bulbous plants, whose flowers appear before the leaves. The bulbs are large, and the flowers are bigger than those of the spring crocus. *C. autumnale*, 8 in., flowers rosy-purple, early September, several flowers from one bulb; *C. byzantium*, 9 in., flowers rose and purple, mid-September; *C. speciosum*, 9–12 in., flowers lilac-purple, September; hybrids of these have large flowers in shades of purple, pink, and white – 'Water-lily' is double. Plant *C. autumnale* in July, and the others in August, during their short dormant season; leaves will not be produced until the following spring, and they will then be large and pleated, dying down in June–July. Borders, in front of shrubs, or near trees are good sites, provided the soil drainage is good. Increase by division in August or by seed sown in August, which will not flower until four or five years old.

Crinum (Amaryllis family). A beautiful, lily-like flower characterizes this bulbous plant, which has several flowers on top of a stout stem. It is slightly tender. *C. × powellii*, 2–3 ft., flowers white, flushed pink, July–September. Plant the very large bottle-shaped bulbs in spring in a well-drained rich soil, preferably in a south-facing border against a wall, or in containers. The necks of the bulbs gradually work above the soil surface, and may need protection in winter. Mulch in spring every year. Increase by

offsets, or by seeds sown in spring in 70°F (21°C), which will take several years to flower.

Crocosmia (Iris family) (montbretia). Easily grown hardy cormous plants, flowering in late summer, crocosmias originally came from South Africa. *C. × crocosmiiflora*, 2–3 ft., flowers small trumpet-shaped, orange-red in a long loose spike, August and hybrids with much larger flowers in shades of orange and red; *C. masonorum*, 2½–3 ft., flowers orange-red, facing upwards, July. Plant in spring in well-drained soil and sun, covering thickly during winter. Corms of most varieties are best lifted in autumn and stored in slightly moist peat. Increase by offsets or seed. *C. masonorum* is fully hardy.

Crocus (Iris family). Although crocus are thought of primarily as being spring flowering, it is possible to grow species and cultivars which ensure a succession from September until April. They are versatile plants, which can be grown on rock gardens, at the edges of beds, in mixed borders, in grass, in containers, and in pans in the alpine house; flower colour is also very varied. Heights vary from 2–4 in. *C. aitchisonii*, flowers bright blue, petals pointed, autumn; *C. albus*, flowers white, autumn; *C. ancyrensis*, flowers orange-yellow February, many flowers per corm, makes a good container plant; *C. aureus*, flowers yellow, January–February, easily increased by seed; *C. chrysanthus*, flowers golden-yellow and rounded, January–March; and cultivars: 'Blue Pearl', blue with orange centres, 'Cream Beauty', creamy-yellow and orange centres, 'E. A. Bowles', yellow, striped brown, 'Ladykiller', pointed petals, purple and white, 'Snowbunting', cream with purple veins, 'Sunkist' deep yellow and lilac, 'Zwanenburg', yellow with brown interior; *C. etruscus*, flowers blue-violet, flowering for a month from February; *C. imperati*, flowers lilac, striped light brown on the outside, January–February, excellent for naturalizing; *C. longiflorus*, scented flowers lilac, striped purple, October–November, needs sun to do well; *C. medius*, flowers lilac-purple, October–November; *C. ochroleucus*, flowers creamy-white with orange base, November–December; *C. sativus*, Saffron crocus, purplish-lilac flowers veined violet with bright red centre, September–October; *C. sieberi* 'Hubert Edelsten', flowers violet-purple with yellow throat, and white bands on outer petals, January–February; *C. susianus* (cloth of gold) flowers orange, veined with bronze, February–March, good for pans; *C. tomasinianus*, flowers blue-violet, grey outside, January–February, good for naturalizing, and 'Ruby Giant', ruby-purple, and 'Whitewell

ABOVE: Crinum × powellii *is rather delicate but worth persevering with for its beautiful pink blooms.*

TOP: Crocosmia masonorum *is very hardy and easy to grow.*

RIGHT: Crocus tomasinianus, *just one of the many different crocuses you can grow.*

Purple', deep purple-mauve outside, pale silvery-mauve in the interior; *C. versicolor*, flowers white, striped purple, March; *C. zonatus*, flowers pale lilac, September, good in grass. Large Dutch hybrids: 'Golden Yellow', long lasting, not for forcing, 'Jeanne d'Arc', white with purple base, 'Kathleen Parlow', white with yellow centre, 'Negro Boy', deep blackish-purple, 'Paulus Potter', magenta-purple, 'Pickwick', silvery-lilac with deep lilac feathering, 'Queen of the Blues', pale blue, 'Remembrance', purple-blue, 'Vanguard', ageratum blue and grey, good for naturalizing. Plant the autumn flowering crocus in July–early August, the remainder at any time in autumn, with about an inch of soil above the top of the corm. The flowers of the autumn kinds will come before the leaves. A steady summer baking will ensure good flowering the following year. They can all be grown in pans, but do not bring into the warm until nearly in flower. Increase by offsets in August, or by seed sown in autumn, from which flowers will be obtained when three to four years old.

Cyclamen (Primula family). The flyaway flowers of the cyclamen are at their most enchanting in the species, which can be had in flower from autumn to spring. The swept back petals are characteristic, and the leaves have many varieties of veining and mottling in grey, silver, and white. Height is 3–6 in., in general. *C. balearicum*, flowers white with pink at the mouth, slightly fragrant, February–March; *C. cilicium*, flowers rose-pink, fragrant, October–November, producing early leaves attractively marbled; *C. creticum*, flowers white, fragrant, February–March, leaves ivy-shaped or rounded, tender, needs shade; *C. cyprium*, flowers white or pinkish, fragrant, October, tender; *C. europaeum*, flowers pink or deep carmine, fragrant, July–September; *C. graecum*, flower variable in colour, pale pink to carmine, September, leaves velvety; *C. libanoticum*, flowers salmon-pink to pale pink, February–March, tender; *C. neapolitanum*, flowers variable in colour, white to pink and mauve-pink, August–September for nine months, attractively marbled; *C. orbiculatum* (includes spp. *coum*, *hiemale*, *atkinsii*, and *ibericum*), flowers white to crimson and magenta, December–March, leaves marbled. *C. persicum*, flowers white or pink, fragrant, spring tender; *C. repandum*, flowers pink, white or crimson, fragrant, March–May, plant in woodland in mild districts, otherwise in pans in the greenhouse, leaves attractively silvered. Plant autumn flowering kinds in June–July, and spring flowering species in September about 2 in. deep and 5 in. apart. Be very careful not to knock the dormant buds off the top of the corm, and cover lightly with

a sieved mixture of leafmould, coarse sand and bonemeal. Topdress with this once a year. In pans, use a compost of 2 parts loam to 1 of leafmould and sand, and keep the plants cool, moist and shaded. Chippings on the compost surface will help with drainage. Dry off and rest the plants in summer. Increase by seed sown in autumn in 50°F (10°C); germination will be slow. The large-flowered greenhouse cyclamen are grown from seed to give a display in December sixteen months after sowing, and with feeding during and after flowering, and resting from May to July, can be induced to flower every year for an indefinite period, provided they are repotted annually in JIP 2 or 3.

Endymion (Lily family) (bluebell). The bluebells are too familiar to need description; *E. non-scripta*, the English bluebell, is rather more graceful and delicate than *E. hispanicus*, the Spanish bluebell, which has stouter stems, and stiffer spikes of larger flowers. Besides blue, both kinds can be had in pink, white, deep blue, and lilac for flowering in May. Plant deeply, in autumn, in woodland; the Spanish bluebell does well also in a border. Increase by offsets.

Eranthis (Buttercup family) (winter aconite). A hardy tuberous perennial, of which the main species grown is *E. hyemalis*, 4 in., flowers yellow, February–March, surrounded with green ruff-like bracts, leaves fern-like. Plant in August 2 in. deep in any soil and a slightly shady place. Increase by division of tubers after flowering.

Erythronium (Lily family) (dog's-tooth violet). These North American bulbous perennials have small lily-like flowers with reflexed petals, in early spring. They do well in woodland, and slightly shaded places in borders and rock gardens. *E. dens-canis*, 6 in., flowers pink or white, March–April, leaves dark spotted; *E. hendersonii*, 6 in., flowers rose-pink, March, stem with purplish markings; *E. revolutum*, 'White Beauty', 2 ft., flowers white marked brown, April–May; *E. tuolumnense*, 1 ft., flowers yellow with plain green leaves, and its hybrid 'Pagoda', 1–1½ ft., flowers yellow with a brown ring. Plant about 3 in. deep in moist soil in autumn, and topdress with leafmould each year. Increase by offsets in August or by seed.

Freesia (Iris family). Autumn and winter-flowering, slightly tender, cormous plants, with wiry arching stems and funnel-shaped flowers in various colours. Most of those available are hybrids in white, yellow, cream, pink, red, violet, blue, and orange. All are heavily and sweetly fragrant, and the yellow and white ones particularly so. Plant the corms in early August, in the containers they are to flower in, which should be at least 5 in. deep, as the plants have long

roots; use JIP 2 and put the corms 2 in. deep and about 1½ in. apart. Put in a cool shady place outdoors until late September and then bring into a cool greenhouse. Support the stems as they grow; flowering will start in December and continue until April. Sow seed in early April, at 65°F (18°C), for flowering from early October to January, also in their permanent containers, and stand outdoors as above, in late May. Bring in in late September. Specially prepared corms planted outdoors in April can be had for flowering in August.

Fritillaria (Lily family) (snake's-head, crown imperial). Two widely different species are commonly grown from this bulbous genus of hardy plants. *F. meleagris*, snake's-head fritillary, 1 ft., flowers drooping bell-like, purplish-pink or white with

chequered markings, stems slender, April. It will grow in grass and open, not too sunny borders in moist soil. Plant in autumn. Topdress every year with rotted organic matter. *F. imperialis*, 3 ft., flowers orange or yellow, bell-shaped in a ring round the top of the stem, surmounted with a cluster of bracts, May. Plant in autumn 6 in. deep, in moist borders. Increase from offsets, or seed sown when ripe in a frame; flowering will be four to six years later.

Galanthus (Amaryllis family) (snowdrop). Snowdrops first appear in flower in January, but it is possible, with different species, to have continuous flowering from October to March. *G. atkinsii*, 6–8 in., late December, *G. elwesii*, 9–12 in., flowers February, leaves broad; *G. nivalis*, common snowdrop, January; *G. n. reginae-olgae*, October,

flowers before the leaves; *G.* 'Straffan', end of March. Double forms are available. Plant in a heavy soil and shade for the later flowering kinds, either just after they have flowered or even while flowering. Increase by division, or seed sown when ripe, which flowers in three to four years.

Galtonia (Lily family) (summer hyacinth). One species of this is commonly grown, *G. candicans*, 3–4 ft., flowers white in a spike summer. It is hardy, and suitable for borders. Plant the large bulbs in spring, 6 in. deep, in moist soil. Lift and replant only when signs of deterioration show; increase by offsets.

Hippeastrum (Amaryllis family). These bulbous plants are mostly tender, but one, *H. pratense*, can be grown outdoors in mild gardens and south-facing sites. Flowers are

ABOVE: *A typically splendid hippeastrum flower.*

TOP: Eranthis x tubergeniana, *the winter aconite, blooms in early spring and is a hardy perennial.*

ABOVE LEFT: Fritillaria imperialis, *the crown imperial, is self-seeding.*

43

red, trumpet shaped, two or three to a 1-ft. stem, in spring or early summer. The more familiar greenhouse hybrids, whose very large and beautiful flowers can be had in bloom for most of the year, are sometimes incorrectly known as amaryllis; bulbs on sale from August will flower from November onwards as they have been specially 'prepared'. The normally early flowering kinds follow them from January to April, and the later kind will continue to July or August with successional planting. Some good hybrids are: 'Appleblossom', white with pink shadings; 'Belinda', dark red; 'Excelsior', orange; 'Fairyland', rose; 'Ludwigs Dazzler', white; 'Hecuba', salmon; 'Minerva', white broadly margined red; 'Peppermint', red and white striped; 'Picotee', white speckled and edged with red; 'Wyndham Hayward', red. There may be two stems to a bulb, with four trumpet shaped flowers at the top of each 3 ft. stem. Put one bulb in a 4–5 in. pot, so that half the bulb shows above the compost – JIP 2 is suitable. Feed liberally after six weeks' growth; the flowers may appear before the leaves. As the leaves yellow, gradually withhold water, and then store them at 50°F (10°C) for about three months. Start into growth by topdressing and watering. Offsets should be removed after the parent bulb has flowered and grown on without resting them. Repot every four years.

Hyacinthus (Lily family) (hyacinth). The two kinds generally grown are the 'Dutch' ones, with stiff, closely-packed spikes, and the 'Roman' hyacinths, whose stems are slender, with loose spikes of flowers; both are strongly scented. Both can be grown outdoors or in a greenhouse.

Of the many Dutch hybrids, the following are especially good: 'Amethyst', lilacmauve; 'King of the Blues', dark blue; 'Delft Blue', 'Myosotis', and 'Queen of the Blues', all pale blue; 'Jan Bos', 'Scarlet Perfection' (double), red; 'Pink Pearl', 'Queen of the Pinks', deep pink; 'Anne Marie', 'Princess Irene', pale pink; 'Salmonetta', salmon; 'City of Haarlem', 'Yellow Hammer', 'L'Innocence', white. The hyacinths called Multiflora are kinds which produce several small spikes to a bulb, after special treatment; the Roman hyacinths are usually sold by colour rather than named kinds. A good species hyacinth for the rock garden is *H. amethystinus*, 8 in., pale blue in late May. Outdoors hyacinths are planted in October–November at least 5 in. deep in sunny borders or beds, 8 in. apart; mulch the soil with peat after planting. If used for bedding, they should be lifted after the leaves have died down, and replaced in the autumn. The Roman hyacinths can be grown outdoors, preferably on rock gardens, but are at their best in the greenhouse.

ABOVE: Lilium 'Sutter's Gold', a very beautiful spotted modern hybrid.
TOP: Lachenalia nelsonii is an unusual plant which needs the protection of a cool greenhouse.
OPPOSITE: The famous Madonna lily, Lilium candidum.

The earliest to flower indoors are the 'prepared' Dutch hybrids, which are potted in August–September for Christmas flowering. Put them singly in 3½-in. pots, in JIP 2, with the tips just uncovered, and keep them in the cool and dark for 8–10 weeks without drying out. Bring them into full light but only slight warmth, when the flower bud is showing, and when it is well up, increase the temperature. They can also be grown closely packed in larger containers or in bowls in bulb fibre; hyacinth glasses can be used, when the bulb is placed over water, into which the roots grow; such bulbs are usually discarded after flowering, but if given liquid fertilizer while flowering and planted out in good soil directly afterwards, it is possible to bring them on to flowering two seasons later. Unprepared bulbs can be potted successively in September and October for January and February flowering. Increase by offsets, or by seed sown in September in a cold frame; it will flower in three years.

Lachenalia (Lily family) (Cape cowslip). Unusual but easily grown plants for the cool greenhouse; it is a pity that they are not seen more often. The narrow tubular flowers come in loose spikes, and foliage is prettily mottled with dark spots and blotches. *L. aloides nelsonii*, 9–12 in., flowers yellow tinged with green, spring; *L. bulbifera*, 12 in., flowers light red, edged green and purple, December–March; *L. tricolor*, 9 in., flowers red, yellow, and green, March, leaves and stems mottled purple. Pot the bulbs five to seven in a 5-in. pot of JIP 2, at 2 in. deep, and plunge outdoors until leaves show, then bring into the greenhouse, with plenty of ventilation; the flowers last much longer if kept at about 50°F (10°C). When flowering has finished, dry off and ripen close to the glass. Increase by offsets.

Leucojum (Amaryllis family) (snowflake). These bulbous plants are very like snowdrops, only a large edition. *L. aestivum*, summer snowflake, 1½–2 ft., flowers white and green, April–May; *L. autumnale*, 8 in., flowers white tinged pink, before the leaves, September; *L. vernum*, 8 in., flowers very large for the genus, February–March. Plant immediately after flowering, 5 in. deep for the spring flowering species, 3 in. for the other one, which requires sun rather than shade. Lift and replant every five to eight years. Increase by offsets at planting time.

Lilium (Lily family) (lily). The lilies have the most beautiful flowers of all the bulbous plants, and many of them are heavily fragrant as well. Colours range over white, pink, red, orange, yellow, salmon, magenta, and greenish-white, and shapes can be trumpet, bowl, cup, and turk's cap with reflexing petals. Their main flowering time

is July–August, but some species will flower as early as May, or as late as September. All the following selection of species and hybrids are very good, and not difficult to grow. 'African Queen', 5 ft., apricot, July–August; *L. amabile*, 2–3 ft., orange-red with black spots, July, smells pungent; 'American Eagle', 4–5 ft., white with many vermilion spots, August; *L. auratum*, 4–8 ft., white with crimson spots and yellow rays, fragrant, August–September; Aurelian Hybrids, 4–5 ft., yellow, pink, white, or salmon, with coloured centres, July; Bellingham Hybrids, 5–7 ft., yellow, red, or orange with maroon to black spots, July, some chalk; 'Black Magic', 5–6 ft., white with outer purple shading, fragrant, June–August; *L. canadense*, 3–6 ft., orange-yellow, July, some chalk; *L. candidum*, Madonna lily, 3–5 ft., white, June–July, some chalk; *L. cernuum*, 1–2 ft., rose with purple spots, fragrant, June–July; *L. chalcedonicum*, 2½–3½ ft., scarlet, July, some chalk; 'Crimson Beauty', 4–5 ft., white with crimson rays and spots, fragrant, August; *L. croceum*, 2½–4 ft., deep orange, July; *L. dauricum*, 2–3 ft., orange or yellow, black spotted, July–August; *L. davidii*, 4–5 ft., orange-red, with brown spots, July–August, a little shade and some chalk; 'Destiny', 3–4 ft., lemon-yellow with brown spots, June; 'Enchantment', 2–3 ft., vermilion red, June; Fiesta Hybrids, 3–5 ft., yellow and orange through to dark red with black spots, July; 'Golden Clarion', 3–5 ft., yellow to gold, July, some chalk; *L. hansonii*, 4–5 ft., orange spotted brown, July, some shade and chalk; Harlequin Hybrids, 4–5 ft., white, cream, pink, rose, lilac, and purple, maroon-spotted, June–July, some chalk; *L. henryi*, 5–6 ft., orange–yellow with brown spots, August, some chalk; 'Imperial Silver', 5–6 ft., white with light red spots, August; 'Imperial Gold', 5–6 ft., yellow with maroon spots, August; 'Imperial Pink', 4–5 ft., shell to rose-pink, spotted pinkish-red, August; 'Limelight', 4–6 ft., greenish-yellow, fragrant, July; *L. martagon*, 3–4 ft., wine-red to light purple, spotted deep purple, June–July, some chalk, and its variety *album*, white; Mid-Century Hybrids, 2–4 ft., bright yellow to crimson, June–July; *L. monadelphum*, 3–4 ft., yellow with maroon spots, fragrant, June, some chalk; 'Mrs R. O. Backhouse', 4–5 ft., yellow-orange with maroon spots, June–July; Olympic Hybrids, 4–5 ft., white, pale pink, or light green, shaded on the outside, fragrant, July, some chalk; Paisley Strain, 3–5 ft., yellow, tangerine, pink, orange, mahogany red with dark spots, June, some chalk; *L. pardalinum*, panther lily, 4–6 ft., orange to red, magenta spots, July, some chalk; 'Pink Perfection', 5–7 ft., fuchsia pink, fragrant, July; *L. pyrenaicum*, 2–3 ft., yellow-green, spotted with black, May–June, some chalk; *L. regale*, 3–5 ft., white, tinted yellow inside, with purple shading on the outside, fragrant, June–July, some chalk; *L. rubellum*, 1–1½ ft., pink, fragrant, June, some shade; *L. speciosum*, 3–6 ft., very variable, but most frequently white with pink suffusion and spots, August–September; Sunburst strain, 4–5 ft., yellow, orange, or fuchsia pink, July–August, and 5–7 ft., white with green or golden throats, August; *L. × testaceum*, 3–5 ft., yellow-apricot, June–July, some chalk; *L. tigrinum*, tiger lily, 4–5 ft., reddish-orange or yellow with darker spotting, July–September, some chalk, produces bulbils. Lily bulbs can be planted any time between September and January, though the sooner they go in the better, so that they have as long as possible to make growth. *L. candidum*, and *L. × testaceum* are, however, moved just after their June–July flowering and planted still in leaf. Actually any lily can be moved after flowering, provided soil is left on the roots; lily roots should under no circumstances dry out, and if lilies are seen for sale in this condition they should not be bought. The bulbs should always be marketed in moist peat or wood shavings. If conditions for planting are not suitable, potting them is just as good until planting outdoors is possible. Lilies are planted at three times the depth of the bulb, i.e. a 2-in. long bulb would be put at 6 in. deep. This is because lilies produce roots from stems just above the bulb as well as from the base. The exceptions to this are *L. candidum* and European lilies such as *L. martagon*, which root from the base only. They should be put at only twice their depth. Good soil drainage is vital, and if at all faulty, coarse sand and extra peat should be worked into the soil before planting. If necessary, special raised beds of suitable soil can be made, so as to keep the roots free of winter waterlogging. Lilies will grow well in thin woodland; they like to have some sun during part of the day, and a ground cover of low shrubs is admirable. Only healthy lily bulbs should be planted, and if the base is soft and mouldy, such bulbs should be destroyed. Grey mould can be prevented from infecting the shoots, leaves and flowers by using a protective systemic spray. Virus diseases can be quite a common trouble in lilies, resulting in mottling and stunting, and eventually death, in some cases; they are spread from plant to plant by greenfly feeding on the leaves, and a systemic insecticide should be used to control them. Increase from seed will help to avoid this, though the hybrids will only come true if grown from scales, offsets and bulbils. Seed from *L. regale* will flower within two to three years, others take about three or four years.

Muscari (Lily family) (grape hyacinth). These are all hardy, small, bulbous plants, with tiny, rounded flowers in closely packed spikes; some are fragrant. Rock gardens, edges, naturalizing in turf, and thin shrub or woodland are all good sites. *M. armeniacum*, 6–8 in., flowers deep blue, honey scented, April–May, and cultivars 'Heavenly Blue', deep blue, and 'Cantab', paler blue; *M. botryoides*, 6 in., flowers pale blue, and *album*, white, April; *M. comosum monstrosum*, feather or tassel grape hyacinth, 12–15 in., flowers violet and dark blue, plume-like, May–June; *M. tubergenianum*, 8 in., flowers pale and dark blue in the same spike, March–April. Plant all 3 in. deep between August and November, except *M. comosum monstrosum*, which is put in 4 in. deep. Any soil, and preferably a sunny place, suits them. Increase by division at planting time, or by seed sown outdoors in September in sandy soil; it will flower at three to four years of age.

Narcissus (Amaryllis family) (daffodil). The daffodils can be divided into two different types for garden purposes: the comparatively tall, large flowered hybrids, and the species and their hybrids, which are miniature in size and flower, looking their best on rock gardens, in short turf and so on. All are hardy, and easily grown; with modern breeding, the typical trumpet flowers have been doubled, flattened or split, and the normal colouring of yellow or yellow and white has been modified to produce pink or orange flowers or flowers with reddish trumpets. The following is a selection of the small species and their hybrids: *N. asturiensis*, 2–3 in., flowers

yellow, miniature daffodil, February; *N. bulbocodium*, 5 in., hoop petticoat daffodil, yellow, wide trumpet, February; *N. cyclamineus*, 8–10 in., yellow, January–February, and hybrids 'February Gold', 'February Silver' (white and lemon), and 'Peeping Tom', yellow; *N. jonquilla*, 12 in., yellow, fragrant, and hybrids with several small, scented flowers to a stem, 'Cherie', white and apricot, and 'Trevithian', pale yellow; *N. juncifolius*, 3 in., yellow, fragrant, leaves rush-like, March; *N. nanus*, 4–8 in., yellow trumpet, paler collar, late February; *N. poeticus*, 14 in., white, fragrant, double, mid-May; and 'Actaea', white collar, and yellow cup edged red, and 'Pheasant's Eye', same colours except for orange edging; *N. pseudonarcissus*, Lent lily, 6–12 in., yellow, late February; *N. obvallaris*, Tenby daffodil, 10 in., yellow, early February; *N. rupicola*, 3–5 in., yellow, fragrant, late February; *N. tazetta* hybrids, many small fragrant flowers: 'Cragford', 14 in., white collar, orange-red cup, March, 'Geranium', 18 in., white collar, orange cup, late April, 'Paper White', 15 in., all white, late February; 'Soleil d'Or', 18 in., yellow collar, orange cup – the last two are tender; *N. triandrus albus*, angels tears, 4 in., creamy-white, late April and *N. t. concolor*, 4 in., deep yellow, late April – 'Thalia' and 'Tresamble' are both white hybrids from *triandrus*; *N. watieri*, 3 in., white February. The large flowered hybrid daffodils include: 'Beersheba', 14 in., all white; 'Binkie', 16 in., pale yellow collar, deep yellow cup, 'Cantatrice', 16 in., all white; 'Carbineer', 18 in., yellow collar, orange cup edged red; 'Carlton', 17 in., all yellow; 'Cheerfulness', 19 in., cream double; 'Chungking', 17 in., yellow collar, red cup; 'Fortune', 19 in., collar yellow, cup orange; 'Golden Harvest', 18 in., all yellow; 'Ice Follies', 16 in., all white; 'Inglescombe', 16 in., yellow double; 'Irene Copeland', 14 in., white and apricot double; 'Kanchenjunga', 14 in., all white; 'King Alfred', 19 in., all yellow; 'Mary Copeland', 14 in., white, yellow and orange, double; 'Mrs R. O. Backhouse', 15 in., white collar, pink cup; 'Mount Hood', 18 in., all white; 'Queen of Bicolors', 18 in., white collar, yellow trumpet; 'Rembrandt', 19 in., all yellow; 'Rustom Pasha', 18 in., yellow collar, orange cup edged red; 'Sempre Avanti', 18 in., white collar, orange cup; 'Unsurpassable' 19 in., all yellow; 'Verger', 16 in., white collar, red cup; 'White Lion', 18 in., white and cream, double.

Daffodils can be grown in a great number of sites, such as in borders and beds for cutting and display, in which they are planted in groups or singly, as formal bedding in rows naturalized in grass in the open and under trees, and in containers both for outdoors and in the home, where they can be

had in flower early by gentle forcing. All these places are suitable for the large-flowered hybrids; the tiny species daffodils and their hybrids look very well in rock gardens, and in short turf and alpine meadows, in miniature gardens in sinks, and in pans in the alpine house. A number of these flower very early, in January and February, without forcing. Grouping the daffodils in this way is for the convenience of the gardener; the official classification is concerned with the characteristics of the flowers and is therefore a botanical one. The colour of the flower, both of the trumpet (corona) and the collar (perianth), and the length of the trumpet are the factors which determine whether the flower in question belongs to Division 1c or Division 9. Those which are commonly called narcissus are white with small cups; those with large trumpets are daffodils, but all belong to the genus *Narcissus*. Planting time for daffodils is September and early October, putting the large bulbs of the garden hybrids in holes

planting time, or by seed sown in autumn in cold frames, which may flower from three years onwards.

Nerine (Amaryllis family). The star-like flowers of the nerines have strap-like petals, and long prominent anthers, reminiscent of honeysuckle or azaleas. They come from South Africa, and there are two species and their hybrids which are commonly grown, but which need quite different treatment. *N. bowdenii* is quite hardy, even in Scotland, provided it has a south facing border, with a wall backing it, to grow in; it grows to 1½ ft., and the flowers are pink from September to November, though the colour can vary in intensity. Plant during July–August at least 6 in. deep; the large bulbs will eventually poke their noses above the surface, and should then be replanted lower, or heavily mulched to protect them from frost. A dressing of bonemeal after flowering, and liquid fertilizer occasionally in growth is beneficial. The leaves will die off in July. *N. sarniensis*, the Guernsey lily, is tender and needs to be grown in a cool greenhouse. Its height and time of flowering are the same as *N. bowdenii*, but there are several hybrids in shades of salmon, scarlet, pink, white, and wine. Plant in pots at the same time, one to a 4-in. pot, with the neck showing, and water only when the leaves begin to show; feed while flowering and growing until the bulbs rest, dry out and ripen thoroughly in warmth. Minimum winter temperature should be 45°F (8°C). Increase both species by offsets at potting time.

Ornithogalum (Lily family). All the ornithogalums have white, star-like flowers coming from bulbs; there are hardy and tender species amongst them. *O. arabicum*, 2 ft., flowers white with black centres, fragrant, summer, for the cool greenhouse; *O. nutans*, 1 ft., translucent greenish-white flowers, April, some shade in greenhouse; *O. thyrsoides*, chincherinchee, 1½ ft., flowers white in long, pointed spike, June–July, mild gardens outdoors or cool greenhouse; *O. umbellatum*, star of Bethlehem, 6–8 in., flowers greenish-white in flattish heads, May, outdoors in shade. Outdoors plant in autumn in sandy soil, topdress in spring every year and feed occasionally while in growth. Indoors, pot in a sandy JIP 1 or 2 between September and February. Good drainage is vital; keep dry while resting. Increase by offsets.

Puschkinia (Lily family) (striped squill). The generally grown species is *P. scilloides*, 6 in., flowers pale blue with a darker stripe, March; there is a white form. Plant 3 in. deep in autumn in a slightly heavy soil, or in pans in the greenhouse in JIP 1. Increase by offsets, or seed sown in a cold frame in August.

6 in. deep, and the small ones of the species and their hybrids at a depth of 3–4 in. The single-nosed bulbs can be planted with a bulb planter, as they will not stick half way down the holes. Bulbs in containers should be planted very close, almost touching, with the noses at or just below the surface. If they are to be forced, keep them in the cool and dark, and always moist until there is plenty of root growth. Where daffodils are naturalized in grass, do not cut the grass until the daffodil leaves have yellowed. If, when bulbs are lifted in summer, they are found to be soft and squashy, with the centres hollow and containing white maggots, they should be destroyed, and the remainder examined very carefully to ensure that they are clean. The maggots are of the narcissus fly, and can do a great deal of damage; dusting the soil in late spring and thereafter at fortnightly intervals until the end of June at least, with g-BHC, will help to control them, putting the material close around the necks of the bulbs. Increase is by offsets at

ABOVE: Nerine bowdenii *may look delicate but it is extremely hardy, even in the north.*
TOP: Narcissus poeticus '*Actaea*'.

Ranunculus (Buttercup family) The tuberous ranunculus produce those very double, rounded flowers in a variety of bright colours which are often sold as cut flowers in summer. They are very attractive, but do need warm sites in which to grow. *R. asiaticus*, 6–12 in., flowers pink, orange, yellow, red, and white, May–June; there are some different strains known as Persian, French, Turban, and peony flowered, which differ in the doubleness of flower, size and height. Soak the tubers for a good 24 hours before planting, and put them in at the end of February, claw side downwards, about 2–3 in. deep. In really warm gardens they can go in during October–November. Soils should be rich and sandy, with plenty of sun. In a greenhouse, JIP 3 with extra grit is suitable. If grown for cutting, make up special beds, with a base of coarse rubble, and 1 ft. of compost on top mixed with rotted manure and grit. Keep well watered until the leaves die down, lift in August and store in paper bags hung in a frostproof place until planting time. Increase by seed sown when ripe in autumn in a cool greenhouse, or by division.

Scilla (Lily family) (squill). The squills are familiar spring flowers grown from bulbs outdoors or in pans, usually in various shades of blue, and white. *S. bifolia*, 6 in., flowers blue, March; *S. sibirica*, 6–8 in., flowers deep bright blue, late February–March, and a white form; *S. peruviana*, 8–10 in., May–June, flowers deep blue, lilac or white in a massed head of 5–6 in. wide; *S. tubergeniana*, 6 in., flowers very pale blue with a deep blue central stripe, February–early March. Plant outdoors in a sunny place, and sandy loam between August and November, 2–4 in. deep, depending on the size of bulb; *S. peruviana* needs to be 4–6 in. deep, in a sheltered place. Indoors, plant in a quick draining compost in pans at the same time, plunging them until growth appears. Keep dry after the leaves have died down and repot every year. Increase by offsets, or seed sown outdoors in September.

Sinningia (Gesneria family) (gloxinia). For the warm greenhouse, these tuberous plants need a minimum winter temperature of 50–55°F (10–13°C). They have very beautiful, trumpet-like, large, flowers, in various colours, and rounded velvety leaves; the following is a selection of named hybrids from *S. speciosa*: 'Blue Ribbon', bright blue with a creamy throat; 'Ceres', dark red edged white; 'Defiance', scarlet; 'Diana', light to deep rose, very large and frilled; 'Dragonfly', white with red spots; 'Prince Albert', violet-blue; 'Reine Wilhelmine', deep pink; Tigrina strain, flowers spotted in a mixture of various colours. Flowering is late July–September, height up to 1 ft. Plant the tubers singly in 5-in. pots, hollow

side up, using JIP 2, covering with about an inch of soil. They can also be started in moist peat; in both cases from January–March in a temperature of 65–70°F (18–21°C). Liquid feed occasionally while flowering and shade from direct sun; lower the temperature and give more air as flowering starts. Increase by leaf or shoot cuttings in warmth, or by seed sown in March. Dry off after flowering, and leave in their pots in a temperature of at least 50°F (10°C) until planting time.

Sparaxis (Iris family) (harlequin flower). Slightly tender bulbous plants which are best grown in the cool greenhouse, though very mild gardens and a south facing border are suitable. They are mainly sold in mixtures of unnamed varieties with a wide colour range of crimson, orange, yellow, copper, wine-purple, and pink, often with two or more colours per flower. Plant in early March in the garden if sheltered, or in pots inside in autumn; flowering will be from April to May; height is 1–2 ft. Feed and ripen well, and be careful when removing the leaves while cleaning. Cormels are produced at the bottom of the leaves, and can be used to increase the plants.

Sternbergia (Amaryllis family). The flowers of these hardy bulbous plants are crocus-like, normally appearing in the autumn. *S. lutea*, lily of the field, 6 in., flowers golden-yellow, egg-shaped and about 2 in. long, August–October, leaves at the same time. Plant in July, 6 in. deep, in a sunny place, as they need a good baking to ripen them during their resting time. Divide when they become crowded.

Tigridia (Iris family) (tiger flower). Exotic and brilliantly coloured, these unusual cormous plants come from Mexico, and are only hardy in really mild gardens and south facing borders. The flowers are three-petalled and spread out flat, spotted red on base colours of orange, deep red, cherry red, yellow, buff, or white; they last only for a day, but open in succession with six to a corm. Height is 1½ ft., and time of flowering is July onwards. They are usually sold as a mixture. Plant 4–5 in. deep in March–April in a sunny place and moist soil, give plenty of water and liquid fertilizer while growing and mulch heavily to protect from frost. Increase by offsets or seed sown in spring in heat.

Tulipa (Lily family) (tulip). Tulips are part of the English cottage garden, and have in fact been grown here and on the Continent since the 1500s. They are now available in a great range of colours, all except blue, and will flower from early March to late May, varying in height from a few inches to 3 ft. The following is a selection of species and their hybrids, and garden hybrids, to cover the variations in colouring, shape and time of flowering as widely as possible:

ABOVE: *Snowdrops, the first flower of spring (see Galanthus).*
BELOW: *A fine show of red-and-white tulips.*

T. clusiana, 10–12 in., cherry and white, late April; *T. fosteriana*, 10–18 in., scarlet and black, mid April, and 'Red Emperor', 15 in., vermilion red, and 'Salmon Trout', 15 in., orange cerise-pink; *T. greigii*, 9 in., scarlet or orange and black, leaves blotched chocolate, April–May, and 'Cape Cod', 8 in., yellow with red stripes; 'Oriental Splendour', 14 in., carmine and lemon yellow; 'Donna Bella', 8 in., creamy-yellow, red, and black; 'Hearts Delight', 8 in., pale rose; 'Red Riding Hood', scarlet; *T. kaufmanniana*, water-lily tulip, 8 in., cream, pink on the outside, March–April, and 'Cesar Franck', 8 in., red and yellow; 'Coral Satin', 7 in., coral pink; 'Johann Strauss', 6 in., cream flushed red, mottled leaves; 'Shakespeare', 6 in., salmon, apricot, and orange; 'Stresa', 7 in, deep yellow and orange-red, and 'The First', 6 in., red and cream, very early; *T. praestans* 'Fusilier', 10 in., vermilion, 4–6 flowers on a stem, April; *T. tarda*, 6 in., white and yellow, 3–6 on a stem, April. Garden hybrids; early singles, April-flowering: 'Bellona', 15 in., yellow fragrant; 'Brilliant Star', 12 in., scarlet; 'Diana', 12 in., white; 'General de Wet', 13 in., orange-scarlet; 'Keizerskroon', 15 in., scarlet and yellow; 'Pink Beauty',

13 in., pink and white; 'Van de Neer', 12 in., plum-purple. Early doubles (seven days later): 'David Teniers', 12 in., violet-purple; 'Elektra', 12 in., carmine-pink; 'Jewel Dance', 12 in., red and white; 'Marechal Niel', 12 in., yellow; 'Murillo', 10 in., pink and white; 'Orange Nassau', 12 in., orange-scarlet; 'Schonoord', 12 in., white; 'Vuurbaak', 12 in., scarlet. Mid-season single (mid-April to mid-May): 'Elmus', 18 in., cherry and white; 'First Lady', 16 in., violet-purple; 'Garden Party', 16 in., white edged pink; 'Sulphur Glory', 22 in., light yellow. Darwin (May flowering): 'Apeldoorn', 26 in., orange-red, black base; 'Aristocrat', 28 in., rosy-magenta; 'Blue Hill', 27 in., amethyst-violet; 'Clara Butt', 24 in., rose; 'Flying Dutchman', 24 in., currant red; 'Gudoshnik', 24 in., yellow; 'Holland's Glory', 20 in., scarlet; 'La Tulipe Noire', 25 in., maroon-black; 'Niphetos', 28 in., lemon-yellow; 'Orange Goblet', 26 in., orange; 'Queen of Bartigons', 26 in., salmon-pink; 'The Bishop', 29 in., violet, blue base; 'Union Jack', 24 in., white with red edging and streaks, blue base; 'Zwanenburg', 29 in., white. Lily-flowered (early May): 'Aladdin', 22 in., scarlet, cream edge; 'China Pink', 22 in.,

pink, white base; 'Golden Duchess', 22 in., primrose-yellow; 'Mariette', 22 in., salmon-pink; 'Picotee', 22 in., white edged pink; 'Queen of Sheba', 19 in., chestnut-red; 'White Triumphator', 26 in., white. Breeder (May flowering): 'Dillenburg', 26 in., orange; 'Louis XIV', 30 in., purple, bronze-edged. Cottage (late single): 'Blushing Bride', 22 in., creamy-white edged red; 'Marshall Haig', 28 in., red; 'Mrs John T. Scheepers', 24 in., yellow; 'Rosy Wings', 22 in., pink; 'Sorbet', 26 in., cream, orange-red and pink; Multiflora (May flowering – several flowers to a stem): 'Georgette', 26 in., yellow edged red; 'Orange Bouquet', 22 in., scarlet and yellow. Broken – the flower colour of these is streaked and patched as they are infected with virus, but nevertheless attractive; keep away from other tulips: 'Absalon', 22 in., yellow, flamed coffee brown; 'May Blossom', 22 in., cream flamed purple; 'Mme de Pompadour', 24 in., white flamed violet-purple. Parrot (deeply fringed petal edges): 'Black Parrot', 22 in., almost black; 'Fantasy', 22 in., soft rose, green markings; 'Orange Parrot', 28 in., brownish-orange, marked old gold; 'Red Parrot', 28 in.; 'Texas Gold', 20 in., yellow edged red, marked green. Late double: 'Carnaval de Nice', 16 in., white with red stripes; 'Mount Tacoma', 18 in., white; 'Uncle Tom', 18 in., maroon-red. Tulips are planted 4–6 in. deep in well drained soil and in a sunny position, in October for the April-flowering kinds, and in November for the May-flowering ones. Feeding with bonemeal, and ripening the bulbs thoroughly will help to ensure good flowers, and with this treatment some of the European species can be naturalized. Most of them, however, need to be lifted when the foliage has died, cleaned, and put in a sunny place to dry off and finish ripening. Increase by offsets or seed sown in February in a cold frame.

Vallota (Amaryllis family) (Scarborough lily). *V. speciosa*, 1–1½ ft., flowers light red, trumpet shaped, several to a head, August, is the species commonly grown, and pink and deeper red forms. Plant singly in 3½-in. pots in JIP 2 with added grit, from May–July. Give sun, and liquid feed while in growth. Repot annually to a larger pot without disturbing the clump until much crowded, and then divide. When the foliage dies down, dry off and rest until repotting time. Increase by offsets.

Zephyranthes (Amaryllis family) (flower of the west wind, zephyr lily). Best grown in a cool house, *Z. candida* is the hardiest, 6–12 in., flowers white, September, like crocuses. Pot or plant the bulbs in autumn in well-drained soil, 4 in. deep outdoors, 2 in. in pots, one in a 5-in. pot. Dry off completely after flowering; increase by offsets.

HARDY FLOWERS THAT BLOOM EACH YEAR

As we have seen, annuals are plants which are sown and die within the same year, while biennials flower the year after they are sown, and then die away. 'Perennials' is an umbrella term for plants which survive for longer than this, but it is not generally applied to trees, large shrubs, and bulbs.

This question of terminology need not worry us too much, for we are only going to deal with perennial plants which show enough colour to be welcome in the borders.

However much you may be tempted to move perennials from the place in which you first planted them, do remember that many will resent this type of interference. In any case, a gardener who is always changing his mind is not likely to have successful results. If a plant does not seem to be doing well, then move it, but it is a mistake to be forever experimenting. Plants, like most people, prefer to be allowed to settle down without disturbance.

Look upon your perennials as part of the long-term planning of your garden. Above all, you want them to flourish for a number of years, so give special consideration to their likes and dislikes before you plant, and then leave them to get on with it. There will be ample scope for year-to-year variety with the annuals which you plant among them.

One reason why perennials have become more popular in recent years is that they do not require much attention. Once gardeners who could afford help would compete with one another for the showiest beds of annuals. Nowadays gardeners, whose time and means are more limited, favour perennials, simply replacing the annuals which they had previously cultivated.

This has resulted in too little consideration being given to the conditions that perennials favour. They were pushed into narrow beds that were not designed for them in the first place, and with little thought given as to whether or not they would get on with their neighbours.

Despite this, most of the perennials that you are likely to choose will adapt themselves quite well to the average garden, especially if you take the trouble to consider their general likes and dislikes, with regard to shady and moist conditions, or dry open situations with plenty of space. Do not make the mistake of planting the shyer kinds next to those which are greedy, rank, and ruthless.

One of the commonest mistakes with perennials is to underestimate the amount of room they need. Any plant, which grows in the same place year after year, must be expected to become bigger, and this must be remembered when siting your perennials. If, in the early days, you are afraid the bed will look empty, just fill in with annuals. Do not, however, overcrowd the perennials, which need room to expand by bushing out. Crowding will create tall and spindly growths, which cannot afterwards be corrected, and weak stems that have to be staked. It has been pointed out, quite rightly, that gardeners who find a great deal of staking is necessary have only themselves to blame, and not the plants.

Be sure then that your borders are wide enough. It is a good basic rule to have a border twice as wide as the height of the tallest plants that it is to contain. This means that if any plants 5 ft. high are contemplated (delphiniums, for example, can easily exceed this height), a 10 ft. bed is necessary. If you have a garden with borders much narrower than this, as they often are, you should consider widening them by any means possible.

A great many of the rectangular gardens found in this country were based on the simple plan of having a border all the way round, with perhaps a gravel path between it and the lawn in the centre. In such a case, you would do well to consider dispensing with the gravel path altogether, thereby possibly gaining another 3 ft. for a border that may only be 4 ft. deep. The path is not, after all, a vital necessity. In the days of wheelbarrows with iron tyres it served, among other things, to prevent the lawn from being damaged. But now that our barrows have soft tyres this is not such a problem.

If walking on wet grass upsets any of the family, you might consider letting some stepping-stones into the turf.

Borders of this depth do, however, create a problem of accessibility if they can only be approached from one side. So it is wiser to avoid running them straight up to the wall and, instead, provide something in the nature of a path between. The plants in the bed itself will grow better away from the wall and many things can be grown up the wall itself, which will appear over the tops of the tallest plants. The path need be no more than a series of stepping-stones along which the barrow can be run and you will no longer have to walk right through the bed to get to the plants at the back. If there is enough space, the turf can be carried round behind the bed instead.

Having shifted the bed further out, and increased its width by several feet into the bargain, you may find yourself looking ruefully at a substantially diminished area for the lawn in which you hoped to take so much pride. This problem must obviously enter into your major planning considerations. You may be able to solve it, however, by getting away from the picture-frame concept of a border all round the garden, and sacrificing some yardage of the previous owner's cramped borders in favour of some really good ones of your own. There is nothing against running the turf close up to a wall. It can produce a very charming effect. The balance of the garden as a whole is a matter for your own eye.

As an alternative, you should remember that there is no need for the edge of the

border to be straight. You can have a wavy-edged border that is considerably deeper in some places than in others. Very attractive layouts can be achieved by this means, with the resulting promontories of plants which can be viewed from both sides, and inlets of turf running in between them. Provided such a plan is not allowed to become niggardly, it can multiply the variety of aspects in a garden to an astonishing extent, and this variation can, in itself, make a garden seem larger. Perennials have been found to do very well in island beds, where there is room for them, and the promontories have at least some of their advantages.

Planning

If you are planning a new garden, or making radical changes to an existing one, this is the time to get out the sketch-plan of the garden. Here you may have indicated the position and shapes of the beds that you want to lay down, and it will be well worth spending some time plotting in, to scale, the positions of all the larger perennial groups that you propose planting. You will then have a chance to give mature consideration to siting, and the space that will be taken up.

In the long run, this approach will give far better results than walking round the garden with a spade, with the 'I think it might look nice here' attitude. Proper planning in advance will also ensure that you get a reasonable distribution of colour throughout the whole garden at all possible times of the year.

Almost certainly, as you become more experienced, you will regret some of your decisions, but then the subsequent adjustments will be *planned* adjustments, and less likely to lead to a major swapping operation among half the perennials in your garden.

Preparation of sites This will present different problems, according to the type of land you have taken over, whether it be old meadow-land, building site, or previous garden. Have a close look at the need for drainage. In many cases, deep digging will be all that is required. This is best done during summer and autumn if the soil is heavy. It should be left in the clod in order to expose as large an area as possible to the beneficial effects of the winter frosts. This works wonders in separating the soil, which can then be worked into a fine tilth for spring planting and sowing.

If there is a pan below the top spit where the soil is compacted very hard, it may be necessary to undertake trenching or double digging. This must be done to provide adequate drainage for the many perennials that depend on it for growth. The loosening up of the soil lower down enables these

PREVIOUS PAGE: *A colourful variety of low-growing perennials: lavender aubrieta, yellow* Alyssum saxatile, *red and cream rock roses and a bright yellow trailing genista.*
ABOVE: *'Pacific' polyanthus, a hardy perennial which comes in a wide range of spring colours.*
ABOVE RIGHT: *A summer border, with a fine display of orange* Helenium autumnale *in the foreground.*

perennials to find a reliable source of water deep down that is unaffected by weather conditions, and so build up a sound root-system. When trenching, keep the top spit at the top and the bottom spit at the bottom.

This not only enormously improves the drainage, but is ideal for cleansing the ground of weeds, which are a particular menace among perennials that are to be permanent residents. While digging, each turn of the spade will disclose long established docks and dandelions which can then be totally eradicated and thrown off the land. Other weeds will be buried deep enough to kill off, and by the time the land has been dug over any perennial weeds that were missed will be all the more con-

then to bury it as you dig, where it will rot down and incorporate humus into the lower levels of the soil. Failure to chop the turf up first will slow down the rotting process. The turfs will gradually shrink and may cause uneven subsidences. Most grassland contains a fairly high wireworm population. Wireworm killers are available, and these can be dusted in while the turf is being buried, or lightly forked in just before planting.

Whether or not the site is old pasture, you should incorporate humus when you are deep digging, in the form of peat, compost, or farmyard manure. If the earth is heavy, it will help to keep it open, and if it is light it will give it body. A liberal incorporation at this time should last for many years, with nothing more than an an occasional booster of top-dressings of fertilizer.

After the kind of preparation that has been described, you should not have to feed the new beds for a year or two. However, the humus content in the soil will gradually disappear, and particularly when it is sand, gravel, chalk, or clay there is a tendency for this to happen. It is wise, therefore, to replace the humus in the form of leaf mould or garden compost, if possible. Failing that, use peat, which is easier to obtain and to apply. This can either be dug in or applied as a mulch, which serves the additional purposes of retaining the moisture in the soil and making life difficult for weeds. It is best to use it in conjunction with an organic fertilizer, but not at the same time. The fertilizer should be given in March at the rate of about 2 oz. per square yard, and hoed in, as it is applied, into the top 2 in. of soil. The mulch must not be applied at this time because it will tend to keep the soil at its existing temperature. At this time of year, the soil will be too cold and a good growing temperature is not likely to be reached until April or May, depending on local conditions.

When using peat for mulching make sure that it is very moist before putting it down, to a thickness of $\frac{1}{2}$ to 1 in. When the sun dries the top surface of the soil, the moisture is absorbed from the level below, and this in turn is dried out by sun and wind, so that there is a constant movement of moisture upwards, and loss by evaporation. A good moist mulch shades the top surface and goes a very long way towards slowing down this process. Probably most of the mulch will have disappeared by autumn or winter, though the benefit of it will continue for some time.

Winter digging Once the beds have been planted out, it will no longer be possible to undertake the thorough deep digging that was done at the time of preparation.

spicuous, and easily dealt with as they are found. Couch-grass should be relentlessly removed down to the last fragment of its runners, and burnt. Mares' tails indicate subsoil close to the surface, and their roots go very deep. But, however numerous, they will generally disappear under continuous cultivation. If you are cursed with ground-elder, you may have to wage war for many years.

Remember that if you do decide to use weed-killers, you must read the instructions carefully. Many of them are persistent, and render the soil unusable for garden purposes for the time it states on the pack. Hormone destroyers for application to individual weeds will be useful for dealing with the convolvulus that comes under the

fence from your neighbour's plot. You can eradicate the evil without trespassing or even mentioning it to your neighbour. But wash your hands thoroughly afterwards if you mean to touch anything you cherish.

Where the ground is really infested with weeds, and you can bring yourself to do so, fallow it for a season. This will enable you to get it really clean, and ready for the planting of a permanent bed of hardy plants.

If the site is old pasture, the turf will have to be dealt with. Old turf can be used to provide a useful source of good loam for potting later, but it should be lifted off and stacked upside down and left until it is fully mature. Otherwise, it is best to chop it up, either with the spade or a rotary digger, and

But a certain amount done with discretion, to avoid disturbing the roots, will help to prevent perennial weeds from becoming established. If you use a spade for this purpose, it will be difficult to avoid cutting through some of the roots. It is better to use a flat-tined potato fork, which will dig quite effectively without much damage.

The other treatment required at this time of year consists in removing accumulations of dead leaves. It is true, these may ultimately become humus, but if left, they will not only look unsightly, but will take a long time to rot down. This soggy mass lying on the bed throughout winter may rot the crowns of plants, and will certainly harbour slugs and other pest or disease infestations. It should be cleared away and composted elsewhere, before being returned to the soil.

Sometime between November and February the dead stems of plants should be cut down to ground level. This applies only to the *dead* stems of the herbaceous kinds that lose each season's above-ground growth. Foliage that remains green over winter only needs tidying up, with the removal of dead or dying outer leaves.

Planting The time to plant is in autumn, whenever you can. At that time of year the soil still retains some of the warmth of the summer, and it is not likely then that it will dry out. Under these conditions, there is a good chance that the roots of newly-installed plants will be able to establish themselves before the winter sets in. They will already be down in the deeper and moister layers, where they are not so vulnerable, by the spring, when there is always a possibility of the soil-surface drying out, and often a need for watering. This means that October is, generally speaking, the best month for planting, except in the coldest districts and the coldest soils. Indeed, in warmer parts, where the soil is dry and well drained, planting can safely be carried through into November. But *Aster amellus*, erigerons, pyrethrums, *Scabiosa caucasica*, nepetas, and some grasses are best planted in spring.

The condition of the soil in autumn must clearly be just right. That is, it should be clean, friable and easy to work. The main problem is likely to be organizing delivery of plants from the nursery at the time when the soil is ready for them.

Supposing, however, that all has gone well. Your beds are fully prepared, with the soil in just the right condition and (if you are wise) marker sticks or labels are pegged out ready, so that a place for everything can be found straight away. As soon as the consignment arrives, unpack the various plants and bundles, stand them upright and sprinkle them with water if they are at all

dry. Do not leave them lying about unwrapped, or the sun and the wind may quickly dry out the roots. If you have a very light soil, and you discover that it is drier than it should be for planting, it is best to puddle in. Dig out the holes for planting with a trowel and almost fill them with water from a can. As soon as this has soaked away, shape out the hole to the correct size for planting. Then spread out the roots of the plant on the moist base, refill the hole with topsoil and make a loose tilth round the plant. If, on the other hand, your soil is inclined to be wet and sticky, it will be difficult, while you are walking about on it, not to compact it or pick up great lumps of it on your boots, thus losing the benefit of some of your careful preparations. This can be largely avoided by having ready some short lengths of plank which can be placed wherever you want them over the plot. With soil of this type you should not tread the plants too firmly in.

Spring planting Should you need to do any planting in spring, the chief problem is drying out, although as a rule the soil is generally moist enough for successful planting until about mid-April. But this will vary from year to year. If the soil *is* dry, use the puddling method described above, and watch the plants keenly from then on. If any seem at all unhappy, they will be in need of water. But it is useless to 'drown' them. Too much water will destroy the tilth around the plants by turning it into liquid mud, which then cakes and dries out very quickly; it will also tend to wash the soil away from the roots, which are trying to establish themselves. The only way to get the water down to the roots is by checking, and reversing the tendency of the moisture to rise, without destroying the soil surface. Soil that is compacted conducts the heat and draws the moisture up. Where the soil is loose, however, there is less moisture-transfer by capillarity and less heat conduction. This is because the separate grains on the top shade those beneath, in the same way as a double-skin tent. Water should, therefore, be applied as a fine spray whenever plants seem to be suffering from drought. It takes longer, but it is infinitely more satisfactory, and sprinklers with fine nozzles are available that will do the job very well. For preference, do the watering in the evening, and when the surface is no longer wet, reinstate the tilth in the top $\frac{1}{2}$ in. with a rake.

HARDY PERENNIALS FROM A–Z
Acanthus (Acanthus family) (bear's breeches). These have long, jagged, glossy green leaves and lavender-lilac hooded flowers tinged with white, growing in 3–4 ft. spikes, which appear from early

ABOVE: Achillea filipendulina 'Gold Plate' is often used as a dried flower.
TOP: The shocking pink 'Carnival' is an unusual-coloured aster.
LEFT: Anthemis 'Grallagh Gold', the golden marguerite.
TOP LEFT: Aster amellus, a traditionally coloured Michaelmas daisy.

July and last for many weeks. Give them a sunny, well-drained position and grow them either in groups by themselves or with other shrubs. But as they eventually encroach beyond their allotted space and will require annual curbing, they are best kept out of the mixed border. Freely flowering kinds are A. mollis and A. spinosus.

Achillea (Daisy family) (yarrow, milfoil). A. filipendulina is the popular form usually offered as 'Gold Plate' on account of the shape of the deep yellow heads growing on stems about 4 ft. high which when cut in their prime can be dried for winter decoration. A. taygetea 'Moonshine' is smaller (18 in.) with canary-yellow heads and silvery leaves, flowering from May to July. A. millefolium is the native milfoil and is deep pink, with variants such as 'Cerise Queen' that are almost red. These grow to about 3 ft. as do the white achilleas, 'The Pearl' and 'Perry's White'. The last three all need support. They should be given well-drained soil, but otherwise demand

little attention beyond dividing in early autumn or spring. Milfoil will need curbing and replanting after one or two seasons.

Alchemilla (Rose family) (lady's mantle). A. mollis forms a neat clump of maple-shaped grey-green hairy leaves with loose sprays of small, yellowish-green flowers spreading out to 20 in. and lasting many weeks. Grow it almost anywhere, either in sun or shade, except in the worst dry situations. It can be divided easily and is free-seeding.

Anemone (Buttercup family) (Japanese anemone). The individual flowers, resembling dog-roses 1½–3 in. across, with yellow stamens, are borne on wiry, branching stems in shades of pink and white from late July until autumn. A. × hybrida (long known as A. japonica) should be given good drainage and a sunny position. It will grow well on chalk. These are favourites whose absence cannot fail to be missed.

Anthemis (Daisy family) (golden marguerite). This has yellow, daisy-like flowers on somewhat twiggy plants about 2–2½ ft. high from June to late August. The A. tinctoria varieties are short-lived, and if the woody rootstock fails to produce new basal growth in autumn, they will not survive. A. 'Grallagh Gold' is particularly difficult. The light yellow 'Wargrave' or 'Mrs Buxton' are less so, and the 20-in. dwarf A. sancti-johannis, with deep yellow flowers, is the most reliable.

Aquilegia (Buttercup family) (columbine). For a good range of colour and large, long-spurred flowers, 'McKana Hybrids' about 3 ft. high and 'Beidermeier' 20 in. high, will carry on for a year or two, but must then be replaced. They do not readily come true from seed. Aquilegias are not over-particular about soil or situation and some can be grown in shade.

Armeria (Plumbago family) (thrift). A. maritima is the common thrift of the sea-coast. The bright carmine-pink 'Vindictive' and the white-flowered variety alba both grow to 8 in. in May and June. They are specially suitable for edging, as within a year or so they produce a continuous ever-green row about 1 ft. wide. A. latifolia 'Bee's Ruby', deep carmine, gives the largest and brightest blooms. Division is seldom possible, and cuttings are not easy to strike. If you attempt it take basal cuttings in early autumn or spring and insert them in a cold frame. Give all kinds full sunshine and good drainage.

Aster (Daisy family) (Michaelmas daisy). There are many varieties of Michaelmas daisies, with different colours, heights and flower sizes, but try to keep to varieties that need no staking. You will want several to keep the garden dressed in autumn. Divide them in spring and replant

ABOVE: Doronicum plantagineum, *known as leopard's bane.*

TOP: Dictamnus albus purpureus *has deep roots and should be carefully placed to give it both sun and drainage.*

OPPOSITE: Euphorbia wallichii *is a herbaceous spurge which adds an unusual look to a border.*

them from the outer, healthier shoots every three years.

Astilbe (Saxifrage family). These have very attractive foliage and plumed flower spikes of many hues from white through pinks, salmons and cerises to fiery and deep reds. The heights vary from 6 in.–6 ft. Generally the taller kinds are the least bright. *A. taquetii superba* is 4 ft. high and has intense lilac-purple spikes in July and August. *A. davidii* and the varieties 'Tamarix', 'Salland' and 'Salmon Queen' are other tall kinds in lilac-rose, pale pink and salmon. 'Cologne', deep carmine-rose, 'Dusseldorf', salmon pink, 'Rheinland', clear pink and early, 'Deutschland', fine white, 'Fire', intense red, and 'Red Sentinel', brick, are all more colourful and about 2 ft. high. 'Glow' and 'Spinell' are reds, 2½ ft. high, 'Federsee', rosy-red, and 'Bressingham Pink' are the same height. 'Fanal', deep red, and 'Irrlicht', white, are 2 ft. *A. simplicifolia* 'Sprite' is a 12-in. ivory pink miniature. The taller kinds do not need staking. All are fully hardy and will go for years without trouble, provided they are not given hot and dry conditions. They all like moisture and enjoy a spring mulch, especially the shorter astilbes, and the dwarfer ones are the longer flowering. Divide them when they are dormant.

Bergenia (Saxifrage family) (pig squeak). These plants have large, shiny leaves which do not die off until late winter, and are much grown for their bright foliage from May to March. The small bell-shaped pink flowers are borne in sprays on 9–12 in. spikes. The modern varieties are the more colourful, such as the dwarf 'Abendglut' (Evening Glow) and 'Ballawley'. 'Silberlicht' is free-flowering and almost white. For ground cover it will be cheaper to grow any *B. cordifolia* varieties or *B. schmidtii*. They will thrive in all except very hot, dry situations, and spread quickly.

Campanula (Bellflower family) (bellflower). There are very many forms, ranging from the prostrate hybrid 'Stella' to forms 6 ft. high. Most of them are various shades of blue, but there are near-pink forms such as 'Loddon Anna' and *alba*, white. Taking them in order of size, the smallest, 'Stella', is suitable for rock gardens, wall-tops, edges and border fronts or as a pot plant. It flowers mainly from June to August, but if cut back, divided, and revitalized it can be persuaded to flower again in autumn. It will grow in most places, given reasonable soil.

Next up in size come the varieties of *C. carpatica*, between 6 and 12 in. with upward-facing cup-shaded flowers varying from white to violet-blue in June and August. To avoid mixed shades you should buy named varieties. *C. burghaltii* attains 15–18 in. from June onwards with pendulous bells of a smoky blue. So does the pale blue *C. van Houteii*. The forms of *C. glomerata* reach 2 ft. The flowers are upturned; *superba* has violet flowers in June and July. Of similar height are the varieties of *C. lactiflora*, of which 'Prichard's' is the deepest in colour. They are long-flowering, and there is a pygmy variety 'Pouffe', which forms a green cushion, flowering from June to September. 'Loddon Anna' is 4–5 ft. high, *alba* about 5 ft.

C. latifolia (syn. *C. macrantha*) is 4 ft., with large blue bells, 'Brantwood' is deep violet-blue and 'Gloaming' pale sky-blue. Campanulas can be grown in both sun and shade.

Centaurea (Daisy family) (cornflower). There is a choice of centaureas between 2 in. and 6 ft. and over. *C. hypoleuca* bears many clear pink flowers on grey-leaved plants 1 ft. tall, flowering from late May to July; *C. dealbata* 'Sternbergii' and 'John Coutts' are improved varieties, also pink, but reaching 2½ ft. in height and freely flowering in June and July. *C. ruthenica*, on 4 ft. stems, is canary yellow, and later flowering, from June to August. *C. macrocephala* is another yellow species attaining 5 ft. on massive leafy plants. The centaureas grow well almost anywhere, even where the soil is poor. They should be divided in early spring.

Centranthus (Valerian family) (valerian). This familiar denizen of abandoned gardens, old walls and neglected borders is available in the brighter red of *coccinea* and the white *alba* form, as well as the somewhat dull pink of *Centranthus ruber*. It gives little trouble as it will perpetuate itself, flowering freely on stems 2–3 ft. tall. Unwanted plants can simply be rooted out.

Chrysanthemum (Daisy family). *C. maximum* 'Esther Read' is the best known of the white-flowered doubles, but there are also 'Thomas Killin' and 'Everest', both with large single white flowers. Other doubles include 'Wirral Supreme', white and very large, 'Cobham Gold' and 'Moonlight', flushed with yellow, and 'Jennifer Read', white. However, *C. corymbosum*, with greyish leaves and bearing large numbers of 1-in. wide white daisies on stems 3½ ft. high from June to August is the best of these perennial chrysanthemums, while the 5–6 ft. *C. uliginosum*, with single white, yellow-centred daisies, is invaluable to grow into late autumn after the Michaelmas daisies are over.

Coreopsis (Daisy family). These are apt to deteriorate after one successful season, but are fortunately easy to divide in spring for replacements after they exhaust themselves. For reliability and distinction grow *C. verticillata*, whose 18-in. bushes produce

yellow flowers from June to late August, or its variety *grandiflora*, in a deeper yellow. *C. grandiflora*, varieties 'Sunburst' and 'Mayfield Giant' are larger, and easily raised from seed. 'Goldfink' is an 8-in. midget with deep yellow, maroon-marked flowers blooming from June to September, which will usually over-winter.

Delphinium (Buttercup family). Generally, delphiniums must be sown outdoors for stock to flower after transplanting in the following year. But if sown under glass in spring some may flower in late summer. 'Pacific Hybrids', which are short-lived, usually come true from seed, but the named varieties usually do not, and will produce various shades of blue. Belladonna delphiniums have more open spikes and are shorter than the others. The tall kinds must be staked in ample time to prevent damage from rain, and should be given rich soil and protection against slugs.

Dicentra (Fumaria family) (bleeding heart). *D. spectabilis* is the true species, with the lush foliage and arching sprays of red and white lockets appearing in May and June.

The roots are brittle, and you will find it worth while to plant them carefully, give them well-drained good soil, some sun, and reasonable shelter from wind. The young shoots, taken with a good base will root in a cold frame. But the plants are not easy to divide.

Dictamnus (Rue family) (burning bush). This is a long-lasting perennial with 3-ft. spikes of lilac-pink flowers appearing from June to August. Remember that *D. albus* has deep roots, so pay extra attention to drainage when installing it and find it a place in the sun. It is not easy to divide. Propagate it by root cuttings in autumn or spring. Growing from seed takes a long time.

Doronicum (Daisy family) (leopard's bane). These appear early, and 'Goldzwerg' flowers from late March to May, 6 in. high. The taller 'Miss Mason' will follow it, also with yellow daisies, but the double-flowered 'Spring Beauty', also 18 in. high, is one of the finest. 'Harpur Crewe' is taller still, with wide-rayed flowers. They are all easily grown, easy to divide (pre-

ferably in early autumn), and should be split up and replanted every few years to do best.

Echinacea (Daisy family) (purple coneflower). The only species grown is *E. purpurea*, 3½ ft. high, an attractive plant whose drooping petals display the central cone. Of the named varieties 'Robert Bloom', in a very warm red shade is one of the finest, and as one of the 'Bressingham Hybrids' does not vary much in colour, as do seedlings. It is more erect than the better known 'The King'. All echinaceas flower from July to September. Give them deep, well-drained soil, which is not too dry, and divide them in early spring.

Echinops (Daisy family) (globe thistle). All of these have grey, jagged, and slightly prickly leaves and light blue flower-heads. They are deep rooted and some of them are rather big, so if space is important, consider *E. ritro*, which is 3–4 ft. high. When divided, the roots remaining in the ground will usually produce further plants.

Erigeron (Daisy family) (fleabane). These grow between 20 in. and 2½ ft. in various shades of pink to blue. 'Darkest of All' is a 20-in. violet-blue single, and 'Foerster's Liebling' is a near-double bright pink the same height. 'Prosperity' is light lavender blue and again near-double. Slightly taller are 'Amity', lilac-pink, 'Gaiety', single pink, 'Sincerity', mauve-blue and long flowering, and 'Dignity', violet blue. Taller still is 'Lilofee', 2½ ft. and mauve blue. Fleabanes flower from May to August. Give them open, well-drained positions and increase by division in spring.

Eryngium (Umbellifer family) (sea holly). There are many species, from *E. pandanifolium* growing up to 10 ft. to *E. bourgatti*, with 20-in. stems. They are unusual in that the flowers have no apparent petals. Colour may appear in the stems as well as the flowers, or both may be green. Other species are *E. serra*, 6 ft., *E. bromeliifolium*, 4 ft., *E. variifolium*, 2 ft., with marbled evergreen foliage, *E. giganteum*, 3 ft. but only biennial, and *E. planum*, which is easy to grow. Particularly good are *E. alpinum*, which has rounded green leaves and large silver-blue flowers, 2½ ft., but best of all is *E. tripartitum* which grows 3–3½ ft. with bright blue flowering tips, and is rather widely branching. Increase them from root cuttings in the spring, or by dividing plants in autumn or spring.

Euphorbia (Spurge family) (spurge). Some garden forms of this large genus are given below. Sulphur-yellow is the characteristic colour. Of sub-shrubs there are *E. characias* and *E. wulfenii* which will grow to over 3 ft. high with masses of yellow heads and blue-grey foliage throughout the year. *E. polychroma* (syn. *E. epithymoides*) is considered one of the best of all spring-flowering herbaceous plants. It reaches 20 in. and flowers in April and early May. It is followed by *E. griffithii* 'Fireglow' in May and June, rising to 2½ ft. There are some vigorous, rapid-spreading species useful for ground cover among shrubs. Such are *E. amygdaloides* and *E. robbiae*.

Gaillardia (Daisy family) (blanket flower). Good named varieties of gaillardias are 'Croftway Yellow', 'Ipswich Beauty', which is yellow with a maroon cone, 'Mandarin', a fiery orange, 'Wirral Flame', a browny red, all of which grow to between 2½–3 ft. There is a 9-in. miniature, 'Goblin'. Although plants are easily grown from seed, these named varieties must be propagated by root cuttings – or rather from roots remaining in the ground after the top growth has been cut off. Their liking for poor soil and dry conditions enable them to be grown in some of the problem corners.

Geranium (Geranium family) (cranesbill). These are true geraniums which are fully hardy. *G. armenum* (syn. *G. psilostemon*) is a fierce magenta from June to August, and if given plenty of moisture will form a dense bush, 3½ ft. 'Bressingham Flair' is pinker, and *G. endressii* can be pale or bright pink with dense mounds of light green, and reaches 20 in. in June and July. Of the blues there is *G. grandiflorum*, 15 in., not very good value in terms of flowers. 'Johnson's Blue' is much better, and the 2-ft. *G. ibericum* produces deep blue flowers with dark leaves. The uncommon *G. wlassovianum* is another deep blue, from July to September. *G. sylvaticum* 'Mayflower' has light blue flowers in May and June. *G. sanguineum* is another magenta, 1 ft. high, with flowers borne in long succession. *G. renardii* is light mauve-blue with crimson veins. 'Holden Variety' is a good clear pink, and *album* is the white form. Geraniums will grow in sun or partial shade and may be divided in spring or autumn for propagation purposes or when the clumps become too large.

Geum (Rose family) (avens). These are not very vigorous, but *G. borisii* is a reliable, 1 ft. tall species with orange single flowers in May and June. 'Mrs. Bradshaw' and 'Lady Stratheden' are popular doubles in red and yellow because they flower very freely, but they spend themselves in a couple of years. 'Fire Opal', orange-red, 'Rubin', deep red, and 'Georgenberg', yellow, are all good cultivars flowering from April to June. They should be divided and replanted every two years.

Helenium (Daisy family) (sneezeweed). They are easily grown and provide a rich display of colour from May to September. 'Bruno' and 'Moerheim Gem' are browny

red, and 'Butterpat' is yellow. These are all about 4 ft. Earlier flowering varieties are 'Bressingham Gold', 'Coppelia', 'Gold Fox' and 'Mahogany', all in orange and browny flame shades. Other earlier kinds are the shorter 'Golden Youth' and 'Wyndley', also brown and orange. Avoid taller varieties than any of these and give them some attention by dividing and replanting every three years in enriched soil.

Heliopsis (Daisy family) (orange sunflower). These do not have the showy immensity of the annual sunflower. The flowers are about 3 in. across and the height is about 3 ft. Colours are yellow-green ('Goldengreenheart') or golden ('Golden Plume'), both of which are doubles. 'Ballerina' and *H. patula* are good singles flowering from June to September. All will carry on for several years, needing no support. Divide them in autumn or spring.

Helleborus (Buttercup family) (hellebore). *H. niger* is the true Christmas rose, which seldom lives up to its name, but we are always thankful for it in January and February. *H. orientalis* is the Lenten rose with hybrids from white to deep pink and even plum-purple. *H. corsicus* is pale greenish-white, and *H. foetidus* has greenish flowers. All are around 2 ft. tall. Give the hellebores shady and moist conditions, but provided they are not baked by the sun they will do well where it is dry in summer. Seed is rather slow to germinate, but in a suitable spot self-sown seedlings will appear. Divide mature plants in autumn, for propagation purposes,

ABOVE: Inula orientalis, *one of the smaller species, has comparatively large flowers.*
TOP: Helleborus orientalis atropurpurea *is related to H. niger, the Christmas rose. Its unusual plum flowers are very distinctive.*
TOP LEFT: Helleborus niger, *the Christmas rose, is the traditional Christmas flower although it often does not bloom until the New Year.*
LEFT: *The beautiful old-fashioned herbaceous peony 'Lady Alexandra Duff'.*
OPPOSITE, TOP RIGHT: Geranium psilostemon *is a true geranium.*
OPPOSITE, TOP LEFT: Helenium *'Wyndley' is an early variety which should be divided and replanted every three years.*

although they are normally best left un-disturbed.

Hemerocallis (Lily family) (day lily). The many varieties of this excellent plant have been much increased recently. The trumpet-shaped flowers are richly coloured, and appear from June to August. The best of their colours are the yellows and oranges, such as 'Hyperion', the golden-yellow 'Doubloon', 'Primrose Mascotte', light yellow, 'Stafford', ruby-orange, 'Golden Orchid' and 'Golden Chimes', dwarf orange, 'Fandango', ruffled light orange, 'Larksong', lemon, and 'Morocco', red. There is a pink one, 'Pink Damask', and the ruby-mahogany, 'Black Magic'. They can be grown in most soils in shade or sun, but the better the treatment the longer the flowers last, and many of them will grow to a considerable size. Divide them in autumn or spring.

Heuchera (Saxifrage family) (coral flower). These all have compact, evergreen foliage and can produce many hundreds of small, bell-shaped flowers on wiry stems in early summer. The colours range through from white to a coppery crimson. 'Bressingham Hybrids' are a mixed strain with a wide colour range. Give them good soil and sun or only partial shade, and every three or four years mulch them deeply with soil or compost, or dig them up and replant the most vigorous shoots deeply. Divide them, after flowering, in July. They do not come true from seed.

Hosta (Lily family) (plantain lily). These hardy, reliable and attractive plants will grow to a considerable size, and develop into solid clumps in which their leaves make a fine show, but the larger kinds can be very space-consuming and need siting accordingly. Otherwise, they are most accommodating, always looking their best in woodland or waterside environments, but still an attractive addition to the edge or border. The leaves of the $1\frac{1}{2}$–$2\frac{1}{2}$-ft. *H. crispula* have creamy margins and the flowers are lavender-mauve from June to August. The leaves of *H. fortunei*, which flowers earlier, are bluish-green, and the flowers are pale lavender. The variety *H. f. picta* is a spring variegated one lasting until midsummer, when the leaves turn green. 'Honeybells', $2\frac{1}{2}$ ft. has scented lavender flowers.

Inula (Daisy family). The daisy-like flowers are yellow, and species grow from 6 in.– 7 ft. high. One of the neatest, *I. orientalis* has finely rayed flowers up to 4 in. across on 2 ft. stems. *I. barbata*, about the same size but with smaller flowers, spreads quite rapidly and flowers for many weeks from June. Similar are *I. hookeri*, another large-flowered species, and 'Golden Beauty', neater, flowering from June to September. You can divide them easily.

Iris (Iris family). The popular *germanicas* or flags are June flowering plants in many colours. The season for these attractive plants can be extended with the earlier 1-ft. tall *I. pumila*, which is at its best in April and May, again offering a choice of yellow, blue and white. For a later show *I. foetidissima*, the wild Gladwyn iris, with violet-blue or whitish flowers, reveals conspicuous orange or scarlet seeds in autumn when the pods open. This may be grown in fairly deep shade. *I. pallida* is a familiar flower in cottage gardens. *I. sibirica* is an erect and rushy-leaved moisture-lover up to 3½ ft. high, with blue, purple or white flowers, which may continue for up to 5 weeks.

Kniphofia (Lily family) (red-hot poker). Where they can be given sunshine, the kniphofias can be selected to give a 5-month spread of colour from June. For the first half of this period there are 'Atlanta', 3 ft., in red and yellow; 'Bee's Sunset', deep orange; 'Gold-Else', 'Springtime', red and yellow, and *K. tubergenii*, a light yellow. Also 'Jenny Bloom', salmon-flushed ivory; 'Maid of Orleans', white; 'Bressingham Torch' and 'Bressingham Flame'. For the second half there is 'Samuel's Sensation' of brilliant flame colour and majestic stature. Divide them in spring, though the early varieties may be divided in September.

Liatris (Daisy family) (gay feather). These also have poker-like spikes, but the colour is bright lilac-purple and the height about 3 ft. There is *L. callilepis*, and the less commonly grown *L. spicata* and *L. pycnostachya*, which are similar. Dig the old plants up in spring, divide them and replant in enriched soil.

Linum (Flax family) (flax). The best of these is *L. narbonense*, which gives the rich blue desired, and is much longer lived than *L. perenne*, which seldom survives more than two years. *L. narbonense* is smaller (20 in.) and in well-drained soil is a valuable dwarf for the border. *L. dolomiticum* has bright yellow rounded flowers, and is taller, but compact, and blooms from mid June to late August, as do *L. campanulatum* and *L. flavum*. Propagate by division in spring.

Lupinus (Pea family) (lupin). There is a vast number of named varieties. The seedling plants are cheaper and likely to be a mixture of colours. Lupins should not be attempted on chalky soils, as they like it acid, or at least neutral. Propagate named varieties by cuttings rooted in a cold frame in spring.

Lychnis (Pink family) (catchfly). There are tall singles, 2–3 ft. such as *L. chalcedonica* with intense red flowers from June to August, and the 10-in. double form *L. viscaria plena* with very bright pink flowers

in June and July. *L. coronaria* has silver-grey leaves. It has a long growing period with sprays of pink or carmine flowers, and prefers a dry situation. All may be increased by division in spring or autumn.

Lysimachia (Primrose family) (loosestrife). There is a white species *L. clethroides*, which flowers in late summer, and the yellow loosestrife *L. punctata*, which has bright yellow, 3-ft. spikes from June to August. These are mainly moisture-loving plants, but they will survive in drier sites. They expand rapidly and require curbing, but flower for longer when small pieces are replanted.

Macleaya (Poppy family) (plume poppy). These make 6–8 ft., strong spikes with powdered stems and leaves that are brownish beneath and bluish above. The small buff flowers of *M. cordata* are borne in large sprays in late summer. Those of *M. microcarpa* are brownish yellow, and 'Coral Plume' is rather more colourful. The plume poppies are easy to grow even in quite dry soils and shade, but their roots are inclined to emerge among neighbouring plants.

Monarda (Sage family) (bergamot). These are later plants, appearing from June to September, whose flowers have upward-pointing petals at the tips of profuse systems of stems. They will grow between 2½ ft. and 4 ft. according to how favourable the site is. This should consist of deep, moist

soil, where they will spread over the surface. There are named varieties of *M. didyma*, such as 'Cambridge Scarlet', 'Adam', 'Prairie Glow', salmon, 'Croftway Pink' and 'Melissa', also pink, and 'Prairie Night', purple. To curb them spreading, either dig over the centres and refill with vigorous pieces from the edges, or dig up and completely replant in early spring.

Nepeta (Sage family) (catmint). *N. faassenii* and its varieties are favourite edging plants, which produce their lavender blue flowers on 1–2-ft. spikes from June to September. 'Six Hill's Giant' has 2-ft. sprays; 'Blue Beauty' is more erect, with shorter, violet-blue flower spikes. Give them good drainage to avoid winter losses. The dead spikes are untidy and unsightly, but giving catmints a 'haircut' in winter, when they look their worst, can be fatal. It should be done either in July or March.

Oenothera (Evening Primrose family). These all have large, yellow or white, cup-shaped flowers. The most distinctive is *O. missouriensis*, which bears 4-in. canary-yellow flowers from July to October. It needs sun and good drainage, and can be increased by seed or by cuttings. Taller kinds are *O. cinaeus*, whose bright leaves of buff, pink and purple-red in spring turn green as the sprays of flowers open. *O.* 'Fireworks' has purplish-green leaves, and 'Yellow River' green foliage. These and 'Highlight', all approaching 2 ft. in height,

ABOVE: Kniphofia 'Springtime', the red and yellow red-hot poker. It blooms in early summer and should be divided occasionally. It likes a sunny position in the garden.
LEFT: One of the great variety of lupins, which can also be grown from seed. Lupins like an acid soil and will not do well on chalk.

are propagated by division in early spring.

Paeonia (Buttercup or Peony family) (peony). Because they live for so long and resent root disturbance, select the site with care and allow plenty of space for expansion. There are numerous varieties of the large-flowered Chinese *P. lactiflora*, whose pink, red and white single, semi-double and double fragrant flowers appear in June. *P. officinalis* is the old-fashioned cottage peony, of great fragrance, in red, pink, crimson and white doubles. Give them rich, deep soil, and mulch them. When necessary, divide old plants between August and October, with a knife, and ensure when replanting that the new buds are 1 in. below the surface.

Papaver (Poppy family) (poppy). *P. orientalis* has enormous flowers with brilliant colours appearing from May until late June. The blood-red 'Goliath' and orange-scarlet 'Marcus Perry' are the most erect. These are brownish-red, pink and white varieties also. Give them well drained, not-too-rich soil and propagate from 3-in. long root cuttings in spring.

Phlox (Phlox family). Of the white kinds there is 'White Admiral', 3 ft. tall, and 'Mia Ruya', still the best dwarf white in the face of new introductions. 'Mother of Pearl' is whitish-pink, vigorous and hardy. 'Mies Copijn' and 'Dodo Hanbury Forbes' are both pink; 'Windsor' and 'Endurance' are both shades of rose. 'Brigadier' and 'Spitfire' are shades of orange, but 'Prince of Orange' is the most brilliant. Of reds, 'Starfire' is the most reliable, and 'Tenor' early flowering. 'Aida', 'San Antonio' and 'Vintage Wine' are all magenta; 'The King', 'Parma Violet' and 'Marlborough' are violet-purples. 'Skylight' and 'Hampton Court' are lavender blue, and 'Balmoral' more lilac-coloured. Give the phloxes light, and not alkaline, soil. Divide them every three years, or propagate them by root-cuttings to avoid attacks by phlox eelworm.

Physostegia (Sage family) (obedient plant). These will continue to flourish without much difficulty in most soils from July to September. The tapering spikes of *P. speciosa* 'Rose Bouquet' are rose-lilac, about 2 ft., and the smaller 'Vivid' is deeper in colour and flowers later. It should be dug up each spring and replanted to prevent it from spreading too far afield. *P. virginica* 'Summer Snow' and the deeper pink 'Summer Spire' are taller. In moist or rich soil physostegias should be curbed after two or three years.

Platycodon (Bellflower family) (balloon flower). They vary in height from 1 ft. (*mariesii*, light blue) to 2 ft. in *P. grandiflorum*, white, blue, and pale pink. The latter open into campanula-shaped flowers. All are long-lived and will grow in most places that are well drained. Although the seed-raised plants do vary in colour, the fleshy roots of the old plants will divide readily.

Polemonium (Phlox family) (Jacob's Ladder). *P. foliosissimum*, 2½–3 ft., is best to grow, as it has a longer flowering period (from June to September) than most, and it is less likely to give trouble through excessive seeding. The heads consist of lavender blue flowers. The dwarf kinds 'Sapphire', 15 in., and 'Blue Pearl', 10 in., both flower during May and June, and respond well to rejuvenation by division.

Polygonatum (Lily family) (Solomon's seal). *P. multiflorum* grows naturally in woods and shady places, and should be given a cool site where it will flower freely in June. The arching sprays of handsome, parallel-veined leaves and pendant green and white flowers grow to over 2 ft. Divide them in autumn or spring.

Polygonum (Knot-weed family) (knotweed). In *P. amplexicaule* the 4–5 ft. poker-shaped spikes top a rounded dense bush of pointed leaves 3 ft. across. *Atrosanguineum* is a dull red variety. 'Firetail' is brighter, and reliable, with a three-month flowering season. *P. bistorta* 'Superbum' is 3 ft. tall with 4-in. pink pokers which appear in May and June. *P. carneum* has smaller spikes of deeper pink, and flowers later, sometimes well into August.

Potentilla (Rose family) (cinquefoil). Most are dwarf plants that will grow well in any open position, with green, grey, or silvery strawberry-like foliage. A vigorous species is *P. atrosanguineum* with bright red flowers ¾ in. across, and silvery leaves. 'Flamenco', 2 ft., has larger flowers and green leaves, and both flower in May to

July. 'Gibson's Scarlet' has equal brilliance, but flowers from June to September. 'Firedance' is orange-salmon, 'Miss Willmott' pink, 'Glory of Nancy' orange or red, 'William Rollison' flame orange, and 'Yellow Queen' yellow. These are all about 18 in. high. Divide them in autumn or spring.

Pulmonaria (Forget-me-not family) (lungwort). These are spring-flowering plants, some with coarse rough leaves and some, like 'Pink Dawn', that are partly grown for their white-spotted leaves. All grow between 9 in.–1 ft. high. *P. angustifolia aurea* bears blue bell-shaped flowers from March to May, and 'Munstead Blue' is a little later. *P. saccharata* and 'Bowles's Red' have large leaves and occupy more space. Propagate them by division.

Pulsatilla (Buttercup family) (pasque flower). The small (9–10 in.) early flowerer produces its goblet-shaped flowers in early spring. They are surrounded by gossamer calyces, and the colours range from lavender, through red, into purple, and some are white. All have prominent golden stamens, and grey-green ferny leaves. The seed-heads also are attractive. *P. vulgaris* can only be propagated from freshly-gathered seed.

Pyrethrum (Daisy family). The flowers are daisy-like and brightly coloured with named varieties in single and double white, several pinks, rich salmon and crimson. They flower from late May until July and seldom grow more than 3 ft. high. The soil should be alkaline and well drained, and the site should be sunny and open, or they

will need supporting. Cut the plants back hard after flowering. This is also the time to lift and divide the old plants for propagation, unless this is done in March or early April for spring planting.

Rudbeckia (Daisy family) (cone flower). The true perennials are all yellow, but the forms vary considerably. The tallest varieties of *R. laciniata* include the 5–6 ft. 'Autumn Sun', which needs support. 'Goldquelle' is not so tall and produces double chrome-yellow flowers 3 in. across from July to October. Shorter still is *R. deamii* (2½ ft.) which, from August to October, bears deep yellow, black-centred flowers. 'Goldsturm' starts flowering as early as June and continues right through to autumn. For long flowering they should all be given a moist soil.

Salvia (Sage family) (sage). The flowering sages mostly produce their spikes of tiny lipped flowers from June to August. *S. × superba* rises to 3 ft., 'May Night' to about 20 in., 'East Friesland' to 1½ ft. The last is a later flowerer. 'Lubeca' is 2 ft. All these are long-lived, hardy, and easy to grow and increase by division or basal cuttings in spring. But *S. haematodes* is sown from seed and may live a great while. It flowers in June and July to 3 ft. high. Give salvias good drainage.

Scabious (Teasel family) (scabious). A tall 2½ ft. scabious in shades of blue, violet, and white flowering from June to September, is *S. caucasia*. It is excellent for cutting. *S. graminifolia* is a 10-in. high species that makes a compact mound of silvery, grassy leaves. Its lavender-blue pincushion heads appear in succession throughout the same months. 'Pincushion' is a pink variety with heads 1 in. across. Give scabious a site where they get good drainage and no winter wet, which they hate. Plant and divide them in spring, or raise from seed. To keep them flowering they should be dead-headed.

Sedum (Stonecrop family) (butterfly or ice plant). *S. spectabilis* has several varieties, 'Brilliant', 'Carmen' and 'Meteor' which are all much the same with wide heads packed with glistening pink flowers in late summer. 'Autumn Joy' is slightly taller and sturdier. In September it opens light pink, but slowly changes to salmon-rose. The heads are 12–15 in. across. *S. heterodontum* grows up to 1 ft. high with burnt-orange heads and bluish leaves. *S. rhodiola*, the rose-root sedum, is also dwarf and bushy. Propagate by division.

Sidalcea (Mallow family). There are several varieties, all pink to rosy-red and sending up spikes of mallow-like flowers between June and September. The lighter pinks include 'Mrs Alderson', 'Wm Smith', 'Rev. Page Roberts' (all up to 4 ft.) and 'Puck', which attains 2½ ft. 'Rose Queen',

'Wensleydale' and 'Craftway Red' are all darker and 3–4 ft. high. Grow them all in full sun with good drainage and divide them in spring. Cut back the spikes after flowering to promote fresh basal growth.

Solidago (Daisy family) (golden rod). These are often seen growing like jungles, having taken over. It is better to grow nothing taller than 'Mimosa' (4 ft.), which is compact and does not seed about. The yellow plumes last until September. The following flower between July and September: 'Golden Mosa', 'Golden Shower' and 'Golden Falls', all deep yellow, and 'Lemore' and 'Leslie', which are lighter shades of yellow. 'Peter Pan' is an earlier variety with horizontal branches to the crested plume. 'Crown of Rays', 2 ft., is bushy, and 'Cloth of Gold', 18 in., is spreading. Neatly growing miniatures are 'Queenie' and 'Golden Thumb', which flower from August to October up to 12 in. high. Their leaves are almost golden. Plant solidagos and divide them in spring.

Stachys (Sage family) (donkey's ears). These are grown mainly for their silvery, furry leaves as *S. lanata*, which also has a non-flowering variety 'Silver Carpet', and they make good ground-cover. *S. macrantha* rises $2\frac{1}{2}$ ft. with short spikes of rosy, purple-lipped flowers, and those of *S. macrantha* 'Rosea' are deep pink. *S. m.* 'Superba' is rich rose-purple, while *S. m.* 'Violacea' is violet-purple. Divide them in spring or autumn.

Thalictrum (Buttercup family) (meadow rue). The attraction of the thalictrums is particularly in their small bluish-grey leaves. *T. minus* (syn. *adiantifolium*) has $2\frac{1}{2}$-ft. sprays of rather insignificant buff-green flowers and is the easiest to grow. *T. speciosissimum* and *T. glaucum* grow from 5–6 ft. and have yellow flower-heads, from June to August. *T. aquilegifolium* is shorter and earlier, appearing in early June with mauve, purple, or white flowers. *T. dipterocarpum* is also mauve-blue, but its 5-ft. stems, which are much branched, will need supporting. A shorter variety is 'Hewitt's Double', but it is less vigorous and needs even richer and moister soil than most of them. Divide thalictrums in spring.

Tradescantia (Tradescantia family) (trinity flower, spiderwort). *T. virginiana* has 2-ft. stems bearing clustered heads of 3-petalled flowers up to 1 in. across from June to August. The leaves are rushlike. The colours are white, light blue, mid and deep blue, purple, or magenta, available as named varieties. There are also smaller-flowered doubles. Grow them in ordinary soil in sun or partial shade. Cut them back in August if they start to lose their looks.

Trollius (Buttercup family) (globe flower). These make a good contribution to the early

summer show, flowering in June and July. *T. europaeus superbus* is light yellow and reliable, 'Canary Bird' has larger and paler flowers, and 'Goldquelle' is mid-yellow. 'Orange Princess' and 'Fireglow' are deeper. The taller *T. ledebouri* has distinctive yellow stamens. All these plants need moisture, especially from flowering onwards, and must not be given hot, dry positions. They are best mulched with peat to save watering. The 'globe' effect is seen just before the buds open.

Veronica (Figwort family) (speedwell). Most of these flower in June and July, and are easily grown. They are usually blue. The varieties of *V. teucrium* include 'Shirley Blue', 1 ft., 'Crater Lake Blue', 'Royal Blue', in order of size up to 'Blue Fountain', at 2 ft. These are all mounded and bushy, topped with short spikes. There are two mat-forming species: the early (May) *V. gentianoides*, and *V. spicata*, both blue and both 2 ft. high. The shorter *V. spicata incana* is violet-purple with silver-grey leaves. The leaves of 'Sarabande' and 'Wendy' are less silvery. 'Baracarolle' and 'Minuet' are pink and 18 in. high. *V. exaltata* is a 4-ft. late-flowering species which may need support. *V. virginica* is also good but does not last long nor does its pink variety 'Rosea'. The handsome 'Alba' is 5 ft. high, and flowers in August and September.

ABOVE: Phlox *'Rosea'* is a beautiful pale pink.
TOP: Romneya coulteri, *the Californian tree poppy, needs plenty of sunshine and is only hardy in southern gardens.*
OPPOSITE: *Pyrethrums may bloom again in the autumn if they are cut back after their first flowering.*

POPULAR GARDEN FLOWERS

Although much of this book is to do with flowers of one sort or another there are certain species which seem to be more widespread in popularity, and this chapter is therefore devoted to providing the reader with fairly detailed advice on how to achieve the best possible results with these firm favourites.

BEGONIAS

There are two forms of Begonia which are used in bedding and they need different treatment. *B. semperflorens* makes a low plant, which is covered with flowers over many months. They are usually grown from seed, although double forms have to be raised from cuttings. A warm greenhouse is essential both for raising seed and for rooting cuttings. Begonia seed is very fine and should be just sprinkled on the surface of a seed compost, in a temperature around 60°–70°F (15°–21°C). As soon as the seedlings are large enough to handle, they should be pricked out in boxes, about 1 in. apart. Soilless compost is very suitable for begonias. The seed is sown at the end of January, and the plants pricked out further apart and kept warm until about mid-May, when they can be hardened off; they should be ready for planting out around early June.

With tuberous begonias, many growers in the past used to put the tubers on boxes of moist peat in January and as soon as the shoots could be seen, the tubers were potted up each in a 3-in. pot of a mixture of loam, leafmould, and sand in equal parts A soilless compost is just as good. As the plants make growth they are potted on to a 5-in. and finally a 6- or 7-in. pot. At this stage they should be given cooler conditions and ample fresh air. The first buds to appear should be removed. With subsequent flower heads, the lateral female flowers, (characterized by the triangular seed capsule behind the bud) are removed, and only the double male flower allowed to develop. Now is the time to start feeding with a potash-rich feed, such as is prescribed for tomatoes. This should continue until September, when no more feeding will be necessary. Towards the end of October, stop watering and allow the plants to dry out thoroughly. It is possible to remove the leaves at this stage. Once the stems have dried out, they can be removed, but do not be in too much of a hurry. Store the tubers in peat and restart them into growth in March. Bedding begonias are treated in the same way, but are hardened off at the end of May and planted out in mid-June, lifted before any frost, about the end of September, and dried off in the greenhouse.

Begonias do not like much direct sunlight, as they scorch easily, and they need plenty of water. Among the best cultivars are: pink 'Roy Hartley' and 'Judy Langdon', white 'Avalanche', yellow 'Midas', red 'Guardsman', crimson and white 'Harlequin', and crimson 'Crown Prince'.

CHRYSANTHEMUMS

Propagation If new plants are purchased, they will arrive in the form of rooted cuttings, but existing stocks need to be propagated yearly. After flowering is complete, cut down the stems to within a few inches of the ground and place the plants in a cool frame or greenhouse. With early varieties, which are grown out of doors, the plants should be lifted, put into boxes, and brought under cover. In early spring shoots start to arise from the roots. These should be taken when about 3–4 in. long, cut off at a node or leaf joint with a really sharp knife; if the cutting is very leafy, remove a few of the bottom leaves and insert it in a box of JIP 1, at least 1 in. deep.

The cuttings need a temperature around 50°F (10°C) to encourage rooting and should be kept reasonably moist but not sodden. The most essential part of growing chrysanthemums is to ensure that there is no check in growth at any stage. With this in mind, take cuttings of mid-season and late cultivars in late January; those for outdoor cultivation are taken in mid-March to April. Once they have rooted, put the early cuttings in boxes of JIP 1, with at least 4 in. between each cutting. The later kinds are potted up in 3-in. pots. Once established in the boxes or pots, they should be put in a cold frame or cold greenhouse for about 10 days, after which they may be stood outside, provided the weather is not frosty, and allowed to harden off.

The soil in which they are to grow should have been well dug during the winter and, if possible, enriched with manure or compost, and a scattering of some complete chemical fertilizer applied at the beginning of April. In May, when the weather is suitable, put out the plants, about 18 in. apart, each one with a cane to which it can be tied later. Once the plants are well established, usually around the start of June, pinch out the growing tip to encourage the production of sideshoots. If the plant is not looking healthy, it is better to delay this. A number of lateral growths will appear; keep four to six of the most uniform, removing the strongest and weakest growths. In the case of plants being grown for spray, or for pompons, you will only need to stop the plants; all the lateral growths can be left. After stopping, a light application of nitrogenous fertilizer may be a help. Eventually the sideshoots will produce a cluster of terminal buds. As soon as they are large enough, reduce the number to one to each branch, and continue to remove any subsequent buds which may be produced. A second application of some fertilizer containing ample potash will make sure that the flowers do well.

Mid-Season and Lates These are usually grown in pots, although it is possible to plant them out, like the earlies, and then lift them and plant them in greenhouse-beds in September. Plants in pots should be

64

stood outside in mid to late May, by which time they will be in 5- or 6-in. pots. As the pots become full of roots, the plants are potted on, first into 5- or 6-in. pots in JIP 2 and finally into 8- or 9-in. pots in JIP 3. Soilless composts would be adequate, but they are so light that tall plants in 8–9 in. pots are liable to prove top-heavy. For the final potting the old gardeners used to ram the soil in hard round the plants, and they got very good results. Late-flowering plants are usually stopped in June and again in July, to obtain what are known as second-crown buds. These lateral growths should still be restricted to only six or eight. The plants will all need staking with the growths lightly tied in, about every 9 in.

Watering should be attended to daily, although it is important to wait until the soil has dried out from the previous watering. A liquid feed containing ample nitrogen should be given until the buds appear, after which a feed containing equal parts of nitrogen and potash is recommended. Bring the plants into the cover of a cool airy greenhouse at the end of September. Ideally, they should not be too crowded, if at all possible. Ventilators must be kept open at all times and heating is only necessary to keep out frost which could damage the blooms. Once the buds start to show colour, you can stop feeding. When the flowers are open, mark the best plants for subsequent propagation and destroy

ABOVE: *'Sugar Candy', an appropriate name for this delicate pale peach tuberous begonia.*

any that are unsatisfactory. Once flowering is over, cut the plants down to about 9 in. from the ground. The stools can be taken from the pots and boxed up in preparation for the new crop of cuttings.

New plants are bought as rooted cuttings and should be treated in the same way, potted into 3 in. pots.

The very large Japanese Exhibition chrysanthemums usually only have three blooms per plant; other cultivars have six to eight blooms.

Earlies
Alice Jones: light bronze, reflexed, September. 'Bernard Zwager': red, Aug.–Sept. 'Cricket': white; 'Primrose Cricket', pale yellow, Sept.; 'Crimson Pretty Polly': red, dwarf plant (2½ ft.). 'Ensign': white, incurved, August. 'Fenny': pale pink, Aug.–Sept. 'Fred Porter': red, August. 'Golden Market': light bronze, Aug.–Sept. 'Grace Riley': bronze, large, Sept. 'Juanita': yellow, Aug.–Sept. 'Karen Rowe': pink, Sept. 'Mexico': red, Sept. 'Oakfield Pearl': salmon, Aug.–Sept. 'Rosedew': pink, Sept. 'Stardust': yellow, Sept. 'Staybrite': yellow, Sept. 'Stephen Rowe': yellow, incurved, August. 'Yvonne Arnaud': purple, Aug.–Sept.

Early Spray
White: 'Adelaine Queen', 'Anna Marie'. Yellow: 'Lucida', 'Lemon Tench', Pink: 'Gertrude', 'Madelaine Queen', 'Pink Rockery'. Red: 'Patricia', 'Aurora Queen', 'Red Rockery'. Purple: 'Nathalie'. Bronze: 'Pamela'.

Pompons
'Fairie', pink and various sports such as 'Purple Fairie'.

Mid Season (Oct. Nov.)
White: 'Snowcap', Oct. 'Ron Shoesmith', Oct./Nov., incurved. 'Alan Rowe', Oct./Nov.
Yellow: 'Goldplate', Oct. 'Golden Gown', Nov. 'John Rowe', Nov., incurved.
Red: 'James Bond', Oct. 'Fireflash', Nov.
Pink: 'Amy Shoesmith', Oct., incurved. 'Joy Hughes', Nov., needs a large pot. 'Lagoon', Nov., incurved. Stop at end of May and end of June.
Bronze: 'Watcombe', Oct. 'Lilian Shoesmith', Nov. 'Minstrel Boy', Nov., incurved. Stop at end of May and July 7.

Singles
These are usually stopped at the end of April and in the middle of June. They flower in November. 'Cleone': pale pink; 'Golden Seal': yellow; 'Jinx': white; 'Mason's Bronze': bronze; 'Chesswood Beauty': red; 'Woolman's Glory': bronze'; 'Red Woolman's Glory': red.

Lates (Dec./Jan.)
Cuttings for these are taken in May and stopped at the end of July. 'Balcombe Perfection' is bronze, but has yellow and red sports; 'Mayford Perfection' is salmon-pink but also has numerous colour sports, while 'Shoesmith Salmon' is found in bronze, cerise, peach, red, and yellow.

DAHLIAS
These are half-hardy, tuberous perennials, ranging in height from 1–6 ft., with flowers of various sizes and shapes. They are classified in 10 groups of which the most important are the doubles and semi-doubles. Some dahlias have daisy-like flowers; among these are the Collarettes, which have two rows of ray florets of different colours. Among the doubles are the Ball in which the flowers are globular; if they are small they are called Pompons. The Cactus and Semi-cactus have long petals rolled in on themselves to give a quill-like impression and the Decorative have flat petals, usually with rounded tips.

Site Dahlias need plenty of light, but have no objection to dappled shade. They will grow in most well-drained soils.

Soil preparation For the best results dig in late autumn and leave rough over winter. In spring, rake down and incorporate a sprinkling of general fertilizer. If compost or manure is available include this in the autumn digging. Dahlia tubers can be planted about 5 in. deep towards the end of April; rooted cuttings should not be planted out until all danger of frost has passed, towards the end of May. Once the plants have made about six pairs of leaves after being planted out, pinch out the growing point. Dahlias need to be supported by stakes and the branches should be tied in at regular intervals. As the buds appear, larger flowers can be obtained by removing side buds and restricting the flowers to one on each stem. Faded blooms should be cut away. The plants should start to flower at the end of July and continue until cut down by frost. An occasional foliar feed will improve their performance considerably. When the foliage is cut down by frost, cut off the stem about 6 in. from the ground and lift the tubers. Remove all surplus soil and store them upside down in a dry airy shed for 10–14 days. Then store (having removed any damaged tubers and trimmed back the stringy roots at the ends of the tubers) in boxes of dry peat or sand in a frost-free place.

Propagation The simplest method is by division. Put the tubers on a box of moist peat or compost in a greenhouse in early April. As the shoots form, you can divide the plant, making sure that each piece has a growth and a tuber. Better results are said

ABOVE: *The perfect round balls of pompon chrysanthemums. This variety is 'Little Dorrit'.*

TOP: *'Lemon Tench' is an early spray chrysanthemum.*

RIGHT: *A splendid, rich orange exhibition chrysanthemum, 'Bronze Tracy Waller'.*

to come from cuttings. These are taken when the shoots are from 3–4 in. long. It is necessary to have a warmish greenhouse for this and to start the stock tubers into growth in early March. Cuttings require a temperature of 59°F (15°C) to root. Cut through the cuttings just below the lowest leaf-joint, and insert about 1 in. deep in cutting compost; the lower leaves of the cutting should be trimmed off. The cuttings should be put in pots or boxes 1½–2 in. apart and must be lightly sprayed twice a day to prevent flagging. They should root in about a fortnight, after which they are potted up singly in 3-in. pots. Once established, they can be gradually hardened off, put into a frame in April, and planted out at the end of May.

Dahlias will also come from seed, although only the dwarf Coltness type are reliable; you have little idea what you will get from other seed. Sow in gentle heat in February, prick out into boxes either of JIP 1 or soilless compost, and then treat as cuttings, hardening off in April and planting out at the end of May. Some of the best sorts are:

Giant Decorative: 'Alvas Supreme': sulphur; 'Hamari Girl': lavender-pink; 'Holland Festival': orange, tipped white; 'Lavengro': lavender-bronze.

Large Decorative: 'Polyand': lavender; 'Shirley Jane': yellow fading mauve; 'Silver City'; white.

Medium Decorative: 'Breckland Joy': bronze; 'Cyclone': cyclamen pink; 'First Lady': yellow; 'Golden Turban': deep yellow; 'Pattern': lilac, tipped white; 'Pink Joy': pink.

Small Decorative: 'Angora': white; 'Amethyst': lavender; 'Dedham': lilac and white; 'Edinburgh': purple, tipped white; 'Rothesay Robin': magenta; 'Twiggy': rose-pink.

Cactus Dahlia Large: 'Polar Sight': ivory; 'Drakenberg': salmon and mauve; 'Paul Critchley': dark rose.

Medium: 'Curtain Raiser': salmon-orange; 'Golden Galator' and 'Yellow Galator', 'Worton Harmony': yellow overlaid pink.

Small: 'Alvas Doris': ruby; 'Klankstad Kerkrade'; sulphur; 'Paul Chester': orange; 'Richard Mare': pink and yellow; 'White Kerkrade': white.

Semi-Cactus Large: 'Arab Queen': coral; 'Hamari Dream': pale yellow; 'Respectable': amber.

Medium and Small: 'Autumn Fire': orange; 'Cheerio': cerise tipped white; 'Goldorange'; 'Hamari Bride': white; 'Hamari Sunset': orange; 'Mariner's Light': yellow; 'Rita Rutherford': pink-bronze; 'Rotterdam': dark red; 'Symbol': salmon; 'Tyros': bright red; 'White Swallow'.

Ball Dahlias Large and Medium: 'Connoisseur's Choice': red; 'Dr John Grainger': golden orange; 'Highgate Robbie': dark red; 'Mrs Anderson': lilac; 'Nettie': yellow; 'Rev Colwyn Vale': purple; 'Rothesay Superb': red.

Pompon: 'Andrew Lockwood': lavender; 'Moorplace': purple; 'Willo's Violet': violet.

Collarette: 'Chimborazo': maroon and yellow; 'Easter Sunday': white and cream; 'Grand Duc': scarlet and yellow.

There are two dahlias which have dark purple ornamental foliage. 'Bishop of Llandaff' grows about 30 in. tall and has scarlet single flowers. 'Yellow Hammer' is single with yellow flowers and only reaches 18 in.

DELPHINIUMS

These are popular herbaceous plants with tall spikes of flowers, mainly blue in colour, although red or yellow may soon be available, and there is also a white variety. They can be grown easily from seed, although named plants must be propagated by cuttings or by division. Seed is usually sown about May and the plants should flower the

ABOVE: *The small round heads of pompon dahlias.*

TOP LEFT: *Collerette dahlia 'Nonsense' has a pretty pink 'collar'.*

TOP RIGHT: *A rich display of dahlias, showing the wide range of varieties.*

RIGHT: *The beautiful shaded pink and orange flowers of the small decorative dahlia, 'Twiggy'.*

FAR RIGHT: *Handsome blue spires of delphinium.*

following year. The 'Pacific Giant' strain, indeed, is usually treated as a hardy biennial, although most delphiniums are long-lived perennials.

Purchased plants can be planted either in the autumn or in early spring. They do not require any special soil, although poor soils should be enriched with compost or well rotted manure. When planting, see that the roots are well spread out and plant firmly. Slugs are the plants' greatest enemy and it is often advisable to cover the crowns with ashes in early spring to protect the emerging shoots. These should be restricted to about six per plant (two for young plants); the other shoots can be used as cuttings. These should be about 4 in. long and cut off close to the crown. The lower leaves are removed, the ends of the cuttings dipped in a rooting powder and the cuttings inserted in a cutting compost, at the rate of five to a 5-in. pot. Place them in 55°–60°F (12°–15°C) and keep moist and shaded. They take about 4–6 weeks to root and are then potted up singly in JIP 1 in 3-in. pots; once established, they should be hardened off outside, and planted out either in a nursery bed or in their final position. Plants can also be propagated by simple division. This is done in early spring; lift the plants and cut the crown, so that each portion has plenty of roots and one or two shoots. The established plants can be encouraged to flower by placing a handful of general fertilizer around each plant in early June, and a tablespoonful of sulphate of potash, when the first buds show colour. They should be kept watered while they are elongating their spikes and while the flowers are opening. Once flowering is over, remove the dead spikes and, with luck, secondary spikes will develop for an autumn display.

Among the best sorts are: 'Betty Hay': pale blue with white eye; 'Blue Tit': dwarfish, deep blue, black eye; 'Butterball': cream; 'Great Scot': pale mauve, black eye; 'Page Boy': dwarfish, mid-blue, white eye; 'Purple Ruffles': purple; 'Silver Moon': mauve with white eye; 'Strawberry Fair': rosy lilac, white eye; 'Swan Lake': white with black eye.

FUCHSIAS

These are mainly half-hardy shrubs, although forms of *F. magellanica* and the plant known as 'Riccartonii' will survive outside in all districts, and make hedges in sheltered ones. A number of others can be cut down to the ground each winter, but will come up again. The others require housing over winter, although they can be stood outside in the summer. They are raised from cuttings, which can be taken either in early spring or at midsummer. Growing tips, which are quite soft, are taken, a few inches

long, cut off cleanly at a leaf joint and the last two pairs of leaves removed. The ends of the cuttings are dipped in a rooting hormone and they are inserted in cutting compost (equal parts of peat and sharp sand, or some proprietary mix), kept humid (if only a few are taken, envelop your pot in a polythene bag) and put in a temperature around 59°F (15°C). They will root in about three weeks, when they should be potted up, individually in 3-in. pots, either in John Innes Potting Compost or in a soilless compost. As they become pot-bound they must be potted on. They will flower in a 5-in. pot, but you will get better specimens in 6- or 7-in. pots. After they are established in their 3-in. pots, they should have the growing tip removed and only the two last pair of leaves left. As growth proceeds you may have to pinch out the side shoots again and again, to get a bushy plant, but this should not be overdone. If flower buds appear on the cuttings or on immature plants, they should be removed. During the winter, cuttings taken at midsummer should be grown on at a temperature of about 54°F (12°C). Older plants can be kept just frost free and dry. Water them to start into growth again in mid-February, when they should be cut back and soon put into fresh soil.

Standard fuchsias are made by preserving only one growth after the first stopping, tying it to a cane, and disbudding it until it has reached the required height; let it produce about three more pairs of leaves, then remove this tip. Let the top sidebranches develop, but rub out any forming lower down. Standards are preserved from year to year. Indoors fuchsias tend to drop their buds if the light is poor, if they are overheated or if they are in draughts, so they are not very suitable.

Plants from midsummer cuttings are overwintered at a temperature of 50°–55°F (10°–13°C), and kept gently growing to come into flower about April.

Hardy Varieties

'Alice Hoffmann': cerise; 'Brilliant': red and magenta; 'Chillerton Beauty': rose and violet; 'Drame': red and magenta; 'Brutus': carmine and purple; 'Lena': pink and purple'; 'Madame Cornelissen': red and white; 'Margaret': carmine and purple; 'Mrs Popple': red and violet; 'Tom Thumb': dwarf, carmine and purple; 'Lady Thumb': carmine and white; 'Peter Pan': dwarf, red and purple'; Susan Travis': erect.

Greenhouse and Bedding Sorts

(1) With ornamental foliage 'Avalanche': with yellowish leaves; 'Golden Marinka': yellow variegated leaves; 'Sunray': with leaves flushed white and pink; 'Autumnale' and 'Thalia': with reddish-bronze leaves.

(2) Singles 'Billy Green': all salmon; 'Bon Accord': white and lilac; 'Caroline': cream and magenta; 'Chang': orange with red tips to sepals; 'Citation': pink and white; 'Dutch Mill': rose and violet; 'Falling Stars': red and scarlet; 'Forget-me-not': pink and blue; 'Golden Dawn': pink and orange; 'Gartenmeister Bonstedt': orange; 'Lady Heytesbury': white and rose; 'Leonora': all pink; 'Mrs Pearson': red and violet; 'Queen Mary': pink and rose; 'Rufus the Red': all red; 'Sleigh Bells': all white; 'Ting-a-ling': all white; 'Tolling Bell': scarlet and white.

(3) Semi-doubles 'Abbé Farges': carmine and purple; 'Pink Flamingo': deep and pale pink; 'Satellite': white and red; 'Snow Cap': red and white; 'Tennessee Waltz': red and violet.

(4) Doubles 'Candlelight': white and carmine-purple; 'Carmen': carmine and magenta; 'Curtain Call': cream and crimson; 'Fascination', 'King's Ransom': white and purple; 'Peppermint Stick': white-striped pink, and purple edged carmine, very striking; 'Prelude': white and purple with white stripes; 'Royal Velvet': crimson and purple; 'Santa Cruz': pale and dark crimson; 'Sophisticated Lady': pale pink and white; 'Swingtime': red and white with pink veining; 'Texas Longhorn': very long flower, carmine and white; 'Torch': pale salmon and salmon-red; 'Winston Churchill': pink and pale blue.

(5) Best sorts for standards 'Cascade': white and carmine; 'Coachman': salmon and orange; 'Flying Cloud': double, all

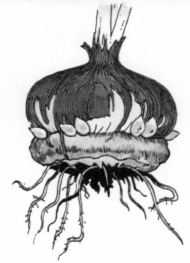

white with pink veining; 'Jack Acland':
pink and rose; 'Mrs Marshall': white and
cerise'; 'Native Dancer': double, red and
purple; 'Pink Galore': double, all pink;
'Red Ribbons': double, red and white;
'The Tarns': pink and lavender; 'White
Spider': all white with pink flush on sepals.

All these have a somewhat pendulous
habit and can also be grown as bushes and
put in hanging baskets.

GLADIOLI

Buy gladioli corms that are of medium
size; the very large ones are not worth the
extra money. They can either be planted in
clumps in the border, or in rows for cut
flowers. Choose a situation that gets plenty
of sun. The soil should be well drained
and, preferably, rich in humus. Gladioli
do not like a very alkaline soil, so lime

ABOVE: *A gladiolus corm, showing the new
corm on top of the base plate, with small
cormlets round the sides.*
TOP: *'Daily Sketch', a delicately coloured
medium-flowered gladiolus.*
OPPOSITE ABOVE: *Fuchsias are very dramatic
plants, with richly coloured flowers against
dark glossy foliage.*

should not be applied. Do not be in any
hurry to plant the corms, as they will not
grow well until the soil is warmed up;
the end of April is quite early enough and
plants will still flower well if planted in late
May. The corms should be planted from
4–6 in. deep, the greater depth for very
light soils, and about 6 in. apart, if they are
planted in rows. Once the leaves start to
emerge, keep the surrounding area clear of
weeds.

Towards the end of September or in early
October, lift the corms, cut off most of the
remaining foliage and hang in an airy position to dry off. Once they are dry, remove
the old corm and the rest of the foliage,
separate any additional corms that have
formed, (the very small cormlets, which
congregate round the base can be discarded,
unless you want to build up a large stock;
they will take 1–3 years to reach flowering size), remove any loose corm fibres, dust
with a combined insecticide and fungicide
dust and store in a dry, cool, but frost-free
situation, preferably in the dark.

The Nanus group, 'Colvillei' and 'The
Bride' are planted at the beginning of March
and flower in early June. They are most
satisfactory outside in mild areas, elsewhere
they can be grown in pots in frames or a

cool house. There are also some late summer flowering dwarf gladioli. The best of these include 'Berta' with red-striped lime-yellow flowers; 'Celeste': lilac with purplish-green blotches; 'Lipstick': purple; 'Orla': pink with deeper blotches; and 'Tampa': smoky brown.

The first to flower are usually the Primulinus hybrids with characteristically hooded flowers. Of these we recommend 'Comic': reddish brown and yellow; 'Essex': red; 'Frank's Perfection': orange-scarlet; 'Hastings': brownish; 'Pageboy': scarlet with yellow spots; 'Pegasus': cream with rosy blotches; 'Red Star': red; and 'Salmon Star'. Next come the Butterfly range with ruffled flowers, slightly hooded, and comparatively short spikes. These include: 'Argus': grey-brown with red veins; 'Bluebird': violet with a white blotch; 'Camelot': pink; 'Greenwich': yellowish-green; 'Foxfire': scarlet; 'Goldilocks': deep yellow; 'Mirth': pink; 'Parfait': salmon and red; 'Rosy Posy': deep pink, rather taller than most; 'Smidgen': red and gold; 'Statuette': yellow with red blotch; 'Tidbit': cream with purple blotch; 'Towhead': cream; and 'Troika': lavender with yellow and pink blotches.

The recommended medium flowered gladioli include: 'Angel Eyes': white with violet blotch; 'Amusing': cerise; 'Blondine': ivory; 'Clio': purple; 'Confetti': scarlet with yellow blotch in throat; 'Daily Sketch': cream; 'Dream Castle': cream edged pink and carmine blotch; 'Madrilene': apricot with red blotch; 'Storiette': salmon with yellow blotch; 'Sweet Song': salmon-bronze; and 'Zenith': crushed strawberry.

Among the best of the large-flowered sorts are 'American Beauty': deep pink; 'Aurora': yellow; 'Blonde Beauty': pinkish buff; 'Cameo': yellow and pink; 'Blue Smoke': smoky mulberry; 'Frostee Pink': pink and cream; 'Isle of Capri': orange-salmon; 'La France': pink and white; 'Limelight': lemon; 'Mount Everest': pure white; 'Orange Chiffon': orange-salmon; 'Orchid Queen': pale pink with white blotch; 'Pompeii': smoky lavender and pink; 'Salmon Queen': salmon with white throat'; 'Simplicity': white; 'Green Woodpecker': yellowish-green with red blotch; 'Winnebago Chief': dark red; 'King David': blue-purple; and 'Chintz Blue': pale violet.

IRIS

Two sorts of iris make popular garden plants; these are the bulbous iris and the bearded iris.

Bulbous Irises are treated like other bulbs; planted in early autumn in a well-drained situation, they can be left for three or four

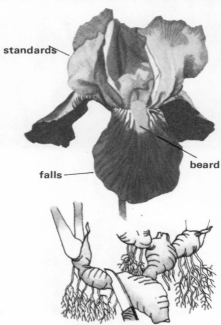

ABOVE: *How to divide an iris rhizome into single fans. The weaker fans should be discarded.*
CENTRE: *The parts of the iris flower.*
TOP: *'Summer Song', an unusual deep orange Tall Bearded variety of iris.*
OPPOSITE: Iris unguicularis *has the traditional colours: violet falls and standards, with yellow beard.*

years without lifting and replanting. They can be divided into two groups. First come the dwarfs which flower very early in the year. The earliest is usually *Iris histrioides* 'Major', which can flower in late January with blue flowers. *I. danfordiae*, with yellow flowers, is usually open in February; after flowering, the bulbs split and will not flower again for a couple of years. The most popular is the violet-scented *I. reticulata*, usually with violet flowers, but pale blue in 'Cantab', dark blue in 'Royal Blue', and purple in 'J. S. Dijt'. The Dutch, Spanish, and English Iris flower in June and July. Dutch and Spanish Iris come in shades of blue, white, yellow, and bronze, the English Iris usually only blue, violet, and white. They are larger plants, to 18 in. tall and are cheap to buy if they have to be replaced. In many gardens they gradually deteriorate.

Bearded Irises (sometimes known as Flags or German Irises) need a somewhat limy soil and full sun. They are greedy plants so the soil should be fairly rich with ample humus, but not with fresh animal manure. Ideally move them directly flowering is over, so that Dwarfs will be received in June, while the Intermediate and Tall Bearded will be received in late July or August. They should be planted shallowly, with the top of the rhizome (the creeping stem) either partially exposed or only just covered. The roots, however, must be encouraged to descend as deeply as possible, so the soil should be well dug. Plant the Tall Bearded Irises about 2 ft. apart, the Intermediates about 18 in. and the Dwarfs about 10 in. About every three years the clumps should be lifted, divided up and replanted as single fans; only the best being retained and the weaker ones discarded. It is easy enough to raise fresh sorts from seed. These take from 3–5 years to reach flowering size, but there is no guarantee what you will obtain and it is better to purchase good named varieties. Any feeding should have more phosphate and potash than nitrogen and should not be allowed to come in contact with the rhizomes. The Dwarf Irises flower in May, the Intermediates in June and the Tall Bearded from mid-June to July. Irises always do best after a hot dry summer as they are Mediterranean plants. Among the best sorts are:

Dwarfs: 'Green Spot': white with green spot on falls; 'Royal Contrast': dark purple with a white beard; 'Tinkerbell': blue; and 'Path of Gold': deep yellow.

Intermediates: 'Langport Honey': standard orange, falls reddish; 'Langport Chief': purple with gold beard; 'Langport Finch': blue; 'Langport Lady': apricot-pink.

Tall Bearded: 'Big Day': mid-blue; 'Canary Bird': lemon yellow; 'Forest Hills':

dark blue, almost black; 'Golden Planet': deep yellow; 'Green Ice': cream with green shading; 'Lady River': standards apricot, falls violet-bronze; 'My Smoky': white with plum markings; 'Happy Birthday': pink; 'Karachi': reddish-purple with white marks on falls; 'Islander': gentian-blue; and 'Foamy Wave': sky blue.

The above are only a selection; the number of sorts is enormous.

PELARGONIUMS

There are a number of different forms of these, ranging from the popular scarlet geraniums of the flower bed to the exotically coloured Regals. Fortunately the majority require similar treatment. Propagation is by means of cuttings, which can be taken at practically any time of the year, except the depth of winter, but are usually taken in late July or early August. They are taken from leading or from side shoots, about 4 in. long (less in the case of the miniatures). Leave them to flag for 24 hours, then cut off clean at a leaf joint. Remove the lower leaves and insert the cuttings fairly thickly in a box or large pot full of cutting compost. If any flower buds appear at this stage they must be removed as soon as detected. As soon as they are rooted they are potted up separately in 3-in. pots either in JIP 1 or in a soilless compost. They are potted on, when sufficiently rooted, into 5-in. pots and if necessary into larger pots. They need plenty of light and should be kept on the dry side. Once they are in 5-in. pots the plants are sometimes stopped to encourage the growth of sideshoots. Normally plants are not kept for more than 18 months, but if planted out in the greenhouse bed (or potted on) they can make large shrubs over 6 ft. in height. Apart from the recognized bedding Zonals ('Paul Crampel', 'Gustav Emich', 'Queen of Denmark' and the like) all pelargoniums flower more freely if kept indoors, but they will all survive outside during the summer months and will tolerate as low as 33°F (1°C) without damage, although they will not stand much frost.

The largest group of pelargoniums is the **Zonals**, which include plants grown for their variegated foliage rather than their flowers. Among the best sorts are: **Nosegay Geraniums:** 'Springtime': pale pink; 'Trull's Hatch': coral with lighter eye; 'Penny': cerise; 'Electra': red; 'Sunrise': pale pink; 'Vera Dillon': magenta; 'Modesty': white; 'New Life': scarlet with white edge. There are also the Cactus varieties, with narrow, twisted petals, Rosebuds, with small double flowers, and Stellar forms with star-shaped leaves.

Among the **Variegated-leaved** forms are: 'A Happy Thought': green with a

white butterfly mark and red flowers; 'Mrs Pollock': with leaves red, cream, and bronze; 'Mrs Quilter': with green and bronze leaves and salmon flowers; 'Caroline Schmidt': with white-edged leaf and double red flowers; 'Bridesmaid': with golden-green leaves and double pink flowers; and 'Daydream': with bright green leaves with copper centre and crimson double flowers.

There are also a large number of miniature Zonals, rarely exceeding 8 in. in height, many with attractive leaves such as 'Fantasy', 'Fleurette', 'Mme Salleroi', 'Petite Blanche', and 'Sun Rocket'. These miniatures are not now grown as much as formerly, but crossed with an Ivy-leaved form they have given rise to the so-called Floribundas, which look like very compact Zonals. They are also known as Deacons as they are called 'Deacon Bonanza': cerise; 'Deacon Coral Reef': coral; 'Deacon Mandarin': orange; 'Deacon Fireball': scarlet; 'Deacon Lilac Mist': lilac-pink; and 'Deacon Romance': magenta.

The **Ivy-leaved Geraniums** flower excellently outside during the summer; they

are trailing or climbing in habit and are often put in hanging baskets or in stone vases. 'L'Elegante' has variegated leaves, but most have plain green leaves. Among the best are 'Ailsa Garland': double pink; 'Blue Springs': mauve-pink; 'Cliff House': double white with reddish centre; 'Jack of Hearts': bright pink with scarlet mark; 'Malibu': cerise with orange flash.

The **Regals** tend to have a shorter flowering season than the Zonals and Ivy-leaved, but make up for this by producing more flowers at a time and with a wider range of colour. They can be stood outside during the summer, but will serve very satisfactorily for room decoration at this period. Among the better ones are: 'Georgia Peach': peach pink; 'Geronimo': deep crimson; 'Aztec': deep pink, white, and maroon; 'Grandma Fischer': orange and brown; 'Nhulunbuy': crimson with white edge; 'South American Bronze': maroon with white edge.

The Regals were crossed with the Scented-leaved sorts to produce the Unique strain, which is now uncommon. These had leaves shaped like the Scented-leaved plants and heads of rather small crimson flowers which are produced throughout most of the year.

The **Scented-leaved** varieties are grown for the sake of the shape and perfume of the foliage, as the flowers are small and usually not so showy. 'Attar of Roses' has rose-scented leaves; 'Crispum Minor' has small crimped leaves smelling of lemons; 'Fragrans' has small spice-scented leaves; 'Prince of Orange' is said to smell of oranges; 'Royal Oak', with rather large leaves smells of peppermint, and 'Mabel Grey' with jagged leaves, smells of Lemon Verbena.

ABOVE: *The Zonal Pelargonium 'Irene'.*
LEFT: Pelargonium *'Maréchal McMahon', a variegated-leaved form. It has few flowers and is grown mainly for the leaves.*

PINKS AND BORDER CARNATIONS

These are rather short-lived hardy perennials, with evergreen, glaucous leaves. They require light, well-drained soil and appreciate lime. The soil should be prepared by incorporating humus and bonemeal, and in the spring sulphate of potash at 2 oz. per square yard should be applied. Established plants will also appreciate a general balanced fertilizer at this point. Carnations are usually kept for not more than three years; pinks can be kept longer. Border carnations require to be staked with a 3-ft. cane and as the flower heads appear, in July, they should be disbudded, leaving only a single bloom to each stem. Pinks usually flower in June and rarely require disbudding.

Carnations are propagated by layering. Select strong sideshoots which can be brought down to ground level. Remove all the leaves apart from the top six pairs. Just below the lowest pair, make a longitudinal cut through the joint below, but do not sever the shoot. Where the cut is, bring the stem to the ground, secure in place with a loop of wire, and cover with a mixture of equal parts of sharp sand and peat. Water in and keep moist until rooting has taken place, which takes about 6 weeks. The shoot can then be severed, but is left in place for a further week. They are then lifted and either potted up or planted out directly. Layering is done in July and August, which means that the layers are not ready until October, so it may be advisable to over-winter in pots in a frame and plant out in the spring.

Pinks are propagated by cuttings, which are usually available from late June till August. Choose strong side-shoots and strip off all but the top six pairs of leaves. Cut the stem at the first joint below these and insert in a cutting compost (or pure sharp sand). Keep in a light, but shady position in fairly humid conditions, such as a closed frame. The cuttings usually take 3–4 weeks to root. Once some growth is seen, harden the cuttings off by bringing them into the open air and either plant out or overwinter in 3-in. pots. If the cuttings show any inclination to start to flower before they have made plenty of side growths, they must be stopped. This entails breaking off about eight joints; it is not enough just to nip out the growing point.

Border carnations and pinks can also be grown from seed, sown in March–April, but will be less 'true'.

Border Carnations: 'Robin Thain': white; 'Merlin Clove': white and purple; 'Alice Forbes': white and pink; 'Fair Maiden': white with red edge; 'Catherine Glover' and 'Thomas Lee': yellow and red; 'Mary Murray': yellow; 'Mendip Hills': pink and red; 'Harmony': grey and red; 'Leslie Rennison': rosy mauve; 'Marvel Clove': violet; 'Gipsy Clove': crimson; 'Salmon Clove': salmon pink; 'Lavender Clove': lavender; 'Beauty of Cambridge': yellow.

Pinks: Laced pinks have a coloured eye and the petals are banded with the same colour.

Old Fashioned Pinks: 'Mrs Sinkins', 'Whiteladies': white; 'Pink Mrs Sinkins' (Excelsior): mauve-pink with dark eye; 'Inchmery': pale pink; 'Dad's Favourite': white laced purple.

Modern Pinks: 'Swanlake': white; 'Show Portrait': crimson; 'Cherryripe', 'Constance', and 'Winsome': bright pink; 'Doris': salmon with red eye; 'Show Aristocrat': pale pink with buff eye; 'London Poppet': very pale pink laced crimson; 'Laced Joy': pink laced crimson; 'Timothy' and 'Freckles': pink with red flecks; 'Show Beauty': deep pink, maroon eye.

SWEET PEAS

To grow exhibition Sweet Peas successfully it is necessary to prepare a trench, double dug, with preferably farmyard manure incorporated in the second spit at the rate of a barrowload to each 15 ft., together with a dusting of $\frac{1}{2}$ lb. bonemeal. If this is not possible, peat at the rate of a bucketful per square yard, with $\frac{1}{4}$ lb of a good balanced fertilizer, provides an adequate substitute. If the sweet peas are grown for ornament in clumps in the border, it is better to choose a strain such as 'Knee-Hi', which makes a bushy plant and does not need much in the way of support, but has good stems for cut flowers. The dwarf strains, such as 'Colour Carpet' and 'Little Sweetheart', are ornamental, but the stems are too short for cut flowers. They all require similar treatment to start with.

Seeds are sown in boxes in a cold frame in late September in the north, up to mid-October in the south. Once they have germinated, they can be exposed to fresh air. If frost is likely, close the frames and cover them with sacks or bracken to protect the plants. Precautions must be taken against mice and slugs. Seed can also be sown in gentle heat in early spring. When the plants have produced three leaves, the growing point can be pinched out. In March, stand the plants outside in a sheltered position to harden off. The seeds are either sown six to a 6-in. pot, or in boxes at 2 in. intervals in John Innes Seed Compost. Some growers chip the seeds before sowing; others soak them for 24 hours. With acid soils it is a good idea to sprinkle some lime over the soil.

The plants are usually set out in April, only one lead being retained for exhibition flowers, while the ornamentals are left to

branch as they wish. Exhibition plants are grown with a single lead, all tendrils are removed, and the plants secured to strings or cane, or wire netting with metal rings or ties of raffia. When planting, reject any plants that show a brown collar under the leaves, and plant at the same depth as the seedlings have already established, with the white collar just beneath the soil. All side-shoots must be removed as they develop. If the season is dry the soil must be watered and the plants sprayed. If temperatures fluctuate considerably, you may get the first buds aborting, but this will soon right itself. Remove dead flowers regularly to maintain a long succession of good quality blooms. Once the plants have reached the top of their supports, they can be untied and let down to ground level; they will soon start to climb again and could be re-attached to canes.

The Galaxy strain may have as many as nine flowers to each stem, but they are not usually as good as those of the Spencers, which are more suitable for exhibition. The Galaxy are perhaps better for home decoration.

There are a large number of cultivars; among the best are: White: 'White Leamington', 'Majesty Cream', 'Hunter's Moon', 'Margot'. Picotee: 'Selena', 'Tell Tale'. Pale Blue: 'Cambridge', 'Larkspur'. Medium Blue: 'Noel Sutton'. Deep Blue: 'Blue Velvet'. Mauve: 'Mauve Leamington', 'Reward'. Lavender: 'Leamington', 'Harmony'. Salmon Pink: 'Splendour', 'Superfine', 'Royal Flush', 'Philip Simons'. Pale Pink: 'Southbourne', Orange-Cerise: 'Herald', 'Clarion', 'Alice Hardwick'. Scarlet: 'Firebrand'. Crimson: 'Gypsy Queen'. Carmine: 'Rosemary Govan'. Maroon: 'Milestone'.

ABOVE: *Sweet pea.* '*Miss Willmott*'. *Lathyrus odoratus. Sweet peas need the support of sticks or netting and should be given plenty of manure to produce good blooms.*
OPPOSITE: '*Ideal*', *a splendidly decorative pink.*

CLIMBERS

The importance of refusing to treat a garden as simply an expanse of ground, and of looking at what can be done with the vertical planes, has been mentioned elsewhere. All gardens have these planes, because the house itself has them in its walls, if there are none anywhere else. The bleakness of a house standing isolated in a beautifully laid-out flat plot brings this lesson home to us at once. We want to be able to reach up to admire and pick our flowers. A flat plot gives us no alternative but to look down.

It is surprising how many of these 'third dimension' surfaces there are if we look around. There may be a garage, outhouses, or dividing walls, or a tree which, instead of cutting down to ground level, we could leave standing to a height where a climber might make a magnificent feature. Some or all of these features should be available.

There are true climbers which will find a way to cling on to almost any upright surface. Others are more particular about the kind of surface on which they will grow. *Hydrangea petiolaris*, for instance, prefers knobbly bark, but will not be so happy growing on ordinary brickwork. There are also shrubs which, although not natural climbers, will enjoy the protection of a wall, responding gratefully to the light as they climb upwards to the top. These will only need a tie here and there by way of support and encouragement.

Among the true climbers we think of actinidia, aristolochia, clematis, honeysuckle, summer-flowering jasmine, *Polygonum baldschuanicum*. Despite the various twining fingers, sucker-pads, or adventitious roots by means of which many of these obtain a foothold, they will often need, or be better for, a little help, especially when they are very small. The young plant that fails to find anything to hold on to often responds enthusiastically if given some assistance. Even the vegetable pea gets off to a quicker start if a twig, thoughtfully placed, is at hand.

Between the true climbers and the wall shrubs a good variety can be found for a wall of any aspect and for any soil. Some, like clematis, give better results when facing north or east. Generally speaking, the soil at the foot of walls and fences tends to be below normal standard. There may have been a certain amount of excavation which has inverted the top and subsoils, or it may have been the dumping ground for builder's rubbish. The soil is often washed out by water from the eaves in wet weather and, in hot dry weather, left without moisture, which is absorbed by the wall itself. Being porous, a wall acts like a lampwick; the sun the wind tend to dry it out, and it absorbs moisture from the soil.

Good soil preparation, therefore, is specially important. The site should be well dug out, and plenty of moisture-retaining compost or peat incorporated, and fertilizer added.

Plant in November or March, and at least 6 in. away from the wall. Climbers like air behind them, and this principle should be followed the whole way up for, unlike ivy, they clearly do not appreciate hugging the wall. Whatever kind of netting, wire, or wire-mesh you use, keep this clear of the walls by mounting it on nails or pegs with spacers, such as cotton-reels; incidentally, this will make tying in a much easier business.

It is possible to plan for flowers all the year round with climbers, provided you have enough space. For the winter, there is *Jasminum nudiflorum*, which will give primrose-coloured flowers from late November until March, and then will continue to provide foliage until the autumn. Overlapping with this, the earlier clematises can be grown, such as *C. alpina* 'Francis Rivas' (blue and white), the evergreen *C. armandii* 'Apple Blossom' (pink), 'Snowdrift' in a warm place, and *C. montana*, which flowers in May, with 'Rubens' as a pink form of the usual white. If you are lucky you may get a fragrant one. The larger-flowered clematises start about May and continue through June: 'Lasurstern' (a deep purplish blue), 'Barbara Jackman' (red-purple), 'Nelly Moser' (carmine, striped mauve), and 'Miss Bateman' (white).

Again overlapping these, you can have the summer jasmine (*Jasminium officinale*) which will start in June and continue through the summer with scented white flowers. This is the period when the honeysuckles will be flourishing, such as *Lonicera periclymenum*, both early and late forms. But with honeysuckle, stand by with a spray gun for aphids. They will flower without this attention, but will respond magnificently to the first-aid. They will also put up with very dry conditions, but if given a good watering regularly, put on a great show. At this time, too, there are all the rambler roses, many of which will flower right through until autumn.

Polygonum baldschuanicum is another climber which will continue to send up its clusters of creamy flowers into October, but do be generous in the amount of space you give it when you first plant it. Then you have all the later-flowering clematises, with varieties in a whole range of extremely beautiful shades for July, and again in August and September. The hydrangea *H. petiolaris* comes out in July (under the right conditions it will go the whole way up a 50-ft. fir tree), and *Schizophragma hydrangeoides* and *Pileostegia viburnoides* are in bloom at the same time.

Just for the leaves alone, consider some of the vines. In summer they will remind you of sunnier climates and, in autumn, many will delight you by turning to superb shades of red, crimson, and orange. *Ampelopsis elegans* is rose-pink on white and green. Others for autumn are *Celastrus orbiculatus* with scarlet seeds, and the pink and white *Actinidia kolomikta* which needs sun. Finally, there are the ivies, with many varieties in variegated and different-sized leaves.

Climbing roses

Roses, as always, are a subject on their own. Personal preferences run strong, but you should always consult a reliable catalogue before making a final choice.

The true climbers and the climbing hybrid-tea roses do not produce a great deal of new growth from the base each year, and so should only be lightly pruned when freshly planted. Once they are established, you should cut out all growth that looks weak or has become so through age. This is replaced by vigorous young leaders, springing from as low down the plant as possible each year. If you arch over mature young leaders, by bending them down, the formation of these new young leaders will be encouraged, and the replacements will be more than the reductions over the years.

When planting new climbers, take the trouble to drive in vine-pegs and set up training wires in anticipation of the future. Extra work at this stage will save you a great deal of labour in years to come. It always seems to be the higher branches whose training tends to be neglected, human nature being what it is. The task of knocking in nails while loose, thorny branches tear at your shirt as you balance on the ladder is very off-putting. But chafing or breakages by wind can do severe damage, and will almost certainly deny you the pleasure of seeing your upper windows enhanced with the scented blooms of your favourite climber.

Wall shrubs and climbers

Pyracantha coccinea is a very popular climber, particularly valued because of its ability to grow on a north aspect. Its vigour is unfortunately one of its drawbacks, for it soon has to be cut back; this process removes all the flowering wood, although plenty of evergreen cover is left. Keep it away from bedroom windows, if the loud chatter of quarrelling sparrows in the morning is likely to disturb you.

Some people do not like the stiff, geometrical growth of *Cotoneaster horizontalis*, whose branches will readily go round corners like drainpipes. Yet the foliage can be very attractive, especially when it turns crimson in November, and it is a shrub that seems to be particularly attractive to bees. It is a strong shrub, up which others, such as jasmine, can be grown.

More unusual, however, is *Garrya elliptica*, which is grown mainly for its remarkably striking catkins in January. This is an evergreen which needs little sunshine, but give it a place where it will be reasonably sheltered from wind and frost, or its leaves will quickly assume a disreputable appearance. At a very dull time of year, it provides welcome interest, and its novelty will attract plenty of attention.

In addition to the true self-climbers, there are a number of shrubs which enjoy growing up walls, or can be persuaded to do so.

Of these, one of the showiest is the evergreen *Magnolia grandiflora*, which is essentially for a house-wall because it will eventually spread up to two, or even three storeys, and there are few garden enclosure-walls of this height. It may even end up darkening the rooms, but that is looking some way ahead! Essentially a long-term

PREVIOUS PAGE: *A beautiful display of red and pink climbing roses, trained to grow round the windows.*

OPPOSITE: *Sweet-smelling honeysuckle,* Lonicera periclymenum, *may require protection from aphids.*

ABOVE: *Clematis—this variety is 'Montana Rubens'—makes an effective cover for sheds.*

project, this magnificent tree, apart from its intrinsic beauty, often proves to be an appealing feature in selling a house.

Similar considerations apply to *Wisteria floribunda* 'Macrobotrys'. For the gardener who does not mind waiting some years, it will give a fine display of beautiful colour and foliage. In the maturer specimens, even the limbs themselves are an attractive feature. Wisterias need careful training, and if you only have a small area for one, you will need to learn to prune it. *Forsythia*, on the other hand, if properly trained, will give an early and pleasing result. Admittedly, this shrub has become something of a suburban cliché, and so has lost its appeal for some gardeners, but like everything else it is a matter of personal preference. Discrimination in the choice of its neighbours is important as it can look most unattractive next door to pink. The quality of the yellow that it so freely provides also varies. *F. ovata* has primrose-coloured flowers that are less harsh than some forsythias can be, and they appear much more delicate and appealing against

a white wall than against exposed brick or other material.

Evergreen *Ceanothus* is another reasonably fast grower which, when young, may put on 3–4 ft. in a season, so it should be sited with some caution. It really needs a wall to grow against, and it can be kept under control if understood. Heavy pruning destroys the flowering growth, and management is more a matter of training. But to keep it tidy it may be clipped immediately after flowering without loss of its riot of attractive blue blossoms. Those of *C. rigidus* are of a particularly dark and attractive shade. Japonica (also called Japanese quince) will flourish almost anywhere, including a north wall. Even if you are in a fairly chalky district, you may still attempt to grow it, but if there is a great deal of chalk do not expect superlative results. It will train well, for the branches can be run along windows as horizontal espaliers. In addition to its quite attractive flowers and foliage, you will get the benefit of the glowing colours of its fruit, a little of which can be added to apple pies for a change.

81

SHRUBS AND TREES FOR THE SMALL GARDEN

The fact that your garden may be small should not deter you from planting a few shrubs and trees. It is essential, however, to give serious thought to your final selection so that you end up choosing the types most suitable for the space available.

It would be foolish to plant a tree which might, in time, grow as high as your house, or select shrubs which would eventually occupy more than their fair share of the garden. Provided that you make the right choice and your tree grows to only modest size, you can look forward to blossom in the spring, berries in late summer, and attractive foliage in the autumn.

If they are thoughtfully chosen, shrubs will enhance any small garden, and can often be used to screen unattractive fences or outbuildings. They can be useful, too, to act as windbreaks in exposed situations.

Below is a list of shrubs and trees which are both decorative and suitable for gardens of limited space.

Acer (Maple family). Maples as a whole are much too large for small gardens, but *A. pseudoplatanus* 'Brilliantissimum', 15–20 ft., is an attractive, very slow-growing standard tree; leaves are variegated in pink, pale green, and yellow in spring, gradually changing to green by late summer. The Japanese maples are also suitable, being shrubby in habit, and are small enough to fit even into a rock garden. They do best with shelter and shade and like acid soil. *A. palmatum* will grow to 8–9 ft., after many years, with lobed leaves; 'Atropurpureum' has dark purple leaves, and 'Dissectum' has very much cut, fern-like light green leaves.

Arbutus (Heather family) (strawberry tree). *A. unedo* is a slow-growing, shrubby evergreen tree, a native of western Europe, including south-western Ireland. It reaches 10–30 ft.; flowers white in late summer and autumn, like lily-of-the-valley; fruit red and strawberry-like a year later. It has attractive, bright brown peeling bark.

It likes chalk soils, well-drained, and withstands strong winds well in seaside gardens. Propagate by tip cuttings or seed.

Berberis (Barberry family). There are many attractive, easy-to-grow shrubs in this genus. Probably one of the best is the hybrid *B. stenophylla*, 6–10 ft., and as much across; flowers yellow-orange in May, leaves prickly, evergreen on arching shoots. Prune to restrict size after flowering. Propagate by heel cuttings, under a frame.

Betula (Birch family) (silver birch). One of the best of these for the smaller garden is *B. pendula* 'Youngii', to 20 ft., a small weeping tree with a mushroom- or dome-shaped head when mature, bark white. The birches are shallow-rooting, greedy trees, best grown in grass and a sandy soil, well enriched. Prune to shape while in leaf, and propagate by seed sown in later winter.

Buddleia (Buddleia family) (butterfly bush). Very easy to grow, the buddleias mostly flower in late summer and autumn. The most popular is *B. davidii*, 10 ft., flowers purple in spikes, leaves grey-green, deciduous; there are cultivars with purple, mauve, and white flowers. Cut back hard in spring. Propagate by seed or semi-ripe cuttings.

Calluna (Heather family) (ling). The callunas, all varieties of a single species, *C. vulgaris*, have purple, white or pink flowers; many of the new hybrids have coloured foliage in yellow, red, grey-green, bronze, and orange as well as dark green. Plants are evergreen, grow 6–18 in. high and flower from July–November according to variety. An acid soil containing plenty of humus and an open position are preferred. Cut back after flowering with shears to encourage new growth. Plant from pots. Propagate by heel cuttings in autumn or by layering.

Camellia (Tea family). The camellias are extremely attractive flowering shrubs, much hardier to grow than is thought, provided they are not planted facing east. The most popular are cultivars of *C.*

japonica, 10–30 ft., flowers pink, white or red, single, semi-double or double, depending on variety, March–April, leaves glossy, evergreen. *C. × williamsii* 'Donation', pink, large, semi-double, is easily grown, also 'Jupiter', bright red, and 'Alba Plena', double white. Neutral or acid soil, with peat or similar material, and a position with dappled shade. Prune to shape only, after flowering, and propagate by half-ripe cuttings in summer or by seed sown when ripe. They also make good container shrubs, if planted in a good acid compost and kept well watered in dry weather. In winter the containers should be well insulated from frost with straw and polythene as the roots will otherwise be killed.

Caryopteris (Verbena family) (blue spiraea). A useful shrub flowering in late summer and early autumn, *C. × clandonensis* grows 3 ft. tall; the flowers are blue and the leaves grey-green and deciduous. Plant in a sunny place and prune hard in April. Propagate by tip cuttings in summer or divide in spring.

Ceanothus (Sea buckthorn family) (Californian lilac). These are blue-flowered shrubs which bloom in early summer or autumn; deciduous or evergreen and mostly hardy. Among the best are *C.* 'Cascade', 20 ft., spring flowering, leaves deciduous; *C.* 'Gloire de Versailles', 10 ft., summer and autumn, evergreen; *C.* 'Autumnal Blue', 9 ft., autumn flowering, evergreen. These shrubs are best grown against sunny walls, though the varieties given are among the hardiest; well-drained soil is needed. Cut back after flowering except 'Autumnal Blue', which should be pruned in spring. Propagate from tip cuttings in summer under glass.

Chaenomeles (Rose family) (japonica). This very easily grown deciduous shrub flowers in March–April (earlier in mild areas). *C. speciosa*, 5–10 ft., depending on variety, flowers pink, red or white, can be grown free-standing or against walls. 'Knap

Hill Scarlet', 'Moerloosii', pink and white, and 'Falconet Charlot', double salmon-pink, are particularly good. The quince-like fruit make good jelly. Prune after flowering, or spur prune in late July. Propagate by layering, ripe heel cuttings, 6 in. long, rooted outdoors in autumn, or by seed sown when ripe in autumn.

Choisya (Citrus family) (Mexican orange) Only one species is commonly grown: C. *ternata*, 6 ft., flowers white, strongly fragrant, borne in clusters in May and September, leaves evergreen, glossy. Choisya forms a nicely rounded spreading bush, growing to about 8 ft. tall; sun and shelter from wind suit it best, but a severe winter may kill it. No pruning is needed. Propagate by half-ripe cuttings rooted under glass.

Cistus (Rock rose family) (sun rose). Aromatic, slightly tender evergreen shrubs from the Mediterranean, these flower May–July. The best kinds include C. × *cyprius*, 6 ft., flowers white with deep red blotch; C. *laurifolius*, 6 ft., flowers white, the most hardy species; C. *purpureus*, 5 ft., flowers rose-pink; C. 'Silver Pink', 3 ft., flowers pale pink. Well-drained soil and full sun are preferred; no pruning is required. Propagate by tip cuttings in August, rooted under glass, or sow seed in spring.

Cornus (Cornel family) (dogwood). A genus containing small trees and shrubs, some with brightly coloured bark. C. *mas* is the Cornelian Cherry, a tree up to 15 ft., flowers yellow February, before the leaves, fruit large and red, will grow in dry soil; C. *capitata*, not quite so hardy, 20 ft., flowers yellow, June, fruit dark red October, edible; C. *alba* 'Spaethii', 9 ft., leaves yellow-margined, bark red and C. *a.* 'Elegantissima', leaves white-margined. A moist soil suits them best. No pruning is needed for the trees, but the stems of C. *alba* varieties should be cut back in March. Propagate by layering, cuttings, or seed sown when ripe under glass.

Cotinus (Sumach family) (smoke tree). Grown for their coloured foliage, these sprawling shrubs also have good autumn colouring. C. *coggygria*, 12 ft., has flowers plume-like and feathery, June, leaves yellow in autumn; var. 'Foliis Purpureis', purple leaves becoming red in autumn. Provide shelter from wind. No pruning needed. Propagate by layering or ripe heel cuttings in September.

Cotoneaster (Rose family) Valuable mainly for their coloured berries, the cotoneasters also have white or pink flowers. They vary from ground-cover forms to large, spreading shrubs or small trees. C. *horizontalis*, leaves small, deciduous, red in autumn, shoots form a herring-bone pattern against ground or wall, red berries; C.

franchetii, 8 ft., arching growth, evergreen leaves; C. 'Hybridus Pendulus', weeping small tree, masses of bright red fruit. Any soil and situation suits them; no particular pruning. Propagate by layering, short, ripe cuttings, or sow seed in October.

Crataegus (Rose family) (hawthorn, may, quick). The thorns grow anywhere. C. *monogyna* is a native tree to 18 ft., or may be used as a hedge, flowers white, June, fruit red; C. *oxyacantha* 'Paul's Scarlet', 20 ft., flowers double rosy-red, May. C. *prunifolia*, 15 ft., flowers white, leaves large and showy, red in autumn, fruits also large, persistent. No pruning is necessary. Propagate by seed sown when ripe outdoors.

Cytisus (Pea family) (broom). These are invaluable shrubs for poor, dry soils and full sun; leaves are insignificant and habit is varied. C. × *kewensis*, 1 ft., flowers pale yellow, May, on very wide-spreading plant; C. × *praecox*, 5 ft., flowers cream, April; C. *albus*, Spanish broom, 8 ft., flowers white May. Varieties of C. *scoparius* have red, yellow, crimson or brown flowers in May; C. *battandieri*, 12 ft., scented flowers, yellow, borne in spikes, June, leaves conspicuous with three leaflets, slightly tender. Prune shoots after flowering by about half. Propagate by seed sown in autumn when ripe, in a frame, or by heel cuttings taken in August and potted on until ready to plant.

PREVIOUS PAGE: Acer palmatum, *the Japanese maple, turns a rich orange in autumn.*

RIGHT: Acer pseudoplatanus *'Brilliantissimum' is a maple which is suitable for the small garden as it is slow-growing, reaching to a maximum height of 15–20 ft.*

BELOW: Cotoneaster glabratus *also has white flowers in the summer. Cotoneasters vary in size from ground-cover shrubs to small trees.*

OPPOSITE PAGE

LEFT ABOVE: *Light pruning.*

LEFT BELOW: *Hard pruning.*

CENTRE: *Remove 'feathers' and 'suckers' from trees as they develop.*

RIGHT: *Before cutting off a large branch, make an undercut with the saw so that the final cut does not tear the bark of the main tree. Dress the wound with a fungicidal paint to resist disease.*

Daphne (Daphne family) (mezereon). The daphnes are low-growing, deciduous shrubs, and *D. mezereum*, 4 ft. is no exception; the fragrant flowers are purple-red, February–March, berries (poisonous) red. Supply shade and moisture, but do not prune. Propagate by layering, or by short, half-ripe heel cuttings rooted in a frame. *D. mezereum* can also be raised from seed.

Deutzia (Mock orange blossom family). Reliable in growth and flowering, the deutzias have small, star-shaped flowers in May–June, and are deciduous, with delicate, twiggy growth. *D. elegantissima*, 5 ft., flowers purple. *D. scabra* 'Candidissima', 8 ft., flowers white, double. Any soil and sunny position – cut out flowered shoots after flowering. Propagate by tip cuttings rooted in July under glass.

Elaeagnus (Oleaster family). Grown mostly for the beauty of their foliage, these shrubs are hardy, with tiny, scented flowers in spring or autumn. *E. pungens* 'Maculata', 9 ft., evergreen leaves, bright yellow-centred, and other varieties with differently coloured variegations; *E. commutata*, 10 ft., leaves deciduous, silver, fruit small and silvery. Cultivation is easy – no pruning is needed except to shape or cut out green reverted shoots. Propagate by short ripe cuttings in late summer.

Erica (Heather family) (heather). The ericas make extremely good ground cover, with their evergreen foliage and long-lasting flowers; by choosing varieties carefully they can be had in flower for almost the whole year. *E. carnea*, 1 ft., flowers pink, 'Springwood White', 'Vivellii', carmine, and 'Winter Beauty', rose-pink, January–April; *E. cinerea*, flowers purple, 'C. D. Eason', pink and 'Alba Minor', white, June–September. Exposed positions and poor acid soils are suitable for most of the species, but *E. carnea* will tolerate alkaline conditions. Clip over with the shears after flowering, and propagate by layering in autumn, allowing a year before separating the layers, or by 1½-in. long sideshoots in August, rooted in sandy soil in a frame.

Escallonia (Escallonia family). Evergreen flowering shrubs, growing particularly well in seaside gardens. Severe frost can damage them badly, but they resist salty gales. *E. × edinensis*, 9 ft., flowers pink in arching sprays; *E.* 'Apple Blossom', pink and white; 'Donard Brilliance', crimson, both 5 ft., all flowering June–July. Ordinary or sandy soil is best, and moderate pruning in July after flowering. Propagate from short, half-ripe cuttings in summer.

Euonymus (Celastrus family). Two kinds of shrubs, grown for berries, or leaves, are included here: *E. europaeus*, spindle tree, 9 ft., pink and orange fruit, and its variety 'Red Cascade', 6 ft., large rosy-red fruit in

ABOVE: *Deutzia 'Magician' is a member of the mock orange blossom family. It flowers in late spring or early summer, depending on the weather.*
TOP: Kalmia latifolia, *the calico bush, produces its beautiful pink flowers in June. It does not require pruning.*
OPPOSITE: Hydrangea *'Blue Wave', a lacecap variety.*

profusion; *E. fortunei* 'Silver Queen', evergreen leaves broadly edged creamy-white, wall shrub, 4 ft., and its variety 'Variegatus', white-edged leaves tinged pink in winter, trailing or climbing; *E. japonicus* 'Aureopictus', 12 ft., shiny evergreen leaves, gold-centred, good for hedges. Any soil and position; no pruning required. Propagate from seed or layers if deciduous, or from tip cuttings in late summer if evergreen.

Forsythia (Privet family). The bright yellow flowers of this easily grown shrub are a familiar sight in spring. *F. × intermedia* 'Lynwood', 8 ft., is the best form; *F. suspensa* has drooping shoots which make it a good wall shrub. Cut out some of the older flowering stems after flowering. Propagate from layers, or tip cuttings or ripe cuttings. Discourage bullfinches from taking the buds by spraying with proprietary bird repellents, especially before Christmas.

Fuchsia (Evening primrose family). The relatively hardy fuchsias will survive outdoors if heavily mulched in winter in mild districts. *F.* 'Riccartonii' is the most reliable, 5 ft. when not cut back by frost, flowers red and purple, June–October. Plant the crowns 2 in. below the soil surface, prune nearly to ground level in late spring. Propagate from tip cuttings without flower buds in spring or late summer, in a frame.

Garrya (Garrya family). An unusual evergreen shrub reminiscent of the hazel nut family, *G. elliptica* grows to 10 ft., with grey-green catkins 6–10 in. long on male plants in winter. Most soils and positions (including walls). No pruning is needed; propagate

from layers or half-ripe cuttings in a frame.
Genista (Pea family) (broom). Very similar to cytisus, but preferring lime, the flowers of these shrubs are always yellow. *G. cinerea*, 15 ft., summer flowering; *G. lydia*, 2½ ft., profusely flowering May–June; *G. tinctoria* 'Plena', dyers' greenweed, prostrate, flowers double, in June. Prune after flowering and propagate by seed or semi-ripe cuttings.

Hamamelis (Witch hazel family). Slow-growing, these shrubs are mostly winter flowering, on bare twigs. *H. mollis*, 10 ft., and as much across, flowers yellow and spider-like, fragrant, late December–February, leaves yellow in autumn. Acid, well-drained soils are preferred and a sheltered position; no pruning is needed. Propagation is by layers or seeds.

 Hebe (Figwort family) (shrubby veronica). The hebes are evergreen and mostly late flowering, sometimes until Christmas. *H.* 'Midsummer Beauty', 5 ft., flowers purple and white in spikes, July–September; *H.* 'Autumn Glory', flowers purple in stubby spikes, July–November. *H. brachysiphon*,

4½ ft., flowers white in spikes, July. Open positions and most soils are suitable. Cut back in spring, and propagate by short ripe cuttings in a frame in late summer.

Hydrangea (Hydrangea family). The large round flowerheads of the Hortensia hydrangeas, and the flat Lacecaps of other plants are a very decorative part of the late summer scene. General height is about 5 ft. Some good varieties are: 'Altona', flowers rose-pink, good blue when treated; 'Ami Pasquier', crimson, 'Marechal Foch', rose-pink or purple-blue; *H.* 'Preziosa', 4 ft., red; lacecaps: 'Blue Wave', 'Lanarth White' 2½ ft., white with central flowers blue or pink. A moist but well-drained soil is liked, and a little shade; red and pink kinds need alkaline soil, others slightly acid. Prune out the oldest shoots only, to the base in spring, and remove flowerheads at the same time. Propagate from tip cuttings in heat in May, or from ripe, unflowered cuttings in autumn.

Hypericum (St Johns Wort family) (rose of Sharon). These are evergreen and deciduous shrubs for any soil and position. *H.*

calycinum, 1 ft., flowers yellow July–August, evergreen, spreading rapidly; *H.* 'Hidcote', 5 ft., flowers large, yellow August, evergreen, needs sun. Prune hard in spring, and divide *H. calycinum* or take short, semi-ripe cuttings in a frame.

Kalmia (Heather family) (calico bush). The evergreen *K. latifolia*, to 8 ft., or more, with pink flowers in June, is the species grown. A round profusely flowering shrub, it needs an acid soil and a part shady position. No pruning is necessary. Propagate by layering or semi-ripe cuttings in a frame.

Kerria (Rose family) (Jews mallow). A tall, leggy shrub, 8 ft., with bright green stems, *K. japonica* has single yellow flowers in April; 'Pleniflora' has larger, double yellow flowers. Thin out dead and crowded wood in late spring. Propagate by detaching rooted suckers in autumn.

Laburnum (Pea family). One of the best small trees, growing in any soil and position. *L. alpinum* has fragrant flowers; *L.* × 'Vossii' has very long trails of flowers. No pruning required. Propagate from seed sown when ripe.

Lavandula (Sage family) (lavender). Poor dry soils and a sunny place produce the most fragrant plants. *L. spica* is the common kind, 2–3 ft., flowers blue-purple in July–August, leaves evergreen. Prune lightly in spring; cut the flowers for drying just as they are fully out. Propagate by heel cuttings in October, or by short half-ripe cuttings in August under glass.

Lonicera (Viburnum family) (honeysuckle). There are shrubby, as well as climbing honeysuckles. *L. periclymenum* is the common one, fragrant flowers, yellow and pink, July–September, leaves deciduous. *L. × tellmanniana*, flowers orange, not scented, June–July; *L. purpusii*, 5 ft. shrub, flowers white and fragrant, January–February. No pruning, any soil and position. Propagate from ripe cuttings or layers.

Magnolia (Magnolia family). The magnolias are beautiful flowering shrubs or small trees, evergreen or deciduous. Some species are very hardy and not difficult to grow. *M. × soulangiana* is reliable, ultimately a small tree to 20 ft., flowers white with a purple basal stain, cup-shaped, in April–May, and intermittently thereafter; varieties 'Alba Superba', fragrant pure white flowers, and 'Rustica Rubra', flowers rosyred, are also good. All flower when about 3 ft. tall. *M. stellata*, shrubby to 10 ft., flowers white with strap-shaped petals

March–April; *M. sieboldii*, 15 ft., flowers white, rounded, from May–August, fruit crimson, cone-shaped. Moist, slightly acid soils are preferred, and a sunny sheltered position; plant in spring just before growth begins. The fleshy roots should be injured as little as possible, and plenty of peat is advisable while planting. Water in well if the weather is dry after planting. No pruning is required. Propagate by layering, or semi-ripe cuttings in heat in summer.

Mahonia (Barberry family). Mahonias are closely related to the barberries but are always evergreen, with prickly, holly-like leaves. *M. aquifolium* (Oregon grape), 4 ft., flowers small and yellow, in clusters, in April, berries green then blue; *M. japonica*, 5 ft., flowers lemon-yellow in spikes, scented like lily-of-the-valley, February–

ABOVE: Magnolia grandiflora *is most commonly grown as a wall shrub. The large creamy white flowers are fragrant as well as beautiful.*

ABOVE LEFT: Pieris formosa forrestii *bears brilliant scarlet foliage in spring which gradually turns to green later in the year. It also has white lily-of-the-valley-shaped flowers.*

ABOVE RIGHT: Lonicera nitida *makes an attractive hedge to border the lawn.*

March or earlier; *M.* 'Charity', 8 ft., upright, similar flowers, in November–December. Mahonias will grow in most soils and situations; *aquifolium* makes good, dense ground cover. No pruning except to shape. Propagate by division or offsets in early October, or winter cuttings in a heated frame.

Malus (Rose family) (crabapple). The apples are used in cooking as well as being decorative. *M.* 'John Downie', 25 ft., flowers white April–May, fruit yellow and red-flushed, good for jelly; *M.* 'Golden Hornet', 20 ft., flowers white April–May, fruit yellow, pear-shaped; *M.* 'Profusion', 25 ft., flowers red, leaves copper-crimson, fruit small and red. Any soil and situation suits the apples – no pruning is required. Propagate from seed or by grafting.

Olearia (Daisy family) (daisy bush). The best of the tree daisies for general use is *O. ×haastii*, 6 ft., flowers white in July–August, leaves evergreen. Town and seaside gardens do not affect it adversely; no pruning is required. Propagate by tip cuttings in late summer under a frame.

Osmanthus (Privet family). A rounded evergreen shrub to 7 ft., *O. delavayi* has strongly scented small white flowers in April, and small glossy, dark green leaves. It will grow in any soil, and in partial shade as well as sun, without the need for pruning. Propagate by short ripe cuttings in September, or layering.

Philadelphus (Mock orange blossom family) (syringa). These heavily fragrant flowering shrubs are easily accommodated in any soil and position; they are deciduous and vary a good deal in size. *P. coronarius*, 10 ft., flowers creamy, June; *P.* 'Belle Etoile', 8 ft., flowers white with purple basal markings; *P.* 'Erectus', 6 ft., flowers small and white, but abundant; *P.* 'Sybille', 3 ft., flowers white and purple, growth neat. Only the older plants need thinning. Propagate by all types of cuttings during summer and autumn.

Potentilla (Rose family) (shrubby cinquefoil). The small rose-like flowers of the potentillas are produced from June–October, on low rounded shrubs, which are

very useful for filling in. *P.* 'Beesii', 1½ ft., flowers yellow, leaves grey, remaining into winter; *P.* 'Elizabeth', 3 ft., flowers primrose-yellow, May onwards; *P. mandshurica*, 1 ft., flowers white, leaves grey; *P.* 'Tangerine', 3½ ft., flowers reddish-yellow, particularly in shade and cool weather. Any well-drained soil and position; prune only to restrict, and propagate by dividing in October.

Prunus (Rose family) (almond, bird cherry, cherry, laurel, peach, and plum). This is a large family, mostly consisting of small trees, many of them grown for their fruits as well as their decorative blossom. *P. dulcis*, almond, 20 ft., flowers bright pink, February–March, fruit not edible; *P. padus*, bird cherry, 30 ft., fragrant flowers white in drooping spikes 5 in. long, May; *P. tenella* 'Firehill', Russian almond, 4 ft., rose-pink flowers in profusion April; *P. sargentii*, ornamental cherry, 25 ft., flowers pink March–April, leaves bronze in spring and red in autumn; *P. subhirtella autumnalis*, 20 ft., flowers semi-double white, from November–February; Japanese cherries: 'Amanogawa', 20 ft., narrow upright habit, flowers pink, semi-double, April–May; 'Kanzan', 30 ft., broad spreading head, flowers carmine-pink, double, April–May; 'Kiku-Shidare Sakura', 15 ft., weeping, flowers pink, double, April–May; 'Yukon',

15 ft., vase-shaped habit, flowers yellow, semi-double, May, young leaves bronze, then red; other cherries: 'Accolade', 20 ft., flowers double white, April–May; *P. avium* 'Plena', 30–40 ft., flowers double white, April–May; *P. cerasus* 'Rhexii', 20 ft., flowers double white, April–May; *P. laurocerasus*, laurel, 15 ft., glossy large evergreen leaves, flowers white in spikes, spring; *P. persica* 'Aurora', peach, 20 ft., flowers rose-pink, double and frilled April–May; *P. cerasifera* 'Nigra', plum, 20 ft., flowers deep pink March–April, leaves deep purple. All are easily grown in any soil, provided the drainage is good – a little lime is preferred but not essential. Pruning is not needed except to shape; do it in summer. Propagate by grafting in spring, budding in summer, by short, semi-ripe cuttings in July in a frame, or by seed sown when ripe outdoors.

Pyracantha (Rose family) (firethorn). This shrubby genus is evergreen, and very prickly. It is quite hardy and grown mostly for its brightly coloured fruits. *P. atalantioides*, 15 ft., flowers white June, hawthorn-like, berries deep red; 'Aurea' has yellow berries, also in profusion; *P. coccinea* 'Lalandei' 14 ft., erect habit, flowers white, May–June, berries orange-red, good wall shrub. Shade or sun suits them and they are not particular about soil. Prune only to restrict size in early spring, and propagate by seed sown when ripe, or by heel cuttings in late summer in heat or under glass outdoors in autumn.

Pyrus (Rose family) (pear). The fruiting pears are mostly rather large, but they are very ornamental, and one less large one is particularly attractive: *P. salicifolia* 'Pendula', 25 ft., but slow growing and weeping, flowers white April, leaves silver and willow-like, fruit small and brown. It is easily accommodated and needs no pruning. Propagate by budding or grafting.

Rhododendron (Heather family) (includes azaleas). The rhododendrons and azaleas are exceptionally beautiful flowering shrubs which can be had in bloom from January to August, though the main flowering time is March–May. A great range of colour is shown, and flower form also varies considerably, from the honeysuckle-like kinds of some of the Japanese azaleas, to the open trumpets and bells of the rhododendrons. All the rhododendrons are evergreen; there are deciduous and evergreen azaleas. Many of the rhododendrons add handsome foliage as well as flowers, and the deciduous azaleas have good autumn leaf colour. Habit of growth varies from the dwarf and prostrate to the magnificent *macabeanum* of 45 ft. and more, with leaves to match. Among the rhododendrons, the following cover a representative selection: *R. ponti-*

cum, 10 ft., flowers purple, April; *R. ciliatum*, 6 ft., flowers pale pink, April; *R. cinnabarinum*, 7 ft., flowers orangey-red tubular May–June; *R. sinogrande*, 30 ft., flowers creamy-yellow April, leaves very large, silvery beneath; *R. thomsonii*, 8 ft., flowers blood-red, March–April; *R. × williamsianum*, 5 ft., flowers rose-pink, bell-shaped in April–May, leaves rounded; *R. yakushimanum*, 2½ ft., flowers white, in May. Some good hybrids include: 'Britannia', red, 'Cynthia', dark rose, with crimson markings, 'Fastuosum Flore-pleno', blue-mauve, semi-double, 'Mrs Furnival', pink with crimson blotches, 'Pink Pearl', rose-pink, 'Sappho', large white blooms, all April–May. Dwarf kinds for the rock garden include *R. impeditum*, purple-blue flowers, free-flowering; *R. calostrum*, purple-red flowers; *R. sargentianum*, primrose yellow flowers, which are rather sparse until the plant is mature; *R. racemosun* 'Forest Dwarf', bright pink flowers, free-flowering, and 'Carmen', deep crimson. These are all under 1½ ft. high.

The azaleas are mostly much smaller

ABOVE: *'Blue Diamond', a dwarf rhododendron suitable for the small garden or rock garden. All rhododendrons need acid soil with some shade. They do not require pruning.*
RIGHT: Prunus dulcis, *the common almond tree, blooms early. It is the best flowering tree to grow in town gardens and does well on almost any soil, given good drainage. Pruning is not necessary, except when the tree gets too large and takes up too much of the garden.*

growing, about 3–7 ft., and there is a great number of hybrids, all good. The main groups are the Ghent and Mollis hybrids which grow to about 5 ft., and come in all shades of red, yellow, orange, pink, and white, the Knap Hill and Exbury hybrids, slightly larger at 6 ft., and the Japanese azaleas, which are evergreen, from 1–4 ft., and with a similar range of colour. They flower slightly later, in April–June. *R. luteum* is an azalea with bright yellow, very fragrant flowers in May, and red deciduous leaves in autumn. Soil for all the genus must be acid, preferably containing peat or leaf-mould, and well-drained though they will not stand drought. A little shade such as that provided by open woodland is preferred, with shelter from strong wind. The fibrous roots should be planted as a complete and undisturbed ball, mixing peat with the soil and watering in well. Pruning is not needed, except to deadhead to prevent seed production. Propagation is by layering, semi-ripe heel cuttings in autumn or seed sown in February–March under glass.

Rhus (Sumach family) (stag's-horn su-mach). The most attractive of the genus is *R. typhina*, 10 ft., leaves fern-like and brilliant orange and red in autumn, striking red fruits in spikes; 'Laciniata' has very much cut leaflets. The habit of the branches and shoots suggests a stag's antlers. Any soil and situation are suitable, and prune only to remove dead wood. Propagate by de-taching suckers in autumn.

Ribes (Currant family) (flowering cur-rant). These are attractive deciduous shrubs, flowering in early spring. *R. sanguineum*, 8 ft., flowers pink in tassels, and 'King Edward VII', deep red. They will grow anywhere, and need no pruning; propagate by ripe cuttings or layers in autumn.

Rosmarinus (Sage family) (rosemary). An evergreen shrub with strongly aro-matic, narrow leaves, used singly or for hedges. *R. officinalis*, 6 ft., flowers blue, May, and 'Fastigiatus', narrow, upright form needing a little shelter. Light soil and a sunny place are necessary – severe cold may kill it. Prune to shape or clip as hedge after flowering. Propagate from short cuttings during summer in a frame.

Ruta (Citrus family) (rue). A dwarf ever-green shrub grown chiefly for its orna-mental leaves. *R. graveolens*, 2½ ft., leaves rounded and small, flowers small, yellow, in clusters, June onwards; 'Jackman's Blue' has marked blue-green leaves. Give it a light soil in sunny position, and clip in spring. Removal of flower buds encourages foliage. Propagate by short cuttings in August under glass.

Salix (Willow family) (willow). There are large trees, thicket-like bushes and dwarf shrubs good for the rock-garden in this genus, which has catkin-like flowers in spring. *S. alba* 'Vitellina', golden weeping willow, 40–50 ft., shoots yellow; *S. a.* 'Chermesina', shoots orange-scarlet, cut hard alternate years in spring; *S. caprea*, goat willow, shrub or small tree to 10 ft., catkins silvery-grey, hairy in bud, later bright yellow; *S. daphnoides*, violet willow, 20 ft., shoots purple, cut hard alternate years in March; *S. matsudana* 'Tortuosa', 35 ft., shoots and branches much contorted and twisted; *S. purpurea* 'Pendula', weeping to 15 ft., shoots purplish; *S. repens argentea*, creeping willow, silver-grey leaves and shoots, catkins small. All are easily grown in moist to medium soil and any position, and can be cut back hard if required in March. Propagate from ripe shoots 2 ft. or more during early winter out of doors.

Santolina (Daisy family) (lavender cotton). The santolinas are aromatic, evergreen, sub-shrubs with finely divided leaves. *S. chamae-cyparissus*, 1½ ft., leaves thread-like and whitish-grey, woolly, flowers yellow, but-ton-like, in July–August. Sun and poor, dry soil is required, together with clipping in spring, to prevent flowering and keep com-pact. Propagate by division in April.

Sarcococca (Box family) (sweet box). The winter flowers of this small shrub warrant it a place in the garden; *S. hookerana digyna*, 4 ft., has narrow evergreen leaves, and fragrant pinkish small flowers in February. It makes good ground cover. Shade and any soil suit it; no pruning needed. Propagate by division in autumn or spring.

Senecio (Daisy family). Two very different small shrubs grown for their evergreen foliage, characterize this genus. *S. cineraria* 'White Diamond', 2 ft., leaves felted, white-grey, much cut, flowers yellow, not com-pletely hardy; *S. greyi*, 3 ft., grey-green rounded leaves, white undersurface, flowers yellow, July. Both like well-drained soil and sun; remove flower buds from both, and clip *greyi* in spring. Propagate by tip cuttings in a frame in summer or by layering in autumn.

Skimmia (Citrus family). The skimmias are slow-growing evergreens with insigni-ficant flowers, and do well in towns and seaside gardens. *S. japonica* 'Foremanii', 3 ft., leaves leathery, berries marble-like, bright red, does not need a pollinator. An acid soil and some shade are required, no pruning. Propagate by layering in summer.

Sorbus (Rose family) (rowan and white-beam). There are two distinct types of small to medium sized trees in this genus; the rowans have feathery leaves with many leaflets, while the whitebeams have oval, entire leaves. The flowers of both are white, in clusters, in May and June. Both are attractive and make good specimens, especially in towns. The rowans include *S.*

aucuparia, 30 ft., fruit bright orange-red in many drooping clusters, and 'Asplenifolia', 25 ft., leaves fern-like as well as good fruit; *S. cashmiriana*, 25 ft., flowers pink, fruit white remaining after the leaves; *S. hupe-hensis*, leaves blue-green to red in autumn, fruit white or pink; *S.* 'Joseph Rock', 40 ft., pyramidal, leaves good autumn colours, fruit pale yellow lasting well; *S. vilmorinii*, 25 ft., leaves fern-like, dainty, fruits small rose-pink. Amongst the whitebeams, *S. aria* 'Lutescens', 30 ft., leaves grey-green, white beneath, fruit orange-red, in upright clusters, and *S. intermedia*, 30–40 ft., leaves grey-green and toothed, denser head, are very good. All these will grow in most soils; the whitebeams do particularly well on chalk. Pruning is not required except to remove shoots from the trunk, or to shape in winter. Propagate by budding, grafting, or the species by seed.

Spartium (Pea family) (broom). The best species to grow is *S. junceum*, Spanish broom, 9 ft., shoots rush-like, leaves in-significant, flowers yellow, fragrant, from June to October. It prefers sun and light soil, and will grow in a limy one, unlike the other brooms. Cut shoots back by half in spring, and propagate by seed sown in

'Mme Lemoine', double white, late May; 'Paul Thirion', rosy-red, early June (all double). The lilacs are not particular about soil though a fertile one will produce the best results, as also does a sunny place. Prune by cutting out some of the oldest stems to ground level in very early spring. Propagate by layering in autumn, or ripe heel cuttings outdoors in October.

Tamarix (Tamarisk family) (tamarisk). Excellent, quick-growing shrubs or small trees for seaside hedges, the tamarisks have insignificant individual leaves which are made up into attractive plume-like foliage. *T. pentandra*, 9 ft., flowers rose-pink in July–August, in feathery plumes. They will grow almost anywhere, including windswept sites, and need to be pruned back to half their growth after flowering. Propagate by ripe cuttings in November outdoors where the plants are to grow.

Viburnum (Viburnum family) (snowball tree, laurustinus). The viburnums have small white or pinkish flowers mostly in clusters, and they may be evergreen or deciduous. *V. farreri*, 9 ft., fragrant flowers, white to pale pink November–February, on bare shoots; *V. tinus*, laurustinus, 8 ft., evergreen, flowers white in flat clusters December–March; *V. × burkwoodii*, 8 ft., scented white flowers in clusters March–April; *V. opulus* 'Sterile', guelder rose, 10 ft., flowers white in snowball-like clusters, May–June; *V. plicatum* 'Mariesii', 9 ft., branches in tiered form, flowers white in upright, flat-headed clusters 2-ranked along the horizontal shoots, May; *V. davidii*, 3–5 ft., flowers creamy-white, May, leaves evergreen, leathery and deeply wrinkled, fruit bright blue, but several plants needed to ensure cross-pollination. The viburnums will grow in most soils and situations, including a little shade; prune to shape only, in spring for the evergreen kinds, and after flowering for the others. Propagate by layering in autumn, semi-ripe cuttings in a frame in July or by seed under glass when ripe.

Weigela (Viburnum family) (diervilla). Late spring flowering deciduous shrubs which are difficult to upset and always provide a good display of their foxglove-like flowers. *W. florida*, 7 ft., rose-pink flowers May–June; 'Variegata', 6 ft., flowers pink, leaves edged creamy-white; 'Bristol Ruby', 6 ft., deep red flowers; 'Eva Rathke', deep crimson with prominent yellow anthers; 'Looymansii Aurea', flowers pink, leaves yellow, best in a little shade for full colour of leaves. Heavy or light soil, sun or partial shade, shelter on an open position are immaterial, and pruning is only necessary to remove the oldest shoots, after flowering. Propagate by semi-ripe cuttings in July in a frame, or ripe cuttings outdoors in October.

ABOVE: Syringa 'Sensation', an unusual purplish-red lilac with white borders to the flowers.

TOP: Skimmia japonica *is a slow-growing compact evergreen which likes a shady situation.*

February under glass in pots, planting from pots, as they dislike root disturbance.

Spiraea (Rose family). A deciduous shrubby genus which contains two different types of plant, the white flowered kind, blooming in spring in arching sprays, and the rose coloured type in erect clusters, in summer. *S. arguta*, 6 ft., flowers white in April–May, *S. thunbergii*, 5 ft., flowers white March–April; *S. × vanhouttei*, 8 ft., flowers white May–June, all with twiggy growth; *S.* 'Anthony Waterer', 3 ft., leaves variegated yellow, flowers crimson, in flat heads in July–August; *S. × bumalda*, 3 ft., flowers deep pink July–September, leaves variegated. Any soil and position are suitable; prune white kinds after flowering, pink ones in early spring, cutting these back almost to the base. Propagate from division, offsets or tip cuttings in summer.

Syringa (Privet family) (lilac). The fragrance of the lilacs is outstanding, and there is now a wide range of colour in the modern hybrids, some of which are: 'Esther Staley', pink, mid-May; 'Maud Notcutt', white, late May; 'Sensation', purplish-red edged with white, May; 'Souvenir de Louis Spath', reddish-purple, late May (all single); 'Mme Antoine Buchner', rosy-mauve, late May;

ROSES

More has been written in praise of the rose than of any other flower. Its delicate beauty, its interest to flower-lovers in every stage of its growth, and its fragrance have intrigued poets, philosophers, and writers from earliest times. In fact, roses have been known for millions of years, although the modern rose only came into existence at the beginning of the 18th century with the introduction of artificial hybridization. The numerous intercrossings which followed made it difficult to designate roses botanically, and the experts resorted to classifying roses in accordance with their qualities and use to gardeners.

In more recent years, because most of us have smaller gardens, there has been a new approach to roses, which will be helped by this new classification. It has become more difficult for gardeners to devote large beds to roses alone and, wherever possible, they have tended to fit them into their gardens, treating them rather as flowering shrubs. They have also become more interested in the many species and types, other than hybrid tea and floribunda roses, which the vast rose genus can offer. The value of repeat-flowering has become more and more appreciated as a result of the modern gardener's wish to achieve the maximum display of colour in the smallest amount of space.

Hybrid tea and floribunda roses These are the two most common types of rose. Until fairly recently, they were very distinct in character. The hybrid teas produced large double blooms one or two to a stem, whereas the floribundas usually produced single or semi-double blooms in clusters. Now, however, the gap between them has narrowed considerably. This change first came about with the introduction of what is known as 'Floribundas – hybrid tea type', which have flowers that are hybrid tea in form, although rather smaller. Later, rose breeders produced hybrid tea roses that grew their rather larger blooms in floribunda clusters. Excel-

lent examples of this latter type are 'Pink Favourite' and 'Fragrant Cloud'.

This important change has been particularly valuable to small garden owners because some varieties can now be intermixed. Rightly or wrongly, it used to be maintained by rosarians that old-time hybrid tea roses were suitable only for formal beds, while floribunda roses could be mingled with shrubs, if so desired. Today, with their increasing likeness, hybrid tea roses can be mixed equally well, which is of great assistance to a gardener with restricted space, who wishes to grow roses. This new characteristic is also helpful because many present-day hybrid tea roses grow up to 4½ ft. high, which makes them unwieldy for formal beds, and they are better planted in a mixed border.

Polyantha pompons and miniature roses Although it is hard to find them, there are still a few low-growing hybrid tea roses, but it is possible to plant either polyantha pompons and miniatures in positions that call for more dwarf plants. The former produce very colourful blooms in clusters. They can be relied upon not to exceed 18 in. tall. Good varieties, that are not subject to mildew, are 'Eblouissant', 'Ellen Poulson', and 'The Fairy'. The miniatures range in height from the 5 in. high, crimson 'Peon' to yellow 'Bit of Sunshine' at 18 in. Mostly their flowers are replicas of hybrid teas and floribundas. They produce a second crop of flowers and are excellent for forward positions in borders and for rock gardens. Standards and climbers are also available.

Species and Shrub Roses Their value in shrub and mixed borders gives them a special appeal. Some very beautiful ones, such as *Rosa moyesii* and the May-flowering *R. spinosissima* hybrid, 'Frühlingsgold', are too large for small gardens, but there are some modest growers, such as the repeat-flowering *R. rugosa*, rose-pink 'Frau Dagmar Hastrup', and *R. gallica*, the dark,

almost black, crimson 'Tuscany Superb', which would be ideal for small gardens. In addition, there are some suitable modern shrub roses, such as the apricot-yellow 'Grandmaster', light crimson 'Elmshorn', the hybrid musks 'Cornelia' and 'Felicia' and the more recent New English Roses, such as crimson and purple 'The Knight', and warm pink 'The Wife of Bath', not exceeding 3 ft. tall.

Rose hedges A hedge of the white *rugosa*, 'Blanc Double de Coubert' (4 ft.), 'Penelope' (5 ft.), the floribunda, 'Queen Elizabeth' (7 ft.) or the hybrid tea rose, 'Peace' (3–5 ft.), gives an excellent chance to have an abundant show of roses in a small garden.

Climbing roses Beautiful as they are, the old-fashioned ramblers, such as 'Dorothy Perkins' and 'American Pillar' have now become outdated because they flower once only in the summer, they are very vigorous and they demand a great deal of pruning and tying in. They have been replaced by more modest-growing roses, for example, 'New Dawn' and its progeny 'Bantry Bay', 'Parade', and 'Schoolgirl'. Also there are the recurrent flowering Kordes climbers, 'Dortmund', crimson with a white eye, crimson 'Hamburger Phoenix', and lemon 'Leverkusen'. Other charming, similar climbing roses are the vermilion 'Danse du Feu' and 'Golden Showers'.

Such climbers can be used in various ways – trained up a post they could form an attractive decoration, and they can be used for clothing fences, walls, unsightly sheds and dead tree stumps. They are effective trained over achways and along draping ropes. Some make excellent, colourful hedges if trained along a wire and post fence. They are space-saving and take little nourishment from the soil. If left untied, they are valuable as ground cover and for the concealment of inspection covers, etc. Particularly good in this respect are 'Excelsa', 'Max Graf', and 'Ritter von Barmstede'.

A beautiful space- and labour-saving way of growing the more vigorous climbers in a small garden is up a tree, to which they will add extra summer colour. For trees up to 10 ft. high, 'Sanders' White Rambler' and rose-crimson 'Excelsa' are excellent; for those up to 20 ft. high, good choices would be the yellow/salmon 'Lykkefund' and the clear pink 'Climbing Cécile Brunner'.

Standard Roses These are very useful in a small garden because other small plants can be grown beneath them. In addition, they afford the gardener the joy of seeing roses in places where otherwise they would not be suitable. Hybrid tea, floribunda, and shrub roses, such as 'Canary Bird', are available in this form. Weeping roses, created by budding true ramblers on a tall briar, can make excellent specimens in a lawn.

CHOOSING AND BUYING ROSES

When choosing roses, you must first decide the purpose for which they are required. You should do this during the summer months to allow ample time to see which are going to be the most suitable for your garden.

There are several important things to avoid when selecting roses:

1 Do not make a final choice from the pictures in a grower's catalogue, because often the colours are not true.
2 Do not order *new* roses from an early Flower Show, like Chelsea, because these would have been produced under glass and the colours might not be faithful.
3 Avoid, if possible, deciding from maiden roses growing in a grower's field, because these will not be fully developed.

Before ordering, try to see your choice in friends' gardens, public parks or rose growers' demonstration grounds. Always buy from reputable nurserymen, avoiding cheap lines.

Be sure your newly purchased roses have several sturdy shoots emerging near the union and have good roots. The British Standard 3936 – Part 2, obtainable from the British Standards Institution, 2 Park Street, London, is a good guide to quality.

Container-grown and prepacked roses are particularly good for out-of-season planting and replacing in an old rose bed. They are, however, more expensive than bare-root roses.

SITING AND PREPARING ROSE BEDS

Suitable conditions

Roses are easy to satisfy, with few dislikes, apart from drainage, shade, roots of trees, and chalky soil.

Choosing a site Ideally, the site should be in the open, with shade for part of the day, and no overhanging trees. The shade of shrubs, however, is sufficient to keep their roots cool.

Good drainage Roses dislike having their roots in saturated soil. Water well, draining through sucks in air, which aerates their roots and activates the beneficial soil bacteria. Drainage is satisfactory if water empties away within a day from a hole, 1 ft. in depth and diameter. If it does not, better drainage can be made by raising the soil in the bed well above the surrounding ground or by making a 2½ ft. deep trench, filled with 1 ft. of stones and then top-soil, across the bed.

Roots of roses Roses have two types of roots: firstly, long, strong tap roots that penetrate the soil, giving anchorage, and able to seek out distant water and nutriment, when required; secondly, fibrous surface roots through which they obtain their main supplies.

The ideal soil for roses Roses need a friable, well-fed top-soil, which retains plant foods and adequate moisture to assist their absorption. The sub-soil should be porous so that it allows drainage and so that the tap roots can penetrate the soil easily. This is the specification of medium loam. Many gardeners have not got this, and they must make the soil in their garden as near as possible to this ideal. Unless they are chalky, most garden soils are sandy or contain much clay. Sandy soil is very porous and allows water to flow through it very quickly, carrying with it any fertilizers. Clay, on the other hand, retains water and plant foods, sometimes becoming waterlogged, and is cold. For worthwhile growing, sandy soil must be made more water-retentive and the clay more porous. In both cases, this is done by additions of well-rotted farmyard manure, garden compost or peat. Clay soil is also improved by adding carbonate of lime or gypsum.

Digging Soil is conditioned by either 'double digging' or 'simple digging'. The first is used when the sub-soil is compacted, and the second when it is easily penetrable, as with stony or gravel soil.

Double digging is done as follows:

1 Dig a trench, 18 in. wide and 1 ft. deep, across the site. Remove this soil to the other end of the plot.
2 Break up the subsoil 10 in. down.
3 Incorporate humus-making material in the upper layer.
4 Dig a similar trench adjacent to it.
5 Fill the first trench with its top-soil, adding some humus-making material to the first layers.
6 Break up the sub-soil and incorporate humus.

PREVIOUS PAGE: *'Blessings', a floribunda—hybrid tea type.*
ABOVE: *'Fantin Latour'.*
TOP: *'Lilac Charm', an unusual floribunda.*
OPPOSITE: *The beautiful 'Eden Rose'.*

7 Repeat this operation until the end trench is reached. This is filled with the top soil taken from the first trench.

To simple dig:

1 Open up a trench as for double digging.

2 Dig an adjacent trench, using the excavated soil, with added humus-making material, to fill the first trench.

3 Repeat until the final trench is reached. Fill this with soil removed from the first trench.

Renovating old rose beds Beds in which roses have been grown for ten or more years should not be restocked with new plants, because the soil will have become 'rose-sick'. This means that while it will support the old roses, newly planted ones will not flourish and will most likely die. When renovation is necessary, you must follow certain procedures to make the soil suitable for roses.

The drastic way is to replace all the old soil to a depth of 18 in. with soil in which roses have not been grown. The excavated soil can be safely deposited anywhere in the garden, where roses are not grown, because other plants are unaffected.

Alternatively, if the bed can be spared,

another solution is 'green manuring'. This consists in sowing successive crops of mustard seed, trampling the plants down, moistening the crushed plants, covering them with sulphate of ammonia, and digging them in.

It is good planning to make provision for making new rose beds and turfing over the old ones, when tackling a new garden.

Planting

Roses are meant to give pleasure for many years, and it is worthwhile paying particular attention to their planting. After about six weeks, newly dug soil is ready for planting.

Usually bare-root roses delivered from a nursery are ready for planting. If they are not, all damaged, broken, and unduly long roots should be cut away. All immature, dead, and diseased shoots and suckers should be removed.

Preplanting preparations:

1 If the roses are dry, with shrivelling stems, steep them in cold water for 24 hours.

2 Remove any leaves left on to minimize loss of moisture before planting.

3 Prepare a planting mixture, consisting of two handfuls of sterilized bonemeal, and one of hoof and bone meal added to a large bucket of moist peat.

Do not plant roses in frosty weather. They will keep satisfactorily in their polythene wrapping in a frost-free place for two weeks. After this, they should be unwrapped, covered with sacking and kept moist. Roses packed in paper should be similarly treated immediately they arrive. If the ground is soggy, place them in a trench, cover the roots with soil, well trod in, until the ground is suitable.

Time of planting It is preferable to plant roses in open weather during autumn or from February onwards.

Container-grown roses can be planted at any time, provided they are well-watered during dry spells.

Planting distance Depending upon their vigour and ultimate size, roses are planted 20–36 in. apart, the shorter distance for average hybrid tea and floribunda roses, and wider apart for more vigorous varieties, species, and shrubs.

Planting procedure Roses either have centrally growing roots or side-growing ones. To plant the former, dig a hole large enough in diameter to allow the roots to be spread out and deep enough to cover the point where they join. The enlarged portion on the stem should be just under the surface of the soil. Mix two good handfuls of planting mixture with the soil in the bottom of the hole and heap it in the centre of the hole. Rest the crown of the rose on this heap and spread out the roots. Cover the roots with more soil and planting mixture, and move the plant up and down to remove airpockets. Fill the hole to one-third of its depth with soil and gently tread in the rose, working inwards towards the centre of the hole. Prevent it from sinking by holding the plant at its tip. The remaining soil can then be added loosely and levelled off. Do not plant roses in very wet weather as the soil may become compacted.

For bushes with side-growing roots, dig a wedge-shaped hole and mix planting mixture into the soil on the sloping side of the hole. Place the rose so that the roots are at such a height that their union is just at the soil level, spread them out and cover with some soil and planting mixture. After this, the procedure is the same as for plants with centrally growing roots, except that treading in begins above the tips of roots.

Planting climbing roses Follow the same procedure as that described for bush roses. As the soil at the base of a wall is usually dry, it is better to plant 15 in. from it and train the rose back to it. It is also more satisfactory to choose a climber with side-growing roots and plant it with the roots pointing outwards, so that they are in a more moist position.

Planting standard roses The depth of planting a standard rose depends upon whether it is budded on to a briar root stock, which has large thorns or a *R. rugosa* one, which has numerous spines. A briar standard is planted to the depth of the soil mark on the trunk, while a *rugosa* one should not be deeper than 4 in. The procedure is the same as for a bush rose.

Standards must be staked. Knock the stake into the bottom of the planting hole, and position the rose beside it. The tip of the stake should be just below where the rose branches. Tie the stem to the stake, using a rose tie or tarred string, and protect the bark at its top, middle and bottom with hessian.

FEEDING ROSES

As roses occupy the same ground for many years, some feeding is very likely to be necessary to maintain the richness of the soil or correct a deficiency. Both organic and chemical fertilizers can be used to achieve this. The real advantage of organic fertilizers, such as farmyard manure, garden compost, bonemeal, fishmeal, and so on, is that they have to be broken down by the soil bacteria into the simple compounds, and as this is a slow process, they supply steady quantities of plant foods over a long period of time. They are thus applied in the dormant season, during autumn and winter. Chemicals supply the requirements quickly and give a boost when growing is at its height or in an emergency.

Roses, like other plants, manufacture their own starch from carbon dioxide from the air and water through the agency of sunlight and the green colouring matter of plants (chlorophyll). This is one reason for keeping roses well supplied with water. In addition to starch, roses need other complicated substances, which include proteins, chlorophyll, enzymes, nucleic acids. These they synthesize themselves from the simple chemicals they absorb from the soil. This means the chemicals must always be in the soil, hence the necessity for regular feeding.

Plant foods are classed either as major or minor nutrient elements. One of the most important major nutrient elements is nitrogen, contained in most vital plant foods. Without a sufficient supply roses appear feeble and have yellowish leaves. It is essential to their good health. You must not, however, use it in excess, for it encourages leaf and stem growth and too much will make the plant lush and weak and extra susceptible to disease and frost. It must not, therefore, be fed later than mid-August. Nitrogen also reduces the production of blooms.

ABOVE: *'Cocktail', a modern shrub rose.*
TOP: *The prize-winning rose 'Peace'.*
OPPOSITE: *'Erfurt', another good shrub rose.*

Phosphorus (phosphate), is another major nutrient beneficial to roses because it encourages the ripening and hardening of wood to resist frost, and better roots. When it is scarce, roses become stunted and their leaves turn a reddish colour.

Potassium (potash) is a major nutrient, without which plants become vulnerable to disease and frost. It also helps to develop their stores of winter foods. Deficient roses have leaves with yellow tips and edges.

Another major element is calcium. This helps to condition soil, reduces acidity and maintains the cell tissues in good order. It is rarely deficient, but when it is, the new young leaves are deformed.

Magnesium is a most important major nutrient because it enters into the constitution of the all important plant substance, chlorophyll. Without it, the older leaves turn yellow.

Of the minor nutrients or trace elements, iron and manganese are the most important because they are essential to the production of chlorophyll. In their absence, the younger leaves become yellow with green veins. Other trace elements are copper, boron, molybdenum, and zinc.

A feeding programme A programme for feeding roses begins late in the winter after supplies of nutrients have become diminished. The first thing to do, preferably in February (providing the snows have gone), is to lay down a foundation for the future by distributing an organic fertilizer. This will break down over the ensuing months into simple chemical compounds and ensure that there is a basic supply that can be steadily absorbed by the plant. If it can be obtained, the substance to distribute is meat and bonemeal at the rate of two handfuls per square yard. Good substitutes are equivalent quantities of sterilized bonemeal, fishmeal, and John Innes Base Fertilizer.

Fertilizer is next applied in the spring, not earlier than April. This time it is a chemical fertilizer, which supplements the elements provided by the organic fertilizer, particularly when heavy rain has washed abnormally large quantities of a particular element away, or rapid growth, due to favourable weather conditions, has suddenly increased the demand for food. Generally it is more satisfactory to put down a proprietary, ready-mixed rose fertilizer, of which there are several on the market. It is important to use one that is blended for roses and not a general fertilizer intended for vegetables, because sometimes the latter contains muriate of potash, which is deadly to roses. Always apply rose fertilizer in accordance with the manufacturer's instructions. Usually these mixtures contain the trace elements that are needed by roses.

Although it is a lot more trouble,

gardeners may mix their own fertilizer for roses. A recommended mixture is: nitrate of potash 3 parts, sulphate of ammonia 1½ parts, superphosphate of lime 8 parts, sulphate of potash 4 parts, sulphate of magnesium 1 part, sulphur of iron ¼ part.

This is distributed at the rate of 2 oz. (about 2 handfuls) per square yard, once in April, and again in May. Twenty pounds of this mixture is sufficient for 200 roses during one season.

It is important that no chemical fertilizer is applied after the end of July, otherwise lush growth might be produced, which will not withstand the winter.

Foliar feeding This takes advantage of the fact that leaves absorb nutrients from liquids sprayed on them. It is not a substitute for the regular feeding programme, but something that can meet an emergency. There are several good foliar feeds on the market. They are best applied in the early morning or in the evening, but never in hot sun.

ROSE MAINTENANCE

Apart from pruning and fighting diseases and pests, maintaining roses is not a difficult task.

Spring Tread in any roses loosened by winter weather; replace or repair any damaged stakes, posts, trellis, etc.; renew any worn sacking protecting bark or replace by rose ties; mulch the rose beds in May, when the soil is warming up and moist, by putting down a 2 in. thick layer of organic material. Leave a small ring around the base of each stem to avoid risk of damage by the mulch heating up as it decomposes. Suitable humus-making materials to use are well-made garden compost, well-rotted farmyard manure, moist peat, and spent hops.

Mulching keeps the soil moist and the temperature steady; it also gives a cool root run, suppresses weeds and provides humus when it is hoed in during autumn.

Summer Weeds steal water and plant foods and they must be suppressed. There are physical methods of doing this, e.g. regular hoeing, mulching, and chemical ones. The two types of chemical weedkillers available are *contact*, which are watered on to the leaves during spring and summer and destroy the weeds when absorbed, and *pre-emergent*, which are applied in winter and prevent the seeds developing so that the weeds do not appear.

Sometimes three shoots will emerge on a rose from one bud centre. Only the central bud should be allowed to develop; the other two should be pinched out.

All suckers should be torn out at their point of origin so that the whole budding system is destroyed and there is little chance

of another appearing. Suckers are essentially shoots that emerge from the rootstock, either low down on the rose or underground. Allowed to remain, they sap nutriment from the budded scion. They are most satisfactorily detected by noting from what position they originate. If from below the union or the root, they are suckers.

Some present-day hybrid tea roses produce three blooms to a stem or in clusters instead of singly. If one large individual flower, suitable for exhibition is wanted, all buds except the centre one should be pinched out at the earliest moment. This is called disbudding. If a beautiful, colourful, massed garden display is desired, no action need be taken.

To ensure repeat flowering, all roses should be dead headed by removing all faded blooms. Avoid removing too much of the foliage in which the plant's food needs are produced, by always cutting off dead heads at the first outward growing leaf with five leaflets and no lower.

Do not wet the flowers and leaves when watering, as the flowers become blemished, and moisture on the leaves might encourage fungus diseases. This can be avoided by

watering the soil with an upturned perforated hose.

Autumn and winter Cut bush roses back to half their size in November to prevent them being whipped by the wind.

MODERN WAYS OF PRUNING ROSES

In recent times, pruning has been a controversial subject, but there should be little difficulty if you think of roses as flowering shrubs, which, of course, they are. The rule is that those that flower on the previous season's growth are pruned immediately after flowering; those that do so on the current year's shoots are pruned in late winter. Most roses fall into the second group. The principal exceptions are the ramblers, which have to be pruned in the summer.

Pruning is carried out for the following reasons:

(a) to encourage growth of new shoots
(b) to shape and restrict size, when necessary
(c) to control habit
(d) to maintain youthfulness by encouraging basal growth.

The technique of pruning Secateurs must be kept sharp, otherwise they crush the stem and may encourage disease infection. A pruning knife is a better tool, but should only be used by the real expert, or after plenty of instruction and practice. Like secateurs, it must be kept continuously sharpened or it will damage the stems and do more harm than good.

When to prune With the exception of ramblers, most commonly grown roses are pruned during late winter, when the sap is just beginning to rise. This usually. means February in southern or warmer gardens, and the end of March in the north and exposed gardens.

Ramblers are pruned in summer, after blooming, and then tied in. `

How to prune If you look closely at the shoot of any rose, the buds are positioned on opposite sides along it. When pruning, the cut is made immediately after a bud pointing in a desired direction, i.e., usually outward in the case of a bush rose, and upwards for a horizontally trained climber.

When pruning, make a sloping cut, which begins level with the base of the bud on the opposite side of it, ending on the opposite side about ¼ in. from the base (see figure 1).

Common faults in cutting are (see figures 2–4):

(a) too far away from the bud, which causes dieback and perhaps infection
(b) too close to the bud, which might damage it
(c) too long a cut, giving excessive exposure of pith, slowing up healing
(d) leaving a jagged edge, damaging the tissues, that might become infected

Before pruning, always first cut out all dead, diseased and weak shoots that use up nutrients intended for the healthy ones. Cut out also all shoots growing in the wrong direction.

Types of pruning There are three ways to prune:

(a) hard pruning: cutting a shoot back to three or four buds from its base
(b) moderate pruning: cutting a shoot back by about half last season's growth
(c) light pruning: remove spent flowers to the first or second bud below the flower stalk

Pruning hybrid tea and floribunda roses in the first year Both should be hard pruned in their first spring, i.e. cut back to the third or fourth outward-pointing bud from the ground, to form a good-shaped bush.

Subsequent pruning of hybrid tea roses The present-day roses, which are mostly vigorous, do not take kindly to hard pruning. In the main, they should be moderately pruned, otherwise they do not bloom so plentifully in the summer.

It is the modern practice to prune hybrid tea roses moderately, i.e. to cut their shoots back by half their previous year's growth. However, because of their great vigour, many will soon become very tall and rather unwieldy for present-day small gardens. This shortcoming can be largely overcome if you remove one or two of the oldest and tallest stems each year. This method seems to keep its size under control without any very serious lowering of the amount of flowers produced later in the year.

Pruning floribunda roses Because the original floribundas stemmed from polyantha pompon roses, they were first lightly pruned, i.e. only the clusters of dead flowers were removed. Because of their great vigour, this resulted in unwieldy bushes. When they were moderately pruned like modern hybrid teas, they lost their repeat-flowering, whereas with hard pruning they failed to grow and tended to die. The modern technique, aimed at keeping them in flower over a long period, is a combination of light pruning to produce early flowers, and moderate pruning, which gives flowering shoots that produce colour later in the season. During the first year they are hard pruned, but the procedure in the second year is slightly different from that in the third, which remains uniform for the rest of their lives. The modern technique is given below.

Pruning floribunda roses in the second year: 1 All the main shoots, which are the

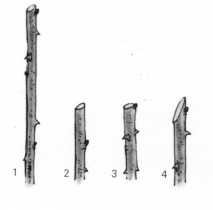

ABOVE: *Floribunda 'Copper Pot'*.
TOP: *'Paul's Scarlet Climber'*.
LEFT ABOVE: *How to prune roses.*
1. *The correct way to prune.*
2. *The cut is too far from the bud.*
3. *The cut is too close to the bud.*
4. *Too long a cut, which may not heal.*
LEFT BELOW: *Where to prune floribundas and hybrid tea roses in their first spring.*
OPPOSITE: *'Duke of Windsor', a hybrid tea.*

previous year's growth and grown from the base of the trees, are lightly pruned by cutting out the clusters of dead blooms at the first or second eye, whichever is growing outwards, below their base.

2 Secondary shoots, which have developed below the clusters, should be cut back to three or four eyes from the main stem.

3 All other shoots, which are emerging from the shoots that were hard pruned in their first year, should be cut back to half their length.

Pruning floribunda roses in their third and subsequent years: 1 All one-year-old wood, that emanates low down on the bush, should be lightly pruned by cutting out the dead flowerheads.

2 All the remaining shoots are moderately pruned, i.e. they are cut back to about half their length.

Pruning standard roses Generally standards are pruned in the same way as their bush counterparts. Hybrid tea standards are best moderately pruned.

Pruning weeping standards The best weeping standards are produced by budding No. 1 Ramblers (see below). All spent flowering shoots are cut back in summer to their base and this year's shoots tied in.

Pruning polyantha pompon roses After removing unwanted stems, cut back the previous year's flowering shoots by half.

Pruning shrub and species roses Remove dead blooms as they fade to encourage repeat-flowering, when they have this ability. Otherwise it is only necessary to control shape and size. If they become bare at the base, this can be remedied by cutting one or two older stems each spring to 9 in. from the ground.

Pruning miniature roses Apart from trimming to size, and shaping, it is only necessary to cut out unwanted stems and spent blooms.

Pruning ramblers and climbing roses There are four groups:

(Group 1 Ramblers): These, such as 'Dorothy Perkins', 'Excelsa', and 'Sander's White Rambler', produce their new flowering shoots to bloom next season from the base. Prune all spent flowering shoots after blooming at ground level and tie in the new growth.

(Group 2 Ramblers): These, which are typified by 'Albéric Barbier', 'Albertine', 'Easlea's Golden Rambler', and 'New Dawn', produce their next year's flowering shoots mainly higher up. These are again pruned after flowering, by cutting back all old wood to a point where a new leader emerges and then tying this in. All shorter laterals should be pruned to two or three buds of their base.

(Group 3 Climbers): This group is composed of the more vigorous climbing sports and the stronger-growing large-flowered climbers, such as 'Coral Dawn'. No main shoots should be removed unless they are damaged or to control size. In late winter, remove all unwanted wood and prune last year's flowering laterals to the third bud.

(Group 4 Climbers): Apart from removing unwanted wood and controlling size and shape, little attention is necessary for this group other than removing dead flowers and a few inches of stem and shoot tip that are soft and leafy in late autumn. Its members include the climbing sports 'Korona', 'Iceberg', and 'President Hoover', some large flowering climbers, such as 'Elegance', 'Golden Showers', 'Handel', 'Rosy Mantle', 'Schoolgirl', and 'White Cockade', the *Kordesii* pillar roses, such as 'Dortmund', 'Hamburger Phoenix', 'Parkdirektor Riggers', and 'Ritter von Barmstede', and the Bourbon Climber, 'Zéphirine Drouhin'.

KEEPING ROSES HEALTHY

Roses are susceptible to certain pests and diseases, and gardeners should be able to identify them. In the main, they are dealt with by insecticides and fungicides.

Pests There are two types to deal with, viz. sap-suckers and leaf- and bud-eaters. These can be effectively attacked with *systemic insecticides*, which are absorbed in the sap and *contact insecticides*, which remain on the surface of the plant, respectively.

Spraying should not begin too early, in order to give the larvae of the friendly insects, such as ladybirds, hoverflies, lacewing flies, and braconid wasps, a chance to destroy as many greenflies as possible.

Sap-Suckers

Greenflies, which can be green, pink, red or brown in colour, breed fast. They suck the sap and impair the vigour of the plants, whose shoots and leaves become crippled, and defoliated. They are also a danger because they are carriers of virus diseases, and exude a sweet fluid, the food of the sooty mould fungus, which prevents the leaves functioning properly.

Thrips are small black insects which, particularly in warm weather, smother the shoots of roses. When young they are reddish. They suck the sap, mottling the leaves, distorting the young shoots and damaging the buds.

Capsid bugs. The green nymphs of these insects suck the sap, distorting the leaves and buds.

Red spider mites are minute, immobile red insects, the presence of which is detected by fine, silken webs underneath the leaves, in which they live and breed. By sucking the sap they turn the leaves off-colour and mottled, causing them to fall prematurely.

Leaf- and bud-eating insects

Caterpillars are the larvae of moths and butterflies and show their presence by holed or rolled leaves, and injured buds.

Leaf-rolling sawflies The adults lay their eggs in the margin of leaves, simultaneously injecting a toxic liquid, which causes them to roll and hang down.

Rose slug sawflies The grubs of these insects skeletonize the leaves.

Diseases

The principal diseases affecting roses are fungal.

Blackspot This disease is well-known to all rose-growers. Its attack is most virulent in August and September, but it can strike at any time in the season. Although some roses are more resistant, none are immune. A list of varieties with the greatest immunity is given below. It manifests itself by black spots on yellowing leaves. The spots eventually join up and the leaves drop.

Until recently, blackspot fungicides have been contact types, that produce a protective coat on the leaves, which must be frequently renewed, particularly in wet weather. None of these are complete cures. More recently, several systemic insecticides have been introduced to deal with both blackspot and mildew.

Mildew When this fungus attacks, the leaves become enveloped in white powder and are distorted. Keeping the roses well-watered helps them to resist attack. More resistant varieties are given below.

Rust attacks roses for about two years and then disappears. It is only active in certain districts in Britain; its spores need to be frozen to germinate. It appears in April as rust-coloured swellings underneath the leaves, turning orange in June, when they germinate freely; in August, they become black, in which form they over-winter.

Dieback and canker Shoots often turn brown and die; they are not necessarily diseased, but their tissues are damaged by frost, bad cutting, snapping off, rough handling, etc. There is, however, a *true* dieback, caused by a fungus disease.

There is also a fungus disease, stem canker, which infects the wounds resulting from any of the above injuries. This can be first detected by yellowish or reddish streaks, and pimply, water-saturated areas on the stems. Eventually they become brown and will often extend to healthy tissues. The only remedy is to cut out affected areas and burn the wood.

Chlorosis This is not a true disease, but an ailment, mainly caused by deficiency of iron and manganese. This can occur, as far as roses are concerned, in soil in which there are ample quantities of these elements present, but where they are in a form in which they cannot be used by the rose, as often happens in alkaline (chalky) soil. The symptoms are yellowing of the leaves and stems in springtime. The leaves eventually shrivel up and drop off and growth is stunted.

The condition cannot be remedied by distributing ordinary, simple compounds of iron or manganese. If it is serious, the soil must be watered in spring with a proprietary formulation, which contains chelates of iron and manganese in a form that can be absorbed by roses, together with active magnesium, which is another vital plant food.

A selection of roses that are more resistant to fungus diseases

Hybrid tea roses Brandenburg, Colour Wonder, Eden Rose, Garvey, John S. Armstrong, Isabel d'Ortiz, Mullard Jubilee, Pink Favourite, Rose Gaujard, Silver Lining, Wendy Cussons.

Floribunda roses Allgold, Arthur Bell,

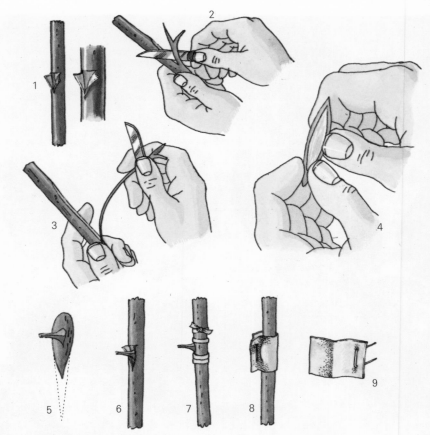

ABOVE: *Budding a rose.*
1. *Make a T-shaped cut and raise the bark.*
2. *Cut out the bud.*
3. *Gently tear away the bud, also taking a thin strip of bark below it.*
4. *Remove the sliver of wood that remains with a twisting action.*
5. *Trim the bark to make a wedge below the end of the bud.*
6. *Insert the bud in the incision.*
7. *Fasten the bud in place with tape or raffia.*
8. *A bud held in place with the Fleischauer Tie, a piece of rubber fastened with a metal staple.*
9. *The patented Fleischauer Tie.*
OPPOSITE: *'Southampton', a vivid orange floribunda.*

Chanelle, Dickson's Flame, Elizabeth of Glamis, Lilac Charm, Masquerade, Orange Sensation, Pink Parfait, Queen Elizabeth, Scarlet Queen Elizabeth, Scented Air.

PROPAGATING ROSES

Hybrid roses cannot be propagated from seeds because they never come true. The usual practice is to bud them, but a few, such as ramblers and the older floribundas, can be reproduced from cuttings.

Growing from cuttings Cuttings, about 1 ft. long and $\frac{1}{4}$ in. thick, are taken in August or September. The lower cut should be horizontal below a bud, the upper cut sloping above one. Insert the cuttings in 2 in. of sand, 6 in. apart, in a wedge-shaped trench, which is then filled and well-watered. They are ready for transplanting in the autumn of the following year.

Budding roses Budding consists of uniting a bud to a well-developed rootstock, either briar or *R. multiflora* (simplex) for bushes or briars and *R. rugosa* for standards.

Seedling rootstocks are planted 8 in. apart during February, with the neck protruding 1 in. above the ground, at an angle towards the position where the budder will ultimately work.

In July, following rain or copious overnight watering, remove the soil from the neck of the rootstock, and rub it clean. Press the rootstock down with your foot, and make a cross cut, $\frac{1}{8}$ in. wide and 1 in. above the root fork with a razor-sharp budding knife. Next make a T-shaped incision by an upward cut, commencing $\frac{3}{4}$ in. below the cross cut. At the finish of this stroke, slightly lift the bark and, using the wedge-shaped end of the handle, lift the bark along the length of the slit.

Select a shoot of the variety to be budded, on which the flowers have just faded. Remove the thorns and trim back the leaves. Take a bud by inserting the knife $\frac{1}{2}$ in. above an eye and thinly cutting behind it, making the knife emerge $\frac{1}{2}$ in. below it. The bud can then be gently torn away carrying a strip of bark with it.

The strip of bark is next pulled away slightly to reveal a thin layer of wood. Remove this sliver carefully with a twisting movement of the thumbnail and trim the bark to a wedge-shaped tongue below the bud. Without delay, holding the small remaining piece of leaf, fit the bud into the T-incision on the rootstock, with the trimmed end downwards. Press back the lifted bark and trim the bud off level with the cross cut. The bud can be secured with raffia or plastic tape tied two turns below and three above, or with a Fleischauer Tie.

About 3 weeks after the bud has been inserted, the raffia tie should be loosened, easily done by running a sharp knife or razor blade down the tie on the opposite side to the bud. If the stub of leaf stalk parts readily when pressed down, the bud has taken. If it stays put and is withered and brown, the bud is dead.

The following January, during open weather, cut away the rootstock to 1 in. above the bud. To prevent the new shoot being torn away by high winds, it should be tied loosely to a stake.

Budding standards Standards are budded in the same way as described above for bush roses. In a briar rootstock, the buds are inserted in the side shoots, whereas with *R. rugosa*, they are put into the main stem. The ties do not rot, as with bushes, and should be removed after 4 weeks. The newly budded standards are ready for transplanting the following October.

ROCK GARDENS PONDS AND POOLS

ROCK GARDENS

Now that gardens are becoming smaller there is much to be said for growing alpine plants. These are naturally small, and so a much greater variety of plants can be grown in a limited space. They are also extremely attractive both for their abundant flowers and, in many cases, for their attractive foliage. On the debit side they do require constant and close attention, but most of them are as easy to grow as any other plants.

We tend to associate alpines with rock gardens but, in point of fact, rocks are the last thing necessary in growing alpines and can easily be dispensed with. The first and most important essential is perfect and very rapid drainage. Many mountain plants have their roots in very damp soil, but the water is never stagnant and it is necessary to ensure perfect drainage before you think of any other preparation. Rocks can look attractive, but they are expensive to purchase, especially if you do not live in a naturally rocky area, and they tend to look rather unnatural, unless you have a slope in your garden. If you are going to insert rocks, you want to be sure that they are seen showing their natural strata; avoid standing them on end like almonds on a cake. They should be buried to $\frac{1}{3}$ of their depth, and particular care must be taken that they are thoroughly well bedded in. Many plants enjoy letting their roots get under the rocks, but if there are pockets where there is no soil, the plants may die. If you have no slope it is possible to raise a mound, but this is elaborate and time-consuming, and you might be better advised to make a raised bed. These look best if irregular in shape, with the sides treated as a dry wall with bits of stone, peat-bricks, or even old railway sleepers at the sides, raised above the ground about 2 ft. This is particularly attractive to the handicapped or elderly gardener who need not stoop so far.

Whatever scheme you decide to go for, you must have at least a foot-depth of drainage material, unless your soil is naturally quick-draining. The simplest method of drainage is to dig out the soil an extra foot deep and fill up this space with clinker, or gravel or rough stones – whichever is most convenient. Ashes are also very suitable. If you have a slope in your garden, you can insert land drains down the slope to carry off surplus water. In the case of heavy clay, many people recommend digging a sump, only about 2 ft. wide, but as deep as 5 ft. It is easier with such soils to construct a raised bed.

Siting As a general rule alpine plants like full sun and all but very few are unhappy under trees, especially where they can be splashed with rain. There *are* shade lovers, but they should be planted under rocks, or in north-facing crevices. Although not all the plants grown in alpine gardens are true alpines, the majority come from the area between the end of the tree line and below the snow-line.

Construction Once you have established your basic drainage, you can then start on your construction, which must be gradual. If you are using rocks, bed the first set; if you are building a raised bed, lay the first course of stone and fill up with a prepared compost. There are a number of these recommended, but the simplest is made up of 3 parts of loam (or any good garden soil) 2 parts of peat, compost, or leaf-mould (moss peat is preferable to sedge peat) and 3 parts sharp sand or fine grit. All these parts are by bulk and a surprising amount of this mixture will be necessary. Five pounds of bone meal can be added to every cubic yard of this mixture. Once the first layer has been put in, add the second layer and so on until your raised bed or rock garden is complete.

For a peat bed, which is ideal for very many plants, the compost is made up of 3 parts moss peat, $1\frac{1}{2}$ parts loam, and $1\frac{1}{2}$ parts sharp sand, but the loam must be acid so, if you live in a limy district, you can omit the loam and increase the amount of sharp sand. Once the construction is finished, give the whole thing a good soaking and leave to settle. You may find some topping up is necessary. It looks neat and helps the plants if the soil is now covered with a layer of limestone chippings or granite chippings, depending on whether you wish to grow lime-lovers or lime-haters. Some people insert a scree in their alpine garden. This is a compartment in which the soil is 3 parts stone chippings to 1 part loam and should be made fairly deep; it is ideal for those plants that are resentful of water lying around the neck, but like water lower down. Such plants are deep rooting. The chippings, although they may look dry on the surface, remain moist lower down, even in prolonged dry periods.

It is a good idea to leave your alpine garden for about 3–4 weeks after construction, so that any annual weeds that appear can be killed off before you start planting.

Planting Most alpines are sold as potgrown plants and, in theory can be inserted at any time, but early autumn or spring are the best times. Autumn planting allows the plants to establish themselves in the new soil before winter comes. Spring planting means that the plants will start to grow away at once, but it will be a year before you see much in the way of results. If the plants are very potbound, loosen the ball gently before planting. Planting should be done firmly in soil that is neither saturated nor dust-dry. After planting, water the plants well in with a fine rosed can and see that they do not dry out until the roots have been able to penetrate the soil.

Watering Once established, alpines should not require watering except in the case of very prolonged drought. If this occurs, water very thoroughly indeed and do this in the evening so that the water can soak through the soil all night.

Cutting back Unless you want to collect seed, most alpines benefit by being cut back

ABOVE: 'Pink Beauty', a cultivar of the rock rose Helianthemum nummularium.

TOP: Pulsatilla vulgaris, *the pasque flower, is a member of the Buttercup family.*

quite severely immediately flowering is completed. This encourages fresh growth, keeps the plants compact and, in some cases, will encourage a second flowering. This applies particularly to alyssum, helianthemum, dianthus, veronicas, and hypericums.

Propagation Seed is the simplest method, although not possible for hybrids. Generally, it is best to sow the seeds as soon as they are ripe, if you have your own; if you are purchasing them, they are usually sown in late winter. Sow them in boxes or pans on fine, rather gritty soil (the soilless mixtures seem to give quite good results), barely covering them. The pans can be covered with a sheet of paper under a pane of glass but, as soon as germination starts, the paper must be removed. However, some alpines take a long time to germinate; the seeds seem to need freezing and such plants (gentians are fairly typical) should have the seed boxes left outdoors in a shaded situation until germination occurs, which may be more than 12 months after sowing. They will need some protection to see them

through the winter.

Most alpines can also be propagated by means of soft tip cuttings. These are from ½ in.–1½ in. long. Strip off the lower leaves, cut the cutting cleanly across at a leaf-joint (or rather where the joint had been before the leaves were stripped) insert it in pure sharp sand and keep shaded and moist until the cuttings root, when they can be potted up separately in JIP 1. With plants such as geraniums and campanulas the cuttings are taken from the base of the plant.

With many alpines propagation by division is the simplest method. The divisions once taken (and be sure that each portion has some root) are potted up individually until they have made sufficient fresh roots to be planted out again.

Feeding and maintenance No feeding should be necessary for two years after constructing the alpine garden. Thereafter, a light application of a balanced fertilizer in late February every other year is beneficial. Care should be taken that the fertilizer does not come in contact with any leaves on the plants. Otherwise maintenance consists of weeding, controlling slugs, one of the main enemies, and cutting back any plant that is becoming too vigorous and swamping its neighbours. Plants with very hairy leaves can have a pane of glass fixed above them during the winter to prevent too much moisture settling on them and causing rot. No alpines are ever killed by frost, but many succumb to too much wet in the winter and early spring.

After care of seedlings As soon as possible after germination, the seedlings should be pricked out in boxes filled either with John Innes Seed Compost or a soilless seed compost, to which ⅓ part extra grit has been added. Once they are fairly sizeable they can be hardened off, and either potted up individually or planted directly out.

SOME BEAUTIFUL ROCK GARDEN PLANTS

Achillea (Daisy family) (yarrow). The dwarf kinds are useful rock garden plants. They include *A. argentea*, flowers white, leaves silvery; *A. chrysocoma*, flowers yellow, leaves grey; *A. tomentosa*, flowers yellow, leaves green. All grow 6 in. tall, flower in spring and prefer full sun and well-drained soil. Propagate by division in autumn or in spring, after the flowers are over.

Aethionema (Cabbage family) (stone-cress). Three kinds are invaluable; *A. grandiflorum*, 9 in., has heads of rose-pink flowers; *A. pulchellum*, 6 in. or so, has paler pink flowers; *A.* 'Warley Rose', a hybrid, 6 in. tall, has bright rosy-red flowers. All are shrubby plants with greyish-green leaves. They begin to flower in early summer. Give them a sunny position and any ordinary soil. Propagate the first two by seeds or cuttings; 'Warley Rose' by tip cuttings.

Allium (Lily family) (ornamental onion). The dwarf kinds described in the chapter on Bulbs are perfectly suitable for the rock garden.

Alyssum (Cabbage family) (madwort). The most popular kinds are *A. saxatile* and its forms; *A. saxatile* itself, to 1 ft. tall, has numerous heads of yellow flowers, leaves greyish-green. The form 'Citrinum' has sulphur-yellow blooms; 'Compactum' makes a denser, less tall plant, flowers yellow; 'Dudley Neville' has buff-yellow blooms. All prefer sun, like lime in the soil and are excellent wall plants, often seen growing together with arabis and aubrieta, as they flower at about the same time.

Anacyclus (Daisy family) (Mount Atlas daisy). A prostrate plant, *A. depressus* makes dense mats of greyish, fern-like leaves. In spring and summer it is covered with large white daisy-like flowers, their petals backed with crimson. It does best in a sunny place and freely-draining soil. Propagation is by seed sown in spring or by cuttings taken in summer.

Androsace (Primrose family) (rock jasmine). There are numerous species and cultivars, many of them easy, some difficult, all beautiful in flower. Among the easier kinds are *A. carnea*, 3 in., flowers pink; *A. lanuginosa*, 6 in. (excellent in a wall crevice), flowers pale pink with red centres; *A. primuloides* (syn. *A. sarmentosa*), 4–6 in., flowers rosy-pink, deeper pink in the varieties 'Chumbyi' and 'Salmon's Variety'. Plant in full sun and in wet winters protect the hairy leaves with a piece of glass (or grow in pots in the greenhouse). Free draining soil is essential. Propagate by detaching rooted rosettes which form on runners (as with strawberries), by seed sown in the cold greenhouse in spring, or by cuttings rooted at the same time.

Anemone (Buttercup family) (windflower). The dwarf kinds, 6–12 in. tall, flowering in spring or early summer, are the most suitable. They include *A. magellanica*, 6 in., flowers creamy-yellow; *A. nemorosa* (wood anemone), 4–6 in., flowers white; varieties 'Allenii' and 'Robinsoniana', have blue flowers; variety 'Alba Plena' has double white flowers. All anemones do best in sunny places, in rich but well-drained soil. Propagate by seeds sown in spring or by division or cuttings taken at the same time.

Arabis (Cabbage family) (rock cress). The most popular and easily-grown kinds are the cultivars of *A. albida*: 'Coccinea', double crimson flowers; 'Flore Pleno', double white flowers; 'Snowflake', single white flowers. All like sun, lime in the soil, and are often grown in conjunction with aubrietas and alyssums. To promote new growth cut the plants back hard after they have flowered. Propagate single varieties by seed sown in spring, or by cuttings or division; double varieties by cuttings or division in spring.

Arenaria (Pink family) (sandwort). *A. balearica* is a mere ½-in. tall; it does well in shade; *A. ledebouriana*, 6 in., has greyish-green leaves and grows well in crevices; *A. montana*, 6–9 in. is a sun-loving plant. All have white flowers in spring. They need well-drained soil and are propagated by dividing plants in spring or autumn, or by seed sown in spring.

Armeria (Plumbago family) (thrift). *A. caespitosa*, 2 in., is best in its form 'Beechwood', flowers delicate pink on very short stems; *A. maritima* (sea pink), 6 in., has various forms, including 'Alba', white flowers; 'Laucheana', bright pink flowers, on somewhat taller stems. They grow in any normal, well-drained soil, do best in sunny places and flower in spring and early

ABOVE: *Armeria caespitosa.*
BELOW: *Cyclamen neapolitanum.*

summer. Propagate by carefully dividing the roots in spring or autumn, or by sowing seed in spring.

Aster (Daisy family). Some dwarf species and low-growing cultivars make good rock garden plants. Of the species, *A. alpinus*, 9 in., flowers blue and golden-yellow is the best; the cultivar 'Beech Wood' has mauve, somewhat larger flowers; *A. natalensis*, 6 in. high, has bright blue flowers. They bloom from mid-summer onwards. Various named cultivars of dwarf Michaelmas daisies, 6–15 in. tall, are available: an up-to-date catalogue should be consulted.

Aubrieta (Cabbage family) (rock cress, purple rock cress). Favourite rock garden plants and probably the most popular of all trailing plants for walls, the aubrietas are available in a wide colour range, from lavender or pale mauve to deep, rich pink, some with a white eye, others with variegated foliage. Those obtainable are cultivars of *A. deltoidea* and a catalogue should be consulted for their names and descriptions. All flower in spring and grow 2–6 in. tall, depending upon soil and situation. They prefer sun and thrive where there is lime in the soil. To encourage the production of new growth, clip the plants over with shears after they have ceased to flower. Propagation of named cultivars is by cuttings rooted in June, or by division of plants after flowering.

Campanula (Bellflower family) (bellflower). Of this large genus there are many dwarf species and cultivars suitable for the garden or for walls. Among the best are *C. aucheri*, 4–6 in., flowers purple, forms tufts rather than trails; *C.* 'Birch Hybrid', 9 in., flowers purple, habit spreading; *C. carpatica*, 9–12 in., flowers large, varying from white to purple according to variety; *C. cochlearifolia* (syn. *C. pusilla*), 3 in., flowers blue (white in var. 'Alba'); *C. garganica*, 3–4 in., spreading habit but not invasive; flowers blue with white centres, fine for walls and crevices; *C. portenschlagiana* (syn. *C. muralis*), 6–9 in., flowers purple, stems spreading to make large but not invasive plants, good for walls or crevices, will tolerate some shade; *C. poscharskyana*, almost prostrate, somewhat invasive, but can be easily controlled, does well in poor, stony soil, flowers blue. All these flower from late spring onwards, do best in sunny places and well-drained soils and may be increased by seeds or by dividing plants in autumn or spring.

Cyclamen (Primrose family) (sowbread). The hardy kinds described in the chapter on Bulbs make excellent rock garden plants, especially for cool, slightly shaded positions.

Dianthus (Pink family) (pink). There is a large number of these delightful plants available for the rock garden: some almost prostrate, with very short-stemmed flowers. others growing up to 9 in. tall, many of them with deliciously fragrant flowers. A good catalogue may list 30 to 40 species and varieties in the colour range from white, through the palest pink to deep red, some with double flowers. Among the best are: *D. alpinus*, 3 in., flowers rosy-red; *D. arvernensis*, 4 in., flowers pink, leaves grey; *D. caesius* (Cheddar pink), to 9 in., flowers pink, leaves grey; *D. deltoides* (maiden pink), 9 in., flowers white, or pale to rich pink, according to variety; 'Inchmery', 9 in., flowers double, soft pink; 'Nellie Clarke', 6 in., flowers double deep red; *D. subacaulis*, 4 in., flowers rosy-red. All these flower from late spring onwards, do best in full sun and with lime in the soil. Species may be propagated by seeds, divisions or cuttings; hybrids by the latter two methods.

Draba (Cabbage family). These are cushion- or rosette-forming plants with tiny leaves. Among the easier kinds are: *D. aizoides*, 3 in., flowers yellow; *D. dedeana*, 1 in., flowers white, leaves grey-green. All grow best in sunny places and good, well-drained soil. They flower in spring and should be propagated by seeds sown in March.

Dryas (Rose family) (mountain avens). *D. octopetala*, is a sub-shrubby, trailing plant with small, dark green, roughly oak-shaped leaves. It is covered with white, short-stemmed flowers in early summer. It is easily grown in sunny places and is increased by division or by cuttings.

Epilobium (Evening Primrose family). The taller kinds are the willow-herbs; one dwarf species, *E. glabellum*, is worth growing in the rock garden. It reaches 8–12 in. and has cream-white flowers from late spring to autumn. Plant in full sun and propagate by cuttings.

Erigeron (Daisy family) (fleabane). Most kinds are more suitable as border plants: but the few dwarf kinds make good plants for sunny places on the rock garden. *E. aurantiacus*, 12 in., flowers orange; *E. compositus*, 3 in., flowers white or lavender, leaves grey; *E. mucronatus*, 6 in., flowers pink and white, excellent for poor soil, will seed itself between the cracks in paving. All flower in spring and summer, though *E. mucronatus* continues to flower well into autumn. Propagation is by seed or division.

Erinus (Figwort family). *E. alpinus* and its forms make fine plants for crevices and often find a foothold in walls and paths. They grow 3 in. tall and bear pink flowers in the species, white in the form 'Albus', deep red in 'Dr Hanele'. Plant in sun or light shade and propagate by seeds.

Erodium (Geranium family) (heron's bill). Delightful little plants, the heron's bills flower throughout spring and summer, thriving for years in any kind of soil and sunny place. *E. chamaedryoides*, a prostrate plant, has white, pink-veined flowers; its cultivar 'Roseum' has deep pink blooms; *E. chrysanthum*, 9 in., has sulphur-yellow flowers and silver-grey leaves; *E. corsicum*, 4 in., a good crevice plant, has rich pink flowers, leaves grey. Propagation is by seeds or cuttings.

Genista (Pea family) (broom). Most of these handsome shrubs are too tall for the rock garden, but there are a few suitable dwarf kinds. They include *G. hispanica* 'Compacta', 1 ft., flowers golden-yellow; *G. pilosa* 'Procumbens'; prostrate, flowers yellow; *G. sagittalis*, 9–12 in., mat-forming, flowers yellow, stems winged. All do best in dry soils and sunny places. Propagation is by seed or cuttings.

Gentiana (Gentian family) (gentian). Where they are grown successfully, the dwarf gentians are among the most spectacularly beautiful of rock garden plants. Some are difficult. Among the easier kinds are: *G. acaulis* (trumpet gentian), 4 in., flowers deep blue, trumpet shaped, spring and summer; *G. septemfida*, 9 in., flowers blue, borne in clusters, midsummer; *G. sino-ornata*, 3 in. flowers azure, August onwards; *G. verna*, 3 in., flowers clear blue, early spring, var. 'Angulosa' has deep blue flowers: both from tufts or rosettes of leaves. Of those described all except *G. sino-ornata* do well in ordinary soil enriched with humus (*G. verna* likes lime) and in sunny places. *G. sino-ornata* must have lime-free soil and prefers a cool position. Propagation is usually by seed, though *G. acaulis* and *G. sino-ornata* may be carefully divided in spring to provide new plants.

Geranium (Geranium family) (crane's bill). There are many of these, some too tall. Of the dwarf kinds, suitable for the rock garden, *G.* 'Ballerina', a hybrid, 6 in., produces pink flowers, veined with deep pink; *G. dalmaticum*, 4 in., has clear pink flowers, its foliage turns red in autumn; *G. renardii*, 9 in., has lavender flowers and greyish-green leaves; *G. sanguineum lancastrense*, to 6 in., is a mat-forming plant with salmon-pink flowers; *G. subcaulescens*, 6 in., has carmine flowers with darker centres. All flower from late spring onwards and thrive in any kind of soil and sunny position. They may be propagated by seed, though it is easy to divide them.

Hebe (Figwort family) (shrubby veronica). Most hebes are more suitable for the shrub border or elsewhere in the garden, than for the rock garden, as they grow 2–10 ft. tall. However, two dwarf kinds are suitable for the smaller rock garden: *H.* 'Carl Teschner', 6 in., has purplish-blue flowers; *H. pinguifolia* 'Pagei', 4 in., has masses of small white flowers and grey foliage. For the larger rock garden, *H. macrantha*, 18 in., with large white flowers, makes a useful shrub. All do well in sun or very light shade, and ordinary soil. They flower in summer, but will produce a later crop of flowers if the dead flower heads are removed. Propagation is by cuttings.

Helianthemum (Rock-rose family) (sun rose). The numerous cultivars of *H. nummularium* are among the best of all dwarf shrubs for the rock garden. Heights range from 6–12 in., colours from white, through all shades of pink, orange, deep red, to yellows. There are many double-flowered kinds. A nurseryman's catalogue should be consulted. All flower throughout the summer and will continue to bloom through the autumn if the plants are trimmed over severely as soon as the first flush of flowers has finished. Give them a position in full sun and well-drained soil. Propagation is by short cuttings rooted in pots in late summer.

Hepatica (Buttercup family). *H. triloba* 6 in. with blue, white, or reddish-purple flowers in early spring; *H. transsylvanica* (*angulata*) similar but slightly larger. All require cool, shady conditions and resent disturbance. Propagate by seed; division is possible but the plants are slow to take.

Hippocrepis (Pea family). *H. comosus* 'E. R. Janes' makes a flat mat covered with heads of lemon-yellow pea-shaped flowers in late spring and early summer. Give full sun and rather poor soil. Propagate by cuttings or division.

Houstonia (Bedstraw family) (bluets). *H. coerulea* makes a mat covered with small, tubular, clear blue flowers in spring. Likes a cool, moist, partly shaded situation. Lift and divide every two or three years and replace in a fresh position.

Hutchinsia (Cabbage family). *H. alpina* about 3 in. high, has dissected dark green leaves and heads of white flowers in spring. Likes a shaded situation. Propagate by seeds.

Hypericum (St John's Wort family). Dwarf shrubby plants, usually flowering late in the summer; *H. olympicum* to 6 in. with large yellow flowers in July–August; *H. polyphyllum* makes a rounded bush to 6 in. with heads of yellow flowers, 2 in. across, July–September; *H. reptans*, creeping plant, best allowed to hang, with orange flowers and coloured leaves later, Autumn. *H. rhodopaeum* to 9 in. with soft hairy grey-green leaves and large yellow flowers in May–June. Propagate by seed or cuttings.

Iberis (Cabbage family) (candytuft). *I. gibraltarica*, 9 in., has flat heads of white flowers, tinted lilac; *I. jucunda* 6 in. has heads of white flowers fading to lilac and flowers throughout the summer; *I. semper-*

ABOVE: Hypericum olympicum.
TOP: *Lewisias grow well in dry walls or crevices.*
OPPOSITE: Geranium sanguineum lancastrense, *one of the dwarf crane's bills.*

virens 'Snowflake' makes a small evergreen bush to 9 in. with white flowers. All need full sun and flower in early summer. Propagate by cuttings.

Iris (Iris family). There are a number of dwarf, tufted species all requiring full sun; *I. chamaeiris*, violet, white, or yellow to 8 in. in April; *I. innominata* with grassy leaves and single flowers on 9 in. stems, golden pencilled with chocolate. There are also a number of *innominata* hybrids with flowers in pastel shades, needing lime-free soil. *I. pumila*, like *I. chamaeiris*, but flowers are stemless. *I. gracilipes* with grassy leaves and branching stems bearing lilac and gold flowers to 6 in. in June. Needs lime-free soil and a cool, slightly shaded position; *I. cristata* has lavender flowers on 3 in. stems in spring and does best in a cool situation and in lime-free soil. Propagate by division or by seeds.

Jasione (Bellflower family). *J. jankae* makes a tuft of grassy leaves from which grow 12 in. stems bearing a scabious-like head of brilliant blue flowers in mid-summer. Propagate by seed or by division.

Leontopodium (Daisy family). *L. alpinum* Edelweiss makes a tuft of silvery, grassy leaves and throws up star-shaped heads of white flannel flowers on 4 in. stems in summer. Best propagated by seed.

Lewisia (Portulaca family). These do best if planted in rock crevices or in a dry wall. They have large showy flowers in late spring and most of the summer. The plants make rosettes of rather fleshy leaves and flower over a very long period. The easiest seem to be the hybrids. The 'Birch Hybrids' vary in colour from pink to deep salmon and crimson. 'George Henley' is brick red, 'Rose Splendour' is deep pink. The stems are from 9–15 in. long, but emerge from the sides of the rosettes and do not ascend vertically, so the actual height is not more than 9 in. They require full sun and to be on the dry side once flowering is finished. Propagate by cuttings of side rosettes or by seed. Best in lime-free soil.

Linum (Flax family) (flax). *L. flavum* makes a stiff little bush to 12 in. tall with yellow funnel-shaped flowers to 1 in. long in late spring; *L. narbonense* bears arching, very slender stems to 18 in. terminated with heads of very brilliant blue flowers in summer; *L. salsoloides* 'Nanum' makes a prostrate gnarled little bush covered with large white, purple-backed, honey-scented flowers at midsummer. All need full sun and prefer alkaline soil. Propagate by seed or by cuttings.

Lithospermum (Borage family). *L. diffusum* 'Grace Ward' makes a prostrate bush with vivid blue flowers which are produced all through the summer. It requires lime-free soil and as warm a situation as possible.

If it becomes bare in the centre, top dress with good leaf soil. Propagate by cuttings.

Lotus (Pea family). *Lotus corniculatus* 'Flore Pleno', Birdsfoot Trefoil, makes a mat of dark green clover-like leaves and heads of deep yellow, pea-like flowers throughout the summer. It thrives in chalky soils, but will grow in any sunny, well-drained gritty position. In rich soil it gets rather too leafy. Propagate by cuttings.

Lychnis (Pink family). *L. alpina* makes a tuft of grassy leaves with heads of pink flowers on 3 in. stems in spring. It is a short-lived plant; *L. flos-jovis* has large white hairy leaves and large carmine flowers on 1 ft. stems; *L. viscaria* 'Splendens Plena' has brilliant heads of carmine flowers on 18 in. stems. This must be propagated by cuttings; the others are better by seed.

Maianthemum (Lily family) (May lily). A creeping plant with deep green heart-shaped leaves and spikes of fluffy white flowers in May. Needs a peaty, lime-free soil, which is cool and shaded. Propagate by division.

Mazus (Figwort family). *M. pumilio* makes a mat of green leaves, studded with lipped blue and white flowers in late summer and autumn; *M. reptans* has bronzy leaves and, mauve, white, and gold flowers. Both spread freely in a cool, moist situation and should be frequently lifted and divided.

Mentha (Sage family) (mint). *M. requienii* makes a prostrate mat of small soft green, mint-scented leaves and tiny lavender flowers in summer. It likes a moist situation and is easily propagated, as the stems root as they grow.

Mimulus (Figwort family) (musk). *M. burnetii*, with red-brown mottled flowers on 9 in. stems. The flowers are large and lipped. *M. cupreus* 'Whitecroft Scarlet' has brilliant scarlet flowers on 9 in. stems. If cut back after flowering, these will probably flower a second time. *M. primuloides* makes a small leaved mat with 1 in. yellow flowers in June; *M. radicans* makes a mat of bronze leaves with stemless white and violet flowers throughout the summer. They all like cool, moist situations, which may be slightly shaded and are all rather short-lived. Easily propagated by cuttings, seed, or division.

Nierembergia (Potato family). *N. repens* (*rivularis*) makes a mat of underground stems from which arise green leaves and large funnel-shaped white flowers in summer. It thrives in very gritty soil and comes up well in gravel paths. During the winter it vanishes underground. Propagate by division in spring.

Oenothera (Evening primrose family) (evening primrose). *O. acaulis* makes tufts of large green leaves to 6 in. with long-tubed, large white flowers which turn pink before they die and continue through summer into autumn; *O. fremontii*, 9 in., has slender greyish leaves and yellow flowers; *O. missouriensis*, throws out sprawling stems to 1 ft. with an endless succession of large yellow flowers; *O. pumila* (*perennis*) throws up 6 in. stems with small cup-shaped yellow flowers in July. Propagate by seed or by cuttings.

Omphalodes (Borage family). *O. verna* runs about underground and has bright blue flowers like a large forget-me-not in early spring; *O. cappadocica* makes a tuft and has brighter blue flowers in larger numbers in April and May. Both like a cool, semi-shaded situation and can be propagated by division or by seed; *O. luciliae* with greyish leaves and pearly-blue flowers in June needs full sun and is somewhat difficult. Propagate by cuttings.

Oxalis (Wood Sorrel family). Plants with clover-like leaves and funnel-shaped flowers arising from tubers. *O. magellanica* makes a small mat with bronzy leaves and pearly flowers in May; *O. adenophylla*, 4 in. has silvery leaves and large pink flowers in April–May; *O. enneaphylla* is similar with greyish leaves and paler flowers; *O. inops*, 4 in. can be a menace as it is more or less ineradicable but has large red, handsome flowers; *O. lobata*, 3 in. produces a flush of leaves in spring, disappears during the summer to reappear in the autumn with golden flowers. Propagate by separating the tubers; *O. adenophylla* and *enneaphylla* are not very free with these and seed may be preferable, if it can be obtained.

Papaver (Poppy family) (poppy). *P. alpina*, 4 in. makes a tuft of rather glaucous, dissected leaves and produces numbers of small poppies in white, yellow, orange, and pink. It is short-lived and is propagated by seed, which will sow itself in some gardens.

Parochetus (Pea family). *P. communis* makes a prostrate mat, covered with clover-like leaves and large gentian-blue pea-shaped flowers in late summer, through to the autumn. It is not too hardy, but rooted runners are formed with great profusion and one or two can be lifted and over-wintered. An excellent plant for crazy paving, as the roots seem to persist under the stones.

Pentstemon (Figwort family). *P. davidsonii* (*rupicola*), 4 in. makes a tiny shrub with large tubular ruby flowers and grey leaves, May; *P. heterophyllus* to 18 in. has spires of blue flowers in June; *P. menziesii*, 12 in. has small, rather fleshy leaves and large purple flowers in May–June; *P. pinifolius* has needle-like leaves and bright scarlet flowers in July; *P. pulchellus* makes a prostrate plant with blue flowers on 3 in. stems in May; *P. roezlii* to 9 in. makes a stiff bush with red flowers; 'Weald Beacon' has crimson flowers to 9 in. All like lime-free soil, a warm situation and shelter from east winds. They are not, usually, very long-lived. Propagate by soft tip cuttings early in the year, or by seed.

Phlox (Phlox family). *P. subulata* makes a close carpet which disappears under the large flat flowers in April and May. Among the best are 'Appleblossom', pink; 'G. F. Wilson', mauve; 'Temiscaming', carmine; 'Fairy', lavender; *P. adsurgens*, with large salmon flowers likes slight shade, as do the taller *P. divaricata* and *P. stolonifera*, with heads of sapphire-blue flowers in May; *P. subulata* requires full sun. Propagate by cuttings or division.

Phyteuma (Bellflower family). *P. hemisphaericum*, 6 in. with a tuft of grassy leaves and a head of small blue flowers in a ball; *P. nigrum*, with large leaves and 12 in. stems of very deep violet flowers; *P. scheuzeri*, 12 in. with rounded heads of purple-blue. All the plants flower in June. Propagate by seed.

Platycodon (Bellflower family) (balloon bellflower). *P. grandiflorum* 'Mariesii', June–July, stems to 15 in. with inflated buds opening to saucer-shaped, purple-blue flowers about 3 in. wide; 'Apoyama' only reaches to 6 in. White forms are known. Propagate by seeds.

Polygala (Milkwort family). *P. calcarea* is a prostrate plant with 3 in. spikes of brilliant blue flowers in May–June; *P. chamaebuxus* is a small 6 in. shrub with evergreen leaves and pea-shaped cream, purple tipped flowers in April–May; *P. calcarea* needs full sun and a very limy soil; *P. chamaebuxus* likes a cool, semi-shaded situation. Propagate by seed or by division.

Potentilla (Rose family) (cinquefoil). *P. alba*, 4 in. with greyish, strawberry leaves and white flowers Dec.–April; *P. aurea* makes a prostrate mat with masses of yellow flowers May–June; *P. megalantha* with large leaves and yellow flowers on 6 in. stems in June; *P. nitida* makes a mat of tiny silver leaves and has pink flowers like small roses in June; *P. verna* 'Nana' has yellow flowers from prostrate stems throughout the summer; *P. alba* has no objection to some shade, the others need full sun. Propagate by seed, cuttings or division.

Primula (Primrose family). *P. minima*, almost stemless pink flowers; *P. auricula*, a crevice plant, with mealy leaves and fragrant yellow flowers in April; *P. pubescens* 'Mrs J. H. Wilson', 3–4 in., rich lilac flowers. Later the leaves get to 9 in. long. *P. frondosa* with farinose leaves and a head of small pink flowers on 4 in. stems in March–April; *P. marginata* with grey, farinose leaves and few-flowered heads of lavender primroses in March; *P. viscosa*, 6 in., rosy-purple flowers; *P. rosea* with brilliant carmine flowers in March–April. Needs ample moisture. Propagate by seeds or division, sowing the seed as soon as ripe. Most primulas need to be lifted and planted in fresh soil every three years.

Pulsatilla (Buttercup family) (pasque flower). *P. vulgaris* has large purple, white or pink flowers in early spring, followed by large, finely-dissected leaves, which are grey in colour; *P. alpina* has white or (in *sulphurea*) pale yellow flowers in June. All plants resent root disturbance and are propagated by seed, which does best if sown as soon as it is ripe.

Ramonda (Gloxinia family). *R. myconii* (*pyrenaica*) makes a rosette of wrinkled leaves from the sides of which emerge heads of flat, mauve, yellow-eyed flowers in June; *R. nathaliae* is somewhat larger. Both will only grow satisfactorily in north facing crevices and are admirable in dry walls. Propagate by seed or by division, which needs great care.

Ranunculus (Buttercup family). *R. amplexicaulis* has 9 in. stems bearing many white buttercups in May; *R. gramineus* makes a tuft of grassy leaves with branching 12 in. stems bearing golden buttercups in May–June; *R. montanus* 'Molten Gold' makes a little mound about 23 in. high with large golden flowers in spring. The double form of the celandine *R. ficaria*, 'Flore Pleno' and the copper coloured 'Aurantiacus' do not spread unduly. Propagate by seeds or by division.

Salix (Willow family) (willow). *S. arbuscula* makes a gnarled shrub, which may eventually reach 2 ft. in height, but which is slow-growing. There are also prostrate forms, which spread quite widely; *S. reticulata* with attractive netted leaves, loves to hug rocks, or ascend north-facing slopes. Propagate by cuttings, selected when the word is half ripe.

Saponaria (Pink family) (soapwort). *S. ocymoides* throws out prostrate trailing stems clothed with dark leaves and masses of bright pink flowers April–June. Propagate by seed or by cuttings.

Saxifraga (Saxifrage family). *S. aizoon* makes rosettes of grey, white-edge leaves with panicles of white, pink, or pale yellow flowers in June; *S. cotyledon* is much larger; *S. cochlearis* much smaller. *S.* 'Tumbling Waters' has narrower leaves and a panicle to 18 in. long. Of the Kabschias, with needle-like leaves, the easiest are *S. burseriana* 'Gloria' with single large white red-stemmed flowers in March–April; *S. irvingii* with pink flowers also singly, in March–April, and *S. apiculata* with heads of yellow flowers in February–March.

The Mossy Saxifrages make mats of green, dissected foliage and bear few-flowered heads on 3 in. stems, which are red, pink, or white. Among the best are 'Four Winds', deep red; 'Winston Churchill' and 'Peter Pan', pink, and 'Pearly King', white. They all flower April–May.

Among others, *S. oppositifolia* makes a prostrate plant with minute leaves and huge single magenta-purple flowers in February–March; *S. granulata* 'Flore Pleno' the double Meadow Saxifrage dies down to a bunch of tubers each winter and has double white flowers on 6 in. stems in May–June; *S. × umbrosa* is an old favourite, 'London Pride', while *S. fortunei* has long-stemmed heart-shaped leaves which are red underneath and a great panicle of white, cyclamen-like flowers in October. It reaches to 12 in.

Propagation by cuttings is usually best, although division is possible, providing plants have several rosettes. *S. granulata* provides plenty of spare bulbets.

Sedum (Stonecrop family) (stonecrop). *S. bithynicum* makes a mat of grey, needle like leaves and has heads of pink flowers in June; *S. album* 'Coral Carpet' makes a mat of pinkish leaves with pink flowers in June; *S. cauticolum* has trailing 6 in. stems ending in heads of crimson flowers in August; *S. lydium* has tufts of leaves which are reddish in summer and green in winter and bears white flowers in June–July on 3 in. stems; *S. spathulifolium* has roundish fleshy leaves about an inch long, purple in 'Purpureum', covered with white meal in 'Capa Blanca'. It has yellow flowers, which are sparingly produced. Cuttings root very readily and sometimes even a leaf will throw out roots and start to grow of its own accord.

Sempervivum (Stonecrop family) (houseleek). These make rosettes of fleshy, pointed leaves and will thrive in practically no soil. There are a vast number of forms of *S. tectorum*, the common houseleek, with rosettes in various colours from green with red-tips to quite bright red. The flowers are pink on 3 in. stems; *S. arachnoideum* has smaller rosettes covered with cobweb-like hairs and deep pink flowers; *S. (Jovibarba) heuffelianus* does not throw out side rosettes on stolons as do all the others, but the rosettes divide. It has glaucous leaves and large yellow flowers on 6 in. stems. Propagate by detaching rosettes, which root readily.

Silene (Pink family) (catchfly). *S. schafta* makes a tuft of slender stems from which arise large magenta flowers on 2 in. stems in late summer; *S. acaulis*, the Moss Pink, makes a tight hummock of grassy leaves, which should be studded with pink flowers in May–June, but is apt to be shy in producing flowers in cultivation. Propagate *S. schafta* by seed, *S. acaulis* by cuttings.

Sisyrinchium (Iris family) (blue-eyed grass). *S. brachypus* with a tuft of grassy leaves and yellow flowers on 6 in. stems in June–July; *S. angustifolium* with blue flowers at the same season; *S. douglasii* with large bell-shaped white or mauve flowers in April. Propagate by seed or by division.

Thymus (Sage family) (thyme). *T. drucei* (*serpyllum*) makes an enormous mat of scented dark green leaves which are studded with mauve, white, purple, or red flowers in June–July. *T. herba-barona* is another prostrate species with pink flowers and leaves smelling of caraway; *T.* × *citriodorus* 'Silver Queen' makes a small upright bush to 6 in. with green and silver lemon-scented leaves. Propagate by cuttings.

Tiarella (Saxifrage family) (foam flower). *T. cordifolia* makes wide mats of soft green heart-shaped leaves and spikes of fluffy cream flowers on 9 in. stems, in May–June. It requires cool shady conditions. Increase by division.

ABOVE: Saxifraga apiculata *blooms in spring. Saxifrages are some of the easiest and best dwarf plants to grow in a rock garden.*
RIGHT: Caltha palustris *'Plena', a rich yellow double kingcup.*
OPPOSITE PAGE, LEFT:
TOP: *Filling a plastic pool. First fill the hole with a layer of sand, then cover with the plastic sheet, held in place by bricks, and gently fill with water.*
CENTRE: *The finished pool.*
BOTTOM: *Water plants can be encouraged to grow on the bottom of the pool by anchoring the roots between bricks.*
OPPOSITE PAGE, RIGHT:
TOP: *Rocks should be carefully inserted in the soil built up over a deep sump to give drainage. The inset shows the wrong angle to lay rocks; the drawing on the right shows the correct angle.*
BELOW: *A section through a pool, showing plants grown in containers on ledges.*

Veronica (Figwort family) (speedwell). Of the vast number available, *V. prostrata* makes a mat covered with spikes of blue, white, or pink flowers in May; *V. teucrium* 'Royal Blue' has spikes of deep blue flowers on 12 in. stems in June; *V. cinerea* has grey leaves and spikes of blue flowers in July. Propagate by seed, division or cuttings.

Viola (Violet family) (pansy, violet). *V. cornuta* makes a tangle of stems to 9 in. high carrying spurred pansies in violet or white throughout most of the summer. *V. sororia* (*cucullata, septentronalis*) has enormous white, grey-veined violets in April–May and grows to about 6 in.; *V. zoysii*, 1 in. wide, rounded buttercup yellow flowers in summer; *V. arenaria* 'Rosea' is like a purple dog violet and flowers March–May; *V. labradorica* has purple leaves and mauve dog-violet like flowers in April. It grows to 4 in. tall. All will propagate easily by seed. *V. sororia* can be divided and *V. cornuta* grows from cuttings.

Zauschneria (Evening-Primrose family) (Californian fuchsia). *Z. californica* makes a shrubby-looking plant with grey leaves and scarlet flowers in August–October. Needs a very dry sunny position. Propagate by soft tip cuttings.

POOLS AND PONDS

Water brings magic to every garden. It is infinitely soothing to jaded nerves to sit beside a pool on a hot summer's day with nothing more strenuous to do than watch

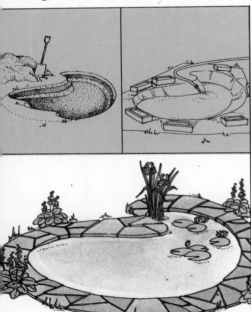

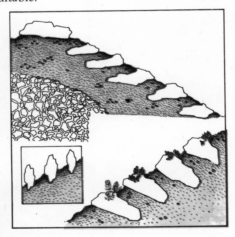

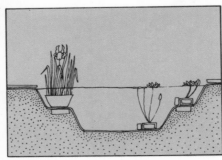

the fish, or to become hypnotized watching the sparkling waters of a fountain. Besides, water in a garden adds to the general interest, for it enables a wider variety of plants to be grown. A pool is like a mirror, reflecting objects inside or outside the garden.

With the modern materials available, pools and ponds can be quite easily constructed by amateur gardeners. Little artistry or skill is needed to obtain a very natural looking effect. A warning should, however, be given to those with young children, for even a few inches of water can be lethal. If a pool is constructed in a garden where children play, strong railings, at least temporarily, should surround it to prevent accidents. An alternative is to raise the pool a foot or two above the ground, but it might be better to postpone its construction until the young members of the family are a little older.

A pool can be formal (figure 1 overleaf), or informal (figure 2), according to the surroundings in which it is to be situated. The former is square or rectangular in shape and can be incorporated in many garden schemes, either in concrete or paving surrounds or in the lawn itself. The latter is irregular in outline and lends itself to the inclusion of other natural features, such as a small stream, that tumbles into it, or a bog garden. It is important, therefore, to decide at the outset which type of pool is most suitable.

Two ways in which a pool can be built are either by installing a prefabricated pool or by using a plastic liner. The costliest method is the use of prefabricated units (figure 3), which are moulded in plastic or glass-fibre. Both formal and informal types are available in the larger sizes, but the latter also come in a wide variety of smaller shapes and sizes.

Their installation is quite straightforward. All you do is dig a hole slightly larger than the unit. After the stones have been removed, some of the excavated soil can be used for back filling when the unit is in place. Care must be taken to see that there is no large area of the pool unsupported, as it could be damaged or distorted when the water is added. Water is very heavy! The rest of the soil removed might be used for the construction of a rockery in the vicinity of the informal pool or for some other construction in the garden.

Plastic-lined pools are very successful. If the tougher grades of plastic are used, many years of maintenance and replacement-free service should be provided. Some of these liners are coloured – usually a pleasant blue. There are some that are reinforced with nylon. One of the toughest and most durable of liners is Butyl, a rubber-based material of exceptional strength. It is black in colour and looks more natural than the coloured liners, making it particularly appropriate for informal pools.

None of the plastic or rubber-based liners are easy to use in pools if the outlines are complex. Therefore, to reduce the number of necessary folds and creases when the material is laid over the undulations, they should be kept to the minimum and they should be as gentle as possible.

A formal pool is quite easy to make from a liner (figure 4) and a careful fold at the corners will be all that is necessary to maintain a reasonable crease-free surface all round the pool.

For all liners, an overlap of material must be allowed for, so that it can be taken over the edges. The amount of material required for a pool can be calculated on the bases of length (overall length of the pool plus twice the maximum depth) and width (overall width of the pool plus twice the maximum depth). Allow 6 in. at the sides and ends for the overlaps.

Where ledges or shelves are required in the pool to provide different depths of water for the various aquatic plants, these must be allowed for as extra measurements. Usually one shelf is adequate all round the sides, about 9–10 in. below the surface of the water. To avoid the necessity for shelves, plant containers can very simply be raised on bricks.

Particular care should be exercised when

113

the excavation for a liner pool is being undertaken and all stones, etc., must be removed to prevent damage to the liner. The base of the site should be lined with about 1 in. of sand, which will serve as a cushion for the liner (figure 5). The installation of a liner is made easier if, when it is in its approximate position, a little water is allowed to run into it. The weight of this water will pull and press the plastic in place, and it is a very useful method when an informal pool is being made (figure 6). The edges of the liner can be held down by several pieces of stone as the water runs in.

To finish off, the edges of the liner in a formal pool can be concealed very attractively if a row of paving slabs is laid all round (figure 5). In an informal pool, crazy paving could be used or the edge of liner can be hidden or trapped by grass turves.

A feature, such as a waterfall, can be installed very quickly if a prefabricated unit (figure 7) is used. Its finish is in a simulated rock face with little rocks protruding in the 'run' to break up the water flow effectively. Several units can be linked to form a series of cascades. A stream can also be easily introduced by the use of preformed units (figure 8). Several can be arranged to form an intriguing course, which could empty into a waterfall basin which, in turn, finally empties into the main pool itself.

A formal pool might be adorned with a fountain from which silvery streams of water could play picturesquely on its surface. Not only does this look attractive, it would also aerate the water to the benefit of any fish.

Another feature that can be installed by the side of an informal pool is a small bog garden, in which moisture-loving plants can be grown. It can be created by allowing the pool to overflow by means of a pipe set in the water level, into the area allocated. To construct a bog garden, the soil should be removed to a depth of 2 ft., and the hole lined with a sheet of butyl rubber, securing its outside edges with rock stones or turves. The lined basin is filled with 6 in. of rough, broken stones, a 6 in. layer of coarse peat and 12 in. or so of a mixture of 4 parts peat, 1 part of light soil and 1 part leaf mould. To take away any surplus water in very wet weather, the butyl liner should be punctured with several small holes at the lowest point near the wall.

The movement of water from the pool to the top of a waterfall or stream course is provided by an electric pump. There are two types, a surface pump (figure 9), which is installed outside the pool with a suction pipe connected to it and into the pool water. The second is the submerged pump (figure 10), which requires less installation work as it is simply placed in the pool water.

Several types are connected to a transformer, which reduces mains voltage to a safe 24 volts or so.

By means of extra piping and gate valves, a powerful surface pump can be used to provide a fountain effect and a waterfall simultaneously. The diagram (11) illustrates such a layout, which uses a preformed stream course, running into a waterfall basin.

The submerged pumps can operate a fountain and a waterfall simultaneously by means of an adaptor, which is often supplied with the pump. For spectacular water effects it is necessary to select a more powerful electric pump.

A raised pool is another effective water feature in a garden. This is ideal when incorporated in a terrace or patio. It is, too, an excellent design for the elderly or infirm gardener, because it can be attended to without stooping.

The height of the pool above the ground level is a matter for personal decision, but generally 1½ to 2½ ft. is adequate. It is necessary to build an inner wall first using breeze blocks or concrete blocks to retain the liner and water. A firm footing of concrete should be provided in a 2-in. deep trench.

An outer wall of the same height is then built up about 3-in. distant from this retaining wall, constructed ideally of decorative

or rough-textured walling stone. This must also have a good foundation. When set the hollow between the two walls can be filled in with some of the excavated soil.

A selection of plants for pools
Bog garden Mimulus 'Whitecroft Scarlet', bright scarlet, 4 in. tall; *Primula denticulata* (Drumstick Primula), lilac flowers in large globular heads, 1 ft. tall; *Primula rosea*, vivid carmine-red flowers, 6 in. tall; *Caltha palustris* 'Plena' (the double kingcup), bright yellow flowers, 9–12 in. tall; *Astilbe simplicifolia* 'Erecta', spikes of pink flowers, 9 in. tall.

Deep marginal plants *Aponogeton distachyum* (Water Hawthorn), white flowers, 6–18 in. deep; *Orontium aquaticum* (Golden Club), yellow, 3–12 in. deep; *Villarsia bennettii*, like a miniature yellow water lily, 4–18 in. deep.

Shallow marginal plants *Alisma plantago-aquatica*, pale rose flowers, 6 in. deep; *Iris laevigata*, large deep blue flowers, 2–4 in. deep; *Mentha aquatica* (Water Mint), deep lilac flowers, helps to keep water clear, 3 in. deep; *Myosotis scorpioides* (palustris) (Water Forget-me-not), blue flowers, 3–6 in. deep; *Pontederia cordata* (Pickerel Weed), spikes of blue flowers, 3–5 in. deep.

Floating plants *Hydrocharis morsus-ranae* (Frogbit), white flowers, rosettes of leaves.
Water-lilies The choice of water-lily depends on the depth of the pool. Here are some suggestions: (4–12 in. deep) *Nymphaea odorata minor*, white, scented; *Nymphaea pygmaea rubra*, red; (6–18 in. deep) *Nymphaea odorata alba*, white, scented; 'Froebellii', red, very fragrant; *N. o. turicensis*, pink, richly perfumed; (9–24 in. deep) 'Albatross', white; 'Escarbonele', red; 'Amabalis', salmon pink; Marliacea 'Chromotella', yellow.

Fish The more common fish are goldfish, shubunkin, golden orfe, and golden rudd. With fish there must be an oxygenating plant like *Elodea canadensis*. Ramshorn snails are also valuable for clearing the water and providing food in the shape of eggs.

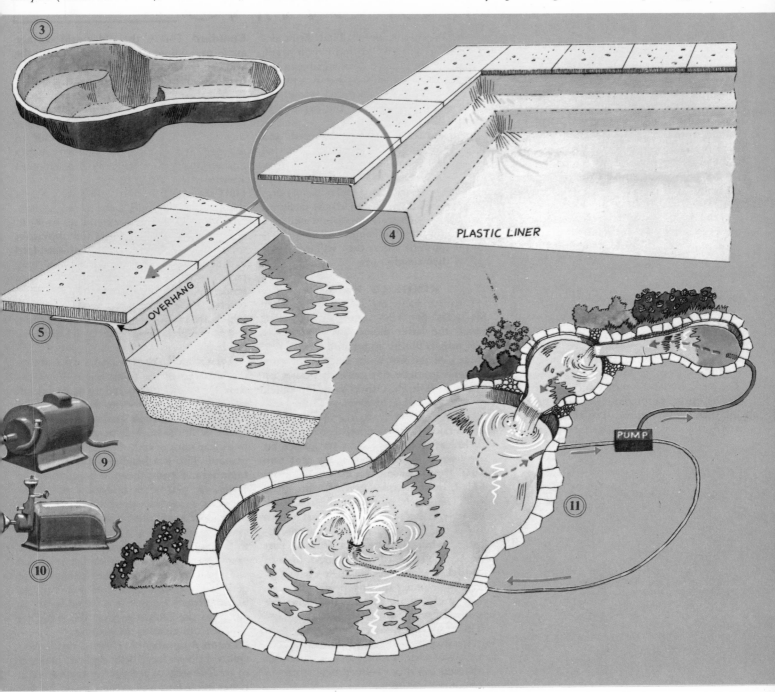

PLASTIC LINER

OVERHANG

PUMP

SUCCESSFUL FRUIT GROWING

People grow their own fruit for many reasons: because bought fruit is expensive, and your own can mean a considerable economy; because they like the varieties of their own choice; because they inherited trees or bushes from the last occupant, or just because they enjoy growing it as a change from the type of gardening involved in growing flowers and vegetables.

They are all good reasons, but perhaps the keenest enjoyment comes from the pleasure of being able to eat the kinds of apples, plums, and so forth, that one likes best.

Some of the most delicious varieties are the products of years of cultivation by enthusiastic private growers long dead, though their names may be commemorated still, particularly in the names of many apples.

Fruit in those times was cultivated more from gastronomic than commercial considerations. The commercial enterprises of today, backed by extensive orchards, packing stations, and marketing organizations, must give major consideration to the cost of picking, spraying, handling, and storage. The result is that the choice and breeding of strains must compromise between flavour and such considerations as thickness of skin and resistance to disease. The private grower can take what risks he pleases to obtain what he prefers.

Inevitably climatic and local factors must be taken into account. So must the size of the garden, and how much protection it affords from wind and frost.

It is always worth while to study the practice of knowledgeable neighbours and what does well in well established gardens nearby. If nobody in your neighbourhood grows plums, find out why before indulging your ambition to grow greengages on an inviting expanse of south wall.

There are few gardens, even patios in the hearts of cities, where fruit of some sort can not be grown. All fruit needs sunshine. Without it they cannot make use of the chemicals in the soil, no matter at what expense these have been added. Fruit deprived of it will give an indifferent yield, be poor in appearance, and lacking in flavour. In a tiny garden it is largely a matter of how much of the restricted sunny sites can be spared for fruit at the expense of other plants.

Small gardens are often sheltered, and there are fruits which will tolerate partial shade better than most, though they may crop late. Such are the cane fruits (raspberries, blackberries, loganberries, and other hybrids), gooseberries and all the currants. Furthermore, tree fruits grown up walls can attain a considerable height and be grown into the sunshine where they will not overshadow their neighbours.

KINDS OF FRUIT

Fruits are generally classified as either 'soft fruits' or 'tree' or 'top' fruits, even though the latter includes relatively soft fruits such as plums, gages, and figs.

Many of the soft fruits such as the currants and gooseberries grow as bushes up to about 3 ft. high. Others grow on canes, e.g. raspberries, blackberries, and allied hybrids. Among soft fruits are also included strawberries, which are herbaceous plants.

Whereas all the soft fruits are grown on their own roots, the tree fruits that you obtain from the nurseryman have been budded, or sometimes grafted, onto their roots. The object of raising the rootstock separately is because it is this part which endows the tree with its growing characteristics, while the upper or fruiting part provides the strain of fruit desired. Lists of rootstocks, with notes on their characteristics appear under the appropriate sections below, and a study of these will give the best idea of which to choose.

The notes that follow immediately concern the shaping of the growing trees. Combinations of various rootstocks and methods of shaping can thus produce trees suited to almost any purpose.

Standard This is the old-world cottage apple tree whose shade is celebrated in the well-known song. Characteristically it has 6 ft. of vertical trunk before the lowest branches appear, and spreads out from there. Although attractive to look at and sit under, such trees are really too large for most gardens, are extremely difficult to manage, and picking the apples is such a business that as a rule a great many of them are lost.

Half-standard In the half-standard tree the main trunk is only 2-ft. shorter, and the spread may ultimately extend up to 40 ft. in each direction, so most of the objections to the standard apply to the half-standard also. Even a half-standard apple tree may crop over 200 lb., and nowadays there is a tendency for people to prefer to grow several smaller trees of different varieties, which are easier for spraying and pruning, and can be picked without the aid of a very tall ladder.

Even a small half-standard, such as weeping varieties of the plum (e.g. 'Warwickshire Drooper') still spread up to 20 ft. each way, according to rootstock, and demand more room than most gardeners can afford.

Bush With the bush form we come down to a clear stem of only 1½ to 3 ft. above the ground. This is a handier form of tree altogether and is now the most popular. When apples are grafted or budded onto weak-growing rootstocks even smaller trees can be produced, and these dwarf bushes can be very convenient when space in the garden is at a premium. Among the soft fruits grown as bushes, such as gooseberries or red and white currants, a stem of about 6 in. is generally allowed. This does not apply to black currants because it is found better to cultivate the bushes so that the branches appear from close to the ground.

Cordon A number of artificial, rigidly disciplined shapes have been evolved in order to get fruit trees to grow tidily against walls, either in the enclosed garden, or up the side

of a house, where they have to be fitted into spaces between windows. These shapes are achieved by means of scientific but relentless pruning and by tying the stems into position as they grow. The simplest of these shapes is the single cordon, in which the tree is confined to a single, vertical stem and the fruiting spurs growing directly from it. No branches are allowed. This form is obviously ideal for growing up between windows and is also specially suited to the pear-tree with its natural tendency to 'tower' to a great height. Cordons need not be vertical but can be planted at an angle of 45°, from which various advantages may result. One is that they will fruit earlier. Another is that when a row of them is grown against a wall the stems can grow much longer than the height of the wall before they reach the top. Another great advantage of the cordon is its compactness, permitting a number of varieties to be grown within a comparatively small space. Cross-pollination requirements can easily be met in this way, and a good seasonal succession of fruit provided for.

Double cordon In the double cordon the tree is trained to grow horizontally on each side of a short vertical stem, and then trained vertically so that the result is in the shape of a pitchfork. Each vertical is then treated just like a single cordon. A triple-cordon, consisting of a central vertical cordon with one on each side of it can also be formed. Both types are commonly employed for gooseberries and red currants.

Espalier The espalier has a central vertical stem from which pairs of horizontal branches are trained at equal vertical distances apart on both sides. Its principal advantage is that it can be kept low, when height is limited. Espaliers of apples and pears can be grown in rows freestanding to form a kind of fence along the sides of paths.

Fan As its name suggests, the fan form has its branches arranged fanwise from the central stem. Although mostly seen trained against walls, fans can also be grown free-standing with their branches held in position by being tied to horizontal wires strained between posts. Most fruits can be trained in this way.

ABOVE: *Even a small orchard can produce a wealth of fruit.*

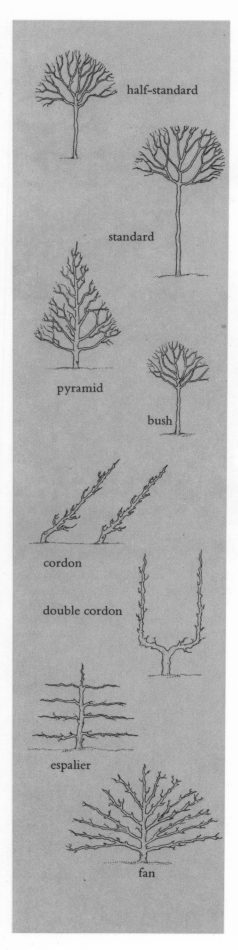

half-standard

standard

pyramid

bush

cordon

double cordon

espalier

fan

Pyramid Unlike the foregoing, the pyramid is a three-dimensional tree in which the apple, pear, or plum is forced to grow into the shape of a Christmas tree with a central vertical stem and branches radiating from it all round and all the way up. Pyramids are often grown on dwarfing rootstocks in small gardens, and even plums, which have no dwarfing rootstocks, are now frequently trained in this way in order to keep them under control.

Family tree Although this has no special shape, the 'family tree' normally obtained from nurserymen is supplied as a bush. Its name refers to the fact that different varieties have been grafted together to form one tree producing several different kinds.

PLANTING AND GROWING TREE FRUITS

For a tree-root to function, the innumerable tiny hairs on the root fibres have to be in intimate contact with the soil-particles in which the roots are growing. In this way the plant is able to absorb the moisture from the soil, carrying the chemicals which it requires.

When a young tree is uprooted for replanting elsewhere there is inevitably some disturbance of the roots, and growth will be checked until they are re-established.

Trees are planted during the dormant months starting when their leaves have fallen and ending when they begin to put out leaf again. Immediately after leaf-fall, which is usually early in November, the soil is likely to be still sufficiently warm to encourage growth of the roots of a newly planted tree. As winter advances, conditions become less favourable. Not only does the soil become colder, but it may also be wet and clogging, and less able to pack closely around the root hairs. Consequently, early planting should always be aimed at, even though it may not always be possible to achieve.

Obviously the first requirement for getting the young fruit trees in early is to be able to get delivery from the nurseryman at the right time. But even if this is achieved, many other obstacles may lie in the way. Heavy rainfall at this time may have rendered the soil quite unsuitable for planting, and the longer planting has to be delayed because of this the greater the possibility that freezing weather may arrive and hold up the planting still further. So it is necessary to be prepared to store the young trees as comfortably as possible while you are awaiting the right conditions to plant.

To take care of them during a short delay, the plants can be heeled in for the time being. For this purpose dig a trench with one side vertical and the other at 45°, lay the young trees along the sloping side of this trench, spread the roots out roughly and cover them with the excavated soil right up to the soil-mark on the stem. Make sure the trench is big enough.

If the trees arrive in bitter weather when frost and snow make it quite impossible to plant, the trees will have to be unpacked and brought indoors. They may be stored in a garage or shed, covered up to keep them frost-free and moist, and somewhere out of the reach of mice.

When the time comes to plant them have a look at the roots, and if they appear very dry soak them in water for a couple of hours before planting.

Staking and supports All tree fruits must be staked when they are planted. If it is intended to grow cordons or fans requiring a system of posts and horizontal wires, the erection of these should have been completed before the trees were delivered. Failure to order and prepare the stakes and other materials beforehand can often be another reason for delayed planting.

It is foolish to economize by trying to make do with stakes that are too flimsy for the job. Aim to give each tree the support of a rock-firm post. This may be of peeled chestnut, or 3 × 3 in. hardwood. In heavy soil it will have to go 18 in. into the ground, and in lighter soils at least 2 ft. The whole of the portion to be buried, and a few inches above, should be thoroughly soaked in a copper-based preservative. It is not good enough to brush this on as the stakes may be in the ground for quite a long time. Trees grafted onto dwarfing rootstocks will need the support of their stakes for the whole of their lives. The stakes must be long enough to extend above-ground to just below the lowest branches.

Planting First have a look at the roots of the tree and with the secateurs cut off cleanly any that are damaged and balance up the root system by shortening any root which appears to have outgrown the rest. It will now be possible to see what size of hole is needed to take the roots of the tree or bush comfortably when they are spread out.

When the hole has been made, break up the soil at the bottom with a fork and build up a small mound of topsoil in the centre on which to place the tree. This is the time to put the stake in. It is helpful to have a cane handy which can be laid across the excavated hole to indicate the level of the soil surface.

The stake can then be driven in to the correct depth before the tree is put into position. It is not easy to plant a tree single-handed as there is plenty of work for two hands without having to spare one to hold the tree in position while stooping over the roots. So it is best at this stage to enlist some

ABOVE: *'Baldwin' blackcurrant bears its fruit later on in the season.*

TOP: *An inviting display of autumn fruit, all of which can be grown in a small garden.*

LEFT: *The main shapes in which to train fruit trees.*

help. The cane will again serve as a guide to ensure that the soil-line on the stem is kept at soil level.

Mix some moist peat with the topsoil before it is returned, as this promotes the growth of the roots.

Simply tipping the soil back into the hole is not good enough. Add a spadeful of soil at a time, gently shaking the tree up and down to filter the soil in between the delicate roots of the tree. Keep firming the soil down as you go along until you reach ground level, when a final firming down can be given with the feet and the surface raked over.

Now is the time for manure. Cover the whole area of the roots with a 2-in. deep mulch of rotted manure, compost, or peat. This will help to preserve the moisture in the spring.

Feeding The 'straight' fertilizers recommended elsewhere provide **the three major** nutritional elements: sulphate of **ammonia** and Nitro-chalk (for nitrogen), **sulphate of** potash (for potassium), and **superphosphates** (for phosphorus). Farmyard manure provides all these requirements and in addition contains the minor minerals which are essential to the tree in very small quantities. Proprietary mixed manures should give every satisfaction provided you use them strictly in accordance with the makers' instructions.

Pruning and thinning apples In order to cover briefly the main elements of pruning, it will be assumed that you are starting with

a 'maiden' tree which you propose to train into the shape you require. In fact, most gardeners buy two- or three-year old trees which the nurseryman has already formed into a cordon, pyramid, espalier, fan, and so on. Those who prefer to do this themselves will pay less, but will obviously have to wait a little longer before they can enjoy, quite literally, the fruits of their labours.

Starting, then, with a 'maiden' which you have just planted in the autumn the first problem is what pruning should be done. Pruning that is carried out while the tree is dormant in winter has the effect of promoting the growth of the wood. By contrast, summer pruning has the effect of encouraging the formation of fruit-buds and at the same time serves to keep the trees under control.

At the beginning of a tree's life growth is what is wanted to build up the framework desired. Consequently winter pruning at this stage can be quite heavy in relation to the size of the tree.

Bush trees You are aiming at a goblet-shaped tree, not a cordon. Therefore you want to encourage branching rather than a vertical central stem. So find a growth-bud 18–24 in. above soil level and cut off the top of the maiden tree just above it. This cut determines the length of the vertical stem below the branches.

During the following summer the result of this beheading process should be a number of lateral shoots. To make a good framework for an open goblet shape, wait until the second winter and then select three or four good shoots as evenly spaced round the tree as possible. These are to form the main branches of the tree, whose arrangement will ensure that later subsidiary branches are reasonably well placed.

Bearing this in mind, cut back the branches that have been selected to between a third and a half of their length at points where growth buds (which will later become subsidiary branches) are pointing in the right direction. Any other shoots which are not destined to form the main structure of the tree may be cut back to five buds if vigorous or one bud if weak.

By the third winter each main branch will have grown longer and produced some laterals. Cut back the extension by half and select two or three of the best laterals to become second generation branches forming the main structure of the tree, and cut these, too, back by half. All other laterals over 5-in. long should be reduced to the fourth bud, and those which were pruned during the second winter should be cut back to one bud of the new growth.

Also remove all feathers (side shoots or stems) from the main stem.

By the fourth winter the tree is essentially

formed, and you will now be less concerned with the growth of the wood than with encouraging fruiting. This means that, in relation to the size of the tree, from now on winter pruning can be less severe, and you can focus your attentions on producing the maximum fruit.

In order to do this properly you should find out (if you do not already know) whether your tree is a 'tip-bearer' or a 'spur-bearer'. Tip-bearers are those varieties which produce most of their fruit-buds at the tips of the young shoots and close to the tips of mature shoots. 'Bramley's Seedling', 'Cornish Gilliflower', 'Irish Peach', 'Lady Sudeley', 'Mr Gladstone', 'Tydeman's Early Worcester', and 'Worcester Pearmain' are all examples of tip-bearers.

Most other trees are spur-forming cultivars, with the exception of a few such as 'George Cave' and 'Crispin' ('Mutsu'), which bear fruit on both tips and spurs. Spurs are readily recognizable from their somewhat arthritic and crinkled texture and shape.

No matter what the variety, the beginning of pruning should always be hygiene. This means cutting out all the dead and diseased wood that can be found, and all shoots that are not growing in the right direction.

With the bush tree, in order to preserve the desired open goblet shape, shoots pointing inwards towards the middle must be cut out. If any shoots show signs of starting to cross one another so that they will rub together and chafe in wind, one of them will also have to be cut out at this stage.

Having got the tree in order, attention can now be turned to pruning for fruit. If you are dealing with a spur-forming tree remove about 2 in. from all the leaders, cut back all new laterals to three buds, and all previously pruned laterals to one bud of new growth. As time goes on the spurs will develop into increasingly complicated systems and may become congested. When this happens, some of the spurs may have to be removed entirely, and the others shortened by half. When growth is weak, cut back more severely, by half or even three quarters of the new growth.

With tip-bearers obviously you do not take off the tips. These should develop fruit buds during the next year, and the year after that they may be expected to produce fruit. However, failure to prune the tips at all would obviously lead in the end to congestion and loss of control. So a system known as 'renewal pruning' may be adopted.

In this system as many shoots are left unpruned as possible so as to produce fruit. But every year some of the laterals that have fruited are cut back to two buds, which are intended to produce two new shoots the following summer. When a tip-bearer has started to fruit there is no further need to tip the leaders.

Oblique cordons To produce a cordon from the 'maiden' that has just been planted a central vertical stem becomes the main requirement. So if it is a spur-bearer the head is not cut off, and no further winter pruning is given. If it is a tip-bearer it should be cut back by a quarter. Any feathers more than 4 in. long should be cut back to three buds.

In forming a cordon the object, of course, is to reduce laterals to negligible proportions. So in mid-July any that have reached a length of more than 9 in. and are becoming woody at the base should be reduced to the third leaf after the basal cluster. Do not touch the smaller laterals now, but wait until mid-September before giving them the same treatment. At this time some of those which you pruned back in mid-July may have produced a secondary growth. These should be pruned back to one bud from the point of origin.

In the summer after this deal with the laterals as in the previous summer, and if any sub-laterals which may have formed have themselves become mature with woody bases cut them back to one leaf after the basal cluster. Again wait until September to deal with laterals and sub-laterals which were not mature in July.

You can now wait until there is no room for the end of a cordon to grow any longer before you need to cut it back again. When that time comes it will have to be shortened to the appropriate length in May. It was mentioned in connexion with planting that cordons can be bent down year by year a few degrees at a time, thereby reducing their height. The cane to which the cordon is tied is unfastened from the wires and re-attached, with the cordon tree, in its new position.

Fruiting spurs that have become too long or congested should be cut back as described for bush trees.

Dwarf pyramids In the dwarf pyramid, as was said earlier, the object is to produce a Christmas-tree-like shape with a central leader up the middle, and branches sticking out all round it.

All the same, you start off from the maiden tree which has just been planted by beheading it about 20 in. above the soil level. The object is to encourage branching to start below this point, but because you want vertical growth to continue, you behead at a point just above a bud, and the shoot from this is to be encouraged to grow as vertically as possible.

To encourage this tendency even further,

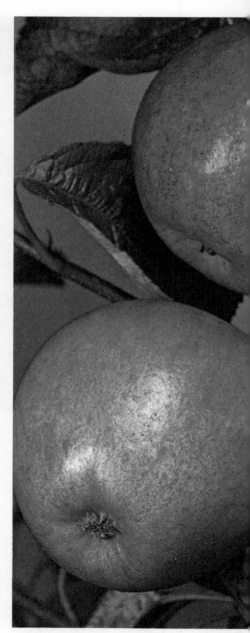

ABOVE: *'Ellison's Orange is a popular dessert apple.*

rub out the bud below the top bud on the tree to prevent a shoot forming which would sap the strength of the bud that was chosen. Below this, look for three or four buds which could produce shoots that will radiate evenly from the stem and rub out any other buds. The uppermost of the radiating buds will tend to grow the fastest, but the ones beneath it can be stimulated by cutting out a tiny wedge of bark ('notching') immediately above each of them.

Feathers between 9–12 in. from the ground can be used to form the first branches if they are cut back to about 6 in. by a downward-pointing bud.

During the first summer following planting it may be necessary to train the leader to grow vertically by tying it to a bamboo cane. It may be found that more than the four side-shoots originally planned for have appeared. Cut the unwanted shoots back to

four leaves after the basal cluster in mid-July.

During the second winter pruning is once again directed at encouraging the growth of wood in the right direction so as to produce a second tier of branches above the first, if possible radiating between them when the tree is viewed from above. The process is similar to that adopted in the first winter, and the central leader is again beheaded between 12–18 in. above the point where it was beheaded in the previous winter and to a bud growing out on the opposite side so as to encourage vertical growth of this central stem.

Again select three or four suitable buds to form the next tier of branches, rubbing out those which are not wanted, and notching the two lowest.

Then turn to the bottom tier of branches and prune their leaders back to downward-

pointing buds about 9 in. from the stem. From now onwards summer pruning of laterals and sub-laterals will follow the same plan as described in the section on cordons.

Winter pruning should continue along the lines adopted for the second winter until the pyramid is as high as desired. After that leave the central leader alone until the following May and then cut it back by half, subsequently restricting new growth to half an inch at each pruning.

Espaliers Espaliers can be bought 'ready made' with two or three pairs of horizontal branches. But if you wish to grow one against the wall of a house at any particular point you may be able to get a better 'fit' if you are prepared to train your own and wait that much longer for the fruit. This may be the appropriate point at which to note that generally apples do not do well against walls except in cold districts.

In ready-trained espaliers the bottom pair of branches may be about 15 in. from the ground, with about that much space from pair to pair, going up the central stem. If you want to do it yourself choose preferably an unfeathered maiden for planting and then cut it down to a bud a little above where you want the lowest pair of branches, and where the lowest horizontal support wire is to be.

Just as in the pyramid, this topmost bud is to provide the next 15 in. of vertical growth. Again, just as with the pyramid, choose buds below this (but in this case two only) which point outwards on each side along the axis of the supporting wire. Stimulate the lower of these by notching, and then rub out all other buds.

Do not attempt to force the side shoots to grow horizontally at once, but tie them to canes on each side at 45° to the ground and central stem, and then fasten the canes up to the supporting wires. To produce a good espalier you want to keep the two branches of each pair at equal strength. If, however, you find that either of the two shoots is tending to outstrip the other it is possible to retard the growth of this shoot by altering the angle of the cane to which it is tied, so that it is a little nearer to the horizontal, and by altering the angle of the partner shoot to a little bit nearer to the vertical in the same way. Then wait until the end of the first season before training both shoots nearer to the horizontal by lowering the canes to about 23°. By the end of the second season it should be possible to bend them down to the fully horizontal position.

Laterals and sub-laterals produced on these horizontal branches are treated just as if these branches were cordons.

Meanwhile vertical growth of the central stem will be continuing, and second, third, and fourth pairs of horizontal branches can be formed in exactly the same way as the first. The leaders should be allowed to grow on until they are as long as they are wanted, but if they are not growing well cut the new growth back in winter by at least half.

Fans Fans consist of a series of straight branches radiating from a single stem like a peacock's tail, and each branch is treated as a cordon. But when planning to grow this decorative shape it should be borne in mind that it is a more rigid form than the true cordon. Cordons can be bent down as they grow longer, but the angles of the fan branches are more or less unalterable, so when they have attained their allotted length the leaders will simply have to be stopped.

Fans can be obtained ready-trained by the nurseryman, but if you are prepared to spend the time and go to the trouble to train your own, you may well end up with a better result because of the tendency for nurserymen to incorporate all possible feathers into the fan-pattern in the maiden year so as to get quick results.

Begin with a maiden planted as early in autumn as possible, and leave it alone until early spring. Then, just before growth starts, cut it down to a sound bud not more than 2 ft. from the ground. Make quite certain that the bud selected *is* a pointed growth bud and not a rounded blossom bud. If there is any doubt look for a triple bud and cut down to this. One of them will be a growth bud.

The pruning plan to produce a fan tree consists in growing first a Y-shaped stem, each branch of which is eventually to produce three more branches, each of which is to produce three more still, and so on until the whole area allotted for the tree has been covered.

Having made this first cut, therefore, two other buds should be selected, about 9–12 in. from the ground, which point out sideways on each side of the main stem. These are to form the first two branches of the fan, so rub out all other buds and cut out any laterals flush with the stem.

The treatment of the two laterals is similar to that described for espaliers: that is, when each is about 18-in. long it is tied to a cane for attaching to the horizontal wire system at an angle of about 45°. Once again, the rate of growth of these two laterals can be kept in balance by adjusting the angles of the canes. While these laterals are growing the top bud is producing a vertical shoot. This is no longer wanted, so once the two laterals are tied up cut out the central vertical leader.

By February of the second winter the original two laterals (which are now the twin branches of the Y-shaped tree) will have made further growth, and they should

now be cut back to between 12–18 in. from where they divide. The cuts should be made just above buds which point either upwards or downwards, but not outwards, to provide extension growth.

You are now trying to produce, not a second generation of Y-formations, but a first generation of three-pronged growths, one on each of the two branches. Look, therefore, for two healthy shoots from above and below each branch to form the laterals and rub out all remaining shoots.

As soon as the new laterals are 18-in. long, they in their turn are attached to canes which are then tied to the wires so as to spread out evenly from the base. In subsequent years the process is repeated until there is no more room for it to continue.

For fruit production rub out any laterals that are growing away from the tree or in the direction of the wall, if the tree is being grown against one. Select suitable buds at intervals of about 6 in. and rub out all the others. Tie in the shoots that have been retained and stop their growing points when 18-in. long.

ABOVE: *Crab apples are often grown today as ornamental trees, but the sharp-tasting fruit can be used in preserves. This cultivar is 'Golden Hornet' which gives abundant crops of small yellow apples.*

OPPOSITE: *Blackberries in various stages of growth on a garden bush.*

Allow replacement shoots to grow out from close to the bases of those currently in fruit, continuing to rub out all the others, and after fruiting allow the best replacement shoot to take over, by cutting back the fruited lateral.

Thinning It is quite normal for apples to thin themselves by shedding a proportion of their immature fruit. However, in good years trees may produce very large numbers of undersized apples, and this can put such a strain on the tree that little fruit may be borne in the year following. As a result of this there may again be another glut the year after that, and for trees to acquire this habit of biennial bearing is quite a well known phenomenon, particularly among certain cultivars.

If you intervene by doing some thinning of your own you may well be able to prevent the development of this bad habit.

Thinning is best done in about three stages. Start by reducing each cluster to one apple. Generally there will be an apple in the middle of each cluster which is larger than the remainder, known as the 'king',

but for all its apparent promise this particular fruit seldom turns out well. So this should be the first one taken out, unless the cultivar is 'Worcester Pearmain'. At the same time remove any fruitlets that are obviously damaged or spoilt in any way. As a general guide, aim to thin out to a point at which one fruit remains for every 25 to 30 leaves. Thin out evenly so that no two apples are closer than 4-in. apart but for cooking varieties allow 6 in.

Watering If any signs of distress appear in the tree, watering has been left too late. This kind of advice is not easy to follow, and you must rely on your experience and common sense. The newly planted and young trees are particularly vulnerable in the spring, and an equable moisture supply in the soil must be maintained. Mulch the trees in early spring with 2 in. of rotted manure, garden compost, or peat to prevent undue loss of soil moisture.

Picking If an apple is held in the palm of the hand, lifted to a horizontal position and given a very slight twist, it will come away from the tree with the stalk on the apple, if

it is ready for picking. Apple picking extends from late July into November, for the late cultivars. The earlier cultivars are at their best if eaten soon after picking. Mid-season and late apples in particular must not be picked too soon, as this results in premature shrivelling if they are kept. Picked at the proper time, keeping improves them.

How to store apples The storage of apples depends on choosing a place where they will have the best humidity conditions and temperature. The air should be moist, ventilation good, and darkness is preferable. Also the temperature should not vary too much on either side of 40°F (4.5°C). If you have one, the average cellar provides excellent conditions for storing apples.

Space the apples out so that no two are touching, stalk uppermost, on clean shelves or slatted racks. A set of such racks will enable best use to be made of the space. If you do not have a cellar, the apples can be stored successfully in a shed, and even if the temperature there should fall occasionally to a few degrees below freezing no harm will be done. Apples should never be handled at such temperatures.

If it is difficult to find enough space, apples can be packed into boxes, provided each is wrapped separately in a square of newspaper or an oiled apple-wrap.

OTHER FRUITS

Blackberries The cultivation of blackberries and other berry fruits that grow on canes is fairly straightforward. They are trained against horizontal wires strained at intervals of 1 ft. above the ground to a height of up to 5 ft.

These fruits appear on canes that were produced in the previous year, so it is important to maintain the supply of these. When planting, all canes should be cut down to a sound bud about 9 in. above the ground to encourage the formation of young shoots, which are to fruit in the second year.

At the end of the picking season all old canes should be cut right down to ground level, and the young canes which are to replace them tied up to the support wires. It is a good thing to be methodical by keeping the old and the new canes separate. This not only avoids getting into a muddle over pruning, but also prevents the old canes from communicating disease to the young ones.

So spread out all the old canes to one side of the plant, and tie the new ones over to the other side, or else keep the fruiting canes spread out over the lower part of the wire system, and tie the young ones in the centre and along the top.

Recommended varieties of blackberries are: 'Bedford Giant' (late July), which is an early cultivar with large berries; 'Himalaya Giant' (Aug.–Sept.), a vigorous with large berries; and 'Oregon Thornless' (Aug.–Sept.) which, though less vigorous than the foregoing is easier to handle because of the absence of thorns.

There are several hybrids, including loganberries. The 'LY 59' strain is the finest cropper, in the second half of July. There is also a thornless loganberry with similar characteristics. The Japanese Wineberry (Aug.) is a decorative species with very sweet crimson berries; 'Malling Hybrid 53–16' has dark purple berries which make excellent jam; Youngberry (late July–Aug.) has large purplish-black berries, is very vigorous, and also thornless. All blackberries and their hybrids are self-fertile.

Blackcurrants Blackcurrants are encouraged to grow their shoots from as close to the ground as possible. Consequently, bushes received from the nursery are planted with the soil-line a little below the ground. They should then be given a mulch of rotted manure, compost or peat, and all the shoots cut down to within one inch of the mulch.

Blackcurrants do most of their fruiting on the young shoots that grew up in the previous summer, although they continue to produce some fruit on the older wood. The object of pruning, therefore is to keep up a constant supply of one-year-old shoots.

In the first year after planting all the shoots will be new, and in the next winter half of these should be cut right down, the remainder being retained for cropping. Thereafter, each year, as soon as picking is over, remove about a third of the shoots that have just fruited. Prune to get even distribution and keep the centre of the bush open.

Blackcurrants are greedy, and should be liberally dressed in winter or early spring with rotted farmyard or stable manure at the rate of 5 lb. per square yard. In addition to this $\frac{1}{3}$ oz. of sulphate of potash and 1 oz. of sulphate of ammonia per square yard should be sprinkled around the bushes in spring. Every third year give 1 oz. of superphosphates per square yard in addition.

As natural manure is often difficult to acquire, garden compost, lawn mowings, or peat can be substituted for the mulch provided the sulphate of potash is doubled and the sulphate of ammonia trebled.

In order to get a succession of fruit 'Laxton's Giant', which is very early, 'Blacksmith', 'Baldwin', and 'Amos Black', which is the latest of all, may be planted. They are all self-fertile.

Cherries Sweet cherries present special problems in gardens because at present they cannot be grown on dwarfing rootstocks, and also because there are no self-fertile

ABOVE: *Morello cherries are easier to grow than the sweet cherries as they are self-fertile and can be grown facing north.*
TOP: *Gooseberry 'Leveller' has a good flavour. It needs good soil and protection from birds.*
OPPOSITE: *An early dessert pear, 'Louise Bonne of Jersey'.*

sweet cherries, and consequently two trees have to be grown. The heavy demands that several trees of this size make on space can be to some extent overcome by growing them as fan-trained trees, but even then in order to keep them under control it may be necessary to resort to root-pruning.

The Morello sour cherry, which can be grown on a north aspect, can be grown singly, being self-fertile. It is also less vigorous than the sweet cherry, and can be grown, if desired, as a bush, or fan-trained.

Pruning should be done in spring, after the appearance of the buds, to encourage new growth. After the tree is established, cut out the old fruited shoots and some of the old branches each summer.

Gooseberries Gooseberries are generally grown as cup-shaped bushes, like the currants. They have a tiresome habit of bowing down their lower branches, which then take root at the tips and rapidly become chaotic unless well disciplined. 'Leveller' and 'Careless' live up to their names by being particularly apt to do this.

When planting, therefore, try to get a leg at least 6-in. high, and always prune leaders to upward-pointing buds.

Gooseberries fruit both on last year's wood and on spurs along the mature branches. The object of pruning is to produce a well-shaped framework in which the wood that has to be removed each year can be replaced by fresh laterals. So for the first years prune fairly hard with this object in mind, cutting branch leaders to half their length and laterals to three or four buds. Thereafter pruning is mainly a matter of keeping a good shape by removing branches that cross one another or are sagging to the ground, and keeping the centre open.

These removals will require replacing by upward-growing laterals selected at appropriate points and cut back to half their length to encourage them to grow on. In late June shorten all laterals to five leaves.

The attacks of birds are often very destructive to gooseberries, as some species are extremely fond of the young buds. This is the reason why many gardeners leave the autumn pruning after leaf-fall until the following spring. When the fruit first develops the birds will not usually attack the unripe berries, but as soon as the fruit begins to ripen protect them with netting.

Gooseberries can be trained as standards, espaliers, fans, or cordons. Pruning the cordons involves reducing the new growth of the vertical leader by a third in winter, or to 10 in., whichever is the less. Reduce laterals to four leaves.

A dressing of $\frac{1}{3}$ oz. sulphate of ammonia, 1 oz. of sulphate of potash, and 1 oz. of superphosphates per square yard should be given in early spring, followed by a mulch of farmyard manure.

As gooseberries are self-fertile the selection of varieties will be on a basis of preference, and succession if several bushes are to be grown. An early variety is 'Keepsake', with a rich flavour, for picking early pale green. For the mid-season 'Careless' is a whitish-green berry and a good all-rounder; 'Leveller' is considered the best for flavour – it is a greenish-yellow berry needing a good soil to grow in. 'Lancer' is a greenish-yellow late variety with a fine flavour, which is good for bottling and dessert.

Pears Growing pears is somewhat similar to growing apples, but they have one or two habits that are slightly different. As they are inclined to be slightly ahead of apples at all stages they are more likely to come into blossom when frosty weather may itself do damage, or by discouraging flying insects hinder the necessary pollination.

On the other hand, they are inclined to be more laggardly in coming into fruit after they are first planted.

In the early stages the pruning technique recommended for apples may be followed, but at this stage it should be less severe. However, once fruit starts to appear give them harder pruning than apples, reducing leaders by $\frac{2}{3}$ to $\frac{3}{4}$, laterals to three buds and sublaterals to one.

Just as with apples, there are spur-bearers and tip-bearers, examples of the latter being 'Jargonelle', 'Joséphine de Malines', and 'Packham's Triumph'. Prune these tip-bearers rather lightly and retain all short laterals for the sake of their terminal fruit-buds. The spur-bearers generally produce denser spur-formations than do apples.

When grown as cordons, dwarf, pyramids, espaliers, or fans the pruning is the same as for apples, but a little earlier because of the earlier maturity of the shoots.

The fruitlets should likewise be thinned out for good-sized pears and regular cropping. If extra-heavy crops occur, reduce the fruit to one or at the most, two fruitlets per spur.

Water the trees in dry weather, particularly when they are young, and give them a spring mulch.

Pears should be picked in the same way as apples, but with considerably more care because of their great liability to bruising and the brittleness of the spurs. Do not wait for pears to become soft. The early cultivars can be picked (and should be eaten) in late July or early August.

The ideal storage environment for pears is very slightly drier and warmer than for apples. It is more important, too, to keep them separate on the shelves or racks. Wrapping and box-storage is not recommended. Do not pick late-keeping cultivars too early, if they are to keep well. They should be brought out of storage when they are nearly ripe and finished off at the normal house temperature.

Feeding: keep the surrounding ground cleanly cultivated, and in spring mulch with rotted farmyard-manure or garden compost. For the latter peat may be substituted but a dressing of 1 oz. of sulphate of ammonia, 2 oz. of superphosphates, and $\frac{1}{2}$ oz. of sulphate of potash per square yard must be applied first. Remember that pears are more likely to be short of nitrogen than apples, and less likely to be short of potash.

Plums and gages The best soil for plums is a deep, heavy loam or well-drained clay. These fruits also are nitrogen lovers and will do well on an old vegetable plot. If they have to be grown in light soil good quality fruit and long life are not to be expected, and there may be an exaggerated tendency for the branches to break.

Both plums and gages may be grown as standards, half-standards, bushes, and fans, but they do not do well as cordons or espaliers. The pruning should be done in summer, spring, or early autumn immediately after the crop has been picked.

For bush trees, freshly-planted maidens in their first year should be beheaded to about 3 ft. from soil level. Do this in the spring, just before growth begins, and then existing feathers may be selected for fruit branches if they are well spaced out.

To counteract the tendency for plum branches to break away from the stem, you should aim for branches that make a wide angle with it, and select laterals accordingly.

In the second year cut the branch leaders to half in the early spring.

In the third year cut the previous season's growth by half. Thereafter, starting between June and August, keep the centre of the tree open by removing all crossing branches, and cut out dead wood before mid-July. It is not wise to over-prune plums, but overcrowding must also not be permitted, and laterals may have to go, or be shortened, during the summer to prevent it. If the growth is behind, hard prune some of the laterals to encourage them to produce new wood.

Always bear in mind that plums fruit on second-year wood and on spurs developing on older wood.

Pyramids Plums cannot be bought as ready-trained pyramids, but have to be produced from a maiden on 'St Julien A' rootstock along the lines described below. Many gardeners consider this is well worth doing because the result is a tree only 10-ft. across and little more than 9-ft. high. In addition to economizing on space, this form of tree, with relatively short branches, is not likely to suffer so severely from branch-breakage, and this discourages the ever-present threat of silver-leaf infection.

Begin in late March by cutting the maiden tree short to 5 ft. above the ground, and removing entirely all feathers that appear up to 18 in. from the soil level. Any feathers above this should be halved. Towards the end of July the growth of new shoots comes to an end, and at that time branch leaders should be cut back to about 8 in. leaving a downward- or outward-pointing bud, and the laterals shortened to 6 in.

Thereafter, the central vertical stem should be controlled as already described in the section on pyramids for apples. That is, it should be cut down to buds pointing in alternate directions out from the tree each year, and reduced to one third of the growth it has made. When growth ceases, again cut leaders to 8 in. and laterals to 6 in., and once the central stem has attained 9 ft. cut it down to 1 in. of new growth every year in May. If it makes any attempt to form a replacement vertical it must be dealt with severely by total removal.

The manner of forming *fans* was likewise described earlier under apples, and the same procedure should be adopted. However, once fruiting has begun, the fact that plums fruit on both old and new wood has to be taken into account. There is no need to cut back laterals as soon as they have fruited. Those which are not required for formation or replacement should be pinched out as soon as they have made six leaves. This is not all done at once, but on several occasions throughout the growing season.

Another point that will require constant attention is the rubbing out of shoots that attempt to grow inwards to a wall or directly away from it, which should be done as soon as they appear.

After picking, all these stopped laterals should be reduced by half, and any vigorous shoots that seem likely to grow vertically should either be trained into a horizontal direction or removed.

As with other fruit, plum trees need to be thinned out. This not only promotes

regular cropping, the main object with glut crops on bush or pyramid trees is to produce better sized fruit, lessen the risk of branch-breakage through heavy burdens of sub-standard plums, and discourage silver leaf disease.

The job should be done in early June, and a second time after the natural crop during stone formation. The stalks should be left on the tree by breaking or cutting off the fruitlets. For dessert plums work to a minimum spacing of 2-in. apart. The smaller cooking varieties may be given a little less space.

Plums should be mulched lightly with rotted farmyard manure or garden compost in early spring, and this should be forked into the top few inches of soil in autumn. They will not require feeding with artificial fertilizers unless growth is slow. In that case, wait until cropping has begun each year, and give a dressing of 1 oz. of Nitro-chalk and $\frac{1}{2}$ oz. of sulphate of potash per square yard in February. Every third year add 1 oz. per square yard of super-phosphates. If peat was used instead of manure or compost the quantity of Nitro-chalk should be doubled.

Raspberries There are two sorts of raspberry: summer fruiting and autumn fruiting. The former fruit on the new canes that were made during the previous summer, and the latter from those which grew in the summer of the same year.

When planting raspberries preparations should be made for their training as described in the section on blackberries (page 123), with wires and stakes. Plant them 2 ft. apart, with 5 ft. between the rows, and after planting cut the canes down to about 2 ft.

When growth begins in spring cut the canes down again to a live bud, this time 10 in. above the soil.

The object is to get a good root-system going, and the whole of the plant's energy should be devoted to this, so there will be no raspberries for the table in the summer of the year of planting. Instead, a number of canes will be produced from which the first crop will be gathered the following summer.

As soon as this has been done, cut all the canes that fruited right down to the ground, select six of the most vigorous new un-fruited canes, and tie these up to the wires. Remove all others. All that remains to be done is to tip these canes to about 4 ft. 6 in. high in February.

The autumn-fruiting cultivars crop, not on the canes of the previous summer, but on the canes produced in the summer immediately preceding the autumn in which they are harvested. New plants that were cut down in April will consequently make fruit in the year of their planting, if they are allowed to.

Just as with the summer-fruiting raspberries, it is important to establish a good root-system, and this first fruiting must not be permitted. It is prevented by cutting off all the blossoms. Thereafter the fruited canes should be cut down each February, including the first February after planting, when the canes that were not allowed to fruit are also cut.

Birds delight in raspberries in the early part of the summer, and in some districts can become so gluttonous that they will almost fight you for a fruit while you are picking. Later in the year their interest turns towards the many other foods available to them, so it is the summer-fruiting varieties of raspberry that are most in need of netting or other protection.

Other treatments required for raspberries, described below, apply equally to summer and autumn sorts.

It is very important to keep the soil around the raspberry rows moist throughout the whole of the growing period, and it will often be necessary to use the hose to water them during June. The soil that they are growing in ought to be well enriched, and consequently the weeds among the canes can present quite a problem, especially as they cannot be hoed away very easily without damaging the root-systems of the raspberries, part of which lie very close to the surface. The weeds must be kept down, however, and a contact weedkiller can be used both to keep down the weeds and to eliminate the unwanted suckers which often appear in large numbers out of the row. If these are not controlled the raspberry plantation can rapidly turn into a jungle.

In the first year mulch the rows at 5 lb. per square yard with farmyard or stable manure in April. Raspberries need a regular supply of nitrogen and potash most of the time, so after the planting year give, with the mulch, 1 oz. per square yard each of sulphate of ammonia and sulphate of potash in February, adding 2 oz. per square yard of superphosphates every third year.

Varieties Summer-fruiting cultivars are available as earlies, mid-season, or late. Of the earlies a good variety is 'Malling Promise', which is a heavily cropping, vigorous raspberry with an excellent flavour. 'Lloyd George' is often preferred, not only for flavour but for its long picking season, and although it is less vigorous than 'Malling Promise' this may be compensated for by planting it at about 1 ft. intervals instead of at the usual spacing. Sometimes 'Lloyd George' will produce a second crop in autumn, and indeed it may be grown as an autumn variety if the old canes are cut down in February.

Of the mid-season varieties 'Malling Jewel' is popular, especially in Scotland as its late flowering can often keep it clear of early frosts. This is another cultivar that can be grown at half-spacing because it is not one of the most vigorous.

The late cultivar 'Norfolk Giant' enables the summer-fruiting raspberry season to be prolonged, but it yields a somewhat sour berry.

Two autumn-fruiting cultivars are worth noting. 'September' yields large berries of excellent flavour, though it is somewhat optimistically named as it most frequently fruits in October. 'Zeba' also has good flavour and large berries. Raspberries are all self-fertile.

ABOVE: 'Denniston's Superb' plums can be trained to grow as a pyramid.
TOP: Raspberry 'Lloyd George' is a good early variety which has a long fruiting season and may even produce a second crop later in the year.
OPPOSITE: A fan-trained plum tree, 'Early Laxton'. Bamboo is used to train the branches.

Red and white currants Red and white currants are treated together here because their cultivation is essentially the same. Both are quite different from the blackcurrant, not only in management but in the kind of soil they prefer.

Unlike the blackcurrant which produces most of its fruit on young shoots, red and white currants produce most of theirs on the oldest wood, that is, on short spurs on old wood and at the bases of young shoots, but not above. Like gooseberries they tend to get their buds pecked out in winter by hungry birds, so pruning is often delayed until early spring when the buds are beginning to make their appearance and you can see what you are doing with your secateurs. Bird-repellent sprays can also be used.

These currants are usually bought as one-year-old bushes, which will normally have three or four branches. All of these should be cut back by two-thirds to outward-pointing buds. As with all currants (and indeed with all bush fruit) the object is to produce a cup-shaped bush with an open centre.

In the second winter cut back by two-thirds again, eliminate laterals which are growing in the wrong direction, and shorten those which are not wanted to one bud.

By the next winter sufficient main branches should have been produced to give the bush its final structure. From now on, therefore, pruning is confined to shortening branch leaders by a half and laterals to one bud. To preserve the open form of the bush always prune to outward-pointing buds. It will be necessary thereafter to maintain the bush by tipping the leaders as long as they are vigorous, or cutting them back somewhat if the growth appears to be weak.

Red and white currants can be grown, like gooseberries, as single or double vertical cordons against walls and fences, wherever there is room. Prune them in the same way, but treat the laterals more severely in winter, leaving only one or two buds.

The easiest way to pick them is to cut off whole bunches at a time with scissors.

The plants should be dressed in February with ¾ oz. per square yard of sulphate of potash, and with 1 oz. of superphosphates per square yard every third year. In late April give them a 1-in. deep mulch of rotted manure or compost, but if peat is used instead incorporate 1 oz. per square yard of sulphate of ammonia with the February dressing.

Suggested very early cultivars are 'Jonkheer Van Tets'; for earlies, 'Laxton's No. 1'; for mid-season, 'Red Lake'; and for lates, 'Wilson's Long Bunch'. Cultivars of white currant are 'White Versailles' for earlies and 'White Dutch' for mid-season.

Strawberries Strawberries should be planted in a well-cleaned bed as once the plants are in position hoeing has to be very superficial to avoid damaging the roots of the strawberries themselves. A contact weedkiller can be used to suppress weeds, but it must not be allowed to touch the leaves of the strawberry plants.

One of the chores of growing strawberries is preventing the rain splashing soil over the growing fruit. The best method is usually to spread clean straw between the rows and tuck it under the plants. Special mats can be bought, at a price, and do the job more neatly. Black polythene sheeting can also be used, but it must be weighted down with soil or stones to prevent the wind getting under it and blowing it away. Technically any of these methods constitutes a mulch, and none of them should be put down earlier than is necessary because they increase the risk of frost damage.

Strawberries reproduce themselves by putting out cord-like runners which produce plantlets at intervals. These take root wherever they can find a foothold to produce new plants. This process starts even while the plants are fruiting and becomes increasingly active as the season goes on. Obviously it makes a considerable demand on the energy of the plant, so unless any are wanted for raising further plants the runners should be cut off as soon as they appear.

Raising new plants from your own runners carries with it the risk of virus infection, and for this reason many gardeners always buy new plants as they require them, and replace the beds once every three years or so.

But to raise your own plants is very easy. Even if you did nothing at all, many of the plantlets on the runners would take root of themselves, but it is much better to sink 3-in. pots of John Innes Potting Compost or soilless compost beneath runner plantlets that have been allowed to grow on, and to pin the plantlet into this with a galvanized wire hairpin, or simply put a stone on it. Pinch out the tip of the runner that is continuing on to form another plantlet. At the end of July you have only to sever the runner between plantlet and parent, and lift out and replant the young strawberry plant a couple of weeks afterwards.

Feed the beds in early autumn with a $\frac{1}{2}$ oz. per square yard each of sulphate of ammonia and sulphate of potash raked in, and spread a mulch of rotted farmyard or stable manure or garden compost at the rate of about 5 lb. per square yard.

By raising some plants in the greenhouse strawberries can be had very much earlier in the year. For this purpose use early-rooted runners, if possible in late July, and plant them in 9-in. pots using JIP 3 potting

compost. These pots can be left in the open on a sheet of polythene until mid-November, when they can either be turned on their sides to prevent over-watering or put into a cold frame.

Transfer them to an unheated greenhouse towards the end of January, and when fresh growth appears water them with discretion and give them a night temperature of 45°F (7°C) to begin with. The night heat may be gradually increased to 50°F (10°C) when the blossom trusses appear. The flowers will need pollinating by dusting their centres with a camel's hair brush, and after the blossom has fallen the night temperature should be brought up to 55°F (13°C). At this point supply liquid feeding with caution until the berries start to turn red.

Good cultivars for this purpose are 'Royal Sovereign' and 'Grandee'.

Another method of getting strawberries two or three weeks earlier is by covering first-year plants with cloches or polythene tunnels at the end of February. It will not be possible to deal with weeds after this is done, so they should be eliminated before the plants are covered. Keep the cloches closed until the blossom opens, when the cloches will have to be pulled apart a little to enable pollinating insects to play their important part.

Close the cloches again by 4 p.m. In April

ABOVE: *The perpetual-fruiting strawberry 'Gento', which yields fruit from June through to October.*

and May there is a risk of a high build-up of temperature so the cloches or tunnels should be kept ventilated at this time. If watering seems necessary in dry weather give the water in the morning to allow the plants to dry before the cloches are closed again later in the day.

Perpetual-fruiting strawberries will yield fruit between June and October. They require slightly different treatment. In the year of planting all flower-trusses that appear before June should be nipped off, but in subsequent years all blossom may be allowed to develop. Some cultivars of this type do not produce runners as freely as the others, and when plantlets appear on them they can be allowed to take root and may flower and fruit in the same season. In the first year cut off all old leaves after cropping, as with ordinary strawberries, but thereafter the leaves can be left to wither off by themselves. Burn all strawberry leaves that are removed.

PESTS AND DISEASES OF FRUIT

Aphids Aphids come in many sizes, shapes, and colours, the best known of which is the common greenfly. They multiply at a phenomenal rate, huge colonies building up apparently overnight as may be seen, for example, when the growing tips of broad beans are found to be coated with the black variety. Aphids go for growing points and young leaves, which they speedily ruin by sucking out all the sap. They are also carriers of strawberry and raspberry virus diseases (see below). Their eggs overwinter on trees.

Woolly aphid.

Caterpillars One of the best known of these predators of fruit is the winter moth caterpillar known as 'loopers' from their characteristic method of perambulation. The adult moths lay their eggs from October to March on twigs behind the buds.

Capsids Capsids also overwinter on the trees, and on hatching out they devour first the leaves and then the fruitlets, particularly of apples, currants, and gooseberries.

Sawflies These attack chiefly apples and pears, boring into the fruit, which drop off the trees as the larvae bore into them. Their activities are recognized by the mass of sticky excreta which they leave around the holes that they make in the fruit.

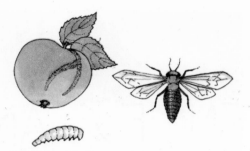

Sawfly and larva.

Codling moths This moth lays its eggs in early summer on the young fruits, into which the larva bores. Often their activities are not immediately evident until the apple is cut and the grub discovered in the core. They will also attack pears, but less commonly.

Codling moth.

Spraying

Only a few of the worst of the insect pests have been mentioned above. The habit of many of them of overwintering on the trees enables them to be suppressed by drenching the dormant trees and bushes in winter with tar oil. Unfortunately this process also kills many useful insects which do no harm to the fruit and which prey on spider mites that will proliferate if their natural enemies are removed. For this reason the tar oil treatment should not be given more often than once in three years.

The pests can also be attacked while they are active. Spraying at the green cluster stage of apples and pears deals with caterpillars and greenfly. Then, at the pink-bud stage of apples, or white-bud stage of pears, a second spraying will help to keep down capsids. Yet a third spraying as soon as 90% of the blossom petals have fallen will deal with sawfly and tortrix caterpillars. Spray in mid-June for codling moth and tortrix, and repeat a fortnight later. For plums spray between bud-burst and white-bud stage for aphids and caterpillars, and again when the petals have fallen and the fruitlets have set, for sawfly.

Colonies of aphids should be sprayed whenever they are seen.

It should be well known that modern pesticides can be highly specific and are often extremely toxic. Some of them are injurious to some plants. However small the print on the pack, the instructions should always be carefully read and followed. Most of them should not be put on garden produce that is shortly to be consumed. But there are substances, such as derris, which are harmless to humans and can be safely used at all times.

Brown rot This fungus disease appears as concentric rings of small pustules on ripe or ripening fruit, and is very contagious. The affected fruit must be burnt, and you should wash your hands after handling it.

Brown rot.

Leaf curl This is commonest in apricots, peaches, and nectarines. Young leaves become puckered and curled, turn first yellow, then reddish, and erupt with 'blisters'. Lime-sulphur should be sprayed in late February or early March just before the buds swell, and again in autumn just before the leaves fall. It must not be applied during growth, when captan should be substituted.

Scab This is a fungoid disease most prevalent in districts where humidity is high. It attacks the skin of apples and pears and can be controlled by regular spraying with captan at the green-cluster, pink- (or white-)bud, and petal-fall stages.

Silver leaf Plums are particularly subject to silver leaf, and some measures that help to control it have already been described in the section on the management of plums. It may also attack apples. The leaves assume a silvery appearance, and if the wood of affected branches or shoots is examined it will be found to have become stained brown. It enters by injuries to the bark, usually between September and May, and is consequently invited by pruning during that period. Cut out infected wood in midsummer. Smooth off all wounds and protect the cut surfaces with tree-pruning paint.

Virus diseases These are likely to be met with most frequently in strawberries and raspberries, whose yield will plummet if they are affected. The warning signs appear as abnormal pigment and pigment distribution in the leaves which most gardeners will find difficult to distinguish from similar markings due to mineral deficiencies.

The best prevention is to buy only new stock from a nurseryman who takes part in the Government Certification scheme.

If abnormal markings are found, it is best to treat the plants for mineral deficiency by watering the leaves with foliar feed containing chelated trace minerals. Do not use any such plants for propagation, and if the above treatment does no good and cropping fails, dig up the plants and burn them.

VEGETABLES – AN A-Z FOR THE HOME GROWER

For even the most amateur gardener, one season's successful attempt at vegetable growing is likely to develop into a lifelong pleasure. A modest amount of effort can be rewarded by really fresh vegetables and salads of a flavour which cannot be matched by any on the greengrocer's shelf. If you are concerned about chemical versus organic fertilizers, it is within your own control how the plants are grown. On economic grounds, too, the cost of a packet of seed or nursery-raised plants is a fraction of the value of the product, even at the cheapest time in the season.

New strains of seed developed for success in the English climate make it possible to harvest such items as corn-on-the-cob, melons and peppers from open ground in a wide area as well as the traditional peas, beans, cabbages, and potatoes. The flow chart on pages 146–7 shows how to achieve self-sufficiency in vegetables throughout the year, and the sowing and yield charts overleaf will help you establish how much space is needed.

Space in the small garden will be at a premium, especially if the vegetables are competing with flowers for the prime positions, but a single 10-ft. row of runner beans, trained on netting along a fence, can produce up to 20 lbs. of fresh beans between August and October – and if that is too much for immediate needs the surplus can be frozen. A dozen tomato plants take up little space but, with lettuce planted as a border in front of them, will provide the two main ingredients of salads from late July to September. With a greenhouse, of course, the span is greatly prolonged.

In the larger garden it should be possible to grow more than sufficient green and root vegetables (except perhaps potatoes), plus salad stuff, for the average family. If you have a freezer, the surplus can be stored.

There are a few basic precepts founded on common sense and simple logic to achieve the best results. Thorough digging should be done in the late autumn to clean the ground of deep-rooted weeds and, in particular, of couch-grass and nettles, which can be persistent pests if not painstakingly eradicated. The other grasses and surface-rooting weeds can be buried, along with slow-acting chemical or organic fertilizers to add to the humus in the soil. Left rough-dug, it will be broken down by winter rain and frost to leave easily worked and fertile ground in the spring. It is not difficult then to produce a fine tilth with fork, hand-cultivator and rake in which the seeds will luxuriate and, hopefully, germinate. By this time you will have planned what and where to grow.

There are three factors which have a bearing on this:

Rotational cropping This is as desirable in the garden as it is essential to the commercial grower. It helps to prevent the ground from becoming stale and it prevents the onset of some pests and diseases associated with taking the same crop from the same ground year after year. An exception could be onions, which do best in very finely worked soil, richer than that needed for most vegetables: to many gardeners the onion patch is always the onion patch. The chart overleaf shows a suggested plan over a three-year cycle.

Successional cropping This is simply the discipline of *not* sowing all the seed at the same time. By planting, say, a row of peas at fortnightly intervals through March to mid-May, and varying the variety, the crop can be gathered from July to September. Early potatoes take a good deal of space, but as they are lifted in June and July, the ground is then available for spinach, late radishes and cabbage for the winter.

Intercropping This is a space-saving device whereby rows of a fast-growing crop are interspersed with ones of slower growth, (which is then also sufficiently widely spaced). Lettuce, for example, can be planted between rows of peas.

More basic principles

(1) Sow small seeds evenly and not too thickly. Pelleted seeds are easier to handle and separate.

(2) Don't cover seed with more soil than is necessary: for small seeds the merest dusting is sufficient.

(3) It is well worthwhile using a string between two pegs to aid in spacing the rows correctly and keeping them straight. Apart from looking better, the practical result is that it is much easier to hoe the weeds without inadvertently decimating the crop.

(4) Frequent light hoeing keeps the weeds down more effectively and with less effort than a massive onslaught when the weeds are higher and stronger than the plants. Not only will the weeds be shading the young vegetables from the light and taking nutrient from the soil, but weeding can then disturb the plant roots and further slow their growth.

Seeds and seedlings

The days of the local seedsman measuring out ounces of seed from bulk supplies have passed. The seed companies make life easier for us by giving at least the basic planting instructions on the packet, and by supplying some of the smaller seeds in clay pellets. These make more uniform sowing easier, which reduces the need for thinning. With pelleted seeds it is important that the ground is both moist and friable at planting time; it must be kept that way during the germination period so that the clay-coating quickly dissolves and does not hinder development.

The term 'F$_1$' hybrid is applied to a number of seeds. It indicates that the variety has been developed under particularly strict conditions, designed to produce very vigorous growth and uniformity. Of value especially to the exhibition grower, the F$_1$ hybrids are also useful for such plants as sweet corn which, not being native to this country, need all the help they can get to achieve a good crop.

Guide to approximate yield of popular vegetables

per 10 ft. row:				
Beans Broad	5 lb.	Kale	15 lb.	
French	2½ lb.	Leek	8 lb.	
Runner	40 lb.	Lettuce	15 heads	
Beetroot	8½ lb.	Onion	6 lb.	
Broccoli	12 lb.	Parsnip	8 lb.	
Brussels sprouts	5½ lb.	Peas	3½ lb.	
Cabbage Spring	7 lb.	Potatoes (main crop)	15 lb.	
Autumn/Winter	15 lb.	Shallots	6 lb.	
Savoy	15 lb.	Spinach (summer)	3 lb.	
Carrot	7½ lb.	Swede	9 lb.	
Cauliflower	10 lb.	Tomato (outdoor)	4 lb. per plant	
Endive	8 heads	(under glass)	6 lb. per plant	
		Turnip	9 lb.	

Crop rotation over a three-year cycle

First year
Potatoes
followed by broccoli, spring cabbage, and leeks.

Second year
Lettuces, radishes, tomatoes, spring onions followed by cauliflower, Brussels sprouts, savoy cabbage.

Third year
Peas, beans, summer spinach.
Carrots, parsnips, turnips, beetroot.

The vegetables described and illustrated in these pages are capable of flourishing out-of-doors without the aid of a greenhouse in the southern half of the country, though some will need protection in the north. In many instances, seeds can be brought on much earlier if sheltered conditions can be given. Using a cold frame or cloches means that some crops, such as lettuce, can be left to mature in them. Even better for seed germination are propagators which, to all intents and purposes, are ultra-mini hot-houses. They provide a controlled environment for the seeds until the seedlings are of a size to plant out. Being portable, they can be kept on a sunny window-sill, and this allows the seeds to benefit from indoor temperatures in the early stages. As the seedlings grow and become stronger, they can be moved to progressively lower temperatures so that they are hardened off by the time they are ready for planting out. The tray of the propagator should have a solid rather than a perforated base and you should line it with an inch of peat to retain the moisture. The seeds are sown in a 1½–2 in. layer of seed compost in ordinary plastic seed trays or individual pots (which can be the fibre type for planting straight into the ground, pot and all), and well watered. As the clear plastic top of the propagator retains virtually all the moisture inside, very little further attention is needed, except to ensure that the compost is kept moist. The main danger with a propagator is that the seedlings can easily grow too quickly and become thin and wasted, because the temperature and humidity in it can be very high. Hardening off to produce strong, sturdy plants is the art of the business.

Although it is not difficult to raise any vegetable from seed, in some instances it is more convenient to buy plants. Tomatoes and cucumbers are examples; those grown by experienced nurserymen are likely to be stronger and ready for planting earlier than those home grown from seed.

A spadeful of garden soil, well sieved and free from weed, will act as a seed bed in a tray, but a bag of special seed compost is a worthwhile investment. The enriched and sterilized loam, which it commonly is, will give the seeds a much better start.

Watering is essential for all plants, and especially young ones. Better too much than too little, but better still, try to achieve overall moistness rather than sogginess. When the plants are large enough, leave the rose off the watering can, and water each plant at its base. The rose gives a fine appearance of wetting everything, but much of the water stays on the leaves, where it is needed less than at the roots.

Soil care

If you have the good fortune to own a garden of loamy soil, which has been grazed by cattle and horses for a generation or so, and is well drained, you have nothing to do except to dig it and weed it. The object of manuring and fertilizing is to achieve ground that is easily worked, full of humus and with a good body to it. Old fashioned farmyard manure, well rotted, is still the best, and thoroughly composted garden refuse comes a very close second. Both add bulk to the soil as well as replacing the nutrients it needs. Compound organic fertilizers add the nutrient in more concentrated and controlled form, but do not have the body. Farmyard manure can be bought, either as a dehydrated product from a garden shop or in its natural form, if you live in the country.

The compost heap is not the same as the rubbish dump: stones, old plastic bags and various bits of broken junk do not make compost. Woody prunings from roses, and fruit trees are not good either as they take a long time to break down. So the compost heap should be exclusively soft vegetable waste of all sorts, including grass cuttings and some kitchen waste, such as tea leaves and eggshells. The heap should be no more than 2 ft. high or 3 ft. across, and should be turned, after about a month, so that all the material rots thoroughly. The addition of a rotting agent, such as Garotta,

ABOVE: *A fine head of Brussels sprouts, one of the most productive vegetable crops to grow.*
TOP: *'January King', a winter cabbage which should be sown as seed in April and transplanted in June. The crop will be ready for harvesting from November through to March.*
OPPOSITE: *Broad beans do well on poor soil and are very hardy plants.*

will help to speed the process, especially if fairly tough items, such as cabbage stalks, are included. If space is a problem, compost bins are available, or a simple wire cage can be made to contain the material. Air and water play their part in the rotting process so an open construction is necessary.

Top dressing is more to aid the plants than the soil, and gives an added boost of fertilizer when and where it is most needed. Allied to this is mulching – spreading a thin layer of compost between the growing rows. This also has the effect of blanketing weeds and helping the soil to retain moisture. Black polythene strips achieve the same result, but add nothing to the humus in the soil.

Insecticides

The first rule about insecticides is *not* to use them except when really necessary. They will not only kill the pests at which they are aimed but also other insects which may be beneficial, or at least harmless: black fly, for example, are food for ladybird larvae and some small birds. If spray you must, the second rule is to use organic rather than synthetic sprays or powders – many of which, such as DDT, are no longer marketed for gardeners. Those with pyrethrum, derris or nicotine as a base are the most common of the traditional 'contact' insecticides, and, if correctly used, are not harmful to pets, except fish. More recently, 'systemic' types have been introduced, which are absorbed by the leaves, and which kill insects feeding on them. The systemics are longer-lasting in their effect than the contact types, but are more toxic to bees and other useful insects; they can also be harmful to domestic pets. Whichever type you decide upon, mix exactly as the manufacturers direct; a solution too diluted will be a waste of time, and one too strong may well do more harm than good. Do the job thoroughly when applying, going under the leaves as well as above with the contact sprays, and remembering afterwards to wash out all utensils with the greatest care. Finally, do not harvest any crop until all toxicity has dispersed, usually 7–14 days.

VEGETABLES FROM A–Z

Artichoke – Globe A splendid, ornamental, thistle-like plant, 4–6 ft. tall, which produces an edible flower-head that is picked before it opens. May be grown from seed sown in a frame in March or outdoors in April, but it is preferable to buy young plants which should be spaced at 3-ft. intervals in an open position. Mulch in May, and cut all the flower stems in the first season. The plants will then crop for two further years, after which there should be a new

planting. Cover the crowns with straw for winter protection.
Varieties 'Vert de Laon'; 'Grand Vert de Camus'.

Artichoke – Jerusalem A hardy perennial of the sunflower family, it has edible, potato-like tubers. Soil need not be rich and the plants will accept a semi-shady position. Plant tubers in February, 6 in. deep and 15 in. apart in rows $2\frac{1}{2}$ ft. apart. The plants grow as high as 10 ft. tall. Harvest from November to February, when some of the tubers can be replanted for the following season.

Asparagus A vegetable for the gourmet, and one which requires patience. Once established, the plants will produce for a number of years and the asparagus bed should therefore be very well prepared and fully cleaned of weeds. Usually the asparagus bed is 4 ft. wide to allow for three rows of plants, each 1 ft. apart in rows 15 in. apart. The bed is built up about 6 in. higher than the surrounding garden to assist in

drainage. Seed can be sown directly onto the bed in April, in drills $\frac{1}{2}$ in. deep; the seedlings can be thinned later to the correct distance. No crop should be taken in the first or second years, except the by-product of asparagus fern, which should be cut down in October. Slightly more speedy results can be obtained by buying one- or two-year-old plants and planting in April. They will need to be ordered in advance and must be planted immediately on arrival in case they dry out. Let them become well established in the first year, but look forward to better things the next. The shoots should not be cut after the middle of June; if there is really more than you can eat, it is eminently freezable. Keep the ground weed-free and apply a 1-in. mulch of compost or manure in the spring. Some growers also recommend 1 oz. of salt at the same time, or using a seaweed mulch.
Variety 'Superior F_1'.

Beans – Broad The hardiest of the bean family and grown solely for its seed. Not too fussy about the soil in which it grows and manure should be used sparingly – no more than 1 cwt. to 15 sq. yd. – or it can follow a crop such as potatoes for which the ground was well fertilized. The plants grow to about 3 ft. so that some staking and tying will be necessary. Pinch out the growing tips when each plant has set two or three clusters of pods. Pick when the pods are young and full, but before they become leathery. Most varieties freeze well. Watch out for black fly, which are most likely to attack late sowings or plants suffering from lack of moisture. It will help, too, to cut off shoots from the base of the plants.

Varieties numerous, e.g. 'Aquadulce'; 'Conqueror'; 'Giant Windsor'; 'Imperial Green Longpod'; 'Imperial Green Windsor'; 'The Sutton' (the only dwarf variety).

Beans – Dwarf (French) Ready for harvesting in between the broad bean and the runner, French beans can be picked when very young and tender. Sow in the open ground, though very early sowings should be protected by cloches. Keep down the weeds and give plenty of water. The plants may need the support of short canes if cropping is heavy.

Varieties numerous, e.g. 'Canadian Wonder'; 'Cherokee Wax'; 'Glamis' (stringless); 'Pencil Pod Black Wax'; 'Masterpiece' and 'Sprite' (stringless) are especially suitable for freezing.

Beans – Runner Nearly always grown as a climber on netting or a bean-pole frame, up which the plants leap with almost measurable speed, especially if planted in well-manured ground. In windy areas, runner beans can be dwarfed by pinching them out at about a foot high, thus forcing them to a bushy habit. Two varieties, listed below, are grown only as dwarfs. Spacing of the plants should then be as for broad beans and some of the side growths also pinched back to give the effect of a low, bushy hedge. Some support from short canes may still be needed.

When left to grow tall the plants should be pinched out when they reach the top of their support. Hoeing the weeds and watering in dry weather is the only attention. Start picking early when the beans are young and not stringy. The harvest can continue over two months.

Varieties 'Achievement'; 'Crusader'; 'Streamline'; 'Kelvedon Marvel'; 'Scarlet Emperor'; 'Enorma', (especially suitable for freezing). *Dwarf varieties* 'Hammond's Dwarf Scarlet'; 'Hammond's Dwarf White'.

Beans – Haricot Similar in habit and requirements to French beans, but the pods are allowed to develop fully until they turn brown on the plants. These are then pulled up complete and allowed to dry; the beans

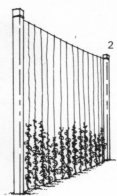
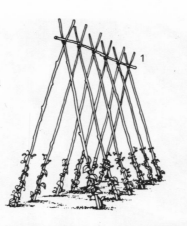
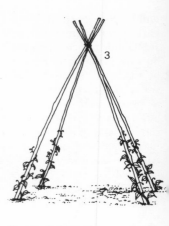

ABOVE: *The pods and flowers of 'Crusader', a good variety of runner bean.*

TOP: *Three ways to train runner beans:*
1. *a double row of plants with 'bean poles' on each side*
2. *a single row grown up strings or netting*
3. *a 'wigwam' of poles.*

OPPOSITE ABOVE: *'June Star' cabbage, a summer cabbage to plant in the spring.*

OPPOSITE BELOW: *'Blood Red' cabbages are grown mainly for pickling.*

are shelled and stored for winter use. Or, given cans and tomato sauce, you can make one of your own '57' varieties, but the crop is not likely to be heavy.

Varieties 'Brown Dutch' (brown beans); 'Comtesse de Chambord' (white beans); or the French bean 'Masterpiece' can be allowed to develop to full maturity.

Beetroot Some older varieties have a tendency to 'bolt' if the seed is sown too early; 'Boltardy' and 'Early Bunch' are examples of varieties bred to resist this. Germination of the seed may be poor, but can be encouraged by top dressing the soil when sowing. Sowings after the end of April are not likely to be affected by bolting. Early crops and the thinnings from the main crop can be used in salads. After lifting the main crop in October, it should be allowed to dry before being stored; alternatively the beets can be boiled, peeled, and sliced and bottled in vinegar.

Varieties Early – 'Boltardy'; 'Spring Bunch'. *Main crop* – 'Crimson Globe'; 'Spangsbjerg Cylinder'; 'Burpee's Golden' (has orange-red skin and yellow flesh).

Broccoli A good crop to follow early potatoes. The seed is sown under cover in March or outside in April; the seedlings will then be ready to plant out between May and August. Heel the plants in firmly as they are planted. A mulch when the plants are about a foot high, and to which they will also root, will give them further strength and support for the winter.

Green sprouting (Calabrese) A central green head forms in August or September and can be cut and treated as a cauliflower. The heads develop very quickly and should be picked before they flower. Thereafter, thick side-shoots are produced, which can be peeled and cooked like asparagus in the late autumn.

Purple sprouting matures later than 'Calabrese' and will withstand the winter to produce its purple shoots in March and April.

Brussels sprouts One of the most satisfying vegetables to grow: it crops well and regularly right through the winter and, as

Planting and Harvesting Chart for Cabbages

	Varieties	Sow	Transplant	Harvest
Spring	Harbinger, April	July/August	September/ October	April to July
Summer	Golden Acre, June Star, Greyhound	February/March (under protection)/April	April (under cloches)/May to June	July to September
Autumn	Autumn Monarch, Autumn Pride	April	June	September to November
Winter	January King, Savoy, Ice Queen	April	June	November to March

well as the sprouts, the tops can be picked before they run to seed. Well-manured ground or, better, ground manured for a previous crop is very desirable. As with all the cabbage family, plant out the seedlings deeply and very firmly. The lowest leaf should be down to soil level, in a hole previously filled with water and the heel of your boot alongside the plant will not be too heavy to firm in. Keep the young plants well watered and weed free. Start picking when the button sprouts reach usable size and leave the smallest to develop further.
Varieties 'Peer Gynt F_1' (early maturing in October, and recommended for freezing); 'Indra F_1'; 'King Arthur F_1'; 'Prince Askold F_1'; 'Bedford Fillbasket' is an older variety which produces larger sprouts.

Cabbage Varieties of cabbage can be sown to produce a crop the whole year round. How much of the year is up to the gardener and the cook, as well as the amount of space to be devoted to the crop. The succession of sowing, planting out and cropping can be seen from the chart, which also lists some varieties for each season. Rich ground produces the best results. The planting technique is the same as for Brussels sprouts.

Red cabbage is the variety grown for pickling. Seed is sown in August and kept under cloches over the winter until planting out in late March or early April. Seed can also be sown in early spring for transplanting in June.

Capsicum (Sweet pepper) The English outdoor climate is unlikely to allow the peppers to develop beyond the green stage (when fully ripe they turn yellow or red), but they are nonetheless edible for all that. The seeds should be started in a propagator in March and transplanted to $\frac{1}{2}$-in. pots when three leaves have formed. Plant outside in a sunny position in late May or early June – when all chance of frost has gone. In the north it is preferable to keep the plants under glass or cloches for their whole season. *Varieties* 'Canape F_1'; 'Ace F_1'.

Carrot There are two kinds of carrot – the stump rooted which mature early in the summer, and the longer 'intermediate', which is sown for the main crop and harvested in October. The seeds are very small and over-thick sowing can be avoided by mixing them with a little fine soil or sand. Pelleted seeds are also available which can be sown individually, $\frac{1}{2}$–1 in. apart. For an early crop, sow in a frame or under cloches in March, having previously warmed the soil by leaving the top on the frame or placing cloches in position a week or so before sowing. Thin the crop as soon as the carrots are large enough: the main crop should be spaced to 4 in. in July. Don't leave harvesting later than October, to avoid the roots becoming tough and woody. They can be frozen or, more traditionally, stored in dry sand in a cool place.
Varieties Stump-rooted (early) – 'Amsterdam Forcing'; 'Early Scarlet Horn'; 'Early Nantes'. *Main crop* – 'James's Scarlet Intermediate'.

Cauliflower The sowing and planting out procedure is the same as for the other brassicas, and the ground should be as rich as possible. Cauliflowers take some time to mature and those planted in April may not develop fully by winter. A sowing can be made early in September which is then transplanted, spaced 3 in. each way, in October, and left under cloches for the winter. It is then transplanted to its final position the following April to be ready for cutting late in the summer.

The cauliflower broccoli (Winter Cauliflower) grows faster, is hardier and has a longer season, though its flavour is less delicate. Seed is sown in March (preferably under cover) and the seedlings transplanted as soon as possible. The crop will then be ready from October to Christmas.
Varieties – summer: 'All the Year Round'; *autumn:* 'Autumn Giant'; 'Canberra'; 'Boomerang'; *winter (Broccoli):* 'Reading Giant'.

Celeriac (Turnip-rooted celery) A substitute for celery in cooking which will grow in poor soil and calls for less attention. The seeds should be sown in a propagator or frame in March or April and planted out

in May (1 ft. apart, with the rows 18 in. apart). If the plants throw up suckers these should be removed. The roots will be ready to lift in October and can be stored in sand until needed.
Variety 'Globus'.

Celery Like some of the other choicer products of the vegetable garden, celery calls for extra care and attention if the crop is to be worth having. There are three types of celery which, in order of their need of special treatment, are: blanched, self-blanching, and green. Sow the seeds in trays or pots in a propagator in February to March, or in a cold frame early in April. Harden the seedlings carefully and progressively until they are ready to plant out in June into well-prepared ground which should have been liberally manured.

For the blanched varieties dig out a trench about 15 in. wide and up to 18 in. deep. The base is filled with compost and soil to the point that the seedlings will be 3 in. below ground level. This method ensures that the

ABOVE LEFT: *Cauliflowers are slow-growing vegetables to grow from seed and take about nine months to mature.*

ABOVE RIGHT: *The 'Burpless' ridge cucumber, which is a good variety to grow outdoors or in an unheated frame.*

RIGHT: *Celery needs more attention than other vegetables, especially the blanched varieties. 'Giant Red', shown here, is a good variety of blanched celery.*

young plants can be liberally watered, which they need, and that the first earthing up, in mid-August, is simply filling in the trench. At the end of August, and again in mid-September, continue the earthing up to create a steep ridge along the row. Leave the plants then to blanch until early November when the first of them can be dug. Take them from the ground as needed through to Christmas.

The self-blanching varieties are best grown in a cold frame (no trench), from which the lights are removed in late June or July. Straw tucked around the plants assists in blanching and the crop will be ready during August and September. American, green, celery is grown in the open, without trenching or strawing, as it is eaten green.

Varieties, Blanched: 'Giant Red'; 'Giant White'. *Self-blanching:* 'Golden self-blanching'. *Green:* 'American green'.

Corn salad (lamb's lettuce) A lettuce substitute to grow through the winter. The seed is sown thinly in a very shallow drill in August and September. The plants are thinned to 6 in. apart – the thinnings can be used in salads – and the leaves picked when young and tender. It will help if the plants can be protected with cloches through the winter.

Cress (American) Not the same as the curled cress in 'mustard and cress', this is a substitute for watercress. The seeds are sown in damp drills between August and October, and the seedlings thinned to 6 in. apart. As the plants over-winter in the ground, cloche protection is desirable.

Cucumber Different varieties succeed in the greenhouse, cold frame, or in the open; only the latter two types are discussed here. For frame cultivation sow the seeds in pairs in 3½-in. pots, the weaker of the two subsequently being pinched off. Sowing can take place late in March in a propagator or late in April directly into the frame, and the spacing should be 2 ft. between plants. When the seedlings have formed four true leaves pinch out the growing point to induce branching, and again pinch out the branch ends when they have formed four leaves. The embryonic fruits can be seen behind the female flowers. The shoots should be stopped one leaf beyond each fruit, and the main lateral branches stopped as they reach the edge of the frame.

Outdoor cultivation is for the ridge varieties. The seedlings can be brought on as described above, or the seeds can be sown direct into the ground in mid-May. Plant out or sow 18 in. apart, and pinch out the growing point after the seventh leaf to induce branching.

Older varieties have both male and female flowers, and may need to be pollinated with a camel-hair brush. Newer strains have female flowers only. Cucumbers need rich soil and benefit from feeding with liquid manure when the fruits begin to swell. They also need plenty of moisture and should be watered freely. Begin cutting as soon as the fruits are of a useful size.

Varieties Suitable for unheated frames in warmer areas: 'Conqueror'; 'Improved Telegraph'. For unheated frames or outdoors: 'Apple-shaped'; 'Burpee F_1'; 'Burpless F_1'; 'Greenline'; 'Long Green'; 'Nadir F_1'.

Endive This hardy plant makes a substitute for lettuce in the winter months. Sow between April and August and thin to 12 in. between plants. Those maturing after October will benefit from cloches. The hearts are partially blanched by tying the leaves together, or total blanching can be achieved by covering the whole plant with an inverted pot. Blanching takes about six weeks.

Fennel (Finocchio) An unusual vegetable akin in texture and flavour to celery when cooked. Sow in shallow drills 1 ft. apart in April, and thin the seedlings to 9 in. apart. The swollen stem bases are ready to harvest late in the summer and the early autumn. (See also under *Grow your own herbs*.)

Hamburg parsley (turnip-rooted) A root crop which looks like, and is grown in the same way as, parsnips – though it has a different and unusual flavour. The tops can also be used as a flavouring in soups. The crop can be left in the ground and dug as needed from September through to February, or lifted complete in November and stored in dry sand.

Horseradish Deep digging and well-broken soil are necessary for successful horseradishes, if they are to have the long, thick roots which are desirable. Small roots are planted in March in holes (made with a long dibber) deep enough to allow the roots to be covered with 4 in. of soil. They will grow and multiply, and will be ready for digging in November. The largest roots are then ready for the kitchen or storing

indoors. The smaller ones are trimmed, tied in bundles and stored outside, buried in sand, ready for the next planting.

Kale (borecole) Hardy, heavy-cropping green vegetable which is easy to grow and which provides a good alternative to cabbage and broccoli right through the winter to Easter. Planting, soil, and cultivation are the same as for sprouting broccoli. Traditionally, kale is not cut until it has survived a hard frost. This may improve the flavour, but it is perfectly palatable earlier in the autumn. Rather than cut the whole plant, take the leaves singly and finally the top, by which time there may well be secondary growth lower down the plant. The crop from only a few plants can be substantial.

Varieties 'Dwarf Green Curled'; 'Thousand Headed'.

Kohl rabi Not very widely grown, kohl rabi is one of the cabbage family, but is grown for its swollen stem, which tastes like a mild turnip. Sowing and cultivation are as for summer cabbage. Keep the growth rate speedy by hoeing weeds regularly and watering frequently. A light top dressing will also help. The plants are ready when the stems have swollen to the size of tennis balls. Do not let them grow too big, or

they will become tough and strongly flavoured. They do not store satisfactorily so that successional sowings are necessary to ensure a regular supply.

Leek Another very hardy winter vegetable which deserves a place in the kitchen garden. Keep the ground well watered after sowing direct into the ground in March or early April. Come June the seedlings will be ready to plant out – about 8 in. apart, in rows 12 in. apart. Use a dibber to make holes up to 9 in. deep, drop the seedlings to the base of their leaves, and fill the hole with water. Do not heel them in, just leave them. The first will be ready for lifting in November, and from then on as required; they can stay in the ground through the winter until April.

Lettuce The basis of nearly all salads, a careful and experienced gardener with a heated greenhouse can produce lettuce the whole year through. With less sophisticated equipment it is still possible to pick them from late April to December. There are three different types: cabbage, cos, and loose-leaf, and of these cabbage are subdivided into butterhead (e.g. 'Unrivalled' and 'May King') and crisphead (e.g. 'Webb's Wonderful' and 'Windermere').

Choose different types of lettuces to make successional sowings which will give continuity and variety. Don't sow too many seeds at one time: the object is to maintain a steady supply, which means sowing at about fortnightly intervals. The seed should be sown fairly thickly in shallow drills, 9 in. apart if all are to be transplanted, or 12 in. apart if the rows are to be thinned. Pelleted seeds are available which should be planted at 1 in. intervals and thinned later.

Keep the plants growing fast by sowing in well-manured ground and giving plenty of water. Cos lettuces will make quicker and tighter hearts if tied loosely with string or raffia when hearting starts.

Melon Although one thinks of melons as a fruit of warmer climes than Britain it is quite possible to succeed with them in a cold frame or under cloches. The seeds, however, should be started in a propagator, as the temperature in the early stages should not fall below 50°F (10°C). Using fibre pots will also help, as it avoids disturbing the roots when planting out. Sow the seeds in $3\frac{1}{2}$ in. pots filled with seed compost early in May. Sow them in pairs so that the weaker of the two can be eradicated after the first true (triangular) leaf has formed.

Growth will be speedy, but keep the seedlings moist, and harden off steadily and progressively until the time for planting out into frames or under cloches in the second half of May. Each plant should be on a small mound to ensure adequate drainage from the main stem and keep in mind that each plant will need 2 sq. ft. of space. After planting out, pinch off the growing stem to encourage lateral growths. Be brutal – retain only four laterals on plants in a frame and two for those under cloches – and pinch them out when they reach the edges.

By July the plants will have grown greatly and the weather should allow the frame lights to be left off or the cloches separated to enable insects to get in and pollinate the flowers. If pollination does not occur naturally, you should do it yourself, using a camel-hair brush.

As soon as three melons have formed on the larger varieties (or four on the smaller), each on a sub-lateral shoot from a different main lateral, refrain from pulling, and prune off all other fruitlets and sub-laterals. The melons remaining should have a piece of slate or wood beneath them to avoid slug damage. Water often and add liquid manure occasionally. Stop the treatment when

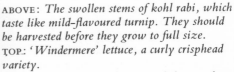

ABOVE: *The swollen stems of kohl rabi, which taste like mild-flavoured turnip. They should be harvested before they grow to full size.*
TOP: *'Windermere' lettuce, a curly crisphead variety.*
LEFT: *Cos lettuces can be persuaded to produce better hearts if they are tied into shape with raffia as they develop.*
FAR LEFT: *Fennel is an unusual vegetable with a delicate aniseed flavour. The swollen stem bases can be eaten raw in salads or cooked, and the seeds are used for flavouring.*

ripening commences – the delicious aroma in August or September heralds its completeness.

Mustard and Cress Of all the vegetables none are easier to grow – perhaps to the point of boredom! Indoors, in a propagator tray without the top, crops can be grown throughout the year. Sow the seed on an inch of seed compost; do not cover – just firm them into the soil. The temperature should not fall below 60°F (15°C). Outdoors, seed can be sown progressively from mid-April till August.

Cress takes 12–18 days to reach maturity; mustard 8–12 days, so that the mustard seed is sown on top of the cress after it has been on the soil for 4 days. Keep the soil moist and harvest with a pair of scissors when the plants are about 3 in. high.

Mustard (Chinese) Another alternative to lettuce for salads, Chinese mustard is sown in shallow drills between April and July. Keep it well watered and thin the seedlings to 8 in. apart.

Onion Onions do best in a well-tilled and reasonably light soil. They are either sown from seed or by planting 'sets' – small immature onions grown from seed in the preceding season, which can be bought from seedsmen in February and March.

Seeds are sown quite thickly in drills 1 in. deep, with the rows 12 in. apart. As they grow to a useful size the rows can be thinned for salad onions until mid-July, by which time the spacing should be 9 in. for those which are to be left to form the main crop.

Sets are planted in March, simply by pressing them into the ground, spaced as above. Keep the rows straight to assist in easy hoeing and water freely if the ground

becomes dry. Liquid manure may be given weekly, but avoid over-feeding and stop when, in August, the foliage yellows and falls. Let it die back completely before lifting the crop, which can be left on the ground for a day or two to dry if the weather is suitable. Then make up into strings, using the straw-like tops, after the fashion of the Breton onion sellers, and hang in a dry, airy position.

For salad only, as it does not attain any great size, the 'White Lisbon' variety is useful and has a mild flavour. Although it will not store as described above, it can be frozen.

Varieties numerous, e.g. 'Ailsa Craig'; 'A1'; 'Autumn Queen'; 'Bedfordshire Champion'; 'Crossling's Selected'; 'James's Long Keeping'; 'Unwin's Reliance'.

Parsnip Being a deep-rooted vegetable, parsnips require well dug ground. Sow the seeds thinly in shallow drills 18 in. apart. The seedlings should be thinned, firstly in April, and again late in June to allow 8 in. between plants. The roots will be ready for digging from November through to Easter, and are best left in the ground until needed.

Varieties (canker resistant): 'Tender and True'; 'Avonresister'.

Pea There are two main types of garden pea; the hardier are the round-seeded, but the marrowfat varieties, with wrinkled seeds, have a reputation for superior flavour. Acidity in the soil will have an adverse effect on pea crops, and if a first sowing is a failure it may be worthwhile testing for this and adding lime.

To achieve an early crop seeds are sown in late October to winter in the ground, protected by cloches, until the following

ABOVE: *Garden peas should be picked as soon as they are ready to get the best flavour. This variety is called 'Pioneer'.*

ABOVE: *'Harvester' onions are just one of the many varieties to grow. They can be grown from seed or 'sets' and like a light soil.*
RIGHT: *'Home Guard' potatoes are among the earliest varieties to be ready for harvesting.*

April. From March until May seeds can be sown successively in the open ground. Cloche protection, however, is worthwhile, not only against the weather, but also to forestall foraging raids on the seeds and the young plants by various birds which find peas quite irresistible. The usual method of sowing is to take out a furrow, with a draw hoe or spade, between 1–2 in. deep, and 8 in. wide, along the bottom of which the seeds are spread about 2½ in. apart. The soil is firmed gently as it is raked back over the seeds. Spacing between the rows varies according to the variety; a good working rule is to allow the same space as the height to which the variety will grow. Most need some support – short sticks with cotton between them (which in the early stages helps to keep off birds) will be sufficient for the dwarf varieties, but those growing to 3 ft. or more will need brushwood, pea netting, or an arrangement of canes and string.

A plentiful supply of water is vital when the pods are beginning to fill and a strawy mulch between the rows will also help to keep the ground damp. Pick regularly and often to enjoy the sugary flavour which is quickly lost.

Varieties First early: 'Early Bird' (1½ ft.); 'Feltham First' (1½ ft.); 'Foremost' (3 ft.); 'Forward' (2 ft); 'Kelvedon Wonder'★ (1½ ft.); 'Little Marvel'★ (1¼ ft.); 'Topcroft'★ (2½ ft.); second early: 'Achievement' (5 ft.); 'Early Onward'★ (2 ft.); 'Kelvedon Climax' (2½ ft.); 'Kelvedon Monarch'★ (2½ ft.); *main crop:* 'Alderman' (5 ft.); 'Histon King-size' (3½ ft.); 'Onward'★ (2 ft.); 'Recette'★ (2 ft.).

★*Good varieties for freezing.*

Popcorn This is sweet corn, or corn on the cob, under yet another name. It applies when the cobs are left on the plant until they are fully ripened and have become dry and brittle.

Potato When the ground is first dug a potato crop can be a good method of breaking it up and helping to clear weeds. It isn't that the potato plants do all the work – you do most of it – but the crop makes it worthwhile, and at the end of the season there will be a well-worked piece of ground ready for the second stage of crop rotation next year. Whether early, main crop, or both are sown, depends upon the space available.

Potatoes need space – 1 ft. between plants and 2 ft. between rows for the early crop and more for the main crop. With some vegetables the recommended distances can be reduced without too greatly reducing the crop to be taken, but not so with potatoes; the space is needed between the rows to allow for earthing up which is a very necessary part of the operation.

Seed potatoes are purchased in early March, and carefully set out in open trays to encourage them to sprout. Any light and frost-proof place will do. By Easter – Good Friday is the traditional planting day – the ground will have been dug and manured, if that seemed necessary (but not limed, as lime is bad for potatoes).

Take out a furrow 6 in. deep, and position

the seed potatoes, 12 in. apart for earlies, and 15 in. apart for the main crop, with the strongest sprouts uppermost, and rake the soil back over them. When the plants have grown to about 9 in. high, draw up the soil in a ridge along the rows to a height of about 6 in. A draw hoe or a cultivator are the best tools for the job. This earthing up can be repeated a few weeks later if the plants are making a great deal of top growth.

Harvesting commences when the flowers have died – usually late in June – on the early varieties. These can then be dug as required through to September. By that time the top growth of the main crop will have died right back, and will look brown and shrivelled. This is the time to lift it, on a bright, dry day, which will allow the tubers a little time to dry before being bagged up for storage. It is important that potatoes are not left exposed to the light – they turn green and are then inedible.

Varieties First early: 'Arran Pilot'; 'Home Guard'; 'Ulster Chieftain. *Second early:* 'Craig's Royal'; 'Dr McIntosh'; 'Great Scot'; 'Maris Peer'; 'Pentland Dell'. *Main crop:* 'Arran Banner'; 'Golden Wonder'; 'Kerr's Pink'; 'Majestic'; 'Pentland Crown'.

Pumpkin Treat pumpkins in the same way as trailing varieties of marrows, restricting the fruits to one or two per plant. They will benefit from copious and frequent feeds of liquid manure, which should be stopped when the pumpkins begin to ripen. Late in September they should be fully ripe, with firm skins; they can be stored in a cool, dry place.

Radish Radishes do best in fairly fertile soil, and can be sown successfully from March to July in open ground to give a constant supply through the summer and autumn.

Keep the plants moist and start thinning as soon as the roots are big enough for use. Initially thin to 1 in. between plants, but those to be grown as a main crop should be further thinned to 8 in. The main crop is ready for lifting in October, and the radishes can be stored in dry sand.

Varieties Summer: 'Scarlet Globe' (round); 'French Breakfast' (tankard shaped); 'Icicle' (long); 'Yellow Gold' (oval). *Winter* (large): 'China Rose'; 'Black Spanish'.

Rhubarb It is possible to grow rhubarb from seed, but more usual to buy roots (or crowns). The plants are perennial and will produce crops for years. The roots are planted either in the autumn or in March, about 3–4 ft. apart, and just deep enough to cover the top part of the crown, but leaving the shoots on it above the ground. Let the plants become well established in their first season and do not take any crop. From then on, the sticks will grow in abundance, especially with the help of a compost mulch each winter.

Early rhubarb can be forced by covering one or two roots with large pots – an up-ended plastic dustbin will do well. Rather pale but very edible shoots will be ready for picking early in March.

Salsify A root vegetable which is rather like a thin parsnip but of very different flavour – it is sometimes known as the 'vegetable oyster'. The seeds are sown in shallow drills in April, and their cultivation is exactly as for parsnips. The crop should be lifted in November, and can be stored in dry sand.

Scorzonera Similar to salsify, and grown in the same way. The root has a black skin.

Seakale An epicurean vegetable, which calls for care and patience by the gardener to achieve a successful result. Although it can be grown from seed, two years will probably pass before there is a crop to be taken, for which reason seakale is usually grown from 'thongs' or root cuttings. These are spaced 18 in. apart in rich soil early in March. The fact that the thongs have no apparent shoot need not be a deterrent, but it is important to plant them the right way up; the bottom is usually cut at an angle and the top square. The thongs are several inches long and must be planted deep enough to cover the top with ½ in. of soil. Mulch with well-rotted compost in

May. In November the foliage will have died back. The roots can then be lifted and transplanted into pots, which should be kept in the dark in a greenhouse or shed. Alternatively, the roots can be left in the ground and covered with large flower pots, or something similar. The important point is to exclude all light so that the shoots are fully blanched as they grow. Un-blanched shoots are entirely unpalatable. Cut the shoots just below soil level, when they are 6–9 in. long. They will be ready in November in the greenhouse.

One or two roots should be lifted in November to provide thongs for the next season's sowing. These, trimmed from the main root, can be left in the open, buried under dry sand during the winter. The main roots will be of little further use once they have been used for forcing.

Seakale beet (Swiss chard, silver beet) Although similar to beetroot, seakale beet is grown for the thick white midrib of its leaves, which are cooked as a substitute for seakale, and the green parts used instead of spinach. Sow the seeds in shallow drills, 12 in. apart, between April and July. Thin the seedlings to 12 in. apart. Pick the leaves as required when the plants are fully grown.

Shallot Of a milder flavour than onions, shallots are also easier to grow. Small bulbs

ABOVE: *Several different varieties of radishes.*
CENTRE: *Pumpkins should be treated like trailing marrows.*
TOP: *Seakale beet is a variety of beetroot, although it looks very different. Both the green and white parts of the leaves can be eaten.*
TOP LEFT: *Forced rhubarb is ready for picking from early March.*
TOP RIGHT: *Sweet corn can be successfully grown in this country with some protection and care.*

are planted about 9 in. apart, the rows 12 in. apart in March and will be ready for lifting in July. The groups of bulbs are separated and spread out to dry. Retain some for replanting next year.

Spinach This is another green vegetable which can be grown outdoors the whole year through. For summer spinach, commence sowing in mid-March and continue through to July; winter spinach is sown in July and August. For both, sow in drills 1 in. deep, 12 in. apart, and thin the seedlings to 3 in. Harvest a few leaves from each plant at each picking.

New Zealand spinach is very different from spinach. It has thick fleshy leaves and a bushy habit. The seed is sown in a cold frame early in April, and planted out in June at 3 ft. intervals. The shoots are picked while they are young and tender.

Perpetual spinach should be sown in the open ground in April, and the seedlings thinned to 8–12 in. apart. Picking commences in July and can go on through the whole winter, taking a few leaves at a time from each plant.

Sweet corn (corn-on-the-cob) The seeds should be started in a propagator in March – one or two in $3\frac{1}{2}$ in. pots, with a view to eliminating the weaker one – or in a cold frame in April. Plant out in a sunny position after the seedlings have been hardened off, in June, at 1 ft. intervals. The plants will grow to about 4 ft. tall. Harvest the cobs when the grains are full but immature in August; the clue is in the 'silks' at the end of each cob. These become brown and brittle when the cobs are ready.
Variety 'First of All' (Suttons) F_1.

Swede The yellow-coloured flesh of this vegetable makes a change from turnips. Sow in drills 18 in. apart and thin the seedlings to 9–12 in. apart. The roots are ready for lifting through the autumn and can be stored in dry sand.
Varieties 'Chignecto' (resident to club root); 'Purple Top'

Tomato For early crops a greenhouse is necessary, and most varieties have been developed to grow with this protection. But there are several which will produce good crops in the open garden, especially if they can be grown against a south-facing fence or wall. 'Outdoor Girl', 'The Amateur', and 'French Cross' F_1 (Suttons) are three examples, the latter two being bush varieties. The gardener has the alternative of growing from seed or buying young nursery-raised plants.

Tomatoes from seed are planted two to a $3\frac{1}{2}$-in. pot (the weaker being pinched out later) in a propagator in mid March. Early growth can be vigorous and result in seedlings which are thin and weedy. Begin the hardening-off process early, when the plants are no more than 3 in. high, to produce plants which will be sturdy and about 9 in. high in June, when it is time to plant them out (after all possibility of frost is past).

This is the time when nursery-raised plants can be bought. Plant out 15–18 in. apart, with a 3 ft. cane behind each plant. As growth progresses, tie the plants to their stakes, especially at points where fruit trusses are forming, and nip off side growths which grow with remarkable speed from the junction of the leaves with the main stem. When the plants have 3 or 4 trusses of fruit – but no later than the first week in August – pinch out the main growing point. Leave the fruits to ripen on the plants as long as possible, although when the weather fails trusses of green fruit can be taken indoors to ripen on the window-sill. If that fails, green tomatoes make good chutney.

Turnip There are two main classes – early for summer and autumn use, which do not store well, and main crop varieties which develop later and can be stored through the winter. One variety in particular – 'Hardy Green Round' – is good for an abundant supply of turnip tops. Sow the early varieties between March and July; the main crop in July. For turnip tops in the winter and spring, sow in August.

The seed should be sown thinly in 1 in. drills, 12 in. apart, and the seedlings thinned to 4–6 in. apart for the early varieties or 9 in. for the main crop. Keep the crop well watered and weeded to reduce the chances of attack from the flea beetle.

Vegetable marrow The gardener has the choice of compact, bushy varieties, which need about 2½ sq. ft. of space each, or the trailing types which can be trained along a trellis. Seed can be sown in a propagator in April, and planted out towards the end of May, or sown directly into the ground in early June. Frost is the main hazard of sowing earlier out of doors. Marrows need rich soil and will benefit from liquid manure feeds while the fruits are developing. Cut the marrows while still young and tender – the thumb nail should easily pierce the skin.

Small versions of the vegetable marrow are **Zucchini**. These can be grown as courgettes, and harvested when small or allowed to develop to marrow dimensions – up to 14 in. long. Treat like marrows.

SOME COMMON PESTS AND DISEASES

Aphids (Green fly and black fly) Tend to cluster under leaves and at the tops of young shoots from which they suck the sap, check growth and cause distortion of the foliage. Spray with derris or pyrethrum, especially

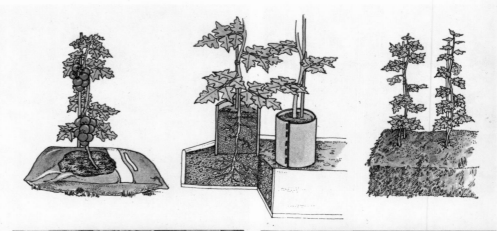

before leaf distortion is so great that the spray cannot reach the aphids.

Blight (Potato and Tomato) A fungus which attacks the leaves, causing black patches which spread rapidly. The disease can spread to potato tubers and tomato fruit, turning them brown and rotten. Bordeaux mixture sprayed early in June is a preventative, but not a cure.

Club root (Cabbage family) The roots swell, then gradually decay with a most disgusting smell. The disease thrives in acid soils; the addition of lime will help to prevent a future recurrence.

Flea beetle (Cabbage family, but only at seedling stage) The small black beetle perforates the young foliage with tiny holes. Keep the seedlings growing fast so that they speedily pass beyond the interest of the beetle, and spray with derris if needed.

Fly (Carrot and Onion) The fly is attracted by the scent of the foliage and lays its eggs at the base of the plant. The maggots bore into the root or bulb. Avoid breaking or bruising foliage, and bury trimmings deep in the compost heap. Early and late sowings often miss attack, and a dusting of napthalene flakes on the soil will deter the flies.

ABOVE LEFT: *'Outdoor Girl' tomatoes will produce a good crop in the open garden. They do best grown facing south so that they get plenty of sun.*

ABOVE RIGHT: *Courgettes or zucchini, a small variety of the large vegetable marrow.*

TOP: *Three ways to grow tomatoes in the greenhouse. Left: plants grown in a specially prepared bag of compost, called a 'Tom-Bag'. Centre: plants grown in individual plastic or clay 'rings'. Right: plants grown in partially rotted straw bales.*

RIGHT: *A fine crop of 'Moneymaker' tomatoes, one of the most popular varieties for outdoor cultivation.*

SOWING AND HARVESTING CHART FOR VEGETABLES

	January	February	March	April	May
Artichoke, Globe					
Artichoke, Jerusalem					
Asparagus					
Beans, Broad					
Beans, Dwarf (French)					
Beans, Haricot					
Beans, Runner					
Beetroot					
Broccoli, Green sprouting					
Broccoli, Purple sprouting					
Brussels Sprouts					
Cabbage★					●
Capsicum (Sweet Pepper)					
Carrot					
Cauliflower					
Celeriac					●
Celery					●
Corn Salad (Lamb's Lettuce)					
Cress (American)					
Cucumber					
Endive					
Fennel					
Hamburg Parsley					
Horseradish					
Kale					
Kohl Rabi				●	
Leek					
Lettuce					
Melon					●
Mustard & Cress					
Mustard, Chinese					
Onion					
Parsnip					
Pea					
Popcorn					
Potato					
Pumpkin					
Radish					
Rhubarb					
Salsify					
Seakale			●		
Seakale Beet					
Shallot					
Spinach, Summer					
Spinach, Winter					
Spinach, New Zealand					
Spinach, Perpetual					
Sweet Corn					
Swede					
Tomato (Outdoor)					
Turnip					
Vegetable Marrow					

★See separate chart   **Sow under protection**   **Sow in the open**   Harvest under protec[tion]

June	July	August	September	October	November	December

Harvest in the open   Store   ● Transplant or plant out

GROW YOUR OWN HERBS

A bed of herbs, preferably handy to the kitchen, can be useful and decorative. If you have no garden, plants such as mint, parsley or chives may be grown in a window box or in pots on a balcony. For many gardeners there is a special fascination about herbs, which are also much loved by bees, and the collection increases until part of the garden is devoted to these most useful plants.

Herbs are accommodating plants, most doing well in rather poor, dry soil and in a sunny position. The mint family is an exception, requiring a moist and rather richer soil.

In planning a herb garden, however small or large it may be, allow one square foot of ground space for each plant. Bear in mind that herbs vary considerably in height. Fennel, angelica and lovage are tall and should be planted at the back, or in the middle of an island bed. Sage is a strong-growing plant and will require ample space. To the front of a bed plant thyme, mint, purslane, chives, sorrel, and other lower growing kinds.

The various mints are invasive plants once they get established and to keep them within bounds grow them in an old pail – plastic or metal – sunk in the ground almost up to the rim. Make some drainage holes in the bottom of the pails before planting the mint.

Some herbs are easily raised from seed – angelica, sweet basil, borage, chives, fennel, sweet marjoram, parsley, summer savory, common thyme – while others, such as mint are increased by division. Mint is a perennial. Sweet basil, borage, and summer savory are annuals. Parsley is a short-lived perennial; sweet marjoram a tender perennial grown as a half-hardy annual.

Lemon balm (*Melissa officinalis*) is a hardy perennial, bushy herb up to 4-ft. high. The white or pale yellow flowers are inconspicuous but are much visited by bees from June to August. It has a lemon odour and a pleasant spicy taste when chopped leaves are used sparingly in salads. Fresh or dried leaves may be used for this purpose. They may also be used with Indian tea in the pot to give lemon-flavoured tea.

Drying balm: If dried balm is required, cut stems of foliage in July or August and dry quickly in full sun outdoors. When dry rub the leaves between fingers and thumb and store in a sealed jar in a dry place. Propagation is by division of the roots in the spring or autumn or by seed sown in the spring.

Basil (*Ocimum basilicum*). A native of tropical areas of Africa and Asia, this herb is treated as a half-hardy annual in British gardens. Sow the seed in boxes in late March or in April and germinate in gentle warmth. The young seedlings are planted out in the open in late May or early June. Alternatively, sow seeds in the open ground in very shallow drills during early or mid-May, where the plants are to grow. Germination will be assisted if the drills are covered with cloches, which should be removed as soon as the seedlings appear. The plant grows to a height of about 2 ft. and bears white or mauve flowers. It is not an easy herb to dry and is therefore generally picked fresh from July to October. The clove-scented leaves should be used when young. Sweet basil is used for flavouring soups and any recipes in which tomatoes are used; also when boiling vegetables or fish and especially when boiling shell fish. When chopped finely it is an ingredient for *fines herbes* in omelettes.

Bergamot (*Monarda didyma*) is a decorative hardy herbaceous perennial plant which has been a favourite in cottage gardens for many years. This aromatic plant has honey-suckle-shaped red flowers over a long period. The leaves may be used, either fresh or dried in the teapot with or without tea. Small quantities of chopped leaves may also be used with green salad. Propagation is easy by division of the roots in spring. It can also be increased by seeds sown in a cool greenhouse or cold frame in March or in the open ground in April. The erect stems are 2–3 ft. high and the plant does best in a moist soil, rather richer than for most herbs. It needs plenty of water in a dry summer when grown in a sunny position, but does quite well in dappled shade.

Borage (*Borago officinalis*) is a hardy annual which may be sown in the open in April in ½-in. deep drills where it is to grow. Seedlings may be transplanted if required. Thin seedlings or space the young plants 10 in. apart in well-drained soil and in a sunny position. The terminal clusters of blue flowers borne from June to September attract bees. Young leaves may be added finely chopped to green salad to give a cucumber flavour and are refreshing in iced drinks.

Salad burnet (*Poterium sanguisorba*) is a perennial herb, a native of our chalk grasslands and thrives in dry, chalky soil. The flowers are pollinated by wind and not by insects. In cultivation it grows up to 2 ft. in height. Sow seeds in April in the open or propagate by division of established clumps in spring. When used with green salad it imparts a cucumber flavour, without the possibility of the windy effects of the hot-house cucumber.

Caraway (*Carum carvi*) is a biennial which should be sown in April, where the plants are to grow. Cover the seeds with ¼ in. of soil. Thin the seedlings to 6-in. apart. Plants will flower and produce seed in the following year in late June and July. When in flower the plants closely resemble 'bolted' carrots. Cut the flower stems then and place them on trays in full sun so that the seed is not lost. The seed is used in flavouring seed cake or is sprinkled over home-made bread or buns before they are baked.

Chervil (*Anthriscus cerefolium*). Sow this hardy annual from April to June in shallow drills where the plants are to grow. Thin seedlings to 6-in. apart. Height is 1–1½ ft. This herb does best in a shady position and in fairly rich soil. The young leaves are used

Dill (*Anethum graveolens*) is a hardy annual which reaches a height of 1½–2 ft. and has grey-green stems, feathery leaves, and clusters of tiny, dull-yellow flowers from June to August. It likes a moist, but well-drained soil and a sunny position. Sow thinly ½ in. deep in April or May where the plants are to grow. Thin the seedlings to 3 in. apart. Harvest the seed in the same way as for coriander. The leaves may be used to flavour soups and sauces. The dried seeds may be used in seed cakes and as a flavouring for pickled cucumber. It is also used for flavouring vinegars.

Fennel (*Foeniculum vulgare*) is a perennial, native herb reaching a height of 4–6 ft. Sow the seeds in March and April in well-drained soil and in sun or light shade where plants are to grow. Thin the seedlings to 1 ft. apart and grow in clumps of several plants. When clumps become overcrowded, lift, divide, and replant in autumn. Fresh leaves are cooked with fish, or finely chopped and used with white sauce for boiled fish. Dry the seed as recommended for coriander. Dried seeds are used for flavouring soups and fish dishes.

Garlic (*Allium sativum*) is a hardy onion-like perennial; height 1–3 ft. The small bulblets, known as cloves, are planted 6–9 in. apart, just beneath the soil, in early March. A light, well-drained soil and full sun is best. Usually one clove is quite sufficient to flavour meat balls, rissoles, and sausages.

Horehound (*Marrubium vulgare*) is a native perennial herb still found in parts of East Anglia where it was used as a base for horehound ale. It is easily grown in poorish dry soil and is 12–18 in. in height. The whorls of white flowers are not produced until the second year after sowing. The woolly leaves when crushed have a pleasant musky smell. It is an attractive plant for the herb garden and is raised from seed sown in early spring, or by cuttings or by division of the roots.

Lovage (*Ligusticum officinalis*). This is a perennial herb up to 4 ft. high, of erect habit. It does well in a moist, rich soil and in semi-shade or sun. Seed may be sown as soon as ripe in September, or in the spring. Thin or transplant the seedlings when they are large enough to handle to 9–12 in. apart. The flavour of the plant is likened to celery and the leaves, seeds, stems, and roots are all used in cooking. The leaves may be used sparingly fresh or dried in soup, stew or salad. The hollow stems are sometimes used as a substitute for angelica. The dried seed may be sprinkled on cakes or on cocktail biscuits and the roots cooked like celeriac. Lovage produces umbels of small yellow flowers in July but if a good crop of leaves is required the flowering stems should be removed before they develop.

fresh in soups, sauces and for garnishing. Chervil is seldom dried. The aniseed-like flavour is retained better if the leaves are placed in a deep freeze.

Chives (*Allium schoenoprasum*) is a perennial non-bulbous onion which forms close clumps, 6–9 in. high, bearing mauve-purple flower heads in June, which should be removed. Chives are often grown as edging plants in the herb or kitchen garden, in sun or partial shade. Clumps are best divided and replanted in September or seeds may be sown rather thinly, ¼ in. deep. Plants can be successfully grown in pots or in a window box. Finely chopped chive leaves give a mild onion flavour to cream soup, salads, and to omelettes.

Coriander (*Coriandrum sativum*) is a hardy annual which grows to a height of 1½–2 ft. and has clusters of white, slightly mauve-tinted flowers in high summer. Sow seeds thinly, in April or early May, ½ in. deep in well-drained soil and in a sunny position where the plants are to grow. Gather the flower heads as soon as the seed is ripening and lay them on a tray so that the seed is not lost while the heads are drying. The seed is used in flavouring curries, chutneys, and for sprinkling on cream cheese. The leaves are also used chopped fresh as a garnish, especially on Indian dishes.

ABOVE: *Bergamot can be used as a tea or a salad herb.*
TOP: *Chives grow well in pots or window boxes.*

Pot marigold (*Calendula officinalis*) is the old-fashioned marigold of cottage gardens. Once you have this plant established it will seed itself freely. It is a low-growing, bushy annual with yellow or orange disk flowers. It is colourful in the herb garden and associates well with sage. It continues to flower over several months in summer and autumn. Sow the seeds thinly outdoors in April in a sunny position where they are to flower. The foliage is pungent, but for culinary purposes it is the flowers that are used fresh in salad, and either fresh or dried in soup.

Marjoram Several marjorams all belong to the genus *Origanum*. The common English marjoram (*O. vulgare*), is a hardy perennial which does well on chalky soil and in full sun and grows 1–2 ft. tall. French (pot) marjoram (*O. onites*), 1 ft. tall is hardy and more sweetly aromatic. Both may be raised from seeds sown very thinly in April at a depth of $\frac{1}{4}$ in. The seeds are very small and are, therefore, best sown in boxes and germinated in a cold frame. Plant out the seedlings 6-in. apart. Sweet or knotted marjoram (*O. marjorana*), height 2 ft. is best grown as a half-hardy annual in the British Isles. Sow seeds of sweet marjoram under glass in March, prick out the seedlings and harden off before planting out in May. Fresh or dried leaves may be used in a home-made herb mixture for stuffing poultry or veal.

Drying marjoram: For drying, cut marjoram foliage just before the flowers open in July and hang in small bunches in the sun. When quite dry rub between the hands and store in sealed jars.

Some garden mints Not all of the different varieties of mint are of culinary value. For mint sauce and for flavouring purposes there are no better forms than the common green mint, *Mentha spicata* (spearmint) and *M. rotundifolia* 'Bowles' (Bowles's mint) or pea mint. The latter is tall-growing and may reach to 5 ft. so should be grown at the back of the bed. A good way to keep mint within bounds is to grow it in a tub on its own either in full sun or partial shade. In dry weather the soil should be kept well watered, but be sure that there is good drainage at the bottom of tub. Young plants may be set out in spring or autumn. Place small pieces of root 6-in. apart and cover them lightly with moist soil. In the first season do not pick sprigs until they are about to flower. Tips may then be gathered for use in the kitchen. Once established, pick as and when required for flavouring new potatoes and green peas in June and July, and for mint sauce.

It is the usual practice to renew a mint bed every three or four years and to replant young pieces 2-in. deep in another part of the garden after the soil has been dressed with garden compost.

Mint is susceptible to the fungal disease mint rust, which is more likely to affect spearmint than other mints. It appears as orange, rusty spots on leaves and stems. Dig up and burn affected plants.

Drying mint: Choose a dry, sunny morning in July to cut stems about 9-in. long before they show signs of flowering. Make small bunches and hang them on a clothes line. Rapid drying is important. Mint that is not dried quickly tends to bleach. The dried mint should be rubbed between the hands and stored in sealed jars. A second harvest may be collected in September in dry, sunny weather.

Parsley. A biennial herb (*Petroselinum crispum*), usually treated as an annual and raised from seed each year. Moss-curled parsley is the most popular type grown in Britain. This herb may be grown in partial shade or in a sunny position and needs ample moisture in a dry summer. Seed should be sown in the open from March onwards. Parsley is slow to germinate, so do not despair if nothing appears for four or five weeks. Covering the seed row with a cloche or two may encourage germination, but keep the soil moist. Sow seed thinly, and cover with about $\frac{1}{4}$ in. of soil. For parsley in winter sow in July and protect the crop with cloches throughout the winter. Never strip a plant of all its leaves. Just cut or pick a leaf here and there.

Drying parsley: Parsley for drying should be gathered in sunny weather in July or August. More heat is needed for drying than for sage or thyme, and it is a good idea to spread the leaves on a fireproof tray above a cooker. It is likely to lose its fresh green colour during drying. Alternatively parsley foliage may be blanched in boiling water for five minutes; pour cold water over it and dry it in a fairly cool oven for 20 minutes. The leaves should then be crisp. Rub the dried parsley between the fingers and bottle it at once. If it is left exposed it quickly reabsorbs moisture from the atmosphere.

Sage (*Salvia officinalis*) is a hardy evergreen herb, native of southern Europe, with a height and spread of about 2 ft. Plant out in March in well-drained soil and in a sunny position. Cuttings taken in May, about 2-in. long with a portion of old wood attached, will root readily in sandy soil in a cold frame. Cuttings may also be taken of young growths, about 3–4 in. long, in August or September and overwintered in a cold frame. To induce bushiness, pinch out the growing point of each young plant as it is making good growth, when about 5-in. high. Transplant 18-in. apart in a sunny position in well-drained soil. Although sage

will withstand drought when established, newly planted specimens should be watered during dry spells. There are several forms of the common sage. Broad-leaved sage seldom flowers and is considered to have more aromatic foliage than narrow-leaved sage of which there are two forms – one with purple and the other with white flowers.

Red sage: *S. officinalis* var. *purpurea*, is more handsome than the ordinary sage and may also be used in the kitchen. There is a choice between a red sage (purple-leaved) which has flowers and one that does not flower. Red variegated sage has purple flowers and is decorative in a collection of herbs for foliage display. Golden sage rarely flowers, but is another attractive dwarf foliage shrub for a herb garden. These varieties also provide useful stems for including in decorative floral arrangements.

Drying sage: Sprigs for drying are cut just before flowering starts in May and further pickings can be made on and off throughout the summer. Quick drying is very important and the process must be completed within a week. In really hot summer weather small

bunches dry rapidly outdoors. If the weather turns dull and cool, bunches may be hung above the cooker in the kitchen or spread out on metal trays above the stove for a day or two. When dry rub the leaves from the stalks and store in sealed jars in a dry place. This herb should be added with discretion to stuffing mixtures because the flavour of sage can override that of other herbs.

Savory There are two kinds, summer savory (*Satureja hortensis*) which is an annual and winter savory (*S. montana*), a perennial of shrubby growth up to about 12-in. high. Summer savory is sown in shallow drills in the open in April where the plants are to grow. Thin the seedlings to 1-ft. apart. Pick for use from July onwards. Summer savory may also be grown in pots indoors for use in winter. Winter savory is propagated by cuttings taken in spring or by division of the roots in spring or autumn. It can also be raised from seeds sown in a pan under glass in April. Aromatic and pungent, it is used in small quantities for seasoning.

Drying savory: Winter savory dries easily if the sprigs are cut in July before flowers

TOP LEFT: *Thyme plants in flower.*
TOP RIGHT: Mentha gentilis, *one of the many varieties of mint.*
ABOVE: *Pot or French marjoram,* Origanum onites.

develop. Hang in small bunches in the sun. The colour also stays well. This trimming keeps winter savory compact. Where older shrubs tend to make too much growth and exceed their allotted space cut back all stems in spring to 4-in. long. The dried herb should be rubbed between the hands and stored in a jar in a dry place. If savory is allowed to flower, it has pretty white and slightly pink tiny blooms, which are much sought after by bees. On the Continent it is known as *benekraut*.

Tarragon (*Artemisia dracunculus*) is an aromatic perennial up to 18 in. high with greenish-white, nodding heads of flowers in August. It thrives in fertile, well-drained soil in full sun and is increased by division of the roots in April. The flavour of *A. dracunculus* (French tarragon) is considered to be far superior to *A. dracunculoides* (Russian tarragon). Plants should be spaced at least 1-ft. apart. To harvest tarragon leaves, cut the tops of the shoots in late July and August. Spread out the shoots and leaves on trays in full sun to dry as quickly as possible. Fresh leaves can be picked throughout the summer and can be used fresh, or dried in *fines herbes* mixtures for omelettes, sprinkled in soup and salad, on egg dishes, in stuffing and in pickles. Green leaves picked young, preferably before the plant flowers, can be frozen. The plant is used in the preparation of tarragon vinegar. It should be used sparingly for flavouring.

Thyme There are numerous varieties, but for kitchen use common thyme (*Thymus vulgaris*) is usually grown and, although it is a sun-loving plant from southern Europe, it is quite hardy in Britain. It makes a 6–8 in. spreading bush with green to greyish-green small leaves and light mauvish flowers. Established plants often seed themselves in gravelly soil or seed may be sown thinly in spring and lightly covered with soil. Thin the seedlings to 1-ft. apart. Spare seedlings will transplant. Established plants may be increased by division. Lift a plant and remove rooted side growths and replant 1-ft. apart. This is best done in spring.

Drying thyme: With small leaves and a woody stem, thyme dried readily in high summer. Small bunches should be hung on a garden line or in an airy room for a few days. When dry rub the sprigs between the hands and store the leaves in covered jars in a dry place.

Decorative thymes: Few plants are more pleasing than the prostrate wild thyme (*Thymus serpyllum*) when grown in paving or on a rock garden. The mauve flowers are a great attraction to bees and there are named varieties with pink, crimson, and white flowers. These will also add interest and colour when grown along the front of a herb bed.

INDOOR PLANTS

Although, for various reasons, the inside of a dwelling house is not an ideal place to grow plants permanently, a surprising number can be induced to thrive provided reasonable care is taken. For practical purposes, we can divide such plants into two sections: those with comparatively thin leaves, usually sold as house plants, and those with fleshy leaves or stems, such as succulents and cacti. Although there are a few borderline cases, such as the Epiphyllums and Sansevierias, generally the treatment for the two sections is quite different and it is convenient, therefore, to deal with the plants in two parts: House Plants and Cacti and Succulents.

HOUSE PLANTS

Most of the plants that are offered for sale as House Plants come from the tropics, usually from the higher rain forests and are, therefore, accustomed to a moist atmosphere. This is not easy to recreate in a room, but it is possible. The easiest way is to place the pot in another, larger container which is filled with some retentive medium. Moss looks the most attractive, but peat is perfectly satisfactory. This medium should be kept moist at all times, and the soil in the plant pot itself is only watered when required. It is also possible to place the pot on a tray of pebbles, filled with water, but this should not come in contact with the bottom of the pot. This ensures that there is always some water vapour around the plant, although not sufficient to make the room atmosphere unhealthy.

Light Having secured an adequate atmosphere around the plants, our next concern is the amount of light available. Although many house plants are forest dwellers in their wild state, the light intensity in a tropical forest is greater than that found in even a well-lit room, as any photographer will know. Plants can be found for most dark conditions, but some light must be present, and very dark corridors and halls should not have plants permanently left in them. You can keep plants there for a few weeks, after which they must be removed to lighter situations, and perhaps be replaced by other plants. In very badly lit houses, artificial lighting can be used.

Generally speaking, most house plants will need to be exposed to as much light as possible indoors, although they need not necessarily be on the window sills. Unless they are in a sun room, it is probable that the plants depend on light from the direction of the window, and they should be turned slightly each week so that they do not all brow toward the light. By rotating them slightly, you ensure symmetrical growth. Plants do require ample light, but most house plants esent prolonged exposure to burning sunlight and they should be moved if they are likely to be exposed to this. Some plants wilt in strong sun, but a slight spraying of the leaves will soon restore their turgidity.

Air All plants require abundant fresh air, but they do not like draughts. If they are placed in very draughty situations, they are liable to drop their leaves and may, eventually, perish. If your plants are not doing as well as they should, it will pay you to check that they are not exposed to currents of cold air. Damage can also be caused by fumes from gas heaters, although North Sea gas seems less lethal than coal gas used to be; but a few plants, such as Begonias, are very susceptible to these fumes and should not be kept in houses where gas heating is used. Fumes from paraffin heaters are harmless, so long as the appliances do not smoke.

Just as plants do not like to be too cold, they also dislike being too hot. There is no use putting plants above a radiator or on a chimney piece. The fierce heat will cook the roots and sear the leaves, and the plants will die.

Composts The four requirements for plant growth are air, light, essential minerals (normally found in the soil) and water.

Many plants nowadays are grown in soilless composts. These are a mixture of peat and sand with added chemicals. The peat and sand mixture makes an easy medium for the roots to penetrate, but contains no plant nutrients. This means that once the plant has absorbed all the added chemicals it may starve, unless more nutrients are added. Thus, when these peat-based composts are used, it is necessary to give a liquid feed once a week during the growing season – roughly from the beginning of April until mid-October. There are a number of liquid feeds available commercially and they should always be used according to the maker's instructions. Resist the temptation to give larger quantities if the plant looks starved or unhealthy. The plant can only take up so much. Any excess is either washed out and wasted, or it accumulates and may eventually cause damage. Liquid feed should never be applied to very dry soil for it could damage the roots if it came in contact with them undiluted. It is best applied about two days after the plant has been watered. During the summer an alternative to applying liquid fertilizer to the soil is to spray the leaves with a foliar feed. This often has satisfying results, but it is not always convenient to syringe plants in the home.

The soilless composts are very light and large plants – or plants in large pots – are liable to be rather top-heavy. For these it is far better to use the conventional loam-based composts. The one in most general use is the John Innes Potting Compost, usually abbreviated to JIP. This is a mixture of loam, peat, and sand with added chemicals. JIP 1 is used for plants in 3-in. pots, JIP 2, with twice as many chemicals, in 5–6-in. pots and JIP 3 in the larger pots. There is a reserve of nutrients in the loam but, even so, it is best to feed during the growing season, at longer intervals than with the loamless mixtures. Once every three weeks is usually adequate.

Feeding should only be applied in John Innes Potting Compost when the pot is well filled with roots. If you have just moved the plant into a larger pot, wait until the roots have penetrated the fresh soil before you recommence feeding. With the loamless composts it is best to wait 3 or 4 weeks before you restart feeding.

Watering The correct use of the watering-can is probably the most crucial item in keeping plants in good health, and it is the hardest to give clear directions about. If it can be obtained, rain water is by far the most satisfactory. A good alternative, but one which is rarely available in sufficient quantities, is the water from the refrigerator after defrosting. Tap water is slightly less good, but quite adequate. The water should be at about the same temperature as the room, ideally between 50°F (10°C) and 59°F (15°C) and in the case of African Violets it should always be round about 59°F (15°C) otherwise the leaves are liable to develop unsightly white blotches. Water is normally applied from above, and the space between the top of the soil and the rim of the pot should be filled to the brim.

ABOVE: Aphelandra squarrosa *'Dania', a striking Danish form of the Zebra plant.*
BELOW: Clivia miniata, *popularly known as the Clivia Lily.*

This should be about $\frac{1}{2}$ in. with 3-in. pots, 1 in. with 5-in. pots, $1\frac{1}{2}$ in. with 6-in. pots, and 2 in. with larger sizes. Water should only be applied once the soil has dried out. Since the top of the soil dries out before the base of the soil ball, it is as well to wait 24 hours after the surface looks dry before applying more water. The frequency with which watering is necessary depends on a number of factors. During the winter, when light is poor and temperatures are low, the plant is not very active in making fresh growth and, indeed, if the temperature falls below 50°F (10°C) may make no growth at all. Under such circumstances the roots will not be taking up any water, so that water is only lost from the soil by evaporation. This means that watering will only be necessary at fairly long intervals. The length of this interval may also depend upon the kind of pot that the plant is in. Clay pots are porous, and the water evaporates from the sides of the pot as well as from the surface of the soil; most plants nowadays are in plastic pots, and these tend to require watering less frequently.

The rate at which plants grow and take

up water will vary according to the size of the plant and the surrounding temperature. Within certain limits, plants are inclined to grow more rapidly in high temperatures. When the temperature is low, growth is either slowed down or stops altogether. The more rapid the growth, the more water the plant will take from the soil. This means that plants will always need more water in the summer than at other times of the year. During cold spells it is best to withhold all water until warmth returns. A safe rule in watering house plants is, if in doubt, don't. Plants very rarely die from lack of water – unless this is taken to ludicrous degrees – but they are often killed from too much water. Excess water clogs the soil and the roots are, almost literally, drowned. It is sometimes possible to arrest this damage by letting the soil ball dry out completely and keeping it as dry as possible for some four weeks afterwards, keeping the foliage turgid by syringing with lukewarm water. This is quite laborious and not always successful, so it is a clear case of prevention being much better than cure.

Temperature As a general rule plants expect to experience the lowest temperatures during the night and the highest around noon. If you live alone and go out to work in the daytime, only lighting your fire when you return home in the evening, you are reversing the usual rhythm of plant growth, and the plants will suffer accordingly. Your selection must therefore be guided by the temperature that your plant will experience in an unheated house. It may be assumed that house plants do not like violently fluctuating temperatures; they will do better if the temperature hovers around 59°F (15°C), than if it fluctuates between 50°F (10°C) and 80°F (27°C). It may not always be possible to achieve this, but it is a goal to aim at. In centrally heated houses a large number of plants will continue to make growth during the winter months. This growth is often spindly and the leaves are small and unsatisfactory, with the result that such growth is usually best removed when the spring comes.

There is a tendency to put plants on window sills where they will get most light. It should be remembered, however, that window sills are often rather cold and draughty and are not necessarily ideal; in frosty weather it is essential to remove plants from such positions. The presence of ice on the inside of windows, even in very warm rooms, is a well-known phenomenon. This does not apply where double glazing has been installed.

Stopping This entails nipping out the growing point of a single stem in order to encourage the production of side-shoots to give a nice bushy plant. It should only be undertaken during the spring and summer when the plant is in active growth and only with well-rooted plants. If the plant is weak or has insufficient roots, you will not get side-shoots forming; only the leading shoot will be replaced. With very vigorous plants it may be necessary to eventually stop the side-shoots that have been formed and so encourage secondary growths. Besides stopping for the sake of obtaining a bushy plant, it is also advisable to remove any unsatisfactory winter growth in the spring and always remove, as soon as noticed, any unvariegated shoots from a plant that should have variegated leaves.

Potting on As plants increase in size, they will require potting on into larger containers. The usual progression is from a 3-in or 3½-in. pot to a 5-in. pot and thence to 6-in, 7-in, and 8-in. After this the plant tends to become too bulky. Most plants require potting on each year, and this is best done when growth starts in the spring – almost any time from March until May. If you want to know whether or not growth has started and you see no sign of new leaves forming, you can knock the plant out of its pot (do not do this when the soil is very dry as it may fall away) and see if the roots are showing white at the tips. If they are, it is a sign that they are active.

Repotting should be done when the soil ball is slightly moist, but not wet. If the plant is dry, water it first, allowing about 8 hours before repotting. In the same way, the fresh soil should be crumbly, but not sticky. It is a good idea to water the new soil two or three days before you expect to do your repotting. If your plant is in a soilless compost, it must be potted on into more soilless compost; if it is in a loam-based type, pot on in JIP compost.

The fresh pot should be clear of all traces of old soil and can be cleaned out with a sheet of old newspaper. If you are using a loam-based compost, put about an inch of drainage material, crocks or pebbles in the base of the pot; this can be omitted with soilless mixtures. Knock the plant out of its pot, add some compost to the new pot and stand the plant in the centre to check that the level is going to be correct. If it is a 5-in. pot, you need about an inch between the top of the soil and the rim of the pot; with larger pots the gap should be greater, with up to 2-in. with a 10-in. pot. See that this level is right, either by adding or by removing the compost. Once this has been achieved, fill up round the plant with the fresh compost, firming it down with your thumbs; soilless composts tend to shrink somewhat so you should fill rather above the required level. Once this has been done, give the plant a good watering. The roots will take a week or so to penetrate the new soil, so that subsequent waterings will be fairly infrequent for a time. If the plant can be placed in a somewhat warmer situation after being repotted for a few weeks, so much the better. Repotting is only necessary when the soil ball is so full of roots that the plant is becoming starved.

Hygiene Rooms are full of dust and this settles imperceptibly on the leaves. Since plants 'breathe' through their leaves this can be harmful to them, and the leaves should be cleaned at regular weekly or fortnightly intervals. This is best done with lukewarm water and a piece of cotton wool. Such luxuries as oil, milk, or flat beer are unnecessary. Young, newly-formed leaves are very soft and tear easily and should not

be touched before they are fully expanded. Both the upper and under surface of the leaves should be sponged. There are one or two plants with waxy leaves, such as the Elk-horn Fern (*Platycerium*) and German Ivy (*Senecio macroglossus*), which should not be sponged. This leaf sponging not only helps the health of the leaves, but will also remove such pests as red spider or green fly, should these appear. Scale insects, which can be very tiresome on rubber plants, are best removed by a match stick tipped with cotton wool. If there are bad infections of aphis or red spider they can be treated with aerosol insecticides, but these should be applied out-of-doors and the containers kept out of reach of children as they may well be poisonous. Leaf mildew is controlled with sprays containing Benamyl. If worms get into the soil ball, immerse the pot in a pail of water with about a teaspoonful of potassium permanganate dissolved in it. After a few minutes the worms will emerge. Sometimes, at the end of winter, when the soil has been dry for a long period, it will shrink, and you will find that the water runs straight through without moistening the soil at all. When this happens, put the plant in a pail of water, with the level of the water the same as that of the rim of the pot, and leave it until bubbles cease to rise. Then take the pot out and firm the soil around the edge of the pot. Watering should then present no further problems.

BELOW LEFT: Nidularium fulgens *is easy to grow indoors and does well without much light.*
BELOW: Azalea indica *flowers indoors in winter and is a popular Christmas plant.*
BOTTOM: Cineraria 'Erfurt' *does well in a cool well–lit room.*

CACTI AND SUCCULENTS

These are mainly plants that are used to desert conditions. One of the most marked of these is the wide fluctuations of temperature that may occur between daylight and dark. It is by no means unusual for the day temperature to be 95°F (35°C) and the night temperature as low as 41°F (5°C). These plants like the dry atmospheric conditions found in most rooms, but they also require considerable light which sometimes presents difficulties. Many will grow in soilless composts successfully, but they do better in a very gritty compost and if John Innes Potting Compost is used, additional grit should be mixed with it. The plants have fleshy leaves or fleshy stems and can go for long periods without water, so should be kept almost dust-dry during the winter months. During spring and summer they should be watered much as other plants, although they will be satisfied with less and you can go on holiday without any fear that they will come to harm as a result of of no water over two to four weeks. Feeding should be done very sparingly if at all. They are ideal for sun rooms. Generally they are quite happy even if the winter temperature falls as low as 44°F (7°C). Succulents can be sponged in the same way as house plants, but this is not possible with prickly cacti and they should be occasionally washed under the tap.

Propagation Almost all succulents and many house plants can be increased by cuttings. With succulents all you need is a tip growth about 2 in. long, which is inserted in a cutting compost (this can be purchased or made up of half peat and half sharp sand), and watered in; it will soon root. Offshoots of cacti must be left to dry out for two or three days before being put into the cutting compost. With house plants that are suitable. Cut a piece of fairly firm stem off at a leaf axil, remove the lower leaves and insert the cuttings in the cutting compost. The whole pot should then be enveloped in a polythene bag, which must be turned inside out every three or four days to prevent the plants damping off. Once rooted, which usually takes from 3–6 weeks, the bag should be removed and, after a further fortnight, the plants should be potted up separately in a suitable growing compost. Succulents do not require the polythene bag and can be inserted right away in the growing compost, although rooting will take a little longer. The compost must be kept just moist.

DESCRIPTION OF PLANTS

In the following descriptions the minimum winter temperatures necessary are indicated by C. for Cool, indicating that 44°F (7°C) is the lowest temperature the plants will tolerate. I. for Intermediate, which indicates a minimum temperature of 50°–53°F (10°–12°C), and W. for warm, which means a winter minimum of not less than 61°F (16°C). Unless a special note is added, it may be assumed that Cacti and Succulents are C.

Acorus (Arum family) C. *A. gramineus* 'Variegatus'. Tufted plants about 6 in. high, with grassy leaf variegated white. Requires moist conditions.

Aechmea (Pineapple family) I. Rosette-like plants with a 'vase' in the centre of the rosette which must be kept filled with water. *A. fasciata*, with grey leaves and a head of blue flowers emerging from bright pink bracts. *A. fulgens* with dark green leaves, purple on the underside and flowers emerging from red berry-like calyces. After flowering the rosette dies, but sideshoots will appear and can be grown on. Mature plants never require potting on.

Aeonium (Stonecrop family) C. Succulent plants with large rosettes of leaf and yellow, almost daisy-like flowers. *A. arboreum* makes a small branching shrub. *A. canariense* makes an enormous rosette.

Agave (Agave family) C. *A. americana* 'Variegata' forms a rosette of spine-tipped leaves which will, eventually, become enormous, but grows very slowly.

Aglaonema (Arum family) W. Attractive marbled leaf, about 6 in. long. *A.* 'Silver Queen', with silver-grey-green leaf, is among the best.

Aloe (Lily family) C. Succulent plants with attractive leaves and often quite showy flowers. *A. variegata*, the Partridge plant has banded leaves and white flowers. *A. jucunda* has white spotted leaf and pink flowers.

Aphelandra (Acanthus family) I. *A. squarrosa* has dark green, shiny leaves, ornamented with ivory veins and pyramidal heads of yellow flowers. 'Brockfeld' and 'Dania' are compact forms, which rarely flower, but have better leaf.

Araucaria (Monkey Puzzle family) C. *A. excelsa* makes a slow-growing, symmetrical, pyramidal tree, with all branches thickly covered with bright green needles. Growth is only a few inches each year. The plant should be turned round regularly so that its symmetrical habit is maintained. It cannot be propagated by cuttings and only needs potting on at 2 yearly intervals.

Asparagus (Lily family) C. *A. plumosus*, 'Nanus', the 'Asparagus Fern', with green, feathery leaves. *A. myersii* has stems like miniature fir trees. Propagate by seed or by division.

Aspidistra (Lily family) C. *A. elatior* is an old favourite which will thrive in very dark conditions.

Asplenium (Fern family) *A. nidus*, W., the Bird's Nest Fern likes warm, moist, shady

TOP: Begonia masoniana, *aptly called the Iron Cross Begonia.*
ABOVE: *Gloxinias need warmth and moisture.*
RIGHT: *Beleperone guttata, one of the Shrimp Plants, is easy to grow in a sunny position.*

conditions and will eventually get very large. *A. bulbiferum*, C. bears little plantlets which can be detached.

Begonia (Begonia family) I. Plants with attractive leaves or flowers of which the best are the *Rex begonias*, with large leaves in grey-green or purple, variously patterned. *B. masoniana*, the Iron Cross Begonia, with green and purple leaves. *B. haageana*, making a small shrub with leaves red below and pinkish flowers. *B.* 'Axel Lange' with velvety dark green leaf with white spots, crimson below. *B.* 'Abel Carriere' with very silvery leaves and red flowers, and many others. They all dislike direct sunlight and do better in soilless compost. Propagate by leaf cuttings.

Beloperone (Acanthus family) Shrimp Plant C.–I. Small shrub with soft rounded leaves and heads of pink-bracted white flowers which resemble the body of a shrimp. 'Yellow Queen' or 'Lutea' has yellow flowers. Requires good light and ample feeding in the summer. Cuttings not easy.

Billbergia (Pineapple family) *B. nutans* C. Tufted plant with grassy leaf and greenish tubular flora emerging from pink bracts. Increases rapidly and is propagated by division. *B.* × *windii* C.–I. slightly tender, but more decorative with larger flowers which emerge from light red bracts.

Calathea (Arrowroot family) I.–W. Handsome foliage plants, rarely more than 9 in. high. *C. bachemiana* with silver-grey, emerald-blotched leaf. *C. crocata* with banded leaf, maroon below and a head of orange flowers. *C. insignis* with light green leaf, purple below and with dark green blotches along the midrib. *C. mackoyana*, Peacock Plant, silvery green leaf with darker blotches, reddish purple below. A very showy plant. *C. ornata* has dark green leaf with pale pink lines between the main veins. Propagate by division.

Chamaecereus (Cactus family) C. *C. silvestrii*, creeping, branching cactus with purplish stems in summer and large scarlet flower in early June. The stems are covered with conspicuous white spines.

Chlorophytum (Lily family) C. Makes a rosette of arching, grassy leaf, green, with cream stripes. At the ends of the flower stems there come small heads of young tufts, which can be detached and rooted, making propagation foolproof.

Cissus (Vine family) C. *C. antarctica*, Kangaroo Vine. Climbing shrub by means of tendrils, with glossy green, toothed leaf which can be 4 in. long and half as wide. Propagate by cuttings of young wood.

Citrus (Orange family) *C. mitis*, I. Calamondin. Small tree to 2 ft. with white fragrant flowers followed by small oranges about 1 in. in diameter. Best grown in JIP

and stood outside in full sun during summer months to ripen wood. Propagation by cuttings is not easy and plants from pips are very slow to come into bearing.

Codiaeum (Spurge family) I. *C. pictum*. Shrub, which can reach 3 ft. with variously shaped coloured leaves in every shade of red, yellow, and green. Very susceptible to draughts and fluctuating temperatures when it will lose its leaves. Requires ample light. Stems filled with white latex, so should not be cut in any way. Propagation by cuttings only possible with warm greenhouse.

Cordyline (Lily family) *C. indivisa* C. makes a palm like plant with a trunk and a head of long, linear leaves with red midribs. *C. terminalis* I. Ti Tree, has brilliant crimson and red leaves mixed with dark green and, sometimes, cream. The leaf may be a foot long in large plants. 'Rededge' has much narrower leaves which are bronze with a cerise margin. 'Tricolor' has the leaf striped with cream and red.

Crassula (Stonecrop family) C. A genus of South African succulents, some of which are slightly shrubby, others nearly prostrate. *C. falcata* has closely set green leaves and heads of fragrant crimson flowers (sometimes sold as *Rochea falcata*). *C. lactea* makes a shrub about 18 in. high with large dark green leaves and heads of fragrant, starry flowers. *C. sarcocaulis* makes a tiny gnarled shrub with pink flowers and can be grown outside in mild areas. *C. teres* is an erect

cone-like plant with closely overlapping leaves, and fragrant white flowers. All propagate easily from stem cuttings.

Cryptanthus (Pineapple family) 'Earth Stars' I. Small rosette forming plants, with attractively coloured leaf. The favourite is *C. bromelioides* 'Tricolor' with inch-wide leaves, which may be 10 in. long, cream striped with green and pink. The plant makes offshoots which can be detached. There are a number of other species and hybrids on the market. They all require good light and must be kept almost dry during the winter.

Dieffenbachia (Arum family) Ornamental leaved plants, most of which require warm conditions. However *D. arvida* 'Tropic Snow' will thrive in Intermediate conditions. It has large oval leaves which are a pale cream, when the leaf is mature. Forms of *D. picta*, W. make larger plants with cream-blotched leaves. The plants are poisonous and should not be kept where there are young children.

Dizygotheca (Ivy family) I. *D. elegantissima* makes a slender tree with elegant, glossy green leaves, coppery when young.

Echeveria (Stonecrop family) C. A genus of succulent plants from Mexico, making compact rosettes of fleshy, usually glaucous leaf. *E. derenbergii* has grey-green, waxy leaf with a red tip and tubular orange and red flower. *E. harmsii* (*Oliveranthus elegans*) makes a small shrubby plant with slightly

hairy leaf and large flower, to 1 in. long, red with a yellow rim. *E. hoveyi* has the leaf variegated with cream and pink.

Echinocactus (Cactus family) C. *E. grusonii* makes a large globose ribbed plant with golden spines. It is very slow growing and never gets large enough in cultivation to flower or to produce offsets.

Echinocereus (Cactus family) C. Cacti with cylindrical, branching stems, usually ribbed. *E. knippelianus* is a smallish plant with minute yellow spines and pink flowers. *E. pectinatus* is larger, with larger, plentiful white or pink spines and purplish flowers.

Echinopsis (Cactus family) C. Plants with globular or cylindric ribbed bodies and large, long-tubed flowers. *E. eyriesii* has whitish aereoles and short spines, flowers white to 10 in. long. *E. rhodotricha* has dark brown spines and white fragrant flowers. 'Golden Dream' with a globular body and long-tubed yellow flowers is a hybrid with a *Lobivia*.

Epiphyllum (Cactus family) C.–I. Plants with this name are usually of hybrid origin. They require treatment somewhat different from other Cacti. They have flat, ribbon-like stems, which resemble leaves in their appearance and they lack spines on mature plants, although these may be present on seedlings. They like a moist atmosphere, as do most house plants, and a winter temperature of 50°F (10°C). The soil compost should be similar to that for house plants.

Euphorbia (Spurge family) I. These are cactus-like in appearance, but require warmer conditions than most cacti or succulents. *E. aggregata* makes a number of short, spiny, cylindrical stems up to 1 ft. high. Flower inconspicuous, borne on spine-like peduncles which persist. *E. hermentiana*, tall plant with vertical branches, which are 3 or 4 angled, spiny at the edges, dark green with white markings. Leaf spoon-shaped, not surviving for long. *E. obesa* makes a globose stem, which is reddish-brown, up to 4 in. high and wide. The green flowers are small but fragrant. *E. milii* (*splendens*), 'Crown of Thorns', spiny small shrub with greyish, succulent stems, rosettes of somewhat fugitive leaf at the tips and heads of flowers, which are surrounded each by two semicircular crimson bracts. 'Tananarive' is larger and the bracts are yellow. They flower more or less continuously, but shed their leaves in cold conditions. *E. tirucalli* is spineless. It makes, eventually, a tall shrub with smooth, round, very pale green branches, thickly produced.

Ficus (Mulberry family). Mainly I. *F. elastica*, 'Rubber Plant'. Eventually a forest tree, but usually grown with a single stem in a 5–6 in. pot. The stem contains a milky latex. 'Decora' and 'Robusta' have very large leaves. 'Schryveriana' and 'Tricolor'

ABOVE: Citrus mitis, *a miniature orange tree, should be put outdoors in summer.*

TOP: Codiaeum *'Mrs Iceton' is a rather sensitive houseplant and requires a constant temperature.*

OPPOSITE PAGE: Cordyline terminalis, *has large crimson and dark red leaves.*

are variegated. They should not receive direct sunlight when the new leaves are unfurling. *F. benjamina* makes an attractive small branched tree with pendulous habit and rather willowy leaves. *F. lucida*, similar to *F. benjamina* but with rounder leaves. *F. lyrata*, Fiddleback, W. large leaves shaped like the back of a violin. *F. pumila*, C. creeping shrub with small round leaves along thread-like stems. *F. radicans* 'Variegata', W. trailing plant with pointed, silver-variegated leaves.

Gasteria (Lily family) C. Succulent plants with strap-shaped leaves arranged in two ranks, usually dark green with white spots, forming numerous offsets. *G. maculata* has red flowers on a very long stem, but only flowers when a large plant. *G. verrucosa* has greyish leaves and red flowers.

Gymnocalycium (Cactus family) C. Very floriferous plants with globular stems, strongly ribbed, with a pronounced chin below each division. Offshoots freely produced. *G. bruchii*, small globes to only 1 in. across with numerous pink flowers. *G. baldianum* with yellowish spines and red flowers. *G. platense* to 3 in. across, with whitish spines and white flowers.

Hamatocactus (Cactus family) C. *H. setispinus* a plant with a globular or cylindrical body, which is ribbed, sometimes spirally. Spines white and brown. Flower funnel-shaped, yellow with red centre. Mature plants produce offsets.

Haworthia (Lily family) C. Succulent rosette plants, with small 2-lipped flowers. *H. linifolia* makes rosettes of dark green, ridged leaf and has white flowers. Side rosettes are produced with freedom. *H. margaritifera* has green leaves spotted with white dots.

Hedera (Ivy family) C. Ivy. A very large number of forms of *H. helix*, English ivy, are grown. Some such as 'Chicago' are self-branching and make an attractive small shrub; others, such as 'Glacier' tend to trail, unless stopped to produce sideshoots. Most ivies require rather shady situations, but 'Golden Jubilee' with attractive dark green leaves and golden centres, likes plenty of light. It is also unusual in making new stems before it makes new leaves. 'Marmorata' and 'Maculata' have larger leaves than most forms of *H. helix*. *H. canariensis*, with variegated leaves with red stems is more vigorous and has much larger leaf. It should be grown as a climber or trailer as it never makes a very bushy plant. Ivies propagate from stem cuttings.

Howeia (Palm family) I. Often known as 'Kentias', these have large drooping leaves divided into numerous segments and up to 2 ft. long. *H. belmoreana* has a close head of pendulous leaves; *H. forsteriana* has a looser head of arching leaves. *H. forsteriana* likes rather shady conditions. Propagation is only by seed.

Hoya (Milkweed family) C.–I. The variegated form of *H. carnosa* is a slow-growing twining plant large fleshy leaves which are variegated with pink and cream. It elongates its new stem before forming any new leaf. A winter minimum of 50°F (10°C) is best. Cuttings require some heat to root. The plant should never be stopped as this seems to discourage it.

Hypocyrta (Gesneria family) I. Clog plant. *H. glabra* makes a small shrubby plant with shining small bright green leaves and orange-red unique pouch-like flowers with a small round mouth, emerging from an orange calyx in the leaf axils. The plant is rarely more than 6 in. high. The leaves are somewhat fleshy, and watering is kept on the spare side. If too much water is given, the flowers fall before opening. Propagation is by stem cuttings.

Impatiens (Balsam family) I. Busy Lizzie. *I. wallerana* is a somewhat straggling plant with elliptic leaves and circular, spurred, red or scarlet flowers. 'Petersiana' has the stems and leaves dark purple. Stem cuttings will root if placed in water and since old plants tend to get leggy, it is as well to re-propagate yearly.

Kalanchoe (Stonecrop family) C.–I. An attractive genus of succulent plants from South Africa. *K. blossfeldiana* with green leaves and heads of scarlet, orange or yellow

159

flowers; can be grown as an annual. *K. marmorata* has large round, waxy greyish leaves with brown spots. It has white flowers and needs rather more warmth in winter. *K. velutina* has leaves and stems covered with velvety hairs and tubular yellow flowers flushed with pink. Propagate by seeds or cuttings.

Lobivia (Cactus family) C. A number of cacti with globular, or cylindrical, ribbed bodies, which are very spiny. Offshoots are produced by mature plants and can be detached. *L. haageana* has white wool at the base of the spines and yellow flowers. *L. jajoiana* has the young spines red or pinkish and deep red flowers.

Mammillaria (Cactus family) C. Plants with globular bodies divided up into tubercles (small protuberances), spines sometimes absent. The fruits are often ornamental as well as the flowers and take a year to ripen. *M. craigii* has yellowish spines and deep pink flowers. *M. prolifera* makes a mass of small spheres, with white spines, creamy flowers and orange-red fruits. *M. spinosissima* is covered with reddish brown spines (although other colours are noted) and has purplish flowers and red fruits.

Maranta (Arrowroot family) I. Much like Calathea and requiring similar conditions. *M. leuconeura* has pale green oblong-oval leaves, which are bright green with maroon blotches in var. *kerchoveana*; similar but with the veins picked out in white in var. *massangeana*; and with larger leaves and bright red veins in var. *erythrophylla* (*tricolor*).

Monstera (Arum family) C.–I. *M. pertusa* (often sold as *M. deliciosa borsigiana*) is a climbing plant with aerial roots and leaves which are both jagged and perforated. In bad light the leaves revert to the juvenile heart-shaped form. A damp atmosphere is necessary when the aerial roots are elongating. Propagation by tip cuttings, taken with an aerial root.

Neoregelia (Pineapple family) I. Rosette forming plants with a central vase which must be kept full of rain water. *N. carolinae tricolor* has the leaves variegated with cream and pink. Just before the flowers appear the innermost leaves turn bright crimson. The blue flowers just emerge above the water level in the vase. *N. spectabilis* has a conspicuous crimson tip to the leaves and red flecks on the upper side and ash-grey below. After flowering, the plants usually die without producing any sideshoots.

Notocactus (Cactus family) C. Also known as *Malacocarpus* these are cacti with round bodies, usually tuberculate. Flowers usually yellow. *N. haselbergii*, with small globular body, covered with white bristle-like spines, which gives the plant a silvery appearance. Flowers red and yellow. *N.*

ABOVE: Saintpaulia *Rochford Pamela, the beautiful African Violet.*
TOP: Rhipsalidopsis *'Electra', a member of the Cactus family.*
OPPOSITE PAGE: Rebutia calliantha krainziana *flowers profusely and easily.*

mammulosus a globular plant, eventually producing offsets, with yellowish spines and yellow flowers.

Peperomia (Pepper family) I. Popular house plants, found either as small shrubby plants, as in *P. magnoliaefolia*, *P. obtusifolia*, and *P. tithymaloides*. Of these the forms with variegated leaves are most often seen, although *P. obtusifolia* with purplish leaves is not known variegated. The others make tufted plants with more or less heart-shaped leaves, which are dark green and corrugated in *P. caperata*; grey-green and quilted in *P. hederaefolia*, and silvery, with dark green veins and leaves shaped like a Rugby football in *P. argyreia* (*sandersii*). They require shady and comparatively dry conditions. They have a small root system and rarely need potting on. Propagation is by leaf cuttings, but some heat is necessary.

Parodia (Cactus family) C. A group of cacti with small, globular bodies and long spines. *P. microsperma* has white and brown spines and orange flowers. *P. nivosa* is somewhat woolly at the top of the plant and has dark red flowers. There are a number of other attractive specimens.

Philodendron (Arum family) Mainly I. Chiefly climbing plants, producing aerial roots as they ascend and so requiring a damp atmosphere around them in the spring and summer. There is one popular non-climber, *P. bipinnatifidum*, which can eventually make a very large plant with huge, very jagged leaves, but which is attractive as a small plant, when the leaves will be about 9 in. long and wide. Among the climbers is *P. melanochryson*, W. with black and gold leaves, which are nearly heart-shaped, *P. hastatum* and 'Tuxla' I., rather slow growing plants with leaves shaped like a spear head, and *P. scandens*, C. with heart-shaped leaves and a slender stem. The climbers can be propagated by tip cuttings, *P. bipinnatifidum* only by seed.

Pilea (Nettle family) C.–I. *P. cadieri*, the Aluminium Plant, has green, silver-spotted leaves and grows vigorously, needing frequent stopping. 'Moon Valley' is slower growing and needs no stopping. Propagate by stem cuttings.

Platycerium (Fern family) C.–I. *P. bifurcatum*, the Elk-Horn, has two sorts of leaf. One is circular and clasps the pot, the others are antler-shaped. Both are waxy, so do not require sponging. The pots should be tilted slightly, as the plant grows naturally on tree trunks. It can also be wired to a block of cork and immersed periodically in a bucket.

Rebutia (Cactus family) C. A genus of small globular cacti, with unribbed bodies. Flowers from the base of the globe, produced very freely on small plants. *R. calliantha* has dark green bodies with white spines and orange flowers. *R. minuscula* makes a cluster of small globes, not more than an inch or so across and scarlet flowers. Seeds germinate very readily and seedlings are often to be found clustered round the base of the plant.

Rhipsalidopsis (Cactaceae) C.–I. A cactus with a ribbon-like stem requiring the same conditions as Epiphyllum. *R. rosea*, the Easter Cactus, is somewhat reluctant to flower, but once started is very profuse. When buds are formed the plant should not be rotated, as this may cause them to abort.

Rhoicissus (Vine family) C.–I. A tendril-making climber with a leaf composed of three leaflets, which are largest in 'Jubilee'. The plant has no objection to quite shady conditions. The young growths are covered in brown hairs; the mature leaves are dark green and toothed. Propagate by stem cuttings.

Saintpaulia (Gesneria family) I.–W. African Violet. There is only one species. *S. ionantha*, normally a tufted plant with velvety leaves and deep violet flowers, but now also other colours from pink through mauve to white and sometimes double flowers. Needs warmth, ample light, but never direct sunlight and a very moist atmosphere. When watering the water should always be around 59°F (15°C). Leaves should not be wetted, nor should they be sponged. Plants rarely require potting on, but can be fed during the summer. Propagation by leaf cuttings, but the plantlets require to be separated subsequently.

Sansevieria (Lily family) C.–I. *S. fasciata laurentii*, Mother-in-law's Tongue, has erect, sword-shaped fleshy leaves, which are dark green with grey bands and a yellow margin. Treat more or less as a succulent, with very little water October–March. A well lit situation is necessary, but the plant is trouble free. Propagate by offsets, which take a year to root and should not be severed before.

Saxifraga (Saxifraga family) C. *S. sarmentosa* Mother of Thousands, makes a small tufted plant with rounded green and grey leaves, variegated with pink in 'Tricolor'. It throws out slender stems with young plantlets at the ends, which can be rooted, and produces white flowers in autumn.

Schefflera (Ivy family) *S. actinophylla* I. makes a slow growing tree with compound leaves on large stems, much like those of a horse chestnut. *S. arboricola*, C. is a new plant with smaller leaves, which will tolerate cool conditions.

Schlumbergera (Cactus family) C. Cacti with ribbon-like stems requiring treatment like Epiphyllums. *C. buckleyi*, Christmas Cactus (often known as *Zygocactus truncatus*) has pink flowers in winter. *S. gaertneri*, the

Whitsun Cactus, has almost scarlet flowers in early summer. None of these require potting on too frequently. Propagate by cuttings.

Scindapsus (Arum family) I. *S. aureus* is much like *Philodendron scandens*, but with leaves variegated with yellow. Treat as a climbing Philodendron.

Sedum (Stonecrop family) C. *S. hintonii* makes rosettes of succulent, bluish-grey, somewhat egg-shaped leaves, and has white flowers in the winter. It must be kept as dry as possible during this period, otherwise it is liable to rot. *S. sieboldii* 'Medio-variegatum' throws out slender stems clothed in rounded grey-blue leaves, with a yellow centre, which produce heads of purple flowers in autumn. After flowering these stems die back and the plant can be left unwatered until February, when fresh growth can be started. Propagate by cuttings.

Senecio (Daisy family) C. *Senecio macroglossus*, German Ivy, is a twining plant with almost triangular waxy leaves, which are variegated with cream. These leaves do not require sponging. The plant is vigorous and greedy and needs ample light. Propagate by stem cuttings.

Spathiphyllum (Arum family) I. *S. wallisii* 'White Sails' makes a tufted plant with shortly stalked, spearhead-shaped bright green leaves and pure white, arum-like flowers about 3 in. long, which may be produced twice during the year. It likes warm, moist conditions and ample feeding.

'Mauna Loa' has larger flowers, but blooms less freely and requires even warmer conditions.

Tradescantia (Spiderwort family) C. Trailing plants with pointed egg-shaped leaves, either without stalks or with very short ones. The Silver Tradescantia, *T. albiflora* 'Albo-vittata', Wandering Jew, has small grey-green leaves with white streaks; the Golden Tradescantia, *T. fluminensis* 'Aurea', has rather larger, dark green leaves with yellow stripes, 'Tricolour' is striped white and pink, with a purplish underside to the leaf. The white variegated plants need ample light. Remove any unvariegated trails at once. *T. elongata* 'Rochford's Quicksilver' has longer leaves with silver blotches, which never revert. Cuttings root very readily and just need to be inserted in a growing compost, about 5–7 in a 5 in. pot. They are very brittle so make a hole for them; do not try to push them into the compost or they will snap.

Zebrina (Spiderwort family) C. Very similar in appearance to the Tradescantias, but *Z. pendula* has grey-green leaves with a purple stripe at the centre. 'Quadricolor' has the leaf striped white, rosy-purple, dark and pale green, but needs warmer conditions and loses its markings in the winter. *Z. purpusii* has leaves dull purple above and bright purple below, so should be placed fairly high up. Propagate as for Tradescantias.

Zygocactus See Schlumbergera.

GREENHOUSES AND FRAMES

THE GREENHOUSE

Greenhouses are of the following types: span or ridge, three-quarter span, lean-to, the newer circular, and ones of irregular designs which are modifications of the span type.

Standing alone and of independent structure, the span type is best for all purposes. Many have glass to the ground and dispense with the base walls of brick, concrete or wood, which minimise the temperature fluctuations to which the all-glass house is subject. Sometimes glass is replaced by plastic, but this is of only temporary value

Wood Should the structure be of wood or metal? Wood is warmer, easier to repair, better for fitting shelves, but it does need painting or, with red cedar, oiling. Teak is durable, but costly. Cheaper wood or red deal is easier to work with.

Whitewood, while cheaper, is susceptible to weather and might split. Western red cedar is particularly durable, but needs to be dressed every 2 or 3 years with linseed oil.

Straight-grained oak, often used with steel, is very durable. It can be painted on the inside with white lead paint to preserve the wood and reflect light.

Metal Steel and aluminium greenhouses are both common, but aluminium is more easily shaped. Aluminium alloys are also satisfactory and stand firm, in spite of their light weight. A metal greenhouse must be perfectly stable and allow for expansion and contraction, otherwise the glass may break and the air leak out. The metal sashes must be sealed with an elastic sealing compound, not putty. Steel needs painting, but not aluminium.

Concrete Although less elegant, the increasingly popular concrete greenhouse is very strong, particularly as reinforced concrete is used in the construction.

Whichever type of greenhouse you choose, make certain there are no ill-fitting joints, doors, ventilators or any other faulty working parts. They only give trouble.

There must be guttering and down-pipes to prevent water pouring off the roof and down wide panes, and also to channel the water into rainwater butts.

Choosing a greenhouse Besides adding value to your property, a greenhouse gives all-the-year-round pleasure. Care must be taken, therefore, to choose the one that best suits your needs from all the various kinds available. Your choice will undoubtedly be influenced by the site available, the plants you want to grow, and the price. The latter governs size, but it is wise to purchase the largest greenhouse that you can afford.

It is a mistake to buy any type of greenhouse until you have decided what plants are to be grown in it. An 8 × 6 ft. greenhouse, for example, is of no use if you wish to grow ornamental plants in addition to grapes or melons. The so-called Dutch light house provides plenty of light and can accommodate tomatoes in summer, followed by chrysanthemums in autumn and winter lettuce, with a succession of other forced vegetable crops.

The unusual span roof greenhouse is ideal for pot plants, like cyclamen and primulas, and raising bedding plants, because the brick or wooden base permits staging. But if you want to grow tomatoes, chrysanthemums or lettuce on one side, you should buy a type with glass to ground level or one which has staging and glass on opposite sides.

ABOVE: *A colourful display of flowers can be grown in a cool greenhouse or conservatory.*

LEFT: *There is a wide range of greenhouses to choose from:*

1. *A span roof greenhouse with low wooden walls.*
2. *A lean-to greenhouse.*
3. *A span roof greenhouse with all-glass walls.*
4. *A circular greenhouse.*
5. *A three-quarter span greenhouse.*

For orchids, you need a special house, as they require extra ventilators, and often two-tier staging so that the plants can be stood on the top lath staging, with pebbles or old coarse ashes which must be kept moist in order to provide the required humidity on the lower. The best choice for a vine or peaches or nectarines is a lean-to house where staging can be erected for ornamental plants.

No matter what type of greenhouse is finally chosen, there must be ample ventilators of the right size, situated on both sides of a span greenhouse, so that some are always leeward.

Siting the greenhouse Choose a position where there is maximum sunshine, especially in winter; avoid overhanging trees that drop leaves and substances that easily soil the glass. If possible, select a site fairly near to the house, where there is a good path and ideally close to a tap.

A greenhouse is traditionally aligned north to south, so that there is both a warmer and cooler side. But some gardeners prefer an east to west siting so that more light is received. Whatever the position, avoid exposure to the north and east winds; these mean draughts and some heat loss, especially if the north winds blow directly into the door. For preference, a lean-to should face south.

163

ERECTING THE GREENHOUSE

The foundation A proper, permanent foundation is all important. The ground plan, usually supplied by the manufacturer, must be strictly adhered to. A simple method for making a satisfactory foundation is to dig a 10-in. deep trench, 1 ft. wide, with vertical sides. In this is built a brick or concrete block footing. The foundation should be stronger in cultivated ground because sinking is more likely. When the superstructure is to rest on brick walls the top of the foundation must be 6 in. below ground level. Any electric cable should be laid before concreting.

A soil floor to the greenhouse is better than a solid or concrete one, because crops can be grown in it. Another advantage is that, during winter, the soil can dry out while, in the summer, it will help in maintaining a humid atmosphere.

Glazing Treat the structure with paint or preservative before glazing. Bed glass on to the glazing bars with putty. Use dry glass, because wet panes stick together and break more easily in cold weather. To avoid subsequent movement, check that the structure is secured to the foundation before glazing.

Plastic has not the same value as glass but is useful for summer protection or providing dappled light. It does not break, but it needs renewing periodically.

HEATING METHODS

Hot water Although this method involves stoking at least twice a day, regular cleaning and ash disposal, it is very satisfactory as the heat is evenly distributed without creating a dry atmosphere. The right fuel must be used.

Electricity Electrical heating is time- and labour-saving and requires no fuel storage. With the right heaters and thermostatic control, predetermined temperatures can be maintained, unless there are fuel cuts. The various methods are (1) a heated wire grid with air blowing over it, (2) a convector heater, producing warm air with no fan, and rapid warmth, but not so evenly distributed, (3) radiating tubes, plates or strips, (4) immersion heater used for hot-water pipes.

Bottom heat, for propagating seeds or root cuttings, which does not substantially heat the air, is provided by electric cables buried in the soil.

Paraffin heaters are widely used and with high quality heating oils, there is little danger of poisonous fumes. To achieve this, however, the burners must be kept clean so that incomplete combustion does not release harmful gases. For large houses, heaters with outside chimneys are essential. For small houses, there are several portable models available, needing little attention,

except re-filling. Choose one producing a blue flame, which results from complete combustion.

Manufacturers usually indicate the period of burning for one filling. More important is how much heat is produced. Heat is lost through ventilation, but stagnant air encourages fungoid diseases and other disorders, particularly with paraffin, so some ventilation is always needed except during the severest weather.

What can be grown largely depends upon the greenhouse temperature. Formerly, in large private gardens, there was a range of houses – the cold house, passing from the cool to the intermediate, and then the hot or stove house. Today few gardeners can afford more than one.

Specialists like to grow particular types of plants, but the less experienced usually cultivate a range, all of which must have similar greenhouse conditions.

TYPES OF GREENHOUSE

The cold greenhouse has only one source of heat – the sun. In it a colourful display can be had. In extra cold weather, some protection is given by blinds, which pull up and down. Many plants killed by winter dampness outdoors will survive the winter indoors.

In such limited space, the staging should preferably be of slatted wood. This allows an air circulation around the pots, avoids atmospheric dampness in winter, and can be erected in tiers. Unfortunately, it also encourages plants drying out in summer. To avoid this, asbestos sheeting can be put over the staging, on which small shingle is placed. This can be kept damp in summer to provide humidity, and be left dry in late autumn and winter.

The cool greenhouse has a constant, minimum night temperature of 40°–45°F (4°–7°C). It must be controlled by adequate ventilation. Generally, it is plants in the smaller greenhouse, particularly where there are insufficient ventilators, that suffer most from bad air conditioning. Fresh air is important, but when the ventilators are opened the temperature falls. It is essential to achieve a balance, remembering that dispersal of stagnant air is vital for plant life.

The intermediate or warm house with a winter-night temperature above 48°F (8°–9°C), allows the cultivation of some exotic plants. Such a house, if possible, should be sited to derive the fullest possible benefit from the sun. In warm greenhouses, automatic ventilation is an investment. Costing nothing to run, it is easily fitted.

ABOVE: *The spectacular flowers of* Amaryllis hippeastrum *which can be grown indoors or in a cool greenhouse.*
OPPOSITE: *Flowering and foliage plants in a cool span roof greenhouse. They need good ventilation and a constant night temperature.*

A hot (or stove) house has a winter temperature never below 60°F (16°C). Few amateur gardeners have this type because of the running costs. Hothouses give you the opportunity to grow the more tender plants. Apart from temperature, the layout and attention needed are as for the warm greenhouse.

PLANTS TO GROW

In the cold greenhouse Choice of the right plants and their proper care are important to success in a cold greenhouse. It is distinctly advantageous to be able to provide just enough heat to prevent the temperatures falling below freezing. Overwatering often causes failures during winter; in frosty weather plants should be kept on the dry side.

Many alpines can be raised from seed and grown successfully in the cold house. These include *Aster alpinus*, aethionemas, aubrietas, campanulas, dianthus, gentians, primulas, saxifrages, and miniature cupressus.

Many bulbs, including crocus and irises, particularly the Dutch varieties, 'Wedgewood', lavender, and 'Princess Beatrix', yellow, and the dwarfs, *I. danfordiae* and *I. reticulata*, violet, do well, giving unblemished blooms. Narcissus, early tulips, fritillarias, liliums, scillas, tritonia, and early gladioli produce a bright display. The lime-loving *Cypripedium calceolus* has very handsome flowers. Daphne, *Erica carnea*, forsythia, prunus, spiraea, and other early flowering shrubs in pots, housed in December or January, give a showy display. *Helleborus niger*, the Christmas Rose, responds well.

In the cool greenhouse Rather surprisingly, numbers of exotic plants become acclimatized and grow in a cool greenhouse. Daisy-flowered plants, like arctotis, dimorphotheca and ursinia, easily raised from seed, will bloom continuously. There is also long lasting brilliant orange-amber *Gerbera jamesonii*. *Erica hyemalis*, the Cape Heath, has long white-tipped, pink bells, while there are species with red, orange, and yellow flowers. Gardenias, daphnes, epacris, and daturas are handsome shrubs.

Interesting among other flowering plants are *Hoya bella*, the flesh pink, wax plant, blue Ipomoea or morning glory, easily raised from seed, yellow *Jasminum primulinum*, *Lapageria rosea*, rich pink waxy bells, the Passion flower, and *Thunbergia alata*, orange with a black throat.

Among the foliage plants are *Lippia citriodora*, the lemon scented verbena, caladiums, with beautifully spotted and veined leaves, grey-green-foliaged *Eucalyptus glo-*

bulus, Grevillea robusta, Maranta leuconeura, with leaves curiously marked and spotted, trailing *Saxifraga sarmentosa.* Ferns and palms can be grown for indoors.

Climbing plants, include the brightly coloured mauve bougainvillea, the fragrant white and pink *Jasminum polyanthum,* and *Cobaea scandens.*

Carnations are important cool greenhouse flowers. Their cultivation is described later.

Fruit in the greenhouse Specially constructed greenhouses are available for growing fruit, but they are mainly used by professional gardeners.

PROPAGATION

Greenhouse and frame plants are raised most easily from seed, but many must be propagated by cuttings, divisions or offsets.

By seeds Most seeds germinate in a temperature of 60°–65°F (15°–18°C). The whole greenhouse need not be kept at this temperature – an independently heated propagator can be used.

John Innes Seed Compost is the best growing medium, because destructive damping-off diseases frequently result from the use of unsterilized soil.

The compost is evenly, lightly compacted in trays, pans or boxes. Sow thinly. Very fine seeds, such as those of begonias and gloxinias, are not covered, but just pressed into the surface. Larger ones are lightly covered. Water, and place in the propagator, and cover the seed containers with glass and paper. When the seedlings appear, remove the glass and paper and keep the surface just moist.

Prick out seedlings early. Keep the pricked out seedlings in the shade for a few days until they are established. When large enough, pot them on.

Stem cuttings These are taken from healthy shoots or tips, with two or three joints, cleanly cutting below the lowest one,

ABOVE: Jasminum mesnyi *flowers in spring and can be grown in a cool greenhouse or outdoors against a warm, sunny wall.*
BELOW: *Several different models of garden frame.*
OPPOSITE: *Constructing the frame light for a home-made garden frame. The top rail can be joined to the side rails either by a mortice and tenon joint or a half-lap joint (see far right of diagram).*

Remove the lower leaves. For good results, insert the cuttings around the edges of pots containing a well-drained, moisture-retaining compost. Water them in and place them in a heated propagator, or alternatively in a polythene bag; close it with a rubber band, but keep it off the cuttings.

When the cuttings have successfully rooted, gradually ventilate the propagating case until the cuttings are at the temperature of the greenhouse. Cuttings with hairy leaves are liable to damp off, and should be rooted on the open bench and shaded to minimize transpiration.

Leaf cuttings Certain plants, like peperomias and saintpaulias, are increased by leaf cuttings. Healthy mature leaves are trimmed so that the stalk is up to 1 in. long. Insert them in compost with their leaf blades just touching the soil.

Rex begonias need their main veins cut in several places. Weight or peg down the leaves onto the soil surface. They will develop where the cuts are made.

Stem sections Ficus, dracaenas and some others are propagated from stem sections where there is a dormant bud in an axil which will develop into a good plant. Place in a mixture of equal parts peat and sand.

Leaf-bud cuttings These are $\frac{3}{4}$ in. long pieces of stem with a centrally situated leaf and dormant bud, taken in August or September, when the plants are mature. This method is suitable for aphelandra, camellia, pilea, and ficus.

Division Chlorophytum and maranta and other plants can be divided in spring. The offsets of many bulbous plants can be detached and planted.

Using frames for propagation When supplied with soil warming equipment, frames may be used to germinate seeds, start cuttings and bring chrysanthemums, carnations, and others through cold periods. When used without heat, frames are useful for blanching endive and for growing a number of vegetable crops and salads.

THE GARDEN FRAME

Types The standard patterns of frames, determined by the size of the lid, are English, measuring 6 ft. long × 4 ft. wide, with four 18 in. × 12 in. panes of glass, or 4 ft. × 3 ft.; Dutch, 59 in. × 31¾ in., with a single pane and French, 4 ft. 4 in. × 4 ft. 5 in. They are usually of deal, cedarwood, cast aluminium or steel, or the body might be of brick, breeze blocks, or plastic. Many are portable, with single or span roofs, and easily removable sliding tops.

The choice depends upon the purpose for which the frame is required, the space available, and the price, but the wisest decision is to buy the largest frame possible.
Making a garden frame A 'do-it-yourself' exponent would have no difficulty in making a frame for himself. Given below are directions for constructing a simple frame, which is capable of extension by removing the end panel and adding to the back and front ones. The main dimensions of this frame are height at the rear 18 in., height at front 12 in., length 4 ft. 10 in., and width 4 ft. 1½ in. The light or 'top' is 4 ft. 10 in. long and 4 ft. 3½ in. wide.

Construction commences with the body of the frame, which is cut from 6-in. wide timber, ¾-in. thick. The back section, of three lengths, is nailed to two corner posts (1 in. × 1 in.), which are placed 1¼ in. in to accommodate the corner posts and thickness of the side sections, with bolt holes drilled in the top and bottom. The front section is similarly constructed except that it is comprised of two lengths of 6 ft. × ¾ in. timber, and the corner posts are 1½ in. × 1½ in.

The side sections are cut from three lengths of 6 × ¾ in. timber. The top length is carefully sawn so that it tapers from a back depth of 18 in. to 12 in. in the front. When shaped, the lengths are nailed to two corner posts placed right up to the outside edges of the side pieces. The top of these are sawn to the angle of the top lengths of timber. Two bolt holes are drilled at the top and bottom through these and the side panels.

The body of the frame is assembled with 8 in. × ¼ in. thick threaded bolts about 3½–4 in. long, so that the end sections are located inside the back and front ones hard up against the corner posts.

The frame light on top has two side rails and a top rail cut from 2 in. × 2 in. timber. The bottom one is cut from 3 in. × 1½ in. timber. The central rail is cut from 2 in. × 2 in. and ½ in. square fillets serve as glazing bars or rebates.

The top rail is joined to the side rails either by a mortice and tenon joint, or a half-lap joint. In either case the joint should be glued and scrwed together.

The centre rail is half-lapped into the centre of the top rail and half-lapped at its base or bottom end so that, when screwed into the top of the bottom rail at its centre, the top of the centre rail sits 1 in. proud of the bottom rail. The bottom is joined to the two side rails by mortice and tenon joints, which are situated 2 in. in from their front end. When screwed and glued in place, the two ends of these side units should extend 2 in. past the bottom edge of the bottom rail, thus providing a useful hand grip when the light is being handled.

The ½-in. square lengths are nailed along the inside face of the top side and centre rails to provide rebates for the glass. These should be placed so that the bottom sheet of glass rests on top of the bottom rail.

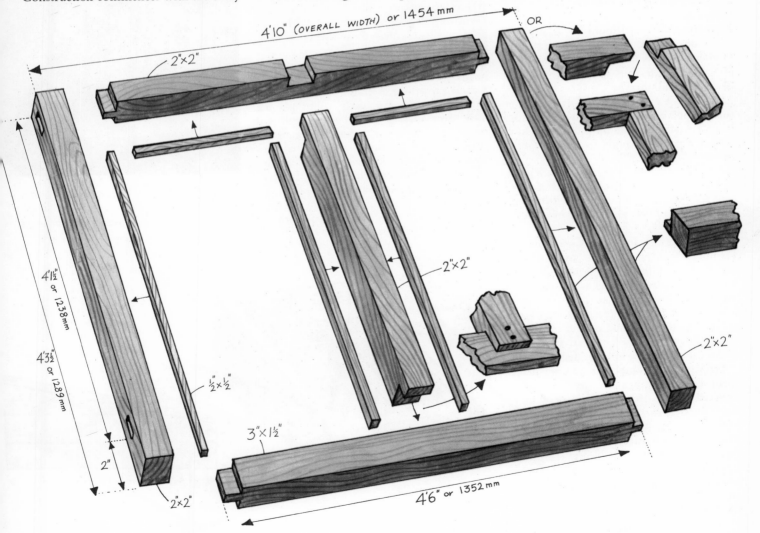

Glazing is done with four sheets of 2 ft. × 2 ft. panes, two pieces either side of the centre rail. They should overlap by about ½ in. Bed well in a generous layer of putty and retain in place by glazing sprigs.

The frame top, which should rest neatly on top of the base section, can be pushed back to allow ventilation.

Although not so durable, a lighter version can be constructed using polythene sheeting.

As an alternative, a frame can be made with sides of plastic; this gives more light and so the seedlings are not drawn up. The sides are made up to the same dimensions as those of the timber frame with strips of wood used to fasten the plastic sheet to the framing. The frame light is made from a simple wooden support, using 1½ × ½-in. timber, and the corners reinforced with plywood angle pieces or galvanized metal corner brackets.

A plastic covering is lightly stretched over the framework and fastened with strips of wood. If desired, a double glazed frame can be made simply by attaching a second layer of plastic to its inside face as well as the sides. A plastic frame should be satisfactory for a few seasons, after which it might deteriorate.

Position A frame should be ideally face due south and not be under or near trees. Good protection against cold winds will be afforded if it is backed on to the greenhouse or other building.

When not a permanent construction, be sure that it is on a draught- and damp-proof base. To facilitate handling during winter or wet weather, provide a path around the frame.

Keep the glass clean and sealed with putty so that rain does not penetrate. Also, make sure that when opening and shutting rain does not get in between the panes or hinge joints.

Water carefully to avoid excess moisture. Dampness can be kept out by placing a lump of quicklime under each light; this absorbs moisture in winter and lasts several weeks.

Heat loss through the bottom of the frame into the surrounding soil can be reduced by a 2–3-in. deep bed of cinders under the site before soil is added.

Propagating frames for raising plants from seed or cuttings can simply be a box covered with a sheet of glass or a more elaborate structure with a wooden or metal base.

Use A garden frame can become an introduction to greenhouse culture. Temperatures are more readily controlled during summer in a frame than in a greenhouse, where they fluctuate readily. This is because the light is easily removable.

Hardening off Frames are invaluable for hardening off greenhouse-raised plants that have to be acclimatized to outdoor conditions. When greenhouses become overcrowded, a frame can accommodate plants at different stages of development.

Heating Frames can be electrically heated by soil cables laid on 2 in. of sand and covered by another 2 in. before the soil is put on. There must be no crossing or touching by different sections of the same element.

Ventilation To minimize mildew and rotting, ventilation is needed daily, except in very cold or frosty weather. Cold winds should not be allowed to blow into a frame. Sliding lights are better than hinged ones, because they can be kept open away from the wind by using little blocks. Protective mats are very valuable during frost, but must not be used wet. It is advisable to have duplicates so that wet ones can be dried.

Forcing With heat, chicory, rhubarb, and seakale can be forced; early potatoes 'Home Guard' and 'Arran Pilot' can be planted in January. Lettuce sown in September will heart by Christmas; partially grown lettuce, cauliflowers and endives can be put in frames to mature. Parsley transferred in October will give winter pickings. Mustard and cress, successively sown, crops continuously.

Drying Onions, potatoes, and haricot beans can be dried in frames.

Catch cropping A frame is excellent for catch cropping, e.g. early tulips planted 4-in. deep early November, overplanted with October-sown lettuce 'Trocadero'; 'Early French Breakfast' radish sown between the plants in January, will mature before the lettuce or tulips are very large.

A greenhouse annexe Frames serve to accommodate plants out of bloom and ones for which the greenhouse is too warm in summer.

ABOVE: Anthurium scherzerianum *is also called the flamingo plant.*
BELOW: *The finished garden frame, showing the dimensions of the panes for glazing.*

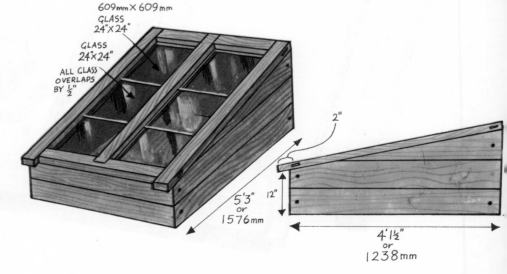

shade. Stop side-shoots at four leaves. Spread growth evenly over the frame area. Remove male flowers, otherwise fruits taste bitter.

Melons For each Dutch Net or Cantaloupe melon, dig a trench 1-ft. wide and deep. Fill it with fermenting manure. Plant the melon in a mould of soil on top of this. Water and keep the frame closed for four or five days. Shade from hot sun; avoid excess moisture. Hand pollinate female flowers and spray with water early mornings. Give liquid manure weekly. Harvest when circular crack appears at base of the stem.

Tomatoes If necessary, excavate soil to give 1-ft. headroom, and replace with a mixture of 4 parts loam and 1 part each, well-rotted manure (or compost), silver sand and mortar rubble or hydrated lime, plus a 3-in. potful of tomato fertilizer per every bushel. Plant in mid-March, 15–18 in. apart. Stake and keep side-shoots removed.

YEAR ROUND INTEREST

A greenhouse and a garden frame give greater value and interest when used in conjunction with one another. There never seems to be enough room even in the largest greenhouse.

Many ornamental greenhouse plants in pots benefit enormously from standing outdoors in the summer, but they must be in a place protected from winds and where watering requirements can be met. Ideally, they can be plunged in a frame, with the light removed during reasonable weather. This applies to Indian azaleas, poinsettias and hydrangeas.

Frames are valuable in their use for the propagation from seeds, cuttings, etc. of many highly decorative greenhouse plants; also for hardening off half-hardy annuals, such as asters, antirrhinums, petunias, sweet peas, and zinnias.

Viola cuttings can be over-wintered; good root growth is developed on bulbs in pots by plunging them into a frame prior to transferring them to a greenhouse. In summer, frames can house greenhouse plants that resent high temperatures, while shaded frames can hold calceolarias, cyclamen, and primulas, such as *P. obconica*, *P. malacoides*, and *P. sinensis*.

Regal pelargoniums and perpetual flowering carnations will benefit from being place in sunny frames from June to mid-September. The lights can be taken off or the sides of the frames raised for tall plants.

Pans of alpines kept in the frame in summer can be transferred to the greenhouse for autumn and winter display.

The use of a greenhouse and frames means that a kind of shuttle service is operated. Many young plants may be started in the

WHAT TO GROW

Garden frames can always be used to grow a variety of edible and ornamental plants. They will give winter protection to cuttings of hardy plants and seedlings of autumn sown sweet peas. Frame-grown violets are always appreciated.

Bulbs Spring-flowering bulbs in containers can be kept in a frame and taken a few at a time into the house to give a succession of blooms. Bulbs and tubers, such as hippeastrum, begonias, freesias, etc. can be allowed to ripen off in a frame, prior to winter storage.

Bulbs in containers plunged in peat or leaf mould in the frame will make good roots.

Greenhouse plants Some popular greenhouse plants can be sown in pots in early summer and kept in a cool frame until September.

In brick- or wooden-made frames, geraniums, heliotrope, fuchsias, and similar plants can be over-wintered, providing there is sufficient heat to keep the air buoyant and damp-free.

Beans and peas Dwarf French Beans, 'Masterpiece', sown in pots every three weeks from September to March, will be ready 10 weeks later. Early peas, e.g. 'Foremost', under glass without heat, are protected from cold winds, wet soil and mice.

Cucumbers To give heat and humidity make a 9-in. deep hot bed of fresh manure in March. Plant greenhouse-raised seedlings in April.

Alternatively dig a 6–9-in. deep trench along the centre of the frame in early May. Fill it with grass mowings, old leaves and fermenting straw. Set out plants, raised in a heated propagator, in early June.

The frame soil should consist of fibrous loam, old manure and leaf mould or compost. One plant is sufficient for a 6 ft. × 4 ft. frame. Provide a humid atmosphere and

greenhouse early in the year, moved to the frame in summer, and taken back into the greenhouse again in autumn.

POPULAR GREENHOUSE PLANTS

Abutilon (Common names: Indian mallow, flowering maple, false maple, lantern flower). Half-hardy evergreen. Propagated by 4–5-in. long young wood cuttings in autumn or spring at 60°F (16°C), half-ripened cuttings in a polythene bag or frame in July or seeds sown in March in warmth. Compost used: two parts fibrous loam, one part each peat and silver sand.

Abūtilons require a summer and winter temperature of 60°–65°F (16°–18°C) and 40°F (4°C) respectively.

Species include *A. darwinii*, 4 ft., orange; *A. megapotamicum*, 2½ ft., orange-pink; *A. striatum* 'Thomsonii', 6–10 ft., mottled green and yellow foliage.

Acacia (wattle, mimosa). A shrub or small tree with yellow flowers in spring. Minimum winter temperature required is 45°F (7°C). Kept moist, pot plants can stand out in the sun during the summer. Pruned after flowering. Propagate by cuttings in a propagator in summer.

Species include *A. dealbata* (most commonly grown); *A. armata* 9–10 ft.; and *A. drummondii*.

Achimenes belong to the same family as the gloxinias and are perfect for hanging baskets, indoor window boxes, tubs, and pots. Periodical stopping produces good bushy plants.

Plant tubers in peaty compost in January at a temperature of 65°–70°F (18°–21°C) in a close, humid atmosphere, giving more ventilation once flower buds are formed. After flowering, dry tubers in a light, airy place at a temperature not falling below 50°F (10°C).

They can also be propagated from seeds sprinkled on the surface of fine compost in pans and gently firmed in at a temperature of 70°F (21°C). Germination takes a fortnight. Pot on in JIP 2 or a mixture of leafmould, peat, silver sand, and some old manure as the plants grow. Leaf and stem cuttings root easily.

Anthurium Their ornamental foliage and brightly coloured flowers from April to August, give them the name flamingo plants. They flourish in rough peat and sphagnum moss (equal parts), shaded from direct sunshine and need a minimum winter temperature of 60°F (16°C). Put in a moist atmosphere and copiously water in spring and summer. Repot in March. Propagate by division in March or seed at 70°F (21°C). Species include *A. andreanum* with heart-shaped leaves and orange-red, red, pink, rose, or white flowers; *A. scherzerianum*,

scarlet flowers with a background of deep green leaves.

Aphelandra A handsome-leafed, evergreen shrub, *A. squarrosa* 'Louisae' has showy flowers and bracts. Flourishes in peaty loam with warmth. Remove unwanted growth after flowering and keep at 50°F (10°C), watering little until spring. Taken as heel cuttings, these new shoots should be rooted in a propagating frame and then planted in 4- or 5-in. pots; left unstopped, it will flower the first year.

Asparagus belongs to the lily family, but nevertheless provides florist's cut 'fern'. Grows in JIP 1, requiring good watering, otherwise the foliage discolours. Sow seed in spring or summer at 60°F (16°C) and transplant to 3-in. pots, discarding any slow or irregular growers.

A. plumosus 'Nanus' has long trails of fine foliage, ideal for cutting and making buttonholes. *A. sprengeri*, producing 1–1½-ft. long, bright green sprays, is valuable for hanging baskets.

Azalea Widely sold as azalea, *A. indica*, correctly called *Rhododendron simsii*, is a most popular winter-flowering plant. Colours include pink, red, and white shades. Plant in a peaty mixture, which must be kept moist as it is difficult to remoisten when dry. After flowering, remove faded blooms, repot as necessary in May and stand outdoors in shelter or plunged in the soil. Re-house in the greenhouse in September maintaining a moist atmosphere. Syringe with water frequently to encourage bud formation. Best to water with rainwater, avoiding lime in the water, and any compost. Propagate by cuttings in summer or early autumn in a propagator.

Begonias This beautiful genus comprises several groups with distinguishing features. Require moist, peaty compost, good light and liquid feeding when growing. See *Popular Garden Flowers*.

Beloperone (Shrimp plant). *B. guttata* is a South American evergreen, with inconspicuous flowers concealed by decorative

ABOVE: *The leaves of bromeliads form a central cup which should be filled with water at greenhouse temperature.*
OPPOSITE: Echinocereus blanckii, *a brilliant pink desert cactus.*

pink bracts, which colour best in the sun, without too much warmth. Needs well-drained, fairly rich soil. Keep dry and cool in winter to encourage rest. Cut back early in the year. Over-watering causes leaf drop. Propagate by cuttings in spring, preferably with bottom heat.

Boronia B. *megastigma*, a sweet-scented Australian shrub. Sow seeds thinly and evenly in sandy compost at not less than 55°–60°F (13°–16°C). Sometimes they take four to six weeks to germinate. At 1-in. high, pot seedlings on to 2½-in. pots, using lime-free, sandy loam, and to larger ones ith growth. Dress occasionally with leaf-mould. Prune in spring or by cutting its maroon and yellow flowers that are produced over a long period.

Bougainvillea have gay flower bracts throughout the summer if given sun, good drainage, climbing room, moisture, and frequent liquid feeds. Do not over-pot. Prune back side-shoots to two buds after flowering, removing weak shoots. Free-

flowering B. *glabra* and B.g. 'Sanderiana' are pink and B. *spectabilis* mauve-pink.

Boussingaultia (The Madeira Vine). *B. basselloides*, hailing from Ecuador and Peru, is a quick-growing, half-hardy, perennial climber, with heart-shaped leaves and sprays of scented, white flowers in autumn borne on reddish stems. Requires very moist, sandy loam and peat in summer. Store tubers in winter, either by drying off in the pot or lifting like dahlias. Propagated by seeds in spring or by division.

Bouvardia are evergreens that display their flowers splendidly on new shoots between September and January – B. *humboldtii* are white and B. *triphylla* scarlet. Grow in small pots, well-watered and fed in summer. Like plenty of light without being in direct sun. Pinch out growths continuously to give bushy specimens. Prune after resting a few weeks. Propagate by cuttings in spring.

Bromeliads have decorative foliage and sometimes colourful flowers. There are two main groups (1) epiphytic, living on boughs of trees (2) terrestial, growing in soil or on rocks. Most epiphytes have leaves in a rosette formation, making a central cup, which collects water. Filled with water at greenhouse temperature, they last long periods of dryness. Keep roots just moist and give liquid fertilizer in the spring.

Easy growing bromeliads include *Aechmea rhodocyanea, Billbergia nutans*, and *Neoregelia caroliniae tricolor. Cryptanthus bivittatus*, one of the smaller ones, forms a star-shaped, prostrate rosette of leaves, which are striped in shades of green and have crumpled edges. Propagated from side-shoots. *C. zonatus* has maroon-green foliage with silver or yellow markings. *Vriesea splendens* has pale green leaves, banded maroon; propagated by off-shoots.

Brunfelsia are evergreen shrubs producing scented flowers freely in spring and summer. Appreciate good light, but not prolonged sunshine, well-drained, rich soil and a warm, moist atmosphere when growing. Propagate by semi-ripe cuttings in a warm frame. Species include: B. *americana*, white; B. *calycina*, purple passing to white.

Cacti and other succulents are very popular, easily cultivated plants, widely grown in greenhouses. Their extensive range of shapes, habits, and in many species showy flowers, make them attractive. See under *Indoor Plants*.

Caladium are tuberous-rooted perennials with richly coloured foliage, liking warmth – a minimum winter temperature of 55°F (13°C) required. Start tubers in March in peaty soil, frequently syringing overhead. When flourishing, transfer to 5-in. pots of two parts loam, one part each peat, decayed manure, and sand. Water regularly when growing, but when leaves discolour, dry off the roots in warmth. Propagate by division in spring, occasionally from seed. Species include *C. bicolor* and *C. humboldtii* and their forms.

Calceolaria are easily-grown plants, succeeding at 50°–60°F (10°–16°C). They are bushy plants with pouch-like, plain, and freckled flowers in yellow, red, and brown. Sow seeds in June and July. Prick out seedlings early and pot in firmly pressed, light, rich soil. Keep them cool and shaded, with overhead spraying and place them on a base of moist gravel or shingle to encourage even growth. In winter provide a temperature of 45°–50°F (8°–10°C) and less moisture. A rather drier atmosphere is needed as flower buds develop. Flowering sized plants are obtained in about nine months.

There are various hybrids – 'C. 'Multi-flora Nana', 9-in. tall, 'Albert Kent' hybrids, 15 in., and F_1 hybrids, and also the species *C. integrifolia* (*C. rugosa*), 3–4 ft.

Callistemon This Australian shrub, *C. citrinus*, (the bottle brush), has leathery, greyish-green leaves and terminal spikes of yellow flowers (crimson in the form *splendens*). Requires well-drained, peaty loam with much sun, light and air. Syringe overhead with water and cut back after flowering. Repot every third year. Stand outdoors during summer. Never expose to temperatures below 40°F (7°C). Propagate by ripe wood cuttings in late spring or summer.

Camellia These shrubby plants are easier to grow than generally believed. They like a summer temperature of 60°–65°F (16°–18°C), plenty of light and sun, sandy loam and leaf mould and frequent overhead syringings when buds swell until colour shows. They dislike being moved, because their buds fail to open or fall. Repot ensuring good drainage after flowering. Feed early in spring. Prune back unwanted shoots after flowering. Propagate from seed or cuttings rooted in late summer in a warm frame. Many named single and double varieties in shades of red, pink, and white.

Campanula *C. isophylla*, a blue trailer, gives a fine display from spring to autumn. Excellent for cooler parts of the greenhouse and outdoors in summer, growing in any good soil. Remove faded flowers. Propagate from cuttings or division in spring. *C. i.* 'Alba' is white.

Canna see *Bulbs for Year-Round Colour*.

Cantua *C. buxifolia* is an easily cultivated branching shrub that can, if desired, be trained as a climber. Its clusters of six to eight large, funnel-shaped, rosy-red, suffused yellow blooms, opening from bright red buds, appear in April and May. Grows in compost of turfy loam, leafmould, and sand. Propagate by half-ripe cuttings at a temperature of 50°–55°F (10°–13°C), during summer.

Carex *C. morrowii* 'Variegata' is a decorative grass with narrow green leaves, edged white. Keep moist and out of bright sun, otherwise it will dry out quickly. Pot in loamy soil, with a little bonemeal in small pots. Propagate by division in spring.

Carnation These are best grown alone. The two main greenhouse groups are 'Perpetual Flowering' and 'Perpetual Malmaison'. Rooted cuttings are planted in spring, or better, established plants in 5- or 6-in. pots. For success, they need good ventilation and a fairly dry, cool atmosphere; even during frost, a temperature around 45°F (7°C) is sufficient. Avoid overwatering, but periodically feed with carnation fertilizer. The varieties and methods of stopping are given in specialist growers' catalogues. Propagate from cuttings or pipings in spring.

Celosia see *Hardy Flowers that Bloom Each Year*.

Ceropegia These fleshy-rooted, twining, semi-climbing plants are best in full light, out of direct sun, planted in a well-drained compost containing much peat and a little bonemeal, with free ventilation. A slight winter rest and restricting roots are beneficial. Propagate by short cuttings in a propagator. *C. woodii* (hearts entangled) has twining growth, small heart-shaped leaves and pinkish-purple flowers.

Chrysanthemum No collection of autumn- and winter-flowering plants is complete without chrysanthemums. See *Popular Garden Flowers*.

ABOVE: Datura suavolens, *the angel's trumpet.*

TOP: Campanula isophylla.

OPPOSITE: *Perpetual-flowering carnation 'Arthur Sim'.*

Cineraria For blooms from December to April, first sow in May and then fortnightly. Transplant seedlings to 5-in. pots, firmly without bruising the stems or burying the crowns, and stand, away from sunshine, in a shaded cold frame. House in September at 50°F (10°C), feeding with liquid manure, when flowering shoots appear. Treat with derris insecticide against white and greenfly. Good strains include C. 'Multiflora Nana', 1 ft. compact, C. 'Moll' strain, 1 ft. compact, enormous heads, C. 'Stellata', star-shaped flowers, immense clusters.

Citrus C. mitis is an attractive branching shrub, 18 in. high, with small, dark green leaves and fragrant, white flowers, followed by oranges. Requires a minimum winter temperature of 50°F (10°C), with a moist atmosphere at fruit-setting time. During the summer ensure good ventilation. Pots may be plunged outdoors in a sheltered sunny situation, to help ripen wood and develop next season's flower buds. Propagate by cuttings in spring.

Clivia see *Bulbs for Year-Round Colour.*
Codiaeum see *Indoor Plants.*
Coleus see *Hardy Flowers that Bloom Each Year.*
Columnea These evergreen, trailing plants require a minimum winter temperature of 55°F (13°C), a compost of equal parts peat, sphagnum moss, and sand, with a little charcoal, also water, warmth, humidity, and regular liquid feeding in summer. In winter they need cool and dry to encourage resting. Leave in same container for several years for effective hanging baskets and cascades. Propagate by half-ripened cuttings in spring. Bushy growth and trailing long stems ensured by stopping twice. Species include scarlet and yellow C. gloriosa and orange-scarlet C. glabra.
Cordyline see *Indoor Plants.*
Cuphea C. ignea (C. platycentra) the cigar plant, is a delightful pot plant, but also grows outdoors. The red tube the flowers form has a dark red ring at one end which, with the wide mouth, resembles a cigar.

Flowers on 12–15 in. stems from July to September. Propagate from seeds in March.
Cyclamen see *Bulbs for Year-Round Colour.*
Cypripedium This orchid grows easily with other plants at a minimum winter temperature of 45°F (7°C). Keep out of draughts and direct sunshine, and keep humid during spring and summer by soaking the pots every five days. Pot from March to July in orchid compost based on osmunda fibre or sphagnum moss and place on a gravel-covered staging or inverted pots. Sphagnum moss round the pots helps. C. insigne, with white, purple, and brown flowers and its hybrids are reliable.
Datura D. suaveolens, the angel's trumpet, is an impressive decorative greenhouse shrub with its white, pendulous, trumpet-shaped blooms in late summer. Water copiously in summer and shade from direct sunshine. Keep almost dry in winter. Grows 10 ft. tall, but can be controlled by hard pruning. Propagate from cuttings in light soil.
Dipladenia An attractive twining plant needing a minimum winter temperature of 55°F (13°C), a moist atmosphere and abundant water in summer. Propagate by young cuttings in warmth in spring. The trumpet-shaped flowers of D. brearleyana are pinkish-red and those of D. splendens pink, in large heads.
Dracaena These variously shaped and coloured, splendid foliage plants thrive in a minimum winter temperature of 55°F (13°C). They grow in rough peaty loam in full light. Propagate from pieces of stems in a propagator with bottom heat. Species include D. deremensis, with silvery stripes; D. godseffiana, creamy spots, and D. sanderiana, leaves edged ivory.
Eranthemum E. pulchellum (macrocephalum), a beautiful blue winter- and spring-flowering, warm greenhouse shrub, 2–2½ ft., grows easily in fibrous loam, leaf mould, and sand. Propagate from basal shoots, taken from plants cut after flowering, planted in a mixture of equal parts, loam, leaf mould, and sand or JIP 2. When rooted, pot on in 3-in. pots of this same compost and keep humid at not lower than 60°F (16°C).
Erica This vast genus includes Cape heaths (E. gracilis and E. × hyemalis), excellent winter-flowering plants for cool greenhouses. They require lime-free compost, regular pinching, and constant watering. Remove dead flowers and stand outside in the summer. Propagate from new growth cuttings in November in peat and sand, preferably with bottom heat 60°F (16°C).
Eucalyptus With silvery foliage, they make excellent pot plants when young. Like open rich compost, copious summer watering and drier in winter. Propagate by

seeds in spring or side-shoot cuttings in June.

Eucharis Requires abundant watering from March to September, less in winter, and a temperature of 60°–70°F (16°–21°C). Plant in John Innes Potting Compost no. 2. Liquid feed when flower buds begin unfolding; dry off as foliage discolours. Leave bulbs in the same pot for three years with annual top-dressing. Repot after flowering. *E. grandiflora amazonica*, the Amazon lily, has white, fragrant flowers in winter; *E. sanderi*, white and yellow.

Euphorbia The most popular greenhouse species is *E. pulcherrima*, which has showy scarlet or pink bracts in autumn and winter. Keep in full light at 60°–65°F (16°–18°C), with moderate watering, reduced when bracts expand. After flowering gradually dry off. At the end of April, soak the roots and cut back to 4 in. Use the shoots that develop as cuttings, dipping their cut ends in powdered charcoal before inserting into compost and maintain at 60°F (16°C). When well-rotted, feed with liquid manure. The 'Mikkelsen' strain is shorter and bushier and has long-lasting bracts.

Eurya *E. japonica* has glossy, dark green, leathery leaves, 1½–3 in. long. A cold greenhouse shrub, it can be grown outdoors in shelter in summer. Propagate by cuttings in spring or summer in a propagator.

Exacum These biennials, flourishing at 55°F (13°C) in winter, are sown early August in sandy compost. Water little from November to February. Transplant to 5-in. pots. *E. affine* has scented lilac flowers; *E. macranthum* blue.

X Fatshedera, a hybrid between fatsia and hedera. Tall with five-lobed, dark green or variegated leaves. Cultivated like Fatsia (below), propagated from stem cuttings in spring or summer.

Fatsia *F. japonica*, false castor oil plant, is a tall shrub with large, dark green, 7 to 9-lobed leaves. Grows outdoors, but impressive in tubs. Propagate by seed or cuttings (this is essential with *F.j.* 'Variegata', with white tipped leaves).

Ferns Ferns, except those with hairy foliage, like occasional, overhead sprayings with tepid rainwater and to be in well-drained, moist compost, containing ample leaf mould and bonemeal. Propagate by sowing spores from undersides of the fronds and maintaining them at 50°–55°F (10°–13°C).

Cool greenhouse specimens include: *Adiantum cuneatum*, the maidenhair fern; *Nephrolepis exaltata*, *Pteris cristata*, *Davallia dissecta* (*trichomanoides*).

Ficus see *Indoor Plants*.

Francoa *F. ramosa*, hailing from Chile, has a stiff main spike, 2–3 ft. tall, of white or pinkish-red flowers throughout late sum-

mer and numerous subsidiary spikes, particularly if the main stem is shortened after flowering. Succeeds in the cool greenhouse at 60°F (16°C) in summer and not below 45°F (7°C) in winter.

Sow in March, with bottom heat. Pot up young plants in compost of equal parts sandy loam and leaf mould. Place in cool, airy frame during summer and house in greenhouse in early autumn. Require copious watering during spring and summer, but little in winter.

Freesia see *Bulbs for Year-Round Colour*.

Fuchsia see *Popular Garden Flowers*.

Gardenia *G. jasminoides* and varieties, with fragrant, white flowers, are excellent for a greenhouse maintaining minimum winter temperatures of 60°F (10°C). Too much watering, or too little, will cause bud drop. Syringe frequently in spring and summer, when not in flower. Plant in equal parts loam, peat, and decayed manure (or leaf mould) with a little charcoal, and shade from direct sunshine. Propagate from side-shoot cuttings in February or March at 70°–75°F (21°–24°C).

Gerbera The Barberton daisy (*G. jamesonii*) flourishes in containers, 15–18 in. deep, containing sandy, humus-rich, free-draining, water-retentive soil, without its crown buried. The best way to do this is to cover the soil with a layer of sand and shingle and plant the crown just above the soil level. Water plentifully in the

summer, sparsely in winter. Never cut the flowers; pull them from the crown. Propagate by sowing fresh seed thinly at 65°F (18°C), with bottom heat. Prick out seedlings into sandy compost, later transplanting them to pots. The Van Wijks' strain is best for size of flower, colour range and constitution.

Gloriosa The glory flower, *G. superba*, is a tuberous-rooted climbing shrub. See *Bulbs for Year-round Colour*.

Gloxinia see *Bulbs for Year-round Colour*.

Grevillea *G. robusta*, silk-bark oak, an evergreen with fern-like leaves in green, bronze, and near red, is easily grown. Requires well-drained soil, free ventilation and copious water in summer. Repot in March or April. Propagate from seed in spring at 65°F (18°C).

Heliotropium see *Hardy Flowers that Bloom Each Year*.

Hippeastrum see *Bulbs for Year-round Colour*.

Hoya *H. carnosa*, the wax flower, has flesh pink flowers and is a climber; less vigorous *H. bella* is a small pendulous shrub with crimson centres, suitable for hanging baskets. Both are evergreen. Needs watering freely in summer, moderately in winter and frequent sprayings overhead, while growing. Prune to remove unwanted shoots. Do not remove flower stalks, further flowers grow on secondary growths at their base. Propagate by layers or cuttings of current growth.

Humea *H. elegans*, the incense plant. Best treated as a biennial, sown in sandy soil in spring. Plants like rich soil containing lumpy peat. Grows 5-ft. tall. Its feathery flower plumes have many pink florets.

Impatiens (Busy Lizzie) The balsams have fleshy stems, 1–2-ft. high, and remain in flower for many months. *I. wallerana* with reddish stems and pink flowers has rose, red, and violet hybrids. Bright scarlet dwarf 'Scarlet Baby' and 'General Guisan', 5–10-in. high, with red and white blooms, are useful pot plants.

Sow from March to May at a temperature of 60°F (16°C). When the first rough leaf appears prick out and pot singly in compost rich in peat or leaf mould.

Kalanchoë Among these succulents with interesting foliage and attractive flowers from March onwards, are *K. blossfeldiana*, bright flame red, its dwarf form 'Tom Thumb', pink *K. carnea* (*laciniata*) and orange scarlet *K. flammea*. Flourish in a loam, leaf mould, and silver sand mixture, with a little bonemeal or old manure, in full light, when watered regularly. To encourage bushiness, pinch back shoots to two good leaves. Flowering time is lengthened until October by keeping plants at 60°F (16°C) from the end of July. Propagate

by seed in February and March or from summer cuttings.

Lantana These evergreens produce large heads of verbena-like flowers from spring to autumn. Species include *L. camara*, yellowish red, white *L. nivea*, and trailing, mauve *L. selloviana*. Flourish in rich soil, containing bonemeal. Cut back by 3 in. in February to maintain bushiness. New growths, produced at 60°F (16°C), are useful for cuttings, which are rooted with bottom heat. Also raised from seed.

Lapageria Standing as low as 40°F (4°C) in winter, *L. rosea*, with bell-like rosy-crimson flowers, is an excellent climber for a cool greenhouse. Although it can be potted, it is better planted out in well-drained, very peaty loam with a little added sand and charcoal. Requires shading from direct sunshine, much water in spring and summer, with overhead syringings until flower buds just break. Propagate by layering in summer.

Lilium Lilies flourish in compost comprising three parts fibrous loam, one part each peat (leaf mould), silver sand, and decayed manure or JIP 3. Plant bulbs for forcing in October and November in 6–7-in. pots, leaving space for top-dressing for stem-rooting species. Plunge in a cold frame. Bring them into a temperature of 40°–50°F (4°–10°C) in January, gradually increasing this to 60°–70°F (16°–21°C). Top dress when 5 or 6 in. high. Without heat,

ABOVE: Lilium longiflorum, *the white Easter lily.*
TOP: Euphorbia pulcherrima *blooms in autumn and winter.*
OPPOSITE: Lantana camara *is an evergreen shrub.*

plant in February for flowering May onwards. Many lilies make good pot plants, including *L. auratum* and *L. speciosum*, the white Easter lily, *L. longiflorum*, white *L. formosanum*, and creamy-white *L. brownii*, with brownish-red markings.

Maranta Marantas like warm, shady, humid conditions, with a winter temperature of 60°–65°F (16–18°C). Need abundant water during spring and summer. Propagate by division of crowns in spring.

The species, *M. leuconeura*, has lovely green leaves with white veins; in the form, *kerchoveana*, the beautiful emerald green leaves are blotched red. Called 'the prayer plant' because its leaves fold inwards and point upwards at night.

Mesembryanthemum This name covers a large group of different succulents, variously tall, bushy, prostrate, and creeping. Included are the lithops, which because of their shape and appearance, are sometimes called 'living stones'. The catalogues of specialists show that there are many types to choose from. See *Indoor Plants*.

Mimosa *M. pudica* is often called the 'humble' or 'sensitive' plant, because its leaflets droop when lightly touched. Although it has spikes of blue purple flowers, its foliage alone makes it worth growing and it is of special interest to children. Propagate from thinly sown seed in sandy compost at 60°–65°F (16°–18°C).

Nerium *N. oleander*, the oleander, is an evergreen shrub that thrives in pots or borders in a light, sunny greenhouse with a minimum winter temperature of 45°F (7°C). Repot in February. Prune previous season's growth to 3–4 in. from the base after flowering. Propagate from firm cuttings in early summer at 60°–65°F (16°–18°C). *N. oleander* has fragrant, rosy-pink flowers, with double white and red forms.

Opuntia Of the several groups of opuntia, the 'prickly pears' are most decorative. They have flat pads, which are stems not leaves. Easily grown in well-drained, rich loam with copious watering while growing, reducing in winter and in sun. Propagate by drying removed pads for three days and planting, and from seed. *O. microdasys* (bunny's ears) is an attractive bright green with red-brown areoles.

Palms Some palms thrive in the warm greenhouse with heat and moisture while growing. Like a compost of fibrous loam, coarse sand, and manure, frequent syringings in summer to develop the fronds and occasional sponging with soapy water to combat scale insects. Avoid overpotting. Useful palms include: *Cocos weddelliana* (reliable in small pots), *Howeia* (*Kentia*) *belmoreana*, *Phoenix dactylifera* (date palm), and *P. roebelinii* (with arching fronds, looks well in the greenhouse or living room).

Pancratium These handsome bulbous plants grow in pots in a cool greenhouse and flower freely when established and slightly pot bound. Repotting in spring-time is rarely needed more than once in three years. Thrive in three-parts loam, one-part decayed manure, and a little silver sand. Copiously water when growing, little in winter, when a temperature of 45°–50°F (7°–10°C) is adequate. *P. illyricum* and *P. maritimum*, both 2 ft., have fragrant white flowers.

Passiflora These very rigorous climbers, the passion flowers, can be grown in containers, but are best in a well-drained border of not too rich soil. Transplant only in spring. A winter temperature of 45°–50°F (7°–10°C) is sufficient. Propagate from cuttings of young shoots in spring. *P. caerulea*, blue, and its white form 'Constance Elliot' are best. *P. edulis* is bluish-purple followed by fruits.

Pilea With close mats of foliage, pileas are useful for the front of staging or draping containers. Like semi-shade, but dislike gas fumes. Propagate by spring cuttings. Grows freely in a moist atmosphere at 50°–60°F (10°–16°C). *P. cadieri* has small silvery marked, green, shiny leaves. *P. microphylla* (*muscosa*), the artillery plant, is so named because it discharges its pollen explosively.

Pelargonium The so-called geraniums are excellent greenhouse plants. See *Popular Garden Flowers*.

Platycerium These look well among colourful cool greenhouse flowers. Their common name, stag's horn fern, describes their shape. Easily cultivated in baskets or pots, but are amazing when growing on wood or bark, which they encircle with their strong, infertile fronds. They grow in damp rough peat and sphagnum moss in a light and moist atmosphere. Propagate by division. Species are *P. bifurcatum*, with 2-ft. fronds; *P. grande*, requiring more heat.

Primula These valuable species are raised from seed in spring and potted on in lightly firmed compost. Do not leave in too small a pot otherwise they starve. To give a long-lasting display they need shade, ventilation, no over-watering, and freedom from pests. *P. obconica* produces lilac, pink, crimson, or white flowers. Those with skin sensitive to touching its foliage should wear gloves. *P. malacoides* has tiers of dainty lavender to deep rose, white, some double, flowers. Sow in June. *P. sinensis* must be planted with their centres exposed to avoid decay. *P. × kewensis* gives fragrant, yellow flowers in winter or late spring.

Rehmannia A half hardy, perennial from China, *R. angulosa*, 2–4 ft. tall, has drooping, foxglove-like, pink flowers. Sow seed thinly from May to August, just covering the seed with compost. Prick out seedlings and pot on gradually to 6- to 7-in. pots. Keep from frost during winter. Water regularly in spring and summer, occasionally liquid feeding. Basal cuttings from good specimens can be rooted.

Rochea These are succulent plants. Their 12-in. stems produce long, thickly arranged, leathery leaves. Produces terminal, tubular, scarlet flowers in summer. Easily grown in rich, well-drained compost with abundant watering in spring and summer, little in winter and a winter temperature of 45°F (7°C). After flowering, trim back. Propagate by cuttings in the spring and give warmth while they become established.

Roses Space permitting, roses can be grown in a cool greenhouse in pots or the border. They need well-drained compost containing fibrous loam and bonemeal and ample decaying manure.

Saintpaulia The African violet is not the easiest plant to grow but understanding its likes and dislikes leads to success. Light is important, particularly winter sunshine. Too little light causes lack of flowering, and too much produces anaemic-looking foliage and short stems. Maintain the warmth at 60°–70°F (16°–21°C) by day and 55°F (13°C) at night, avoiding draughts and stagnant air. Dislikes gas fumes. Water carefully using tepid water. Cold water causes leaf spotting. Propagate by leaf cuttings, also from seed at 70°F (21°C). When sowing, press the seed into the compost and sprinkle a little silver sand over the surface to prevent damping off. Prick out and pot up. Repot from February to May.

The main species grown, *S. ionantha*, has violet-blue flowers, but there are many double and single blue, pink and white hybrids available.

Salpiglossis *S. sinuata* has brown, deep violet, orange, yellow and white funnel-shaped flowers, covered with darker veins. Sow seeds thinly in John Innes Seed Compost at 55°–60°F (13°–16°C) in late August for winter and spring and in February for summer flowering. Prevent soil drying out by covering with paper. Pot seedlings with three rough leaves. Pot on with growth. Shade from direct sunshine. August sowings, placed in the cold frame, can be brought indoors when cold comes. Good strains are 'Superbissima' and F_1 'Splash'.

Sanseviera Mother-in-law's tongue. This favourite foliage plant has narrow, erect, pointed, fleshy leaves. See *Indoor Plants*.

Schizanthus The butterfly flower or poor man's orchid is a showy, easily grown cool greenhouse plant. Sow seed in August and September, or spring, in pots of John Innes Seed Compost in a cold frame. When large enough, transplant the seedlings to small

ABOVE: Pilea cadierei *'Moon Glow'*.
TOP: *The beautiful waxy white flowers of* Stephanotis floribunda.
OPPOSITE: Tibouchina semidecandra, *the Brazilian spider flower*.

pots in the cool greenhouse. Give them plenty of air, light, but little water during winter. Pot on in spring into 5- or 6-in. pots. Pinch out growing points when necessary and support. The compact bush, *S. × wiseto-nensis*, 1½–2 ft., has large flowers. In the strain 'Dwarf Bouquet Mixed', 1 ft., colours range from crimson to apple-blossom pink.

Smithiantha (formerly *Naegelia*) A beautiful pot plant, it has rich velvety foliage, attractively marked in contrasting colours. The flowers of its cultivars are like small foxgloves, in spikes well above the leaves, in the colours cream, pink, rose, and salmon. Propagated by separating the rhizomes, or by sowing seeds in spring in a temperature of 65°–70°F (10°–21°C). Seed-raised plants flower in seven or eight months.

Start dormant tubers, shallowly buried in peaty compost at 60°–65°F (16°–18°C) in spring. Liquid feed when flower spikes appear every ten days. Keep water off foliage as it marks. After flowering, the rhizomes are dried off and stored out of frost for the winter.

Solanum Winter cherry, *S. capsicastrum*, has bright scarlet berries, which makes it popular at Christmas. Sow from January, every fortnight, at a temperature of 60°–65°F (16°–18°C), covering the boxes with paper and glass. To encourage bushiness, transplant the seedlings, when large enough, to other boxes. Plant into 3-in. pots in early May and pot on accordingly. Keep under cool conditions and subsequently move them outdoors. Encourage setting of berries by regular spraying of water and by giving dilute liquid feeds. Take indoors in September, shortening long growths. Avoid dry atmosphere and spray with an insecticide if aphids or red spider appear.

Stephanotis Not an easy plant to grow, *S. floribunda*, the clustered wax flower, likes a peaty compost, plenty of moisture in summer, almost complete dryness in winter and a minimum winter temperature of 55°F (13°C). Grows tall in a warm greenhouse border, but in containers it can be restricted to 8 or 9 ft. It is an evergreen with white, fragrant flowers. Remove weak shoots in spring and top dress with rich soil. Propagate by cuttings of the previous season's growth at 72°F (22°C) with bottom heat.

Strelitzia The showy *S. reginae*, the bird of paradise flower, has handsome, long-stemmed leaves and large purple and orange flowers, resembling a bird's head in summer. Requires well-drained loam containing peat and coarse sand, to be kept moist in summer, dry in winter, and a minimum temperature of 50°F (10°C). Propagate by detaching and planting suckers in late winter or early spring.

Streptocarpus The Cape primrose likes cool humid, well-ventilated conditions. When growth slows down in October, reduce watering so that soil is dryish, but not dust dry. Repot in March using porous, moisture-retentive compost containing decayed manure. Feeding liquid manure to established plants is beneficial. Propagate by seed sown in succession to prolong flowering. December or January sowing gives flowers between June and September; sown in June and July, overwintered at 50°F (10°C), blooms come from April onwards. Various hybrids have 2-in. mouthed, trumpet-like flowers with unique throat markings, contrasting with the dominating purple, violet, pink, and white colours.

Streptosolen An evergreen climber, *S. jamesonii*, valuable for a frost-free greenhouse, has showy clusters of orange-red flowers in autumn. Grows well in containers or a rich, well-drained greenhouse border. Regular watering and syringing in summer is beneficial. Prune as necessary when dormant. Propagate by young cuttings in a propagator.

Tibouchina The Brazilian spider flower, *T. semidecandra*, an interesting cool greenhouse, evergreen climber, bears clusters of rich purple flowers, individually 4–5 in. across. Thrives in equal parts loam and peat with a little silver sand in containers, but preferably in a greenhouse border. Needs full light, water, and good feeding in summer, with little moisture in winter. Prune in February. Propagate by half-ripe cuttings in a propagator.

Torenia Treated as an annual, *T. fournieri* is a charming, free flowering pot plant with large, blue, antirrhinum-like flowers with a deeper blue and gold blotch in July and August. Sow seed in March. Transplant to small pots and support with canes.

Trachelium Best treated as a biennial because younger plants are the more floriferous; *T. caerulea* is a half-hardy, shrubby perennial, producing heads of fragrant, blue flowers from June to April. Likes light, sun, and a compost of sandy loam and leaf mould. Sow seeds thinly from February to June in boxes, greenhouse beds or sheltered frame. When seedlings are flourishing, pot firmly and pinch out leading shoots. Transfer in late September to 5-in. pots and keep at 47°F (7°C) minimum during winter.

Zantedeschia Variously called calla lily, arum lily, and formerly Richardia. Pot in July in equal parts of loam, sharp sand, and decayed manure. Keep outdoors until mid-September, water sparingly, but syringe overhead as growth increases. House in the greenhouse, giving free ventilation and constantly moist compost. After flowering and foliage discolours dry off roots. Propagate by suckers. *Z. aethiopica*, the lily of the Nile, white flowers, and *Z. elliottiana*, yellow, require a minimum temperature of 55°F (13°C) and spring planting.

BASIC TOOLS AND EQUIPMENT

There are many important tasks which must be carried out throughout the gardening year. It is a wise gardener who decides to reduce the amount of time and effort spent on these activities to the minimum! This can be done if a careful selection is made of those tools which will be required to carry out this work efficiently.

Tools can be expensive, however, and it is as well to reduce expenditure as much as possible. Economies can be made bearing in mind that some tools are veritable 'maids of all work', and can be used for several diverse operations. The beginner will be able to start off with a basic set of tools to which further equipment may be added from time to time.

The most important basic tools are those which cultivate the soil – the spade and fork for example. Careful selection is important with these tools and weight and balance are two features which must be appreciated. If possible, go through the motions of digging with these tools when you are making your selection in the shop or garden centre. In this way you will be able to choose the right spade or fork for you *personally*.

Digging spade and fork and border tools.

There will be several designs available. Some will have shiny stainless steel blades and prongs, whereas others may be of duller metal. The former slip through the soil more easily and are especially useful on the wet, sticky types of soil, although they are quite expensive. Those made of duller metal are less expensive and will prove just as useful, but they *must* be regularly cleaned. Another useful feature to look out for is a comfortable handle – many handles are now made from plastics and moulded to fit the hand. Some shafts are made from alloys to combine strength with lightness.

The woman gardener especially will appreciate the smaller types of spade and fork. These are called border tools and have much smaller working heads. Ideal for working between plants in the borders, they are equally efficient as ordinary digging tools.

Garden rake.

Other important basic tools include the rake and hoe. The former is quite a versatile piece of equipment and is used for breaking down of the soil ready for sowing and planting. It can also be used on its edge for taking out seed drills. After sowing, the rake is then used to pull back the soil to cover the seeds. The more teeth a rake has, the finer the tilth or surface it can produce. A rake with a minimum of 10 teeth should be selected. Some special rake designs have many more teeth than this and the head can span some 40 in. These types are excellent for the lawn for their big sweep will quickly remove fallen leaves, mowings, general thatch or debris.

Hoes come in all shapes and sizes and their selection will depend on what job they have to perform. For taking out seed drills and for earthing up work, the draw hoe is ideal. It can be used on its edge to take out quite a narrow, shallow drill, or used to its full width; it is an excellent tool for those wider and deeper drills, which are required for sowing such vegetable crops as peas and beans.

Draw hoe, standard dutch hoe and cutting dutch hoe.

When it comes to weed control and surface tilling to prevent the surface becoming hard or panned, you will find that the dutch hoes are very useful. Some special designs have a two-edged blade so that, with a push-pull action, they can deal with weeds very quickly and efficiently. Some have small side-guards to the blade, and this prevents damage to plants in the row; it is especially useful where the hoe has to be used between closely-spaced rows or in between more mature crops.

There is a lot to be said for the soil cultivators – those tools with a number of curved prongs or teeth, which are pulled through the soil to keep the top inch or so nice and friable. They are excellent for working in top-dressings along the plant rows. Some designs can have extra tines quickly clamped onto the head, which give variations in working widths.

In many gardens, especially the new or neglected ones, a considerable amount of carrying about is necessary and a wheelbarrow can be a vital piece of equipment. Rubble, soil, sand, cement and paving stones are some of the many materials which have to be moved by wheelbarrow.

There are several good designs available and many have the weight distribution directly over their wheels, which means better balance and control. Twin wheels also ensure easier pushing and some designs can be tipped forward so that debris, leaves, etc. can be conveniently swept into the barrow. Strength is also important and many wheelbarrows are manufactured from steel. A capacity of about 3 cu. ft. is generally adequate for most gardens, but barrows of larger capacity can be purchased.

Two-wheel wheelbarrow.

Another useful piece of equipment is the two-wheel truck – so handy for the transportation of paving materials, bags of cement or peat, etc. One design can be quickly converted to a hose reel carrier, or can have a large-capacity plastic bag attached, so that weeds can be put in as the gardener works round the borders.

Pruning tools will be required and a good pair of secateurs is a sound investment. Many different types are available and the capacity required (i.e. the size of cut) will depend on the average type of growth which will need cutting. A general-purpose design will be adequate for most gardens, but it may be a good idea to purchase two pruners – a heavy-duty model for the really tough wood and the general-purpose secateurs. Some gardeners find the small, lightweight secateurs very useful and the flower-gatherers – those types which cut and hold the flower in one action – and very handy for the flower-arranger.

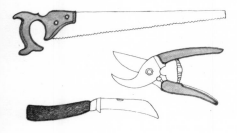

Pruning tools: pruning saw, general-purpose secateurs and pruning knife.

A hand trowel and fork are indispensable tools for the garden. These are the planting tools and they can be obtained in stainless-

Hand trowel and fork.

steel finish or ordinary steel. It is important to make certain that their handles are as comfortable as possible. Don't forget a garden line too! This is very essential when rows of plants are set out. An all-plastic design with reel is convenient and easy to use.

Lawn edging is just as important as mowing – it gives that 'finishing touch'. Long-handled shears are ideal for the small to medium-sized lawn, but for larger areas the push-along edger or the electric or battery-operated type would be a better proposition.

When it comes to the selection of a mower for grass-cutting, the range is somewhat bewildering. The final choice will depend largely on the area of grass which has to be cut and to a great extent on the type of grass – whether it is close and reasonably fine or tall and coarse.

For the best of both worlds in cutting efficiency, the rotary mower is the one which can tackle both long and short grass equally well. Some designs have grass-collection facilities. For a finer and closer cut or finish, nothing can compare with the cylinder machine and the more blades it has, the better the cut.

For the average lawn, a 12–17 in. cylinder model is adequate. For large areas the 14–18 in. machines will be necessary, and the ride-on machines make light work of extensive areas. An 18 in. rotary machine will cope with quite large areas of lawn or rougher grass conditions.

Ease of starting is an important feature, and the mains electric and battery-operated machines should be considered from this viewpoint; the woman gardener will find some of the small versions ideal for her purpose. The battery machines are somewhat heavy and are quite difficult to negotiate over steps. They are, however, easy to re-charge as they are supplied with a built-in re-charging unit. During the winter, it is important to make sure the battery is kept fully charged.

You will find that care of the lawn is simplified by the use of leaf-sweepers. These are push-along models with a large revolving stiff brush which sweeps the leaves, mowings, and debris backwards and into a canvas or plastic collection bag.

The use of a fertilizer distributor is invaluable on the larger lawns where quick

and accurate lawn dressing applications can be given. The machine is pushed up and down at walking pace and a useful range of application rates is provided.

Efficient watering is vital if plants are to grow well both indoors and outside in the garden. If you own a greenhouse, you may have a problem at holiday times if an obliging neighbour is not available to attend to this work.

The use of a capillary mat watering system has much to commend it to the greenhouse owner. It is a relatively cheap form of automation and thoroughly reliable. A special absorbent mat (1 sq. yd. can hold about 1 gallon of water) is laid on the staging and kept constantly moist via a water trough, water level controller, and mains water tank with a ball valve and float system. Pot plants stood on this damp mat automatically take up their own individual water requirements, and can be kept watered for months without attention.

Outdoors, an efficient sprinkler will be adequate for most requirements. This can range from a simple rotating type with adjustable nozzles or the more sophisticated model with oscillating action and setting control to regulate the throw of the water. Strong reinforced wall hose pipe should be used, and it must be kept in good condition and neatly stored on a hose reel.

Hose reel and hose pipe.

The efficient control of pests and diseases in the garden and under glass depends not only on the use of a suitable spray material but also on the type of equipment used to apply the preparations onto the plants. For small gardens and in confined areas such as a greenhouse, the 1 pint capacity hand sprayer is quite adequate. Larger areas need bigger sprayers and the 1 gallon capacity sprayer is a wise choice.

The pressurized designs reduce effort because, with a few initial priming pumps, sufficient strong pressure is built up to provide several minutes of useful spraying. Some are made from anti-corrosion plastics, and are light to carry around. There is even a battery-operated sprayer to reduce time and effort still further. Long-reach lances enable the gardener to get right into trees and shrubs, and also to attain height.

GARDENER'S DIARY

JANUARY

General work

Winter gales may loosen trees, shrubs, and roses, particularly newly planted specimens, so firm the soil around the base where necessary. Check stakes and ties on standard and half-standard young trees. Pruning of apples and pears can continue. Summer-fruiting raspberry canes should be tipped and ties renewed. Order your vegetable and flower seeds so that you have them to hand when the weather is favourable for sowing.

Tipping raspberry canes.

The greenhouse

Cuttings of late-flowering chrysanthemums and of perpetual flowering carnations can be taken now and rooted in sandy soil in a warm greenhouse or propagating frame. Anchusa, oriental poppy, phlox, gaillardia, and perennial mullein (verbascum) can be increased by root cuttings treated in the same manner.

FEBRUARY

General work

The popular purple *Clematis × jackmanii*

should be cut hard back to within 3–4 ft. of the ground, for it will quickly make vigorous new flowering shoots. The early summer flowering clematis varieties should only be tipped and weak growths thinned out. Lightly clip winter flowering hardy heathers as they finish flowering. Where there was trouble last year with canker on apple shoots, black spot on roses, powdery mildew on chrysanthemums and on the other plants, use appropriate sprays according to the maker's instructions.

The greenhouse

A sudden fall in greenhouse temperature can do untold damage in just one night, so not only listen to the weather forecast but use your own judgement on local conditions. On the other hand, ventilate the greenhouse whenever the weather is favourable, or grey mould may quickly spread.

Half-hardy annuals, such as ageratum, cobaea, celosia, nemesia, petunia, may be sown towards the end of the month for bedding out in May. In a greenhouse or frame with a temperature of 60°F (16°C), sow for an early crop of French beans, Brussels sprouts, carrots, radishes, lettuce, cauliflower, and broad beans. If not sown in the autumn, sweet peas raised now from seed will flower from July onwards.

Clematis.

MARCH

General work

Newly planted conifers should be protected from perishing winds with a screen of sacking or polythene. Spray the shrubs overhead with water in dry weather and keep the soil moist around the roots. Rose pruning will be in full swing and they can still be planted. Hedging plants usually do well if planted early in the month. Where there is moss in the lawn, treat with lawn sand, but if drainage can be improved this will be a better long-term remedy. When giving the lawn its first mowing of the season have the mower blades raised to give a light cutting.

Hardy perennial plants can be lifted from the border, divided, and replanted. Shrubs, which were layered last spring or summer, such as rhododendrons, magnolias, and lilac (syringa), can now be detached from the parent plants and put in their permanent positions. Start planting gladiolus corms in well-drained soil and in a sunny position.

Sow in the open, later in the month, broccoli, spinach beet, summer spinach, carrots, sprouts, cauliflower, leeks, onions, lettuce, peas, and radish.

The greenhouse

Rooted chrysanthemum and carnation cuttings will need potting in 3-in. pots, and pelargoniums rooted from autumn cuttings may need potting on. Dahlia tubers should be brought into a warm house or frame to produce cuttings. Last month's sowings of half-hardy annuals will need pricking out into wooden or plastic seed trays, placing the seedlings 2-in. apart each way. Alpine plants growing in pans can be seen at their best when staged in a cold greenhouse or frame.

APRIL

General work

Continue to plant gladioli for a summer display. Plant in groups, not in straight lines unless they are being grown merely for cutting. Hardy annual seeds should be sown where they are to flower. They are most useful for filling gaps which may have occurred in a sunny border. Lawn grass seed may be sown for a new lawn or for renovating worn patches. A dressing with a combined lawn fertilizer and weedkiller will make all the difference in the appearance of a lawn. Use according to the maker's instructions and do not give a bit extra for luck. The same applies to moss killer on lawns. Your roses will appreciate a feed with rose fertilizer.

Cloches should be placed over strawberry plants to ensure an early crop. On sunny days the cloches should be removed to allow bees to pollinate the flowers and watering may be necessary. After weeding the ground around raspberry canes and currant bushes a topdressing of straw as a thick covering to the soil should keep down weeds for the rest of the season and also help to retain moisture in the ground.

Asparagus beds and Jerusalem artichokes will benefit from a dressing of a general compound fertilizer. Greenfly and other pests may mean that spraying is necessary, so keep a close watch in the garden and catch 'em young.

The greenhouse

Plants and seedlings in the greenhouse will require more water. Try to keep an even temperature with the ventilators open on sunny days. Close them in good time if the night is likely to be frosty.

Tomatoes can be planted out in the border or grown in pots so long as a night temperature of about 55°F (13°C) can be maintained, and a moist atmosphere by day. Freesia seed can be sown, eight to a 7-in. pot in which they are to flower from October onwards, when these fragrant blooms will be most welcome. Primula seed may also be sown to provide colourful pot plants for next winter. If dahlia tubers were not started into growth in a greenhouse last month, this may now be done in an unheated frame.

MAY
General work

Gladiolus corms planted now will prolong the succession of spikes produced by earlier plantings. From mid-May onwards plant out chrysanthemums in the open or pot-grown plants may be stood in the open in a sunny position. Towards the end of the month, plant out dahlias and other summer flowering bedding plants.

Freesias grown from seed may be stood in the open in a shady position for the summer. Biennials for flowering next year can be sown this month, such as polyanthus, wallflowers, forget-me-nots, Sweet Wil-

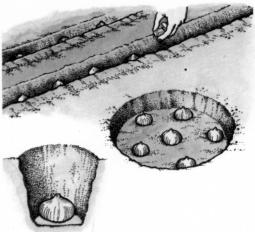

Planting gladiolus corms.

liams, Canterbury Bells (*Campanula medium*), foxgloves and pansies.

Evergreen and tender shrubs can still be planted, but don't forget watering if the weather becomes dry. Waterlilies and other aquatics can be planted, and this is a good month to introduce fish to a pool. Forsythia, kerria, and early flowering spiraeas and berberis should be pruned when they have finished their display. A compost heap is a valuable source of natural plant food and can consist of vegetable material, leaves, soft shrub prunings and grass mowings (as long as a hormone weedkiller has not been used on the lawn); in the autumn, beech and oak leaves are excellent material.

Main crop potatoes should be planted and more sowings made of lettuce, radish, peas, runner beans, and French beans. Marrows will germinate under glass and can be planted out towards the end of the month.

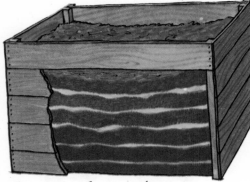

Cross-section of a compost heap.

The greenhouse

Shading may be necessary for the greenhouse, particularly where tomatoes, begonias, and gloxinias are grown. Damping down paths and staging in the greenhouse in the middle of the day will become a routine on bright, sunny days. A humid atmosphere is essential for tomatoes, cucumbers and melons to set fruit and it also discourages the spread of red spider. Peppers

and aubergines will make rapid growth in a warm house. Cinerarias and primulas may also be sown to provide decorative winter pot plants.

JUNE
General work

Sweet peas growing on canes will require tying, or a quicker method is to use sweet pea rings which are squeezed gently around the stems. These fast growing plants will require ample water in a dry spell and liquid manure will encourage flower production. Roses will be in full flower and dead heads should be removed regularly. Where necessary, spray rose bushes to control black spot, mildew, caterpillars, and greenfly. Biennials can still be sown in the open for next year's display. The small seedlings will require watering in hot dry weather; this is best done in the evening.

Quick growing hedges can be given their first clipping in early June – privet, *Lonicera nitida*, blackthorn, hawthorn, and gorse. June and July are good months to visit a rose nursery and assess new varieties to add to your collection. Where space permits, shrub roses are admirable when growing in a sunny mixed shrub border. Many of these shrub roses are delightfully fragrant and they require the minimum of attention.

Tall growing dahlias will need regular tying and later on disbudding if exhibition blooms are desired. Make further sowings of lettuce, radish, and a final sowing of green peas. Winter greens, such as savoy, broccoli, kale, and drumhead winter cabbage, should now be planted out.

The greenhouse

Trying to keep the greenhouse at an even temperature may prove a problem, and shading and damping down to maintain a moist, growing atmosphere will require constant attention. In really hot weather watering will be necessary twice a day. Sideshoots must be removed from tomato plants, and when the plants have set at least eight trusses the plants should be stopped by breaking off the leading growth on the main stem just above the leaf joint.

JULY
General work

Check that plants requiring staking and tying are secure against summer gales and thunderstorms, which can play havoc in the flower border. Chrysanthemums and dahlias will need regular disbudding if specimen blooms are desired. Both will be the better for spraying for capsid bug and greenfly early in the month.

Conifer hedges can be cut now as well as decidous hedges, such as beech, hornbeam,

Layering strawberry (top) and blackberry plants.

hazel, and the evergreen holly and euonymous. The pruning of early flowering summer shrubs should be completed. Wisteria can be summer pruned this month or next, cutting back long sideshoots to leave five buds or leaf joints. Rock roses (helianthemums) should have the straggling shoots cut hard back after flowering to keep them bushy.

Bulbs such as tulips, hyacinths, bulbous irises, and daffodils, if overcrowded, can all be lifted, cleaned, and stored in a dry place for replanting in the autumn.

Border carnations and pinks can be layered. Overcrowded clumps of Madonna lily (*Lilium candidum*) should be lifted, divided, and replanted immediately after flowering.

Remove strawberry runners as they appear, unless required for new stock, when they should be pegged down to form study young plants. During dry weather remove the grass box from the lawn mower.

The greenhouse

As tomato plants mature it may be wise towards the end of the month to cut back some of the larger leaves, which overhang ripening trusses. Where space is available in the greenhouse, herbs can be dried for culinary use, and home-saved seeds ripened before being packeted and carefully labelled.

AUGUST
General work

Hardy heathers should be lightly clipped with shears after they have finished flowering, or in spring for those that flower in late summer and autumn. Heathers can be increased by layering side growths which are pegged down into moist soil. When rooted the layers should be severed from the parent plants and put in their permanent positions.

At the end of the month cuttings of geraniums (pelargoniums) can be rooted in sandy soil in pots in a cold frame or cool greenhouse. Freesia corms for winter flowering can be planted early in the month,

about 2-in. deep in pots, and stood in a shaded cold frame until early October, when they are brought into gentle warmth. Prepared hyacinths for flowering around Christmas should be put into pots or bowls of moist bulb fibre and kept in a dark, cool place for about three months before bringing into light and warmth. Cyclamen corms should be repotted and when they start into growth they will need careful watering. Only half cover the corm with soil.

Vegetable seeds which can still be sown in the open include spring cabbage, lettuce, radish, spinach beet, winter spinach, and endive. Young plants of broccoli, winter cabbage, and savoys can all be planted out. The leaves of onions should be bent over to ground level to assist ripening.

Rope onions for storage. They ripen quicker if you bend over the leaves.

The greenhouse

Keep the greenhouse staging and paths free from litter, dead leaves, and the like, which only encourage pests and diseases. Damping down will also be frequently necessary during hot sunny weather.

Disbudding chrysanthemums.

Reverse broken turfs at the edge of the lawn.

SEPTEMBER
General work

For a new lawn or for renovating worn patches sow lawn grass seed and during the second half of the month turf can be laid so long as there is no drought. If dry weather does occur newly laid turf should be well watered. Be careful to use reasonably weed-free turf or you will be importing a load of trouble. Established lawns can be given an autumn dressing with a compound lawn fertilizer high in potash and phosphate.

Hardy annuals for flowering next May and June can be sown in the open where they are to flower, including larkspur, nigella, calendula, Shirley poppies, annual scabious, and coreopsis. Sweet peas can also be sown in pots or boxes and overwintered in a cold frame, for flowering in June next year. Beware of mice, they not only eat the seeds but will also devour the young plants. This is a good month to transplant conifers and other evergreens. Cuttings of shrubs, using half-ripe wood can be taken and inserted in sandy soil in a cold frame. They should be well rooted by next spring. Layering of shrubs can also be done this month.

The vegetable garden will require attention with a good tidying and forking of the soil where crops have been cleared. Apple and pear picking will be in full swing; both are ready to pick if the stalk detaches easily when the fruit is lifted up gently in the palm of the hand.

The greenhouse

Tomato plants should be cleared of their remaining fruit and pulled out to make room for chrysanthemums, azaleas, carnations, fuchsias, and other tender plants which have been in the open for the summer months.

OCTOBER
General work
This is the month to plant bulbs of narcissus, hyacinths, scilla, crocus, grape hyacinth (muscari), chionodoxa (glory of the snow), and other early flowering spring bulbs. Tulips are best planted in November. Complete the pruning of rambler roses and tie in securely the new growths for future flowering. Where new trees and shrubs are to be planted, fork over the sites and add garden compost or peat to improve the soil where necessary, for once planted they will become permanent features therefore and require a good start in life.

Plant out spring bedding plants such as wallflower, forget-me-not, polyanthus, and double daisies, perhaps leaving space for tulips to be interplanted next month. Towards the end of the month, lift dahlia tubers and when cleaned and dried store in a frost-free place. Gladiolus corms should also be lifted, cleaned, and stored in an airy, but frost-free place.

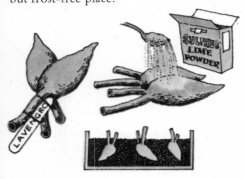

Dry, clean and store away lifted dahlia tubers.

Hardy perennials will mostly have finished flowering and towards the end of the month the border should be cleaned, the plants cut down and any stakes stored away in a dry place for the winter. Large clumps should be lifted, divided, and replanted, discarding the old woody parts of the clumps.

Apples for picking, eating, and storing this month are 'Bramley's Seedling', 'Charles Ross', 'Blenheim Orange', 'Egre-

Heel in trees if they cannot be planted out.

mont Russet', and 'Laxton's Superb'. Bramley's is a particularly good keeper when stored in a cool shed.

The greenhouse
By this time the greenhouse will be filled with plants and bulbs to provide colour during the winter. These may include freesias, azaleas, primulas, cyclamen, saintpaulias, and chrysanthemums in a variety of colours.

Protect grey- and woolly-leaved plants with cloches.

NOVEMBER
General work
A busy month for planting trees, shrubs, roses, fruit trees, hardy perennials, also bulbs, in particular tulips. Firmness is essential to prevent the wind rocking tall plants, so tread the soil down around the newly planted trees and shrubs. Staking may also be necessary. Hardwood cuttings of shrubs, including roses, can still be taken and put in a trench in the open ground in a sheltered place, lining the bottom of the trench with sharp sand to assist root formation. Strip the lower leaves of the cuttings before inserting them in the soil. Climbing roses can be pruned, and rambler roses given the finishing touches.

This is a good month for laying turf for a new lawn. When estimating your requirements a turf measures 3 × 1 ft., that is three turves to a square yard.

Some of the woolly-leaved grey foliage perennial plants do not like prolonged wet wintery weather and will appreciate the protection of a cloche.

As soon as the leaves have fallen, start to prune apples, pears, and other top fruits and when completed give a spray to control pests and diseases, choosing a windless day, if possible. Mulching can follow pruning and spraying. The vegetable garden will need digging and manuring and left rough to get the frost to break up heavy soil.

The greenhouse
To get as much light as possible in the greenhouse during the dark months the glass should be cleaned; also clean garden frames. Pelargoniums and fuchsias require the

minimum of water during the winter. Watch out for greenfly on various pot plants coming into flower or they may spread rapidly in a warm atmosphere.

DECEMBER
General work
So long as the ground is not too wet continue planting trees, shrubs, roses, hardy perennials, and the like. Pruning and spraying of fruit trees can also continue while they are dormant. Slug bait will be needed around delphiniums, lupins, pyrethrums, and other succulent shooted border plants.

Construction work, such as making a garden pool, laying paving or building a rock garden, can be carried out, but do not do cementing during frosty weather.

Autumn-sown sweet peas overwintering in a cold frame should be stopped just above the third leaf. Fruit in store should be examined, also dahlia tubers and gladioli, removing any that show signs of rotting.

Have the motor mower overhauled, also electric hedge cutters and other equipment. The battery of an electric mower should be kept charged and the mower blades oiled.

Aphelandra squarrosa.

The greenhouse
There should be a useful supply of pot plants to bring into the house for Christmas decorations, but do not make the mistake of standing such plants too near radiators where the dry heat will soon spoil them. Buds and flowers will shrivel and drop if the room atmosphere is dry and hot. Careful watering is essential and once an azalea, cyclamen, *Aphelandra squarrosa*, or primula has been allowed to get too dry the damage has been done. Return it to the moist, warm atmosphere of a greenhouse, soak the soil thoroughly and it may revive. Never leave tender plants on a windowsill, behind drawn curtains at night, where the temperature may be near freezing. It takes many months to produce a colourful pot plant, but only hours to ruin it.

INDEX AND ACKNOWLEDGMENTS

The publishers would like to thank the following individuals and organizations for their kind permission to reproduce the photographs in this book:

A–Z Botanical Collections Ltd: 70–71, 77, 80, 98 above, 133, 141–142, 144 above, 149 above, 150–151, 160 below; Bernard Alfieri: 140, 145 right: J. Allan Cash: Charles de Jaeger 123; P. R. Chapman: 161; W.F. Davidson: 155 below right, 156 above, 176 below; J. E. Downward and E. L. Crowson: 19, 47 below, 65, 66 above, 81, 85 below, 98 below, 101, 103, 120–121, 137 below, 139 below, 141, 143 below left; Valerie Finnis: 51, 69 below right, 79, 87, 107 above, 109, 122, front flap and back flap; Brian Furner: 13, 128, 134 below, 135 above, 143 centre left; Will Green: 117; Iris Hardwick: 33 above, 38 below, 40 below, 54 above; Peter Hunt: 15 left, 24, 43 below right, 56 below, 62, 85 above, 88 left, 160 above, 164, 172 below; Anthony Huxley: 22, 28 above, 44 above, 55 below, 58–59 below, 99, 108 below, 135 below, 139 centre, 175 above, 177; George Hyde: 30, 119 below, 168–169, 175 below, 176 above; Jackson & Perkins: 165; Leslie Johns: 96 below, 97, 149 below; D. J. Kesby: 27 below, 31 above, 59 above right; Elsa Megson: 100 above, 174; D. F. Merrett: 68 above; John Mitchell: contents' page; NHPA: B. Alfieri 153 above, 155 above right, H. R. Allen 45, Valerie Finnis 23 below, 35, 48–49 below, 88–89, 111, A. Huxley 57, 105 above L. Hugh Newman 69 above, M. Savonius 60; E. A. Over: 170; Ray Procter: 44 below, 126; John Rigby: 14; Wilhelm Schacht: 153 below; Kenneth Scowen: 166 above, back jacket; Harry Smith Horticultural Photographic Collection: 8–11, 13 above right, 15´right, 16 below, 17, 18, 20, 21, 25, 27 above, 28 below, 28–29 below, 29, 31 below, 37 above, 38 above, 39, 40 above, 41–43, 46–47, 48 above, 52–53, 54 below, 55 above, 56 above, 58 above, 59 above left, 59 below right, 61, 63 above, 66 below, 67, 68 below, 69 below left, 71 above, 72 above, 73–76, 83, 86, 89–91, 92–93 above, 93, 95, 96 above, 100 below right, 105 below, 106–107 below, 108 above, 110, 112, 119 above, 124, 125, 127, 134, 135, 138–139, 143, 144 below, 145 left, 156 below, 157–159, 163, 171, 172 above, 173, front jacket end papers; Spectrum Colour Library: 154–155; Jeremy Whitaker: 18